BE FIRST CLASS !

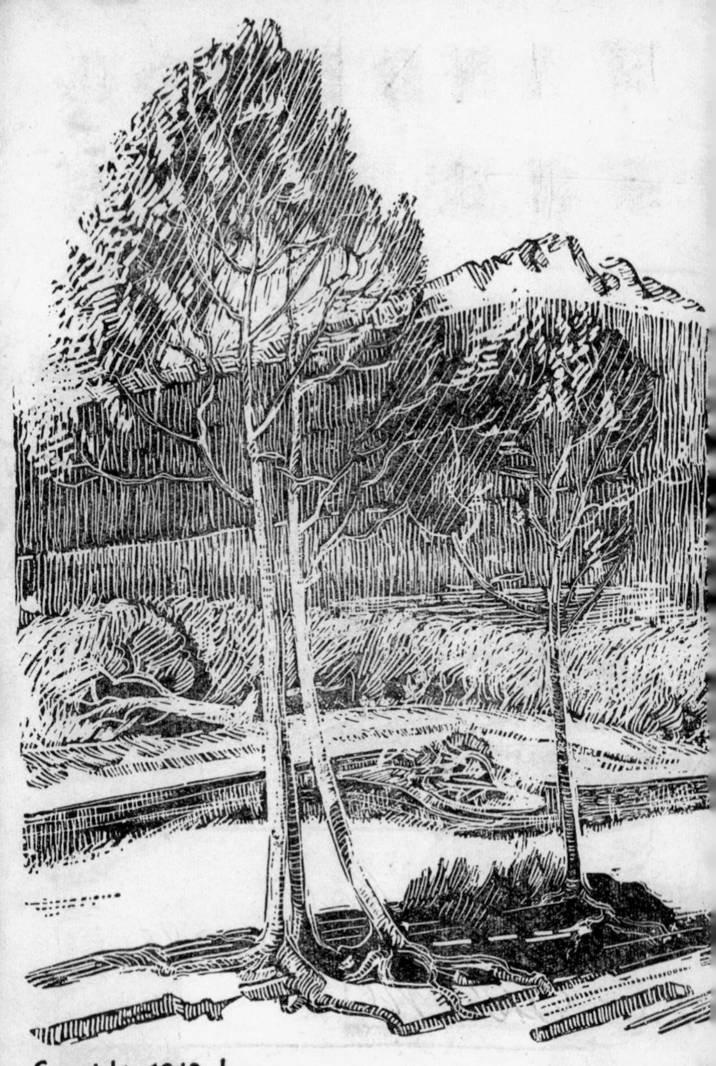

BOY SCOUTS

NATIONAL COUNCIL NEW BRUNSWICK, N. J.

HANDBOOK FOR BOYS

OF AMERICA

NO. 3225

PRINTED IN U.S.A.

FIFTH EDITION — TWELFTH PRINTING
September 1958 • 525,000 copies
Total printing since 1910 • 16,550,000

ABOUT THIS BOOK

We take pleasure in presenting to you, the boys of America, this fifth edition of the *Handbook for Boys*. If you are a Scout or Explorer you will find it a helpful guide along the trail to self-reliance, citizenship, and physical fitness—along the trail to Eagle rank. If not, you will find it a handbook of ideals, information and outdoor skills that you surely will find interesting.

General editor of the book was Ted S. Pettit, using material especially prepared by experts in many fields. A number of nationally known outdoorsmen provided the manuscript for the Wildlife and Woodlore Chapter: Grassland Scouting by E. Laurence Palmer, Professor of Rural Education at Cornell University; Bogs and Marshes by William G. Vinal of Massachusetts State College; Forests, E. G. Cheney, Professor of Forestry, University of Minnesota; and Desert Living by H. L. Shantz, Division of Wildlife Management, U. S. Forest Service. The Chapters on Woodsman's Tools, Handicraft, and Signaling were written by Ted S. Holstein; those on Fire Building, and Camp Cooking by Paul W. Handel. Dr. Laurance M. Thompson prepared the Chapter on First Aid, and Fred C. Mills those on Swimming and Physical Fitness. M. R. Greene contributed to Chapters 2 to 5 and developed the Chapters in Part V. The balance of the material in the book was written by the editor, Ted S. Pettit.

You should understand that the writing of these experts was based not only on their own long experience in Scouting and special fields, but also on the best experience of many hundreds of thousands of Scouts and leaders in this country and all over the world.

Format and art work, under the direction of Don Ross, was done by a group including Remington Schuyler and George Goddard.

The mammal drawings by Walter A. Weber in Chapter 12 were taken from "Meeting the Mammals," and used with the permission of The Macmillan Company, Publishers.

Belmore Browne, nationally known expert in mountaineering, contributed background material for the Chapters on Preparation for Hiking and Camping and on Tents and Outdoor Shelters.

The Editorial Service is grateful to many Scouts and Scouters who contributed helpful advice and criticism. William E. Lawrence, National Director of Volunteer Training, followed the book through its entire production.

Thus this Handbook represents the experiences of many people — experts in Scouting and experts in technical lines. It is written for the boys of the nation. It is our hope that it will inspire you and help you to be watchful for opportunities to help other people, to be tolerant and respectful of the rights of others, to be courageous and self-reliant — in other words, to be a good American.

CONTENTS

Part V—On to Eagle

APPENDIX

TENDERFOOT REQUIREMENTS

To become a TENDERFOOT SCOUT, you must be at least eleven years of age and do the following:

	Check in Boxes When You Have Met the Requirements — Numbers Are Page References
I. SCOUT SPIRIT — Learning about the ideals and traditions of Scouting:	☐
1. Repeat from memory the Scout Oath or Promise and the twelve points of the Scout Law, the Scout Motto and the Scout Slogan, and explain the meaning of each in your own words.	19 26 40 42
2. Describe the Scout Badge and explain its meaning.	47
Tell when to wear the Scout Uniform and how to use and care for it.	50
3. Give the Scout Sign, Salute and Handclasp.	45 46
II. SCOUT PARTICIPATION — Knowing about the Patrol and Troop, the community and the country of which you are a part:	☐
1. Explain the name of the Patrol you will join and give its call or yell.	56
Tell who your Scout leaders are, and what they do in the Troop.	61
Explain, in a general way, what you have to do to become a Second Class and a First Class Scout.	104 109

2. Tell how, in an emergency, you would get in contact with the doctor or hospital and the police or sheriff's office nearest to your home.	65
Explain how, in your community, you would report a fire.	67
3. Describe The Flag of the United States of America and tell its history in brief. Tell when to fly it. Show how to hoist, lower, display and fold The Flag. Show how to salute it.	69

III. SCOUTCRAFT — Setting out to learn a few simple things that all Scouts should know: ☐

1. Tell why it is important to care for a cut or a scratch, and show on yourself how to do it.	82
Tie a bandage with a square knot.	84
2. Explain what care should be taken before building a fire in the open.	86
Describe the harm to a live tree that results from hacking it with an axe or other sharp tool.	87
3. Whip the ends of a rope at least one-quarter inch in diameter.	91
Join two ropes with a sheetbend.	92
Attach a rope to a post or rail with a clove hitch, then untie it and fasten it again with two half hitches. Fasten one end of a rope around your waist with a bowline.	92 94

When you have met the Tenderfoot requirements before your Scoutmaster (or have been reviewed in the Cub Scout Webelos requirements by your Scoutmaster), and have proved to him that you thoroughly understand the Scout Oath or Promise and Law, he registers you as a Boy Scout. **You take the Scout Oath or Promise at a ceremony in front of your Patrol and Troop,** and are then entitled to wear the Tenderfoot badge and the Official Uniform of the Boy Scouts of America.

SECOND CLASS REQUIREMENTS

Check in Boxes When You Have Met the Requirements

Numbers Are Page References

To become a SECOND CLASS SCOUT, you do the following:

I. SCOUT SPIRIT — While a Tenderfoot Scout, satisfy your Scout leaders that you do your best, in your everyday life, to live up to: ☐

1. The Scout Oath or Promise. 118

2. The Scout Law. 119

3. The Scout Motto. 40

4. The Scout Slogan. 42

(Your Troop leaders, both the boy and man leaders, will decide whether you have done your best to live up to the Spirit of Scouting. They will know after watching your actions and your behavior. Your Scoutmaster may want to talk with your parents, teachers, religious leader, and others. Work on your own church or synagogue Religious Award will demonstrate your Scout spirit.)

II. SCOUT PARTICIPATION — While a Tenderfoot Scout, show to the satisfaction of your Scout leaders, that you: ☐

1. Work actively in Patrol and Troop meetings, outdoor activities and service projects. 123

(Your actions and behavior while a Tenderfoot Scout are important. Troop and Patrol records will show your attendance. Statements of your Troop Leaders will show how actively you have taken part.)

2. Do your share in helping in your home, your school, your church and your community. **127**

(Your Scoutmaster may check with your parents, your teachers and your religious leaders to see if you have been helpful, in the spirit of the Daily Good Turn.)

3. Take care of things that belong to you, the property of others, and your Country's natural resources. **129**

(A check with your leaders and your parents will show whether you have met this requirement, taking proper care of your personal belongings, protecting other people's property, and helping protect wildlife and forests.)

4. Maintain a personal savings plan (such as regular payments into a savings account or into a savings project sponsored by your family or Troop). **132**

(The regular practice of thrift counts more than the amount. The amount may be in the form of a savings bank account, savings stamps or bonds, or insurance. Regular payments into a family savings project or a Troop project such as for camp, uniform, equipment, will be accepted.)

III. SCOUTCRAFT

1. PREPARE FOR SCOUT HIKING

a. *Clothing and Equipment* — Present yourself for inspection suitably clothed for the locality, season and weather, and equipped for a five-mile hike. ☐ **136**

(Clothing will depend upon the time of year; equipment upon the type of hike and the place. Your Troop Leaders will give you that information.)

b. *Hiking Methods* — Tell the safety precautions to take on the highway and cross-country for day and night hiking. **150**

Show correct way of walking and proper care of feet. **149**

Demonstrate at least six Silent Scout Signals for formations and field work. 380

Demonstrate how to purify water for drinking. 152

Explain how to make a one-man latrine. 153

Identify local plants that may cause skin poisoning. 154

Tell what to do if lost. 155

("Tell" and "explain" mean just that. Using your own words, explain how to do these things. "Show" and "demonstrate" mean to *do* those things. "Identify" means to recognize from pictures or in nature.)

c. ***First Aid*** — Demonstrate artificial respiration. 354

Demonstrate first aid for shock and fainting and, on yourself, for the following: 357

Arterial bleeding of arm and leg. 358

Common cuts and scratches. 361

Bites of insects, and chiggers and ticks. 366

Blister on heel. 366

Burns and scalds, sunburn. 367

Skin poisoning from poison plants. 368

Objects in eye. 368

Sprained ankle. 369

(You must actually demonstrate first aid for each item. Use proper first aid materials where necessary, and practice on yourself.)

2. FIND YOUR WAY ☐

a. Compass — Explain how a compass works and give its eight principal points. 255

Set a compass and take a degree reading with it. 256

(Tell in your own words, how earth's magnetism attracts the compass. Recite the principal points. Using a compass, actually take a degree reading.)

b. *Measuring* — Determine the length of your step. 259

Walk a course for which you must take three compass degree readings and measure three distances with your step. OR 260

Lay out, in this manner, and stake a four-acre tract of land. 261

(These are all things that you must actually do.)

c. *Map Reading* — In the field orient a map preferably a topographic map and follow a route far enough to prove that you know how to use the map. 263

Read at least ten different conventional signs on a map, including contour lines. 277

(This is a project that you must complete, to show that you can use a map.)

3. COOK A MEAL IN THE OPEN

(The four parts of this requirement should be met in the order given. You may sharpen your knife and axe ahead of time, but you should do the rest of the requirements at one time, in camp or on a hike.)

☐

a. *Preparing Fire Wood* — Sharpen a knife and an axe, and use these sharpened tools to prepare kindling and fuel. 284 285

(Prepare enough wood to cook your meal.)

b. *Fire Building* — Locate and prepare a suitable fire site. 288

(Clear fire site. When dry wood is used, two matches should be sufficient.)

Keep the fire going for cooking a meal. 292

c. *Hike Cooking* — Cook a meal from raw meat (or fish or poultry) and at least one raw vegetable. 305

(You have your choice of cooking your meal without utensils as kabob, on broiler or in the ground, or using utensils stewing, frying, baking.)

d. *Clean-up* — Dispose of garbage in proper manner. 161

Clean utensils. 161

Put out fire. 303

Clean up the site thoroughly. 243

(Garbage should be burned: utensils cleaned in hot water. Put out fire by sprinkling water on it. Clean site so that it is almost impossible to find signs of the fire and camp.)

4. BE OBSERVANT

a. *Observation* — Do ONE of the following: ☐

TRACKING. Follow the track of a person or animal in soft ground or snow for 1/4 mile, reading the main meaning of the track. OR 245

TRAILING. Follow a track made with trail signs for 1/2 mile. OR 250

STALKING. Follow another Scout, who knows that you are stalking him, for a distance of 1/2 mile, without being seen by him. 251

b *Wild Life* — Find evidence, in natural surroundings, of at least six different kinds of wild mammals, birds, reptiles or fish. Identify them. 164

(The simplest "evidence" is the discovery of the animal itself. Other evidence: tracks, burrows, nests, feathers, skulls, and "pellets," snake skins, turtle eggs, etc. Name the animal from the evidence discovered.)

5. TAKE A HIKE

The Second Class Hike* ☐

After you have done the above, prove yourself a Scout Hiker by taking a hike, properly clothed and equipped with your Patrol (or, if this is impossible, with at least one companion approved by your Scoutmaster). On this hike, cover a total distance of not less than five miles following a route indicated on a map or map sketch; show correct hike style and highway safety, cook a meal, clean up, and return in good condition.

(This is the *last* requirement to meet in working for Second Class. It is a separate hike, taken after you have proved your Scoutcraft ability on previous hikes. The "one companion" may be a junior leader, a fellow who has already become Second Class, or your own father. The hike should cover all the activities of a real hike as listed.)

* NOTE on the SECOND CLASS HIKE:
If a physician certifies that the Scout's physical condition for an indeterminable time does not permit the Second Class Hike, the Advancement Committee of the Local Council may authorize the following substitution for the hike: The requirements for any one "outdoor" Merit Badge (selected from the NATURE or CONSERVATION groups) which the Scout is capable of meeting. In EACH individual case, application for a substitution must be made in advance by the Scoutmaster to the Advancement Committee and the specific substitution must be approved in writing by the Committee, after thorough review.

FIRST CLASS REQUIREMENTS

To become a FIRST CLASS SCOUT, you do the following:

I. SCOUT SPIRIT—While a Second Class Scout, satisfy your Scout leaders that you do your best, in your everyday life, to live up to: ☐

1. The Scout Oath or Promise. 118

2. The Scout Law. 119

3. The Scout Motto. 40

4. The Scout Slogan. 42

II. SCOUT PARTICIPATION — While a Second Class Scout, show, to the satisfaction of your Scout leaders that you: ☐

1. Work actively in Patrol and Troop meetings, outdoor activities and service projects. 123

2. Do your share in helping in your home, your school, your church and your community. 127

3. Take care of things that belong to you, the property of others, and your Country's natural resources. 129

4. Maintain a personal savings plan (such as regular payments into a savings account or into a savings project sponsored by your family or Troop.) 132

(As for Second Class, your Troop leaders will decide whether you are trying to live up to the rules of the game of Scouting in your everyday life. Having watched your actions and behavior while you were a Second Class Scout, they can tell if you are doing your best. A check with your parents, teachers and church leaders will show to what extent you share in home, school and church duties; whether you take care of the things that belong to you and others, and whether you make a regular practice of thrift. Continue on the Religious Award Program of your own church or synagogue so that you can receive the award as soon as you are First Class rank.)

III. SCOUTCRAFT

1. PREPARE FOR SCOUT CAMPING ☐

a. *Clothing and Equipment* — Present yourself for inspection suitably clothed for the locality, season and weather, and equipped and packed for an overnight camp. 136

(Equipment may be packed in a knapsack, pack basket or pack frame, or in an improvised pack to carry on the back. Your equipment and clothing should include all things you will need in camp, for the time of year in which you are camping.)

b. *Health Protection* — Explain methods used in camp for care of food and drinking water, fire protection and waste disposal. 159 161

(You must show that you know how to do these things, so you will be able to do them in camp.)

c. *First Aid* — Give artificial respiration for three minutes. 354

Explain danger of taking laxative for pain in stomach. 370

Improvise a sterile dressing. 85

Use triangular bandage for arm sling and as binder for wounds on head, hand, knee and foot. 85 359 361

Demonstrate first aid for one problem from each of the following groups (problems to be chosen by your leader after you have trained for all of them).

Arterial bleeding from face, throat, arm, leg. 359

Shock, heat exhaustion, sunstroke, frostbite, internal poisoning. 357 370-371

Puncture wounds from splinter, nail, fishhook, dog bite, poisonous snake bite. 362

Fracture of collarbone, upper arm, forearm, lower leg. 372

Explain under what circumstances a person should or should not be moved. Improvise a stretcher and, with helpers under your direction, transport a presumably unconscious person. 376 377

(Read Chapter 20 before taking part in Patrol or Troop first aid problems. Practice all these problems so that you can do them on *yourself*, if possible, and on someone else. After you have trained in all problems, your leader will ask you to demonstrate first aid on a few problems from the groups described in the requirement. You will not know what these problems are ahead of time.)

2. GET THE LAY OF THE LAND

a. *Directions* — Lay out on the ground a true north-south line with the help of the sun by day and the North Star by night, and a magnetic north-south line using a compass. 267

(The line may be scratched on the ground, or may be a pole laid in the proper direction. You should have a general idea of the difference between true North and Magnetic North.)

b. *Measuring* — With simple means and using your own personal measurements, determine a height you cannot reach (such as a tree) and a width you cannot walk (such as a river or a canyon). 271

("Simple means" may involve such things as small sticks, rustic poles or stakes driven in the ground. "Personal measurements" may be the length of your step, span of your hand, width of your thumb, or length of your reach.)

c. *Map Sketching* — Select a site suitable for a Patrol camp and make a map sketch for laying it out. 275

Make a map sketch by which someone unfamiliar with your camp location can find his way to it over a distance of at least two miles. 275

(Map sketch of camp should use proper conventional signs for natural features with tents, fireplaces and other camp features, indicated by simple signs. The map need not be drawn to exact scale.

The two mile map sketch may be made from memory, after you have been over the route. *It is not a map*, but a sketch, and specific distances and compass degrees are not necessary. The main features will be landmarks that show where turns are made, types of roads or trails and other marks to show how to reach the campsite. Draw a North arrow to show the general lay of the land.)

3. LIVE IN CAMP

a. *Camp Making* — Sharpen an axe and use it for cutting light wood into tent pegs. 282

Locate a tent site and pitch a tent, fastening the guy line with a taut-line hitch. 332

Prepare a comfortable ground bed. 339

Improvise a piece of camp equipment requiring lashings. **351**

(A ground bed may be made of grass, leaves or boughs; or may be a piece of ground cleared and smoothed, with hip and shoulder holes scooped out, and covered with a waterproof ground cloth. Improvised camp equipment, using lashings, may be such things as camp broom or rake, fire crane, table, kitchen rack, or wash stand.)

b. *Wood Lore* — Find and identify ten different trees or shrubs. Tell their uses. **176 to 229**

("Uses" may be suitability for fuel, poles for engineering, wood for tool handles, edible parts, food for animals, shelter for animals, or use in soil control. You may identify ten trees only, or ten shrubs only, or a combination of trees and shrubs totaling ten in all.)

4. COOK YOUR MEALS

☐

a. *Camp Cookery* — Prepare in the open, for yourself and a companion, from raw ingredients: a complete breakfast of fruit, hot cereal and bacon-and-eggs (or griddle cakes); **316**

A complete dinner of meat (or fish or poultry), vegetable, dessert and bread (or biscuits, or twist baked on a stick). **317**

(Second Class cooking provides for an individual meal and First Class asks you to cook for another fellow. Breakfast may be prepared on one trip, dinner on another. The dishes are to be served as a complete meal, in their proper order. Fruit may be served raw. Dessert for dinner must be a cooked dessert, such as stewed fruit or pudding. Bread may be cooked in a reflector oven, pan, Dutch oven, or on a thick stick.)

b. *Edible Wild Plants* — Find and identify four different edible wild greens, roots or fruits. **329**

(Greens range from watercress to dandelion leaves; roots from cattail to Indian cucumber; fruits from wild grape and numerous berries, to a great variety of nuts. Even in winter snow country, you should have little trouble finding edible plants. Certain lichens and tree bark. It is not necessary to collect and cook the plants, but you will probably want to try it.)

5. GO SWIMMING

☐

Swimming*

Tell what precautions must be taken for a safe swim. **391**

Jump feet first into water over your head in depth. 397

Swim fifty yards. 395

During the swim, stop, make a sharp turn, level off and resume swimming. 398

(By precautions are meant: 1. Have medical examination and follow doctor's orders; 2. Know your swimming ability and stick to the swimming place that fits your skill; 3. Always swim with a buddy; 4. Wait two hours after a meal; 5. Follow all rules and orders given by waterfront directors; 6. Never dive into unknown water, never take a dare to show off in the water, and never swim long distances, unless someone goes along in a boat.

6. GET A MESSAGE THROUGH

☐

Morse Signaling—Know the International Morse Code, including necessary procedure signals. Using that code, send and receive, by any suitable means, a message of 20 words (100 letters), over a distance of at least 100 yards. 378

Morse Signaling — Suitable means are flags, blinker or sound device. No speed is required. No more than 5 errors are permitted, and none that destroy the sense of the message. Procedure signals include: For sending: Attention, Error, End of Word, End of Sentence, End of Message. For receiving: Go ahead, Repeat, Word received, Message received.

7. THE FIRST CLASS CAMP

☐

After you have done the above, prove yourself a Scout Camper by camping, properly clothed and equipped on a suitable camp site for not less than twenty-four hours with your Patrol (or if this is impossible, with at least one companion approved by your Scoutmaster). During this camp, cook at least one hot meal, sleep in a tent or improvised shelter or under the stars, keep camp clean and safe, and leave camp site in good condition.

(This requirement must come last. It is a separate camp, taken after you have proved your Scoutcraft ability on previous hikes and camps. The companion may be a junior leader, a First Class Scout, or your father. The camp must include all the activities listed.)

*NOTE on the FIRST CLASS SWIMMING REQUIREMENTS

Under certain very exceptional conditions, where the climate keeps the water cold the year round, and/or where there are no suitable and accessible places within a reasonable traveling distance to swim at any time during the year or in cases where a physician certifies that the Scout's physical condition for an indeterminable time does not permit swimming, the Advancement Committee of the Local Council may authorize a substitution for the First Class Swim (as indicated on the "Application For Substitution For Basic Scout Requirements," Cat. No. 4434). In EACH individual case, application for a substitution must be made in advance by the Scoutmaster to the Advancement Committee on the special standard form provided for this purpose, and the specific substitution must be approved in writing by the Committee, after thorough review.

FUN AND ADVENTURE IN SCOUTING

Have you ever dreamed of hiking the wilderness trails that were worn down under moccasin feet hundreds of years ago? Do you hear in your imagination the almost noiseless dip-dip of Indian canoe paddles in that stream where you fish today?

Have you stopped to think of the pioneer wagons whose great wheels cut the tracks for our present roads?

You can follow those trails, those streams and tracks! You can have your share of that adventure.

Wherever you live, you are not too far from the woods and prairie, the desert or mountain—the country where once the Indians roamed and where the great Scouts of yesterday did their part in making America. There is some place where you can go camping and feel that you are in company with men like

Rogers' Rangers, Lewis and Clark, Daniel Boone, Davy Crockett and Pere Marquette.

This adventure awaits you in Scouting!

* * *

The first streaks of the sun slant down over the ridge and rouse you from deep sleep to greet a new day. You stretch and worm out of your bedding to dress. Outside your lean-to or tent you pause to drink in the glory of the sunrise, and fill your lungs deep with the clean morning air.

Suddenly you notice a slight movement in an up-wind thicket. Gradually you make out a young deer grazing peacefully. Why, with all its sharp sense of smell and hearing, has it not noticed you?

You know—because you're a Scout.

It has rained during the night, but inside your tent you have been dry and comfortable. The rivulets racing down the hillside have failed to get in under your shelter. How did you protect yourself?

You knew how—because you're a Scout.

Breakfast time. How do you get dry wood? How do you build your fire? How do you fry bacon and

flip your flapjacks?

You know—because you're a Scout.

Camp cleaned up, you and your buddies hit the trail with a light pack and a silent step. You see birds and animals, insects and fish, at home in their natural haunts. Are those raccoon or mink tracks in the muddy trail? Why is this tree trunk badly scarred, that one full of tufts of animal hair? Is that a teal, a mallard or a loon?

You leave the trail behind you. You chuckle together as you recall the lost Indian who, when found by his friends, said: "Ugh! Me no lost. Wigwam lost!" You're not lost either. You can find your way with your map and compass, and by reading the signs of the woods.

Evening falls, and you sit around the campfire with the other fellows. You spin yarns, sing old favorite songs, plan big things for tomorrow. Perhaps you don't know why you feel so good all over.

But you do—because you're a Scout.

* * *

Yes, it's fun to be a Scout—to hike, to camp, to

live in the open . . . to swim and paddle a canoe . . . to follow in the footsteps of pioneers who led the way into the wilderness . . . to look up at the stars and dream.

But Scouting is more than camping. What else do Scouts do?

"Be Prepared"

That is the Scout Motto. From the day you become a Scout, you set about preparing yourself to help other people. Your ability to help them depends upon how well you learn each Scout skill.

Every day, in countless ways, Scouts show that they *are* prepared—to point the way to strangers in town or country . . . to prevent accidents . . . to give first aid to the injured . . . even to save life. In disasters of all kinds—fires, floods, earthquakes and storms—Scouts have mobilized to give aid to rescue and relief authorities. And when the United States Government needs widespread help, as it so often did in World War II, the Boy Scouts of America are called upon. They are prepared. Remember, the Scout uniform stands for the spirit of service.

Your Patrol and Troop

As a Scout you will belong to a Patrol, which is the Scout name for a small gang of your best friends in the Troop you join. Every week, probably, you will have a Patrol and Troop meeting. Here there will be time for games and contests, and songs and stunts—lots of fun. You will plan and get ready for hikes and camping trips—learning how to pitch a tent, pack your knapsack, how to use a compass and read a map; how to tie useful knots and bandage a wound. There's always plenty to do.

From time to time your Troop will also have parties or outings for the families of all the Scouts, perhaps a picnic, a barbecue or clambake. Sounds swell, doesn't it? Mother and Dad will like it, too.

Then there are times when all the Scout Troops in your community will get together for a big Scout circus or a rally or "camporee." You will enjoy meeting your brother Scouts in these big events.

Scouts Around the World

When you join a Scout Troop, you are a part of a great world-wide movement. The same day that you are on a hike, building a bridge, meeting with your Patrol, Scouts in many other countries of the world will be doing the same thing. For there are Scouts in almost every country, from Canada to the Argentine, from Iceland to Australia, from China to South Africa.

Every four years thousands of these Scouts of the World meet in one tremendous camp, the World Jamboree. There, they have two weeks of real adventure and fellowship, showing each other their favorite games and how they camp back home. There are large pageants with flags flying, and bands playing the tunes of many lands. At a Jamboree you see Scouts who cannot speak the same language living as friends together. They talk by means of signs and gestures, laughing and joking as if they belonged to the same Patrol in the same Troop. It is a living example of the fourth Scout Law, "A Scout is friendly . . . a brother to every other Scout."

How Scouting Began

Have you heard the story of how Scouting began and how it came to this country? It's an interesting one, beginning in South Africa in the early 1900's.

A young British army officer, Robert Baden-Powell, was stationed in the wild South African country to train new soldiers from England in the skills of tracking, trailing, and wilderness living.

He found that his men were so used to city living that they could not stand the vigorous life of the outdoors. He recalled his own early days, his love of nature and outdoor living. He remembered tracking

Scouts of the World—Brothers Together

wild boars and tigers in the jungle; hunting wild buffalo, elephants and rhinos in West Africa and the Sudan.

Remembering his own training, he worked out a series of games and activities to make his men physically strong, self-reliant, and able to live comfortably in the wilderness. The men enjoyed these games and quickly became skilled. The idea soon went back to England. There, boys picked it up, and started to practice Scouting for themselves.

When General Baden-Powell returned home to England he was persuaded to develop his idea into a great game for boys. He studied many organizations, like those of Dan Beard and Ernest Thompson Seton in the United States. In 1907 he took a group of twenty boys to camp on little Brownsea Island, off the coast of England to try out the new program. That was the first Boy Scout Camp. In 1908 he published the first Boy Scout Handbook, *Scouting for Boys.*

How Scouting Came to America

It was on a very foggy day in 1909, that William D. Boyce, an American publisher, was searching for an address in old London. All day long the city had been covered with a heavy fog. Street lights had been turned on before noon. Now night was coming on, and it was almost impossible for the stranger to find his way.

Mr. Boyce was surprised when a boy approached and asked if he might be of service. He told the boy where he wanted to go, and was more surprised when the boy saluted him, and said, "Come with me, sir."

Upon reaching the address, Mr. Boyce reached into his pocket and offered the boy a shilling. He was more surprised than ever when the boy refused it.

"No thank you, sir. I am a Scout. Scouts do not accept tips for Good Turns."

"Good Turns? Scouts?" asked Mr. Boyce. "What are the Scouts?"

The boy told him, and showed him the way to Baden-Powell's office nearby. There, Mr. Boyce found out about the Boy Scouts, and decided that American boys would like the great game of Scouting.

On February 8, 1910, Mr. Boyce and others interested in the idea, formally incorporated the Boy Scouts of America. This day, February 8, is celebrated today as the birthday of Scouting in the United States.

So it was that Scouting began in South Africa as an idea for training young men in outdoor skills, and came to America by way of England, because of a Good Turn. Today, in America, there are Scouts in nearly every city, town and village, from coast to coast.

There stands in Gilwell Park, England, a Bronze Buffalo statue, in memory of the unknown British Scout. The inscription reads:

"To the Unknown Scout whose faithfulness in the performance of the Daily Good Turn brought the Scout Movement to the United States of America."

THE DECLARATION OF INDEPENDENCE

laid down basic ideas about the
rights of man (your rights):
"We hold these truths . . .
. . . all men are created equal
(have equal opportunity)
. . . endowed by their Creator
with certain unalienable Rights . . .
(which cannot be given or taken away)
. . . Life
. . . Liberty
. . . the pursuit of Happiness
. . . Governments . . . deriving their
just powers from the consent
of the governed . . . (The government's power is granted
by the people.)

HOW TO BECOME A SCOUT

PART I

WHAT TO DO FIRST

CHAPTER 1

You have had a little glimpse of Scouting, how it began, what fun and adventure it holds for you. The next question is: how to become a Scout.

If you are eight, nine, or ten, you can join the Cub Scouts and have a lot of fun.

On the other hand, if you are fourteen and in the ninth grade, or fifteen — regardless of grade — you may become an Explorer.

If you are eleven or over and want to become a Boy Scout, this Handbook will help you get started right and get the most fun and value out of Scouting.

Find a Troop

Tell your Mother and Dad that you want to be a Scout. They want to know all about this new adventure, and help you find a Troop or a neighborhood Patrol.

Possibly some of your friends are Scouts, and have

asked you to join their Troop or Patrol. Perhaps your church or synagogue sponsors a Troop. You may discover that a Troop meets in your school or that your Dad knows of one in the neighborhood.

If there is no Troop nearby, the Scout office will tell your parents how to get one started. Your parents can find out where the Local Council Scout office is, or write to the National Council, Boy Scouts of America, New Brunswick, N. J. No matter where you live, you can be a Scout. If there are no Troops or neighborhood Patrols nearby, you can be a Lone Scout.

When you have found a Troop, take your Dad or guardian and visit one of its meetings. The Scoutmaster can tell him about Scouting.

Joining a Patrol

A Troop is made up of two or more Patrols of Scouts. A Patrol is a group of fellows who are good friends, and who can work and play together as a team. It has a name, its own officers, and its own meetings. Much of the fun you find in Scouting will be with the other fellows in your Patrol.

Candidate Scout

To become a Candidate Scout, you must be at least eleven years of age, and:

1 — Repeat from memory the Scout Oath or Promise and the twelve points of the Scout Law, the Scout Motto, and the Scout Slogan, and explain the meaning of each in your own words.

2 — Give the Scout Sign, Salute, and Handclasp.

3 — Present your application.

Having met these requirements, you may become a member of a Patrol. You may receive your membership card, wear the uniform, and start working on the rest of your Tenderfoot Requirements.

TENDERFOOT REQUIREMENTS

To become a TENDERFOOT SCOUT, you must be at least eleven years of age and do the following:

I. SCOUT SPIRIT—**Learning about the ideals and traditions of Scouting:**

1. **Repeat from memory the Scout Oath or Promise and the twelve points of the Scout Law, the Scout Motto, and the Scout Slogan, and explain the meaning of each in your own words.**
2. **Describe the Scout Badge and explain its meaning. Tell when to wear the Scout uniform and how to use and care for it.**
3. **Give the Scout Sign, Salute and Handclasp.**

II. SCOUT PARTICIPATION—**Knowing about the Patrol and Troop, the community and the country of which you are a part:**

1. **Explain the name of the Patrol you will join and give its call or yell. Tell who your Scout Leaders are and what they do in the Troop. Explain, in a general way, what you have to do to become a Second and a First Class Scout.**
2. **Tell how, in an emergency, you would get in contact with the doctor or hospital, and the police or sheriff's office nearest to your home,**

Explain how, in your community, you would report a fire.

3. Describe The Flag of the United States of America and tell its history in brief. Tell when to fly it. Show how to hoist, lower, display and fold The Flag and how to salute it.

III. SCOUTCRAFT—Setting out to learn a few simple things that all Scouts should know:

1. Tell why it is important to care for a cut or a scratch and show on yourself how to do it. Tie a bandage with a square knot.
2. Explain what care should be taken before building a fire in the open. Describe the harm to a live tree that results from hacking it with an axe or other sharp tool.
3. Whip the ends of a rope at least one-quarter inch in diameter. Join two ropes with a sheet-bend. Attach a rope to a post or rail with a clove hitch, then untie it and fasten it again with two half hitches. Fasten one end of a rope around your waist with a bowline.

When you have met the Tenderfoot requirements before your Scoutmaster (or have been reviewed in the Cub Scout Webelos requirements by your Scoutmaster), and have proved to him that you thoroughly understand the Scout Oath or Promise and Law, he registers you as a Boy Scout. **You take the Scout Oath or Promise at a ceremony in front of your Patrol and Troop,** and are then entitled to wear the Tenderfoot badge and the Official Uniform of the Boy Scouts of America.

Your Patrol Leader and your Scoutmaster will help you prepare for the Candidate and Tenderfoot requirements. Your Dad can help you, too.

When you are ready your Scoutmaster will go over them with you, to make sure that you know and understand them. When he is satisfied, he will give you an application blank to take home and fill out, and will explain the registration fee to you. Bring the completed application and the registration fee back with you to the next meeting, and he will send it to the National Council of the Boy Scouts of America, through the Local Council office.

Then comes the big day for you—the day when you are formally received into the Troop. There will be a special ceremony called an "Investiture Ceremony." There, in the presence of all the Troop and its leaders, and your folks, too, you will take the Scout Oath or Promise. It will not be memory work; it will be your promise to live like a good Scout. There your Scoutmaster will present you with the Registration Card which says you are a registered member of the Troop. At the close of that ceremony you will be a full-fledged Scout, starting out on a wonderful trail.

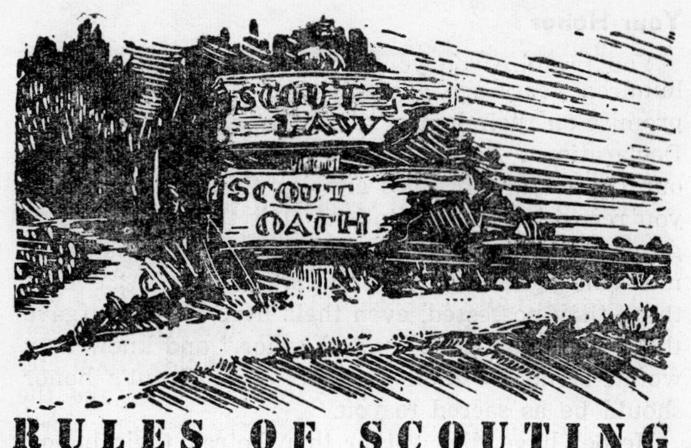

RULES OF SCOUTING

CHAPTER 2

You know that there must be certain rules to play any game, whether it is football or checkers. You and the others have to follow those rules, or there just isn't any game.

In the game of Scouting there are certain rules too. These rules are the Scout's code; they are the Scout Oath or Promise and Law, the Scout Motto and the Scout Slogan. When you take the Scout Oath, you promise to play the game according to these rules.

Of all the requirements to meet to become a Boy Scout, understanding and keeping these rules is the most important. If you don't know the Scout's code, and do your best to live up to it, you are not a Scout, no matter what badge you wear on your uniform. When you promise to follow these rules, you start a new life. Therefore, it is important that you know them, and understand the meaning of each part.

Your Honor

You promise "on your honor." It was almost two hundred years ago a group of men made a solemn promise on their honor. "And for the support of this Declaration . . . we mutually pledge to each other our Lives, our Fortunes and our Sacred Honor." Do you recognize this quotation? It is the closing paragraph in the Declaration of Independence. The brave men who signed it knew that they stood to lose everything they possessed, even their lives. But they gave their pledge on their "sacred honor," and knew they would stand by their promise. Your Scout's honor should be as sacred to you.

Heroes have died rather than betray their honor. In the last war, the Germans were constantly hindered in France by the Underground, the loyal Frenchmen who resisted them and destroyed their equipment. The Germans knew that one house in a certain little town was the center of resistance in that district, but they did not even know the names of the loyal Frenchmen who were using the equipment. So they arrested a young Boy Scout who was

"We . . . Pledge . . . Our Sacred Honor"

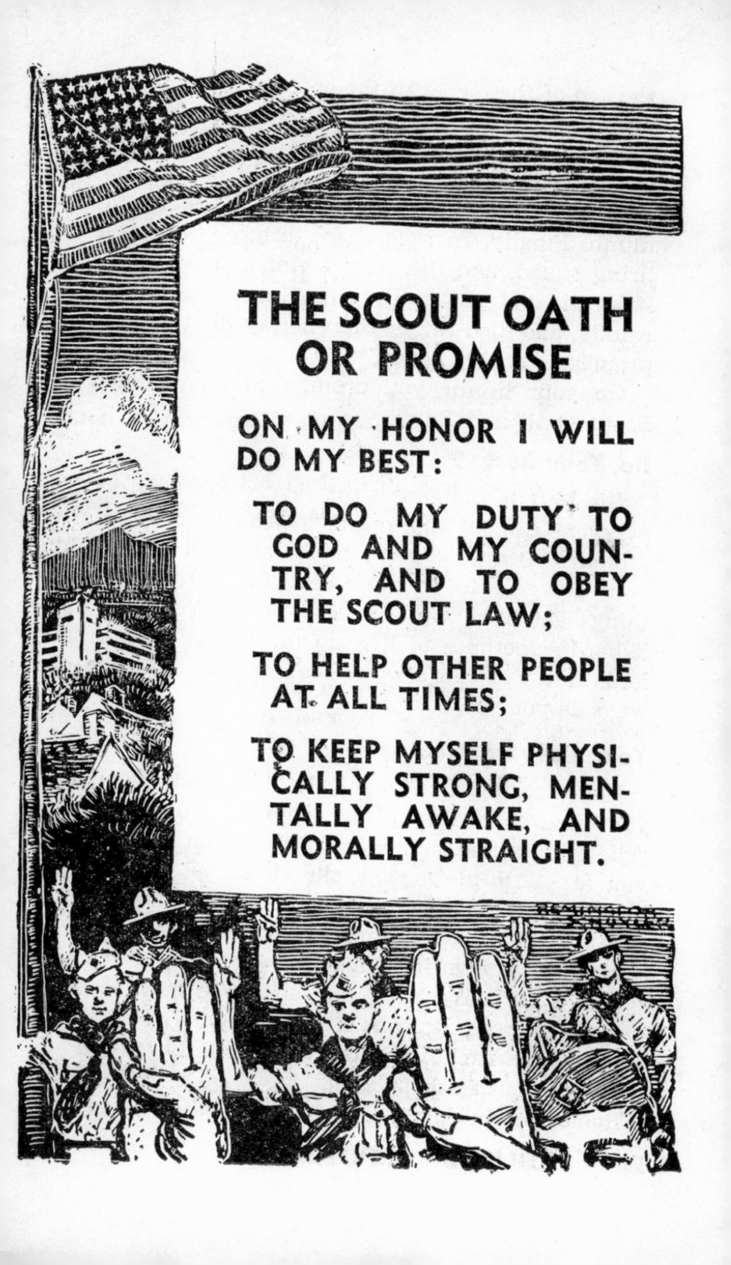
THE SCOUT OATH
OR PROMISE
ON MY HONOR I WILL
DO MY BEST:
TO DO MY DUTY TO
GOD AND MY COUN-
TRY, AND TO OBEY
THE SCOUT LAW;
TO HELP OTHER PEOPLE
AT ALL TIMES;
TO KEEP MYSELF PHYSI-
CALLY STRONG, MEN-
TALLY AWAKE, AND
MORALLY STRAIGHT.

the son of the owner of the house. "He must have the information we want, and being only a boy, he will break easily," they said. First they tried coaxing, and offered bribes. The Scout would not speak. Then they tried starvation and beating. The Scout was dumb. Finally, in rage, they dragged him before a firing squad, and threatened him with instant death if he did not speak. But the Scout faced the rifles calmly, and died rather than betray his trust. He had promised "on his honor."

On your **honor** you promise to try to keep the Scout Oath and Law.

Do Your Best

His **best** is something that every boy can do. Not everyone can get high marks in school, or be a star in athletics. But this more important thing is within your power — to do your best. Slackers quit when things get hard. Not the Boy Scout. You may find it hard sometimes to live up to all you have promised. But you can always keep trying. You can always do your best.

Your Duty to God

You worship God regularly with your family in your church or synagogue. You try to follow the religious teachings that you have been taught, and you are faithful in your church school duties, and help in church activities. Above all you are faithful to Almighty God's Commandments.

Most great men in history have been men of deep religious faith. Washington knelt in the snow to pray at Valley Forge. Lincoln always sought Divine guidance before each important decision. Be proud of your religious faith.

Remember in doing your duty to God, to be grate-

A Scout is faithful to his religion

ful to Him. Whenever you succeed in doing something well, thank Him for it. Sometimes when you look up into the starlit sky on a quiet night, and feel close to Him—thank Him as the Giver of all good things.

One way to express your duty and your thankfulness to God is to help others, and this too, is a part of your Scout promise.

Duty to Country

Every Boy Scout wants to help his Country. During the last war, they proved it by hours of back-breaking work. They collected thousands of tons of paper and metal; they travelled thousands of miles in various other services.

In peacetime they serve their Country too, less dramatically, but faithfully.

Your Country is made up of thousands of neighborhoods like yours. When you serve your community you serve your Country. When you put torn paper and trash where it belongs, instead of throwing it in the street, you serve your community.

Scouting will train you in many ways to be an asset to your community. Knowing how to report a fire correctly may save valuable property and even human life. When you learn how to give first aid to injured animals and people, you are helping your community and through it, your Country.

You will have many opportunities with your Troop to do Good Turns to the community. Scouts have made traffic counts, taken health surveys, set out trees, planted gardens around railroad stations, performed many services for which their community had no funds to pay, and no men available to work. So can you in your Troop.

Obey the Scout Law

In order to obey the Scout Law and live up to its twelve points, you should understand each part thoroughly. You should be able to explain how you use it in your daily life. If a man makes a promise, he should know what he is promising. Although you need not memorize all the text, you should be able to explain it in your own words.

We speak of the Scout Law, meaning all its twelve parts or points. The Scout Law is something positive. There is not a "Don't" anywhere in it. Be sure you understand it.

To Help Other People At All Times

Captain John Smith, who came over with the early settlers in Virginia, and whose life was saved by Pocahontas, was a tough and seasoned soldier. He had fought in every part of the world, but he had a good, kind heart. He was a fine Scout. One of his favorite sayings was, "We were born not for ourselves, but to do good to others, for the love of God," and he carried it out all his life.

Remember it was the Good Turn of an unknown British Scout which brought Scouting to the United States.

Baden-Powell, the founder of Scouting tells this in the British Handbook, *Scouting for Boys.*

> "I often think that when the sun goes down the world is hidden by a big blanket from the light of heaven, but the stars are little holes pierced in that by those who have done good deeds in this world. The stars are not all the same size; some are big, some are little, and some men have done small deeds, but they have made their hole in the blanket by doing good before they went to heaven.
>
> "Try and make your hole in the blanket by good work while you are on earth.
>
> "It is something to *be* good, but it is far better to *do* good."

Physically Strong

To be physically strong does not mean that you have to be a superman with bulging muscles, who devotes most of his time to developing a physique that is useful only in the prize ring or the athletic field. But you should have your body under control, you should be supple, and quick and easy of movement, with strong heart and lungs. Such a body helps you to carry through whatever you start, and you can develop it.

Your Scouting activities will help. Camping is a wonderful builder of a sturdy body. There is no more joyful nor effective method, especially if you make it an adventure.

Even if you are not as tall or as well developed as you wish, don't be discouraged. Have a physical check-up to find out what you should do to correct your weakness, then do it. Turn to Chapter 23 in this Handbook and read the simple rules of diet, sleep, fresh air and exercise and cleanliness, and follow them. It is up to you.

President Theodore Roosevelt was a puny, sickly boy. He was handicapped by deafness in one ear and half blind besides. He went to a ranch and lived in the open like the old scouts, worked hard, and built himself up till he was outstanding as a strong, virile man, one of the greatest explorers and hunters of his time.

Mentally Awake

The boy who is mentally awake lives more in a day than a dull boy does in a month. He has more adventure. He gets more out of life, and he gives more to other people. You want to have friends. Of course you do. You want to excel in games, have interesting hobbies. If you are dull and uninteresting, you will never get all that is coming to you out of life.

As a Scout you will be helped to be mentally awake by your training in observation. A Life Scout, because he was mentally awake, once helped capture two dangerous criminals. As he watched from his living room window, he saw two men. He thought they were acting suspiciously. As a part of his Scout training he noted their clothing, their appearance and the number of their car license. Later the police came to make inquiries and he was able to furnish information that led to their capture.

Morally Straight

George Washington said that morality cannot be lasting without religion. A morally straight Scout knows how to love and serve God in the way He wants him to. We are created by God and we owe certain duties to this Heavenly Father of all of us. You learn to perform these spiritual duties in your home and in your church or synagogue. Some Scouts learn these most important duties in the schools they attend. On Mt. Sinai God gave to Moses the Ten Commandments. He laid down certain definite Laws for all. Not to steal, not to lie, not to abuse your body are some of these Laws. Keeping these Commandments is an important step towards being morally straight.

A loving Scout son always asks his Heavenly Father's pardon before he goes to bed at night for any offense he may have committed in thought, word or deed during the day. This is a Scout's way of saying: "I am sorry, dear God, and with your help I will not offend you again." Your own spiritual leader, minister, priest or rabbi will teach you how to know God better.

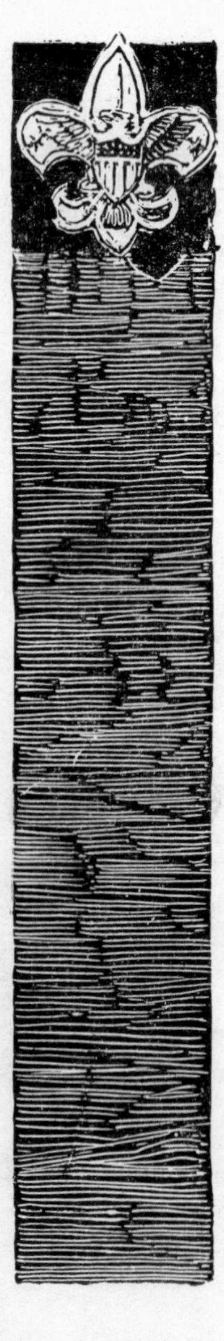

THE SCOUT LAW

1. A SCOUT IS TRUSTWORTHY

A Scout's honor is to be trusted. If he were to violate his honor by telling a lie, or by cheating, or by not doing exactly a given task, when trusted on his honor, he may be directed to hand over his Scout Badge.

2. A SCOUT IS LOYAL

He is loyal to all to whom loyalty is due, his Scout leader, his home, and parents and country.

3. A SCOUT IS HELPFUL

He must be prepared at any time to save life, help injured persons, and share the home duties. He must do at least one "Good Turn" to somebody every day.

4. A SCOUT IS FRIENDLY

He is a friend to all and a brother to every other Scout.

5. A SCOUT IS COURTEOUS

He is polite to all, especially to women, children, old people and the weak and helpless. He must not take pay for being helpful or courteous.

6. A SCOUT IS KIND

He is a friend to animals. He will not kill nor hurt any living creature needlessly, but will strive to save and protect all harmless life.

7. A SCOUT IS OBEDIENT

He obeys his parents, Scoutmaster, Patrol Leader, and all other duly constituted authorities.

8. A SCOUT IS CHEERFUL

He smiles whenever he can. His obedience to orders is prompt and cheery. He never shirks nor grumbles at hardships.

9. A SCOUT IS THRIFTY

He does not wantonly destroy property. He works faithfully, wastes nothing, and makes the best use of his opportunities. He saves his money so that he may pay his own way, be generous to those in need, and helpful to worthy objects. He may work for pay, but must not receive tips for courtesies or Good Turns.

10. A SCOUT IS BRAVE

He has the courage to face danger in spite of fear, and to stand up for the right against the coaxings of friends or the jeers or threats of enemies, and defeat does not down him.

11. A SCOUT IS CLEAN

He keeps clean in body and thought, stands for clean speech, clean sport, clean habits, and travels with a clean crowd.

12. A SCOUT IS REVERENT

He is reverent toward God. He is faithful in his religious duties, and respects the convictions of others in matters of custom and religion.

Trustworthy

Our whole world is based on trusting other people. You trust the storekeeper from whom you buy your baseball mit to sell you a good one, and the manufacturer who made it to use honest materials. You trust the Postal Department when you put a stamp on a letter to deliver it for you. You trust the plumber who mends the kitchen sink to do a good job. Sometimes people fail in their trust, but they live up to it far more often. Unless we trusted people the whole machinery of living would break down.

As a Scout, your parents and teachers and friends know you tell the truth and act honestly in what you do. If your ball broke the window in the parish house, you own up. If you did see someone else's examination paper, you tell the truth, even if it means flunking the course.

You do "exactly a given task." When your mother trusts you to look after the younger children in her absence, you stay with them instead of joining the ball game in the next lot.

A store manager once wanted some handbills delivered to private houses, and hired some boys to do the job. Half the notices never got there; they were dumped, torn and mutilated. Next time he hired a Patrol of Boy Scouts. The notices got to the places for which they were intended. There was no wastage, no complaints. A Scout does exactly a given task.

Sometimes an apparently little thing becomes very important. Some years ago there was a boy who wanted to be a Scout. His knot requirement gave him a lot of trouble. He practiced until he could produce a knot that passed inspection, but he knew that he had not really mastered the sheetbend. After he had joined the Troop, some of the things his Scoutmaster had said to him about the First Law made him serious. Entirely on his own, he practiced his Tenderfoot knots till he knew he was qualified. Then came his real test.

A steeple-jack, by a series of accidents, was stranded at nightfall on a chimney two hundred feet in the air, with no way to get down. He was exhausted and unnerved, and could not hold on to his dangerous perch much longer. His tackle was on the ground, but he remembered that ropes were too short, and he had not spliced them. He called down to the crowd to ask if anyone could make a knot that would hold. There was silence. Then someone called, "Here comes a Boy Scout." The Scout called up that he could make a sheetbend, and tied the knot.

The tackle was sent up to the steeple-jack by the lead rope. The steeple-jack went over the edge in his "chair" and prayed all the way down that the Scout knew what he was talking about. But the steeple-jack reached the ground safely. The crowd cheered and shook his hand. But one member of the crowd was nearly in tears. It was the Tenderfoot Scout who had tied the sheetbend and saved his life.

Loyal

Loyalty starts in your home. Show that you are proud of your parents and appreciate what they do for you. Maybe your house isn't the finest on the street. Still it is your home, and if you show respect for it, others will too. It is never smart or clever to make "wisecracks" to others about your home or your family.

The success of your Patrol and Troop depends on the loyalty of each member. If you kick, grumble, or fail to pitch in with the team, you are disloyal. If things are not quite to your liking, get to work with the others, and make them better.

A Scout is loyal to his Country. As a Scout, you show respect for your Country's Flag, for its laws and its government and institutions. You prove your loyalty by helping in your community.

Helpful

In your Scout Oath you promised to help other people at all times. The third point of the Scout Law suggests a definite way to do it—the Daily Good Turn. Start today to do at least one helpful thing for some one. The knot in the Scout Badge is a symbol of your Good Turn, and you tie a knot in your Scout neckerchief to remind you to do it.

At first it may be a little difficult to remember it; you may even have some trouble finding a job that will be helpful to someone. But stick to it, and the Good Turn will soon become a good habit. It need not be large, the spirit is what counts. This spirit is illustrated by something that happened one Christmas Eve in the city of New London, Conn.

The father of a family of seven children had been injured and was in the hospital. The children were sure, however, that Santa Claus would fill their stockings while they slept. To the mother, the situation was desperate, because the family needed food and clothing, and there were long weeks ahead before her husband could leave the hospital. While the children chattered of roller skates, dolls and Christmas trees, she was trying to figure out how to scrape enough together to keep the home going.

Then there came a knock at the door. "Santa Claus!" shouted the children. It was not Santa Claus, but a Boy Scout with a smile extending clear across his face. In his arms a bag overflowed with toys. Behind him stood another Scout, and another—a whole Troop of Boy Scouts, bringing toys and food and clothing, enough to carry the family through the weeks ahead. The Troop had heard of the plight of this family and had adopted them as their Christmas Good Turn.

Because you are a Scout, you will have many op-

In a World Jamboree all Scouts are "brothers"

portunities to do Good Turns with your Patrol and Troop in addition to your own personal Daily Good Turn.

A Scout's Good Turn is not doing regular home duties about the house or farm such as any boy expects to do cheerfully because it is his job. A Good Turn is something off the beaten track, something you go out of your way to do. It may be something planned, like feeding the birds during the winter, or taking used magazines regularly to the hospital, or serving as a Den Chief in a Cub Den. Or it may be something done on the spur of the moment, such as straightening the noisy manhole cover, helping a motorist change a tire, or doing an errand for a stranger. It may involve giving first aid, or saving a life.

One more thing. Keep it secret. Good Scouts never boast about their Scouting spirit. They don't ask for glory. Once a Baltimore Scout saved a boy from drowning, and swore all his friends who were there to silence. Only months later did the story leak out. That is typical of the true Boy Scout.

Friendly

The best way to have a friend is to be one. You take the new Scout into your Patrol, and try to make him welcome. If you are in camp, you do your share of the chores and help others if necessary. To be a good leader, you must first be a good friend, make the other fellows know you care about things that interest them.

A smile helps you to feel friendly. Try it and see.

The World-wide Scout Brotherhood is based on friendship. To it belong boys that go to different churches, have different colored skins, speak different languages. Some come from rich homes, others wear patches on their clothes. But in Scouting they are all friends and brothers, though they gather from all corners of the earth.

Courteous

This is just another way of saying "A Scout is a gentleman." Courtesy comes from the heart, and goes hand in hand with friendship.

The caveman was all right in his day. He squatted beside the fire, snatched his lump of meat, pulled it apart with his hands and teeth. If he saw anything he wanted he grabbed it. If someone was in his way, he knocked him down.

But who wants a caveman around today? Along with houses, tables, knives and forks, we have developed standards of friendship and courtesy which make life a lot more enjoyable.

Part of the training of plebes at West Point and Annapolis includes training in the courtesies of "an officer and a gentleman."

Kind

Naturally you are kind to pets, the family cat, your dog, to the poultry and the farm livestock. As a Scout, your care extends further. As you study wild animals and birds, you will become as much interested in protecting and helping them as you are in the animals around your home. Birds especially need protection and help. You will set up feeding stations and keep food in them, build bird houses. Perhaps with others in your Troop you can take part in a state conservation project. Read the chapter on Conservation to learn how.

Obedient

After George Washington had successfully defeated the British Army, an officer asked his mother how she had managed to raise so brilliant a son. You know Washington's character, his fame for truth, his honor, his bravery. But his mother's reply to the question touched none of these qualities. She answered "I taught him to *obey*!"

This was not only the case with Washington. The great men of history learned to obey when they were

young. They learned to discipline themselves before they could give orders to others. Obedience is a manly quality. It shows self-control, strength of character. Great men know how to take orders. Weaklings whine and grumble about them.

Obedience is something everyone has to learn. How successful would the school football team be if the players disobeyed their coach's instructions, and ignored their quarterback's signals? What fun would you have on a hike if half the Patrol straggled off the road, and the rest had to waste the afternoon looking them up?

If everyone is to have a good time in Scouting or in life, he must learn first to take orders and carry them out, cheerfully and promptly.

Cheerful

You know the fellow who is all smiles as long as he gets what he wants but who grouses like a spoiled child, if he doesn't. He likes to cook the camp meal on a fine day, but not when the wind blows the smoke in his eyes. He's a good pal as long as you play the game he wants. He's a smiling son if his mother offers the gang a plate of cookies; but if she wants the eggs collected—he doesn't act like a Scout.

You have lived long enough to know that you can't have your way all the time. You also realize that you are going to have to do a certain number of things you don't particularly like. Everybody has to. All right, face it; be cheerful about it. You'll make your home duties, school work or any other job easier and pleasanter if you are pleasant. The time will pass more quickly and the job be easier. Cheerfulness is more or less a habit, and it will help you a lot to have more friends, and enjoy life more.

Thrifty

Every Scout wants to pay his own way in everything he does, but especially in Scouting. You work to earn the money to help buy your uniform and equipment for hiking and camping, and to pay your Troop and Patrol dues. Take good care of the things that belong to you, for uniforms and other things represent money. Make them last as long as possible. On hikes and on camping trips be careful not to waste food. Take only what you need.

Real thrift is not just saving money. It is saving with a purpose and spending wisely the money you save. Thrift actually consists of four things: earning, saving, spending wisely, and sharing. It takes hard work to earn money. When you work for it, you appreciate it. If you save it toward your education or toward a future ambition, you are saving with a purpose. When you spend it, spend it carefully and wisely. Remember always to share what you have with those less fortunate than you.

Brave

Not long ago, a fourteen-year-old Boy Scout performed such an outstanding act of bravery that newspapers all across the country printed the story. He was a Star Scout of Syracuse, New York, and he saved the life of a child from a burning launch. To do this, he had to swim twice under a patch of blazing oil. From his boat he dived in and swam under the flames. He climbed aboard the blazing launch, and, holding the child with one arm and keeping his other hand over her nose and mouth to prevent her from inhaling the water, he dived again and swam with her twenty-five feet under the water covered with blazing oil, to safety. For this extraordinary act of courage, the National Court of Honor of the Boy Scouts of America awarded him a Gold Medal with Crossed Palms.

Thousands of other Scouts have shown extraordinary bravery and quick thinking in times of dan-

ger. Their Scout skills have given them the knowledge which helped them to save life. Their character as Scouts has helped give them courage to do so.

Perhaps you will not have the opportunity to prove your bravery in such fashion. But there are tests of your bravery that you face every day.

You know the ideals of the Scout Oath or Promise. You know right from wrong, and in spite of urging and "wise cracks," you can do what is right. You can be brave in the face of danger, and brave in the face of temptation.

Clean

You know how good you feel after a bath, with plenty of soap and hot water. As a Scout you keep clean in thought and speech too, and the feeling is just as satisfying. Keeping clean in body is a part of being physically strong. Keeping clean in thought, speech and habits is necessary to be morally straight.

A little soap and water and rubbing will remove the dirt from the outside of your body. But no soap will remove dirt that gets inside in your mind.

The best way to keep clean in thought, word and actions, is to go with those fellows who are trying to do the same thing. It is much easier to keep clean mentally, if your friends are the right sort.

You will find that if you do your best to live up to the other points of the law, and if you live an active, worthwhile life, it will be easier to keep clean in thought and action. Fellows who hang around street corners or waste their time in other ways are the ones generally who have time for dirty stories and thoughts. The fellow who keeps busy with worthwhile things, who is thrifty with his time and his energies, is also clean in his thoughts and actions.

Reverent

Reverence is that respect, regard, consideration, courtesy, devotion, and affection you have for some person, place or thing because it is holy. The Scout shows true reverence in two principal ways. First, you pray to God, you love God and you serve Him. Secondly, in your everyday actions, you help other people, because they are made by God to God's own likeness. You and all men are important in the sight of God because God made you. The "unalienable rights" in our historic Declaration of Independence, come from God.

That is why you respect others whose religion and customs may differ from yours. Some fellows think they are smart by telling stories or making fun of people of other religions or races. All your life you will be associating with people of other beliefs and customs. It is your duty to respect these people for their beliefs and customs, and to live your own.

You will find help in living this Twelfth part of the Scout Law in the Scout Religious Awards (see page 441). Work with your minister, priest, rabbi, or religious adviser to earn this Award. It is given under the authority of your own religious leaders.

This true story happened to a family in Oklahoma. It was a cold winter morning and a gas heater had been lighted to warm the young children while dressing. One of them thoughtlessly stepped too close, and in an instant her flimsy clothes were in flames. The little girl shrieked and the other children cried. The mother stood filled with horror. The father and his thirteen-year-old son came running upstairs. The son was a Boy Scout and had been taught in his first aid training what to do. He was prepared. He caught up a small rug from the floor, and rolled the screaming little girl in its folds. In a moment he had smothered the flames and had prevented serious injury.

When the Scout's father told the Scoutmaster about what had happened, he said "Thank God, my son is a Scout. He knew what to do when I stood confused." Said the Scoutmaster, "He was prepared."

The Scout Motto means that a Scout is prepared at

any moment to do his duty, and to face danger if necessary, to help others. In the Middle Ages the Knights had a similar motto "Be Always Ready." Another well-known motto of a famous group is that of the United States Marine Corps, "Semper Fidelis," (Always Faithful).

Someone once asked Baden-Powell, the founder of Scouting, "Be Prepared for what?" "Why," said he, "for any old thing." That is just the idea. Accidents or emergencies are continually happening and Boy Scouts are prepared to help. Learn what to do in all kinds of emergencies, and how to do it. Wherever you are, whatever you are doing, think through in advance what you ought to do. It will be too late if you wait until the emergency happens. Suppose that Scout who saved his little sister had had to run to consult his Handbook to find out what to do! He would have been too late.

As a Scout it is your duty to Be Prepared.

Scout Slogan

DO A GOOD TURN DAILY

When people hear the word "Good Turn" they almost always think of Boy Scouts. Not that the idea of helping others started with Scouts, because of course it didn't—the Bible story of a Samaritan's Good Turn is known to millions, as are the adventures of King Arthur's Knights bringing help to those in distress. But in this modern world people do associate the words "Good Turn" with "Scouts."

This is true because since the beginning of Scouting every new member has proudly accepted the obligation to do a Good Turn to someone every day. It is the Scout Slogan just as "Be Prepared" is the Scout Motto. Together they carry much of the meaning and spirit of the Scout Oath and Law.

A Good Turn means doing something helpful, but it means more than that—it means doing something extra, beyond what you would do ordinarily.

This takes watchfulness on your part. As a Scout you are expected to be on the lookout for Good Turn opportunities. You can develop that type of "observation ability" just as you can that of seeing faint trail signs.

Along with this ability to recognize Good Turn

opportunities will come your own daily check-up on yourself. "Have I done a Good Turn yet today?" (Of course you should not stop at one Good Turn. But it often is surprising how much special attention it takes to find that first one each day.)

Here are some ways Scouts keep track of their Good Turns: In many Troops Scouts make a practice of putting on their Scout Badge or their neckerchief slide upside down each morning, turning it right side up when they have done their first Good Turn of the day. Many others put the Scout Good Turn pocket piece in their left pocket each morning and move it over to the right one when they have done that Good Turn. Whether or not you use some such reminder plan, do keep the Good Turn in mind every day. Gradually it becomes a habit that will give you a lot of satisfaction. It's good citizenship and it's good Scouting.

Those are the ideals of Scouting. Those are the qualities that make great and successful men. Those are promises that you make to yourself, and live up to in your daily life. Those are the promises that make up your code of honor, as a Scout.

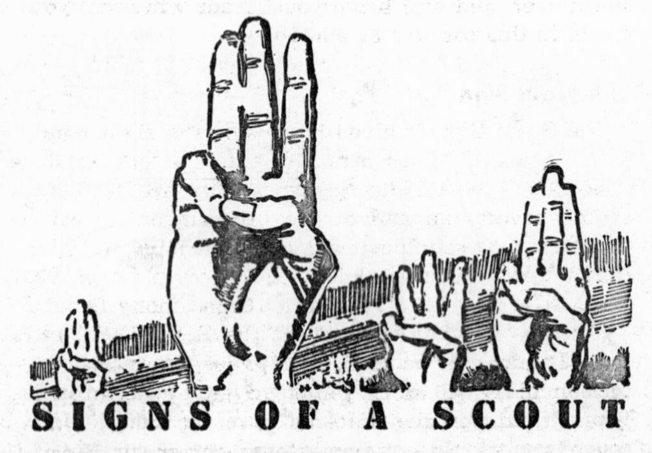

SIGNS OF A SCOUT

CHAPTER 3

Once an American, homesick for his family and friends, was making a trip to far-off India. As his boat entered the harbor he scanned the crowd of strangers' faces and felt lonelier than ever. Suddenly he snapped to attention and raised his right hand. There in the crowd stood a dark-skinned, turbaned boy with a big smile, and this boy was holding up his right hand to give **the Scout Sign.** The Indian Scout did not know whether there was another Scout on the big ship, but if there was, he wanted the Scout to know that here was a friend.

The American was the late General Theodore Roosevelt, an active Scout leader, and he often used to tell how his heart leaped when he realized that he had found a Scout brother.

All Over the World

The signs of a Scout set forth here are used the

world over, and will bring you friends wherever you travel in this country or abroad.

The Scout Sign

The Scout Sign is given by raising the right hand, palm forward, upper arm straight, and out to the side. The three middle fingers are upward, and the thumb covers the nail of the little finger. Be sure your arm is at shoulder level, and your hand straight.

The three fingers stand for the three parts of the Oath. It is used as a recognition sign among Scouts.

You use it when you repeat the Scout Oath and Law. It may also be used by your leaders to call attention in Troop or Patrol Meetings, or when on a hike. When you see a leader give the Scout Sign, stand at attention, be quiet, and return the Scout sign, waiting for the instructions which follow.

The Scout Salute

To give the Scout Salute, hold your right hand as in the Scout Sign. Bring it up quickly and smoothly to

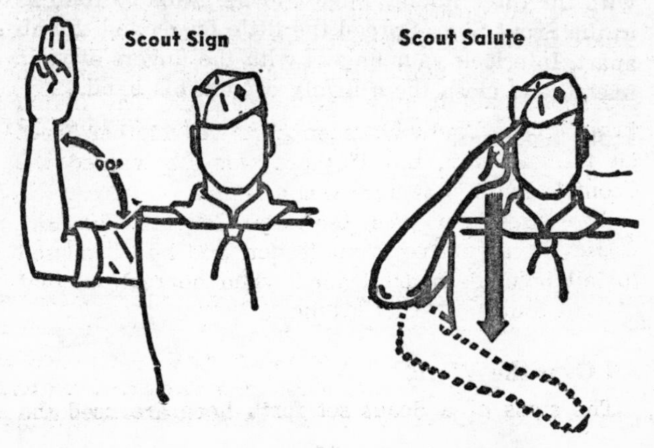

your head, palm sideways, until the forefinger touches your hat, or head, above the right eye. Snap it down, quickly and smoothly. Be sure, while saluting, that your upper arm is at right angles to your body, and your forearm at a 45 degree angle to your upper arm. Nothing looks better than a smart salute—and nothing worse than a sloppy one.

The Scout Salute is used to salute The Flag of the United States of America. Use it when you are in uniform, instead of tipping your hat. You give the Scout salute when you approach a Scout leader, before you speak to him. A salute as you leave him is courteous too.

The Scout Handclasp

The Scout Handclasp is made with the left hand, the hand nearest the heart, the hand of friendship. When you travel in foreign countries, or when you greet a Scout from another country, you use a straight lefthand clasp. In America you use your left hand with the three middle fingers in the same position as in the Scout Sign. Spread the little finger and thumb apart. Interlock your fingers with the fingers of your friend, and clasp them firmly around his hand.

SCOUT HANDCLASP

The Scout Badge*

The design of the Scout Badge is the sign of the north taken from the mariner's compass. The mariner's compass helps ships steer their course. The Chinese claim they used it two thousand years before Christ. It is known they used it as early as 300 A.D. (after Christ). Marco Polo, a famous explorer, brought the compass back to Europe on his return from Cathay (China) at the close of the thirteenth century.

In the centuries of adventure when men of courage sailed strange seas and made trails across unsettled continents, the north was their one and only fixed point, and this three-pointed sign came to stand for the north with the explorers, pioneers, and trappers, woodsmen and Scouts. It became the Scout emblem, only slightly changed as centuries passed by.

What Does the Badge Mean?

With slight changes in different countries, the Scout trefoil badge is used around the world as a mark of the Scout Brotherhood, of good citizenship, and friendliness.

The three points like the three fingers of the sign, refer to the three points of the Scout Oath.

---

* The Boy Scouts of America reserve the right to recall at any time, any badge awarded, if the Scout proves unworthy to wear it.

The two stars symbolize the ideals of truth and knowledge, which are foundations of strong Scout citizenship. The stars guide the Scout by night, as they do the mariners on the seven seas. They remind the Scout of the wondrous out-of-doors, which he enjoys on hikes and camping trips, sleeping beneath the boundless open sky.

The eagle is the national emblem of the United States of America. It symbolizes freedom and readiness to defend that hard-won freedom.

The scroll, at the bottom of the badge (which is used as the badge of the Second Class Scout) is turned up at its ends like a Scout's mouth, because a Scout smiles as he willingly does his duty or enjoys his play.

The knot at the bottom of the badge—a simple overhand knot—is a reminder that a Scout must do at least one Good Turn for somebody every day.

A Tenderfoot wears the trefoil, a Second Class Scout the Scroll, and a First Class Scout the trefoil and scroll combined.

The Scout Uniform—What It Stands For

The Scout uniform stands for Scouting. It shows that you belong to the biggest boys' organization in the world. Only Scouts may wear it. Congress authorized it, and it is protected against unlawful use by Act of Congress. It is a constant reminder that you are a Scout.

It stands for your *character* as a Scout, your Scout Promise, and your Scout Law.

It stands for *service*. It means that the Scout is "prepared" to help others. An accident occurs, a crowd gathers around. No one knows just what to do. A uniformed Scout steps quietly forward. The crowd lets him through, for he's supposed to know what to do in an emergency. He administers first aid and slips away, probably without his name being known. The Scout uniform quietly says that here is a fellow who is ready to be "helpful to other people at all times."

The Scout uniform stands for *friendship*. No matter what nationality or race or religion a Scout belongs to, he is a brother to every other Scout.

The Scout uniform stands for the *out-of-doors*. It is made of rugged, tough material, that is suited for outdoor use.

The Scout uniform *helps you to be a better Scout*. It is a thrill to wear the uniform, when you know all it stands for. It makes you want to go hiking and camping. It makes you want to be of service to your fellow man. It makes you want to live according to the Scout Oath and Law.

Wear Your Uniform!

You do not have to have a uniform to be a Scout, but you will be a better Scout if you do own one. Start now to earn the money for it. Talk this over with your parents, Scoutmaster and others in your Troop.

When you get your uniform wear it with pride. Take good care of it. Wear it when you go Scouting.

Wear it correctly. There is only one correct way to wear the uniform and badges, and that is the way shown in the illustrations on the following pages. All the members of the Troop must wear the same articles of the uniform; that is all wear hats or all wear caps; all wear long trousers, or all wear shorts. Your Patrol Leader will tell you what you need.

When to Wear the Uniform

1. In all formal Scouting activities such as Patrol, Troop or Tribe meetings, hikes, camps, demonstrations, etc. At special Church services for Scouts.

2. When appearing before formal Courts of Honor.

3. During Boy Scout Week (February 7-13).

4. For special Scouting or civic service.

5. On other occasions when requested.

When the Uniform Should Not Be Worn

1. When soliciting funds or engaged in any selling campaign, or in any commercial operation. This does

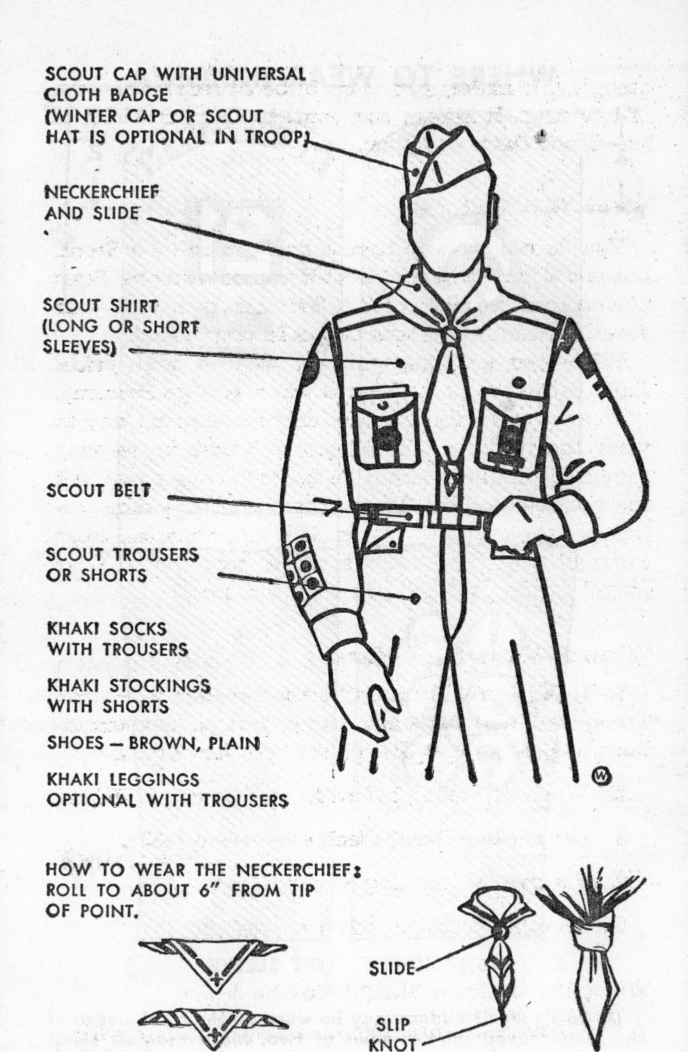
SCOUT CAP WITH UNIVERSAL CLOTH BADGE (WINTER CAP OR SCOUT HAT IS OPTIONAL IN TROOP)
NECKERCHIEF AND SLIDE
SCOUT SHIRT (LONG OR SHORT SLEEVES)
SCOUT BELT
SCOUT TROUSERS OR SHORTS
KHAKI SOCKS WITH TROUSERS
KHAKI STOCKINGS WITH SHORTS
SHOES — BROWN, PLAIN
KHAKI LEGGINGS OPTIONAL WITH TROUSERS
HOW TO WEAR THE NECKERCHIEF: ROLL TO ABOUT 6" FROM TIP OF POINT.
SLIDE
SLIP KNOT

WHERE TO WEAR INSIGNIA

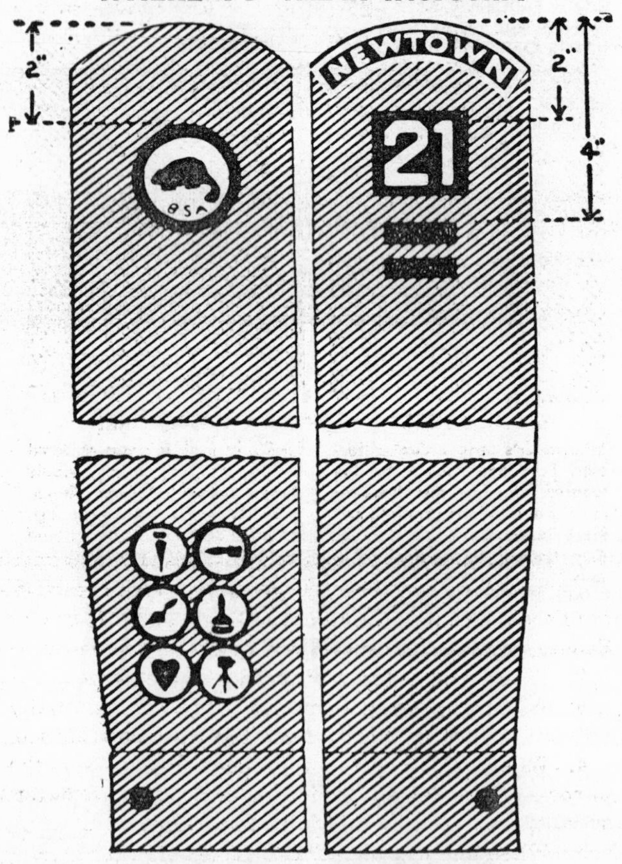

RIGHT SLEEVE LEFT SLEEVE

Up to six Merit Badges may be worn on the right sleeve of the long-sleeved shirt in rows of two. More than six Merit Badges should be worn on a sash.

RIGHT POCKET

Interpreter's Strip indicates foreign language spoken by the wearer who has met Requirement 5a of World Brotherhood Merit Badge.
One Council temporary badge may be worn.

LEFT POCKET

Badge of rank is worn centered on left pocket, except Eagle Badge suspended from ribbon, which is centered on left breast. Webelos Badge is worn centered and touching bottom seam of left pocket.

not forbid Scouts in uniform selling tickets to or for Scout Circuses, Rallies and similar Scout events.

2. When engaged in any political endeavor.

3. When appearing upon the stage professionally without specific authority from the National Council.

4. When taking part in parades, except for the purpose of rendering services as a Scout or Scouter, or when representing officially the B.S.A.

5. When one has ceased to be a Scout.

Care of the Uniform

A Scout is careful of his clothing. It represents money and "A Scout is Thrifty." He carefully folds it or hangs it on hangers when not using it.

Instructions for washing—The material used in the Official Uniform of the Boy Scouts of America has been selected after most careful testing to provide best colorfastness. It should not fade or shrink if washed with normal precautions. Bleaches or harsh alkalies should not be used.

Attendance Pin: worn by Cub Scouts, Boy Scouts, Explorers. Requirements for earning shall be set by unit committee and leaders.

Service Stars: Cub Scout—Yellow; Boy Scout—Green; Explorer —Red; Scouter—Blue; Plain stars for one year; numerals indicate years of tenure.

Unit Numeral

Community Strip

Senior Strip: worn by Boy Scouts over age fourteen centered above the Boy Scouts of America strip.

Webelos

Patrol Emblem

Den Chief Cord

Tenderfoot
2d Class
1st Class
Star
Life
Eagle
Eagle Palm
Honor Medal
Medal of Merit
Ass't Patrol Leader
Patrol Leader
Senior Patrol Leader
Scribe
Bugler
Quarter-master
Librarian
Jr. Ass't Scoutmaster Bronze on Green
Scoutmaster Silver on Green Asst. SM. Gold on Green
Chaplain
Commissioner Blue and Silver Scout Executive Red and Silver

TAKE PART IN SCOUT ACTIVITIES

CHAPTER 4

Your Patrol

Your Patrol is your gang, with whom you scout, hike and camp. Each Patrol has its own name, flag, call and badge.

Your Patrol may be named for the Tiger, the Bear or some other animal. Or it may be named after a pioneer like Kit Carson, or a hero like George Washington. The name stands for something the Scouts admire—like the cleverness of a fox, like the courage of Washington, or some quality in a local hero. Ask your Patrol Leader what the name of your Patrol stands for.

Your Patrol flag displays the emblem of your Patrol. How proud you feel to belong when you see it fluttering in the breeze! You wear your Patrol badge on your right sleeve for the same reason—to tell the world where you belong, who your buddies are, and what you stand for. Probably you stencil it on your pack, your tent and other equipment. The best Patrol in the Troop—you are part of it!

Your Patrol has a call—the cry of your Patrol animal. Softly you give your Patrol call under your buddy's window, and no one knows why he suddenly slips away to join you. In the silence of the woods, your Patrol Leader sounds a sharp call for his Patrol to gather, but it is a secret to the rest. In a game, at night, you hear that call and know it is a warning to you and your buddies.

Around the campfire you give your Patrol cheer, then sing your Patrol songs as the flames burn low.

The strength of your Patrol is the strength of each Scout. Do your share to make it strong.

Leaders in Your Patrol

Every Scout in your Patrol has a job, and so will you.

Your Patrol Leader is a First Class Scout, or working towards it rapidly, because part of his job is to help train the others. He leads the Patrol at Patrol and Troop meetings, on hiking and camping trips.

He selects (or the Patrol elects) his Assistant Patrol Leader to help him.

Your Patrol Scribe keeps the record in the Patrol Log (history book of the Patrol).

The Patrol Treasurer collects dues of Patrol members and keeps a financial record. He turns over these dues to the Troop Scribe or to the Troop Committee member who is Treasurer.

The Patrol Quartermaster has charge of Patrol equipment—tents, cooking gear, first aid kits and the

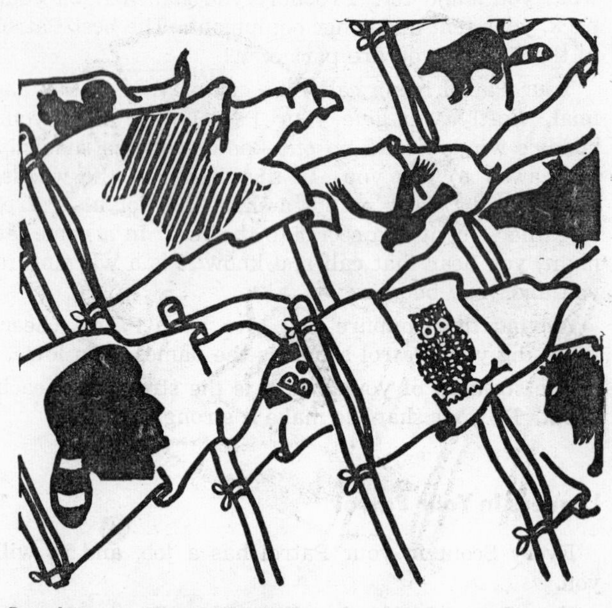

Patrol Names, Flags and Calls

Seal—sharp bark
Crow—"caw-caw-caw"
Otter—"hoi-oi-oik"
Raven—"kar-kaw"
Hawk—shrill high whistle
Panther—"keeook"
Eagle—shrill "kreeee"
Porcupine—teeth chatter
Buffalo—lowing "um-mooww"
Gull—"kow-howk"
Bob White—whistle Bob Bob white
Moose—"oh-ah, oh-ah, oh-ahhh"
Raccoon—whine "mm, mm, mmm"
Antelope—shrill snort
Woodpecker—"tap, tap, tap"
Bat—high squeak
Cookoo—"cook-koo"
Flaming Arrow—"whsssss"
Whippoorwill—whistle "whip-poor-will"

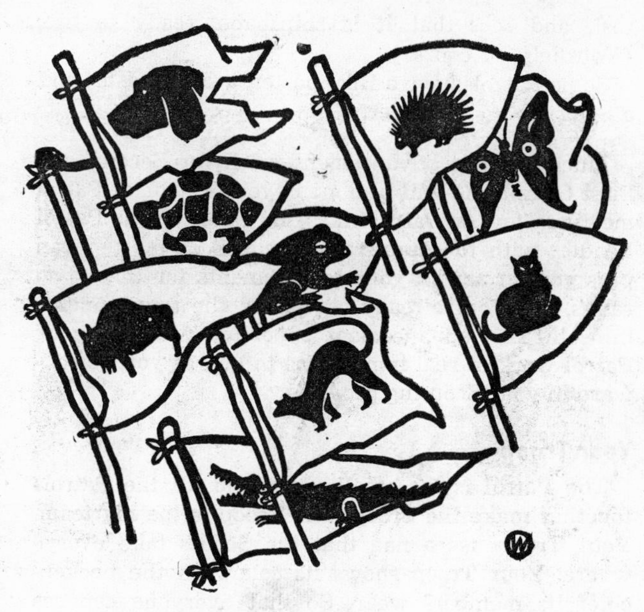

Heron—"quawk quawk"
Flying Eagle—shrill "kreee"
Bear—growl
Rattlesnake—rattle pebbles in can
Beaver—clap hands once
Owl—loud coo
Alligator—grunting hiss
Pelican—clap-clap-clap
Wolf—howl "how-ooo"
Pine Tree—rustle paper
Fox—bark

Other names, make up your own calls

Pioneer
Dan Beard
Kit Carson
Dan'l Boone
Ranger
Iroquois
Robinson Crusoe
Woodsmen
Paul Bunyan
Mohawk
Apache

rest, and sees that it is shipshape, ready to use. (You help, of course).

Some Patrols have a Hikemaster, a Grubmaster and a Song or Cheer Leader.

Much of your advancement work for Second and First Class Rank will be done in your Patrol, at Patrol meetings, and on Patrol hikes and camps. Your Patrol Leader, with the approval of your Scoutmaster, can pass you on any of your requirements for these two ranks, if he has already completed the requirements himself. This advancement opportunity makes your Patrol work of real importance to you as you go forward in your Scouting progress.

Your Troop

The Patrol is the small gang, and all the Patrols together make the Troop. The Troop is the big team. Your Troop has a flag that the Scouts take everywhere. Your Troop shows its colors on the neckerchief its members wear. So that everyone can see what Troop you belong to, you wear the Troop numeral on your left sleeve. Troop 21, "Old 16," the "Hiking 63"—what memories those numbers recall to the Scouts who have gone before you! Troop songs around the fire on a cold winter's night, swims at camp, treasure hunts, fellowship! Father and Son camps, Parents' Nights, Scout Sundays, Courts of Honor, the Troop Hallowe'en party, the Troop's Christmas Good Turn!

You are now a member of that good old Troop, carrying on its traditions and making new history.

Your Senior Patrol Leader

The key boy leader of your Troop is the Senior

Patrol Leader, selected for this high honor because he is a First Class Scout, a good leader and a swell Scout.

Junior Assistant Scoutmasters

Another leader may be the Junior Assistant Scoutmaster. He must be at least fifteen years old. He was probably appointed because he is an expert in some activity, such as signaling, bird study, or handicraft. Some Troops have more than one Junior Assistant Scoutmaster.

Other Boy Leaders

Your Troop has a Scribe, a Quartermaster, perhaps a Librarian, (look up their badges on page 55). Perhaps it has a Song and Cheer Leader too.

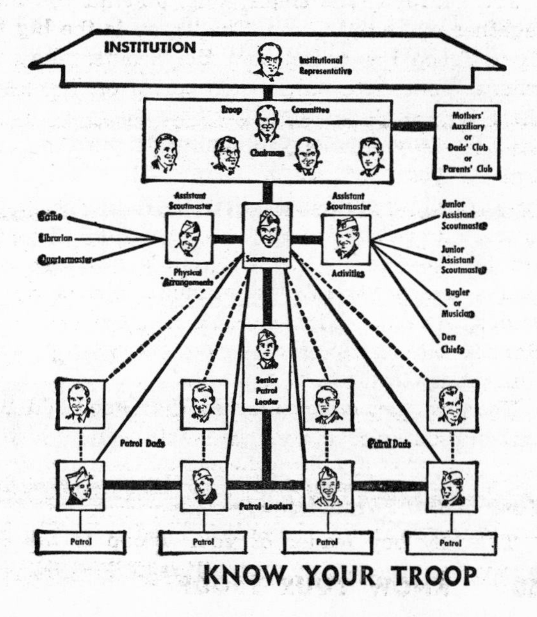

Your Scoutmaster

What a man your Scoutmaster is! He comes to every Troop meeting to help you get Scouting. He spends hours figuring how to give you fun and adventure in your Troop. He takes special training to learn exciting new things for you to do. He takes you hiking and camping on his holidays and weekends and often spends his vacation with his Troop. He is the friend you go to for the advice every boy needs sometimes. He coaches the Patrol Leaders, and they teach you. Without him there would be no Troop. Why does he do all this? Because he likes boys and wants to see them grow up to be real men.

Your Patrol Dad

Many Troops have Patrol Dads assigned to work with the Patrols. These Patrol Dads don't run the

The Patrol Leaders' Council plans the program

Patrol, but try to help the Patrol Leader in making Patrol work really worth while. The Patrol Dad is usually the father of one of the Patrol members.

Your Assistant Scoutmasters

Your Assistant Scoutmasters help the Scoutmaster, and take charge of the Troop when needed. They help you in many ways. Like the Scoutmaster, they spend a great deal of time in training and planning and work in your behalf.

Your Patrol Leaders' Council

Your Scoutmaster does not run your Troop alone. All of you Scouts help him through the Patrol Leaders' Council. This Council is made up of the Patrol Leaders, Senior Patrol Leader and Scoutmaster. Other leaders may be invited if the meeting requires their help. They meet regularly to plan what the Troop will do, camping trips, Good Turns. Before the Council meeting, your Patrol Leader talks this over with the Patrol, so if you have any good ideas, pass them on to him.

Your Troop Committee

Your Troop Committee was appointed by the church, grange, club or whatever group sponsors your Troop, to see that you have fun and profit in Scouting. This Committee consists of fathers of Scouts in your Troop, and other interested men, and helps the Scoutmaster run the Troop, get it a comfortable meeting room, a good place to camp, and a chance to go camping.

Scouts are ready to help their community

KNOW YOUR COMMUNITY

Here is a true story that shows how a group of Scouts, some no older than you, served their home town when disaster came.

It was a fine March day in a small Illinois town. Children dashed up and down on roller skates; on the baseball field the team was getting in its first practice; housewives chatted over the back fences. Suddenly the wind began to blow hard. The sky grew dark. Faster and faster the wind blew and a tornado struck the town, driivng 90 miles an hour. When it had passed and the stunned people crawled out of their refuges, two thirds of the town was completely destroyed.

One of the first groups to report for duty was the Boy Scouts. "What do you want us to do?" their leader asked one of the town officials. "Help these men dig in the ruins over there where a family is buried. Some of you build a fire in the square and see if you can fix some food for the workers. Those who know first aid, get over and help that doctor. The rest stand by to carry messages."

All night the Scouts worked, carrying supplies, transporting the injured, helping the Red Cross and town officials. Next morning Troops from three neighboring places reported. Their Scout neckerchiefs were their passport through police and military lines, and hospitals.

Scouts carried stretchers, scrubbed in hospitals, located lost children, transported Red Cross supplies and delivered clothing to undertakers. One hundred Scouts were turned over to Western Union to deliver the thousands of telegrams that poured in. Fifty Scouts worked under the Red Cross and canvassed the entire devastated district, making a list of missing people and cross-checking it with the morgue and hospitals.

It was not just by chance that these Scouts were so effective. They were prepared from the time they were Tenderfoot Scouts to help other people. They had learned to take their part in their community and so can you.

CALLING DOCTOR, HOSPITAL, POLICE OR SHERIFF

Every Scout should be able to help in his community, particularly in case of an emergency—fire, flood, tornado, hurricane or earthquake. Start by learning how to get in contact with the nearest doctor or hospital, and to reach the police or sheriff's office nearest to your home.

Telephoning

Of course the easiest and quickest way to get help is to telephone. Learn by heart the telephone numbers of the doctor, hospital, police and fire department, nearest to you; because when you are excited you may forget them, you should write them down in a permanent place too, such as your *Scout Diary,* or in a notebook near the telephone. Write them also on a small card and paste it in your first aid kit.

When in camp or on a hike always Be Prepared, and find out and write down this information in advance. Find out in advance whether the nearest hospital will send an ambulance at your call, or if they send one only at the request of a doctor or the police, so you will know whom to notify.

Make Your Report Clearly

You know how it is when you try to tell something if you are nervous or excited. You are likely to forget the most important part. Therefore, practice out loud what you will say in making your report.

Give your name—"Scout John Smith of Greenville." Tell why you called; "I want to report an accident. My brother slipped and fell downstairs. I think he has a broken leg."

Then tell where he is. "He is at 28 Southport Road. I will meet you in front of the house." Or, "It is a red house with white shutters."

Next, ask the doctor what to do until he arrives, and tell what first aid has been given. Carry out his instructions to the letter.

If you are on a hike, or in camp tell the doctor exactly where to meet you, so that you may take him to the scene of the accident.

When Telephones Fail

Sometimes there may be no telephone available, or the telephone wires may be damaged by wind or

Scouts act quickly in time of trouble

fire. You should know the location of the nearest doctor, hospital, police or sheriff's office so that you can go there yourself. Learn the quickest route by foot and by bicycle. Practice going over it.

Do this from your Troop meeting place, school, church and camp. Remember to practice giving a clear account of the accident, too.

Reporting a Fire

In large towns and cities, there are fire alarm boxes. Learn the location of the nearest fire alarm to your home, school, Troop meeting room, and how to operate it. Stop at the fire station, and ask the man in charge.

You may also report a fire by telephone to the nearest fire station or fire warden's office, or by going yourself over the shortest route.

In other communities, you report a fire by sounding an alarm, either a large bell, an iron ring or a

Know how to report a fire in your community

fire siren. Volunteers hear the alarm, and come to fight the fire. You stay by the alarm to direct them.

Find out exactly how to report a fire where you live. In addition, know what to say when you report it.

First tell the exact location of the fire, either the street and number, or the location on the road if there is no number. Be sure to give the nature of the fire—a small house, a large house, a barn or farm building, a grass or forest fire. Practice reporting. Your ability to do this may save lives and valuable property.

People Turn to a Boy Scout

Because people know a Boy Scout can do these things, they will look to you in case of an accident.

So learn well, and practice on problems that your Patrol Leader or Scoutmaster may give you. You can never tell when an emergency may occur, and when you will be able to save property and even a life, by knowing what to do, at the right time.

LOVE OF COUNTRY

CHAPTER 5

Breathes there a man, with soul so dead
Who never to himself hath said,
"This is my own, my native land!"
Whose heart hath ne'er within him burned,
As home his footsteps he hath turned
From wandering on a foreign strand?

—Sir Walter Scott

If you haven't read Edward Everett Hale's *The Man without a Country,* don't lose any time in looking it up. You'll enjoy it. You'll thrill to Nolan's words: "And for your country, boy, and for that Flag, never dream a dream but of serving her as she bids you, though the service carry you through a thousand hells. No matter what happens to you, no matter who flatters you or abuses you, never look at another flag, never let a night pass but that you pray God to bless that Flag. Remember, boy, that behind all these men you have to do with, behind officers and government, and people even, there is your Country Herself, your Country. and that you belong to Her as you belong to your own mother."

Ways of Helping Our America

It is not likely that you will ever be in a spot like that in which Philip Nolan found himself. There will be many opportunities for you to serve your country, to be proud of and helpful to your nation. Every time you are a good citizen you help to strengthen your nation.

Turn back to page 21 and read again about "Duty to Country." In addition to ideas presented there, keep in mind that everyday activities reveal how good a citizen you are. Do you obey traffic signals? Do you do your share at home? Are you doing your best in school? Do you take care of your clothes and other possessions? Are you friendly with others? Do you play a team game? Do you volunteer to do a job that needs doing? That is what a good citizen does. Every time you do these things and many more like them, you help to make your country stronger.

Our Flag — A Symbol of Us

"The red for valor, zeal, and fervency; white for hope, purity, cleanliness of heart, and rectitude of conduct; the blue, the color of the sky, epitomizing heaven, for reverence to God, loyalty, sincerity, justice, and truth."— *Your Flag,* U. S. Army Recruiting Service

Franklin K. Lane in *The Makers of the Flag* makes

Queen Ann Flag

Grand Union Flag

the flag say to us and to all Americans: "I am whatever you make me, nothing more. I am your belief in yourself, your dream of what a people may become.... Sometimes I am strong with pride, when men do an honest work, fitting the rails together truly.... But always I am all that you hope to be, and have the courage to try for."

Queen Ann Flag

When the first explorers and settlers came from Europe to the New World, they brought with them the flags of their native lands. Many flags flew over our country before it became the United States of America—the flags of Spain, France, Holland, Sweden, and England. When the Thirteen Colonies came under the control of England, they all displayed an English flag, known as the Queen Ann Flag.

Grand Union Flag

As their troubles with England increased, the Colonies felt that they needed a flag of their own. Two years after the Boston Tea Party, Benjamin Franklin was made chairman of the committee that designed a flag of thirteen red and white stripes, with

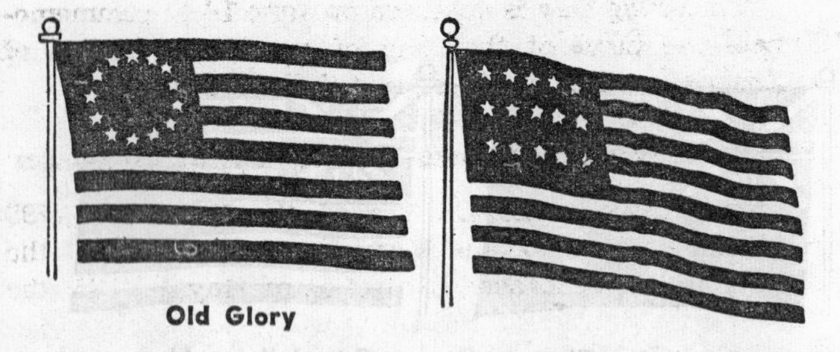
Old Glory

a Union composed of the crosses of St. George and St. Andrew—still English because of that emblem. This flag was first unfurled over Washington's headquarters in Boston on January 2, 1776. It was called the Grand Union Flag.

Another flag was used at this time by the Navy—the Pine Tree Flag. Later the Navy used a rattlesnake on thirteen stripes.

Old Glory

The Declaration of Independence on July 4, 1776, put an end to the Grand Union Flag, and the Colonies wanted a new flag. General Washington had been in Philadelphia in May of that year. According to tradition Betsy Ross suggested five-pointed stars as part of the design. In the presence of Robert Morris and George Ross, General Washington actually penciled the design of thirteen stars and thirteen stripes, from which she made Old Glory.

Origin of Flag Day

On June 14, 1777, Congress passed the following resolution: "Resolved that The Flag of the thirteen United States be thirteen stripes, alternate red and white; that the Union be thirteen stars, white on a blue field, representing a new constellation."

Thus Flag Day is observed on June 14 to commemorate the birth of the Flag of the United States of America, which is its correct full name.

Fifteen-Striped Flag and the Star-Spangled Banner

Two more states had joined the Union by 1795 (Vermont in 1791 and Kentucky in 1792), and the Flag Act of 1794 decreed that as of May 1, 1795, the Flag should include 15 stars. It was this fifteen-striped flag that flew over Fort McHenry, near Baltimore, during the War of 1812. Francis Scott Key, an American, was a prisoner on a British warship in the harbor. During a night of heavy bombardment he feared the American fort had fallen, but by the dawn's early light on September 14, 1814, he saw the broad stripes and bright stars still floating in the air over Fort McHenry and wrote the words of the National Anthem, the *"Star-Spangled Banner"* (page 115).

Back to Thirteen Stripes

By the time five more states had been admitted to the Union, it was clear that the Flag would become awkward in shape and lose its beauty if more stripes were added. Therefore, in 1818, Congress passed a law restoring the thirteen stripes, representing the original Thirteen Colonies, and a Union of stars, one star for each state. This is our Flag today.

Pledge of Allegiance

I pledge allegiance to the Flag of the United States of America and to the Republic for which it stands, one Nation under God, indivisible, with liberty and justice for all.

Color Guard Formation

In taking this pledge, the Scout in school uses the procedure authorized by the school authorities. The following is the procedure authorized by Congress. The pledge shall "be rendered by standing with the right hand over the heart. However, civilians will always show full respect to the Flag when the pledge is given by merely standing at attention, men removing headdress. Persons in uniform should render the military salute."

The procedure used by Scouts in Scout meetings is set forth in the next paragraph.

Salute to the Flag — in Uniform

Stand facing the Flag. Come to attention. Give Scout Salute.

Not in Uniform

Come to attention. Remove hat. Hold hat over heart during entire ceremony. If without hat, hold right hand over heart. (Women use this salute on all occasions.)

Showing Respect to the Flag

In hoisting and lowering the Flag, all persons face the Flag and follow the procedure for saluting. When the Flag is passing in a parade, or in review, spectators follow procedure for salute a short time before the Flag arrives and hold it for a few moments after the Flag has passed. Do this each time a United States Flag passes in a parade.

When passing the Flag, come to salute six paces before reaching the Flag and hold salute for six paces after passing.

When the National Anthem is sung or played, use procedure for salute. If the Flag is displayed, face it. If Flag cannot be seen, face the music.

When Scouts are in ranks, for the sake of uniformity all Scouts salute at the direction of the leader.

Laws Protecting the Flag

State and Federal Laws protect the Flag from mutilation, desecration, and improper use.

Trademarks may not use either "The Flag or the Seal. It should never be used for advertising purposes in any manner whatsoever. It should not be embroidered on such articles as cushions or handkerchiefs and the like, printed or otherwise impressed on paper napkins or boxes or anything that is designed for temporary use and discard; or used portion of a costume or athletic uniform. Advertising signs should not be fastened to a staff or halyard from which the Flag is flown." (Joint Resolution by Congress, December 22, 1942.)

If the Flag is used on envelopes, it must be placed so that the cancellation stamp will not desecrate it.

"Persons tearing down, mutilating, abusing or desecrating the Flag are subject to arrest and imprisonment." (Presidential Proclamation, April 6, 1917.)

Worn Flags

Flags should be cleaned when soiled, and may be neatly mended if torn. Do not display the Flag (unless as an historical relic) if it is in poor condition. That is disrespectful.

Congress has authorized that worn-out flags may be privately destroyed by burning, in a way lacking any disrespect or irreverence.

When To Fly the Flag

The following is from a Congressional Act, Dec. 22, 1942. (a) It is a universal custom to display the Flag only from sunrise to sunset on buildings and on stationary flagstaffs in the open. However, the Flag may be displayed at night upon special occasions when it is desired to produce a patriotic effect.

(b) The Flag should be hoisted briskly and lowered ceremoniously.

(c) The Flag should not be displayed on days when the weather is inclement.

(d) The Flag should be displayed on all days when the weather permits, especially on New Year's Day, January 1; Inauguration Day, January 20; Lincoln's Birthday, February 12; Washington's Birthday, February 22; Armed Forces Day, third Saturday in May; Easter Sunday (variable); Mother's Day, second Sunday in May; Memorial Day (half staff until noon) May 30; Flag Day, June 14; Independence Day, July 4; Labor Day, first Monday in September; Constitution Day, September 17; Columbus Day, October 12; Navy Day, October 27; Veterans Day, November 11; Thanksgiving Day, fourth Thursday in November; Christmas Day, December 25; such other days as may be proclaimed by the President of the United States; the birthdays of States and on State holidays.

Fold the Flag into a "Cocked Hat"

(e) The Flag should be displayed daily, weather permitting, on or near the main administration building of every public institution.

(f) The Flag should be displayed in or near every polling place on election days.

(g) The Flag should be displayed during school days in or near every schoolhouse.

Hoisting and Lowering

The Flag should always be hoisted briskly and lowered slowly. When the Flag is lowered, take the greatest care that no part of it shall touch the ground nor anything beneath it. It is carefully folded into the shape of a cocked hat.

When flown at half-staff, the Flag is first hoisted to the peak and then lowered to the half-staff position. Before lowering the Flag for the day it is first raised again to the peak.

Where the Flag Flies Continuously

There are five places in America over which the Flag flies night and day continuously; the east and west fronts of the National Capitol; Fort McHenry, Baltimore, Maryland; the grave of Francis Scott Key, Frederick, Maryland; World War I Memorial, Worcester, Massachusetts; and Flag House Square, Baltimore, Maryland.

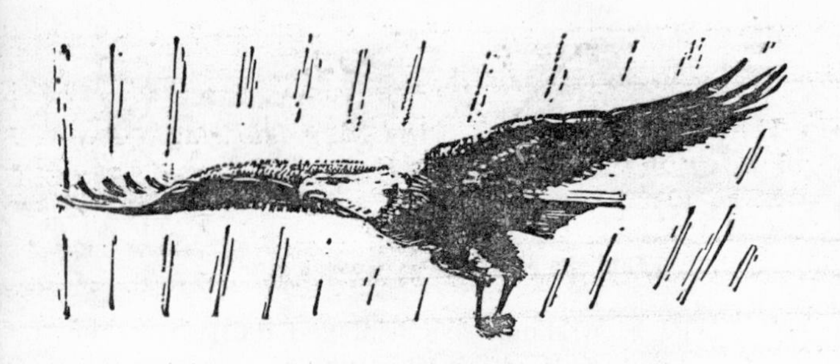

THE AMERICAN'S CREED

I believe in the United States of America as a government of the people, by the people, for the people; whose just powers are derived from the consent of the governed; a democracy in a republic; a sovereign nation of many sovereign states; a perfect union, one and inseparable; established upon those principles of freedom, equality, justice and humanity, for which American patriots sacrificed their lives and fortunes.

I therefore believe it is my duty to my Country to love it, to support its constitution; to obey its laws; to respect its Flag, and to defend it against all enemies.

William Tyler Page

THE FLAG CODE

The following section, "Displaying The Flag," is a summary of the official Flag Code adopted by Congress in 1942.

DISPLAYING THE FLAG

1-9

In a Group of Flags—The Flag of the United States should be in the center, or at the highest point.

2-3

With Another Flag, with Crossed Staffs—The Flag should be on its own right, its staff in front. Do not cross two United States Flags.

4

On an Automobile—The Flag should be flown from a staff attached to the right side of the front bumper, as you sit in the car. It may also be flown on the radio aerial.

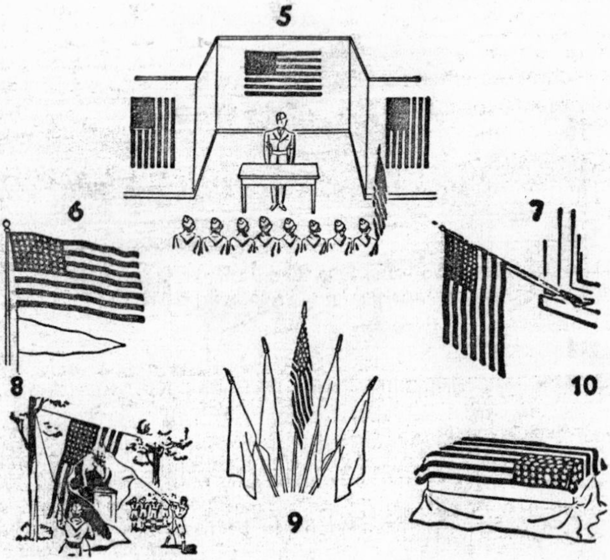

5

6

7

8

9

10

5-12

Horizontally on a Wall—The Union of The Flag should be on top, to the Flag's own right—to your left as you face it. Hang it flat.

5-8

Vertically from a Window or Wall—The Union of the Flag is on top, to the Flag's own right—to your left as you face it.

5

In the Audience—The Flag is on the right end of the first row of the audience or congregation.

6

Hoisted with Troop Flag—The Flag is always at the peak. Troop, State or City flags are below it. Flags of two or more nations are never flown from the same staff.

7-11

From a Staff—displayed from a staff projecting from a window or wall, the blue field should go to the peak of the staff, except when at half-mast.

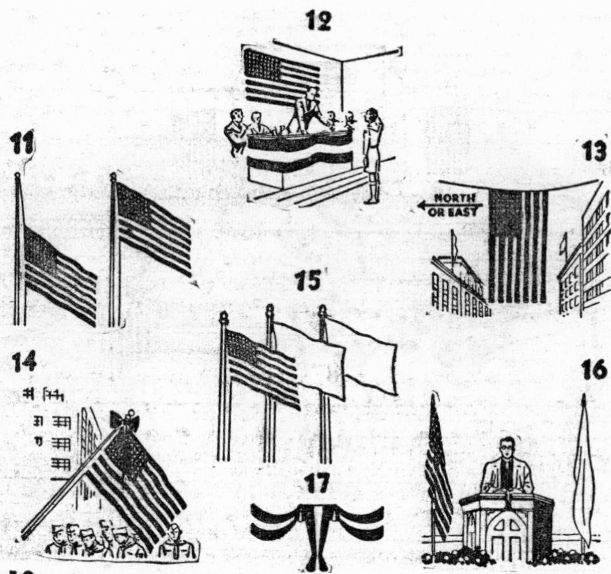

10

Covering a Casket—The Flag should be placed so that the Union is at the head, and over left shoulder. It should not be lowered into the grave, or touch the ground.

13

Across a Street—The Flag is hung vertically with the Union to the north or east, depending upon how the street runs.

15

In Line with Other Flags—The Flag goes to its own right and is hoisted before state or other flags. Flags should be of equal size and the staffs of equal height. Flags of different nations are always flown at the same height.

16

On a Platform or beside Speaker—The Flag is placed on the speaker's right, as he faces the audience.

14-17

The Flag Is Never Draped—Do not use The Flag for decoration. Instead, use blue, white and red bunting, with the blue stripe on top. Use black bunting for mourning.

TENDERFOOT SCOUTCRAFT

CHAPTER 6

Every Scout should know a few simple things that will make outdoor living easier. Of course, there are many skills to learn before you will be a real hiker or camper. But simple first aid, how to build a fire, how to protect living trees, and what knots to use in hiking and camping, are all among the first things to learn before going out to the woods, or open fields.

When the time comes to use these skills you want to be able to do so quickly and easily. If you have to experiment in putting a bandage on a cut, you may let germs get in that cause infection. There are many times when your knowledge of the right knot will make a lot of difference. You should know the precautions to take before building a fire, and why living trees must be protected.

FIRST AID

Anyone who uses a knife or axe, or who does much hiking in rough country, is likely to get a few scratches or small cuts. A real Scout in a moment or two can take care of these wounds, and be as fit as ever.

Skin breaks are caused by a number of things. You may slip on a rock and scrape the skin on your elbow or knee, or you may cut yourself with a knife or axe. You may scratch your legs on briars or sharp twigs, or you may puncture your skin with a thorn, fishhook, or nail. All skin breaks may be serious for two reasons —germs may get in the blood through the break and cause infection. A large artery or vein may be cut, so that too much blood escapes.

Later on, in Chapter 20 you will learn what to do for deep cuts and serious bleeding. But in the beginning, you should know why a break in the skin may be serious, and why it must be cared for immediately.

Keep Out the Germs

Most small cuts and scratches will stop bleeding in a few minutes when the blood has clotted. But germs are everywhere—on your skin, on your clothing, in the air, and on the briars or rocks through which you walk. Prompt first aid will help to keep germs from getting into the cut or scratch.

First, let the cut bleed for a minute. The flowing blood will wash most of the germs out of the wound, if it is a small one and not too deep.

Then place a sterile dressing over the wound, and fasten it on with bandage or adhesive tape. The important thing is that the dressing be sterile—that is, free of all germs. In your first aid kit, there should be sterile dressings securely wrapped in cellophane or other containers. When handling these dressings, do not touch the part which will cover the wound. Handle them by the very edge, and place the center over the wound. Ready-made dressings attached to adhesive tape, are handy to have for small cuts and scratches.

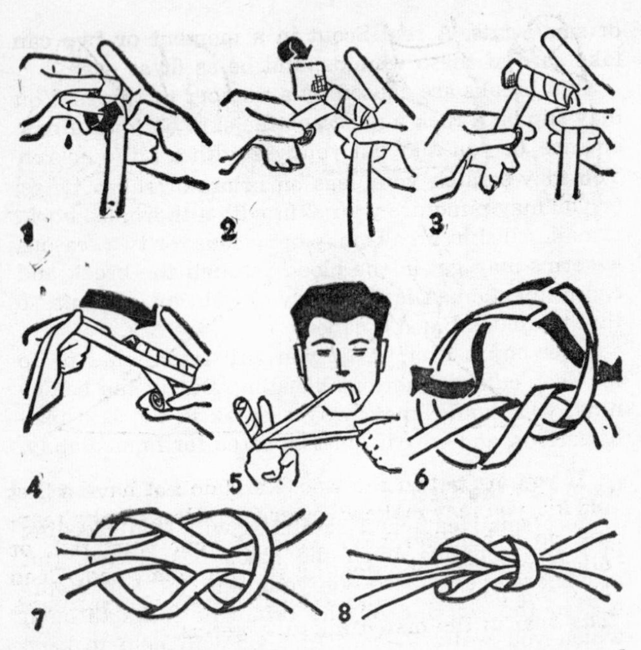

Personal First Aid—Bandage a cut on your own finger by covering the cut with a sterile dressing. Hold dressing in place with a bandage tied with a square knot as shown in 6, 7 and 8.

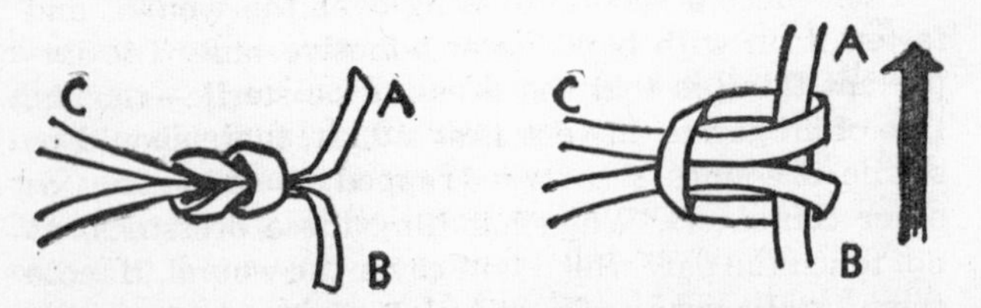

"Trip" or untie a square knot by pulling a short end (A) and a long end (B) on same side of knot. Then slide the half hitches off the short end (A).

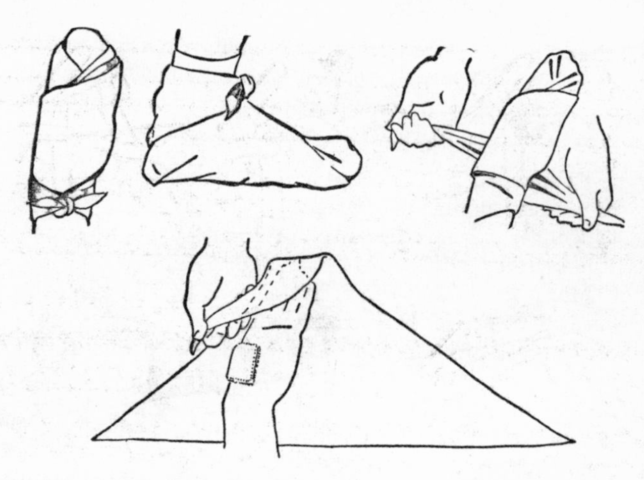

If you are out in the woods and do not have a first aid kit, you may make an emergency dressing by tearing up a handkerchief, piece of your shirt tail, or other material, and folding it in a small pad. Then hold this pad over a lighted match until it is scorched. The heat of the match kills the germs.

A Square Knot for the Bandage

The best knot to use in tying a bandage, is a square knot. Once it is pulled tight, it will not slip. It is easy to tie with one hand, either your right or left.

The illustrations on these pages show how to tie a bandage using a square knot. Practice it with both hands first. Tie it with your right hand alone, then your left hand. Practice tying a bandage on your right index finger. Then practice on your left hand.

You can never tell when you may need to know this simple bit of first aid. It may be at home or in the schoolyard. It may be in Troop meeting or in camp. Be ready to take care of cuts and scratches, whenever or wherever they happen. Practice so that you can take care of yourself as well as someone else.

FIRE BUILDING CARE

Every year in this country forest fires cause millions of dollars damage to valuable timber trees. This is especially serious because for many years to come, this country will have a shortage of lumber.

Many times these fires are caused by the carelessness of campers. No Scout should ever be the cause of a forest fire. On the other hand, every Scout will want to do all he can to prevent fires, and to show other campers how to guard against them.

There are two precautions that must be taken every time a fire is lighted out-of-doors.

Clear Away!

The first is to clear away all material that will burn, for a distance of five feet around the fire site. In the woods this means clearing away leaves, needles, and other plant material down to real soil or rock. In some sections, the plant material is quite deep. Layer upon layer of leaves have been built up on the forest floor. In such areas, fires will burn underground, suddenly coming to the surface hours later, to ignite trees and shrubbery.

In a place such as this, you may have to build a platform of rocks upon which to build the fire. The rocks must fit together, so that sparks cannot fall into the plant material. The best plan however, is to look for a place where you can build a fire right on soil or rocks.

In fields or prairies, dig up the sod and lay it aside. Build your fire on the soil or sand. Then when the fire is thoroughly out, replace the pieces of sod.

Clear fire site of anything that will burn

Put It Out

The second precaution is to have water or dirt on hand to put out the fire. You should have it ready, *before you light the fire.*

Never leave a camp fire unguarded. Someone should watch it continually, so that it cannot get out of control. Never leave a camp fire until the fire is thoroughly out. Frequently, fires have started up again hours after campers have left them. Use water, or dirt, to put out every glowing coal. Stir up the coals and turn over pieces of charred wood to soak them thoroughly or cover them with dirt.

If you take these precautions, there is no reason why you should ever be the cause of a forest fire.

Protect Living Trees

In the same way that germs get into your blood stream through a cut or scratch, and cause infection, disease may enter a break in the bark of a tree. It may cause the death of the tree. If the tree does heal from the wound, the wood may be weakened underneath, or distorted so that it is of less value as lumber. This is one reason why real Scouts never hack a tree with an axe, drive nails into it, strip off bark, or carve initials.

There is another good reason. Every tree belongs to someone. It is the property of the person who owns the land, either an individual, or all the people, as in the case of a park or State or National forest. Every Scout respects the property of other people.

Every Scout who goes camping, does so because he likes to be out-of-doors. He likes the rugged life of a real camper. He does not like to camp where there are unsightly scars on trees. Every Scout should look upon the trees as the walls of his wilderness home. He would no more mark them with axe or knife, than he would chop the walls of his home or Troop meeting room.

Axe scars, Troop numerals, initials, and peeled bark are signs of inexperienced outdoorsmen. When real Scout campers leave a campsite, they leave not a sign of having been there.

KNOTS AND ROPE WORK

One way to tell a real outdoorsman and camper, is by his ability to know the right knot to use at the right time and to tie it quickly. The Scout camper knows several knots. Each was designed for a definite purpose. He can tie them in pitch dark, as well as in broad daylight. The knots required of the Tenderfoot Scout, are those that are most generally used in camping and outdoor work.

The Test of a Knot

Here are the tests of a good knot.

(1) It fits the purpose for which you need it.

(2) It will hold until you untie it.
(3) It is easily tied.
(4) It is just as easily untied.

Keep these qualities in mind, when learning to tie knots. Learn to tie the right knot for your purpose, not just any knot that comes along.

Learning to Tie Knots

Follow the steps shown in the pictures, and you can learn easily to tie knots. Here are two hints to make learning easier. First, use a real piece of rope. Get a six-foot long piece of one-quarter to one-half inch rope. Use **real rope,** not twine or string, in learning your knot tying.

Second, tie knots in real situations. If a knot is to be used for tying a rope to a post or rail, practice tying it on one.

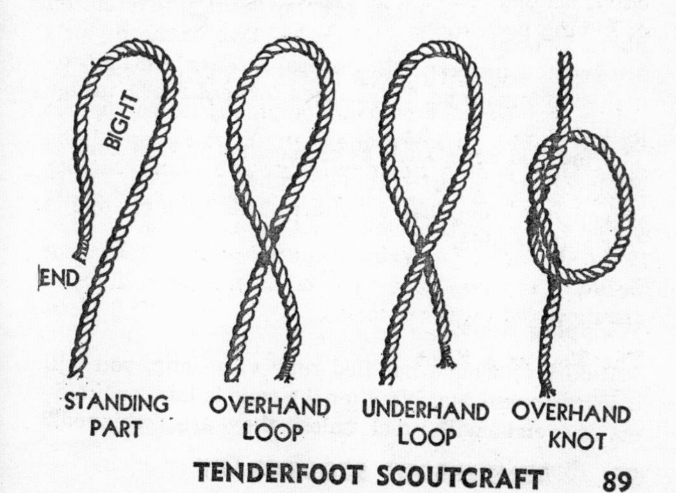

Parts of a Rope

The first step in handling rope and tying knots, is to learn the names of the parts of the rope and the parts of a knot. The rope has two parts. The **end** is the short, free part with which knots are tied. The **standing part** is the rest of the rope.

All knots are made by combining **bights, loops** and **overhands** in different ways. A **bight** is formed by turning the end of the rope so that the end and the standing part lie alongside each other. An **overhand loop** is made by crossing the end over the standing part. An **overhand** knot is a loop through which the end has been passed.

If you understand these terms, the instructions given here will also be easy to understand. Get your rope, and form a bight, a loop and an overhand knot.

There are, speaking generally, two kinds of rope: (1) laid rope used for most pioneering and camping; (2) braided rope used for life lines, lariats and the like.

Laid rope may be made of hemp, sisal, jute or cotton fibers, twisted together into yarn. Two or more yarns are twisted into strands. Several strands are laid together to form rope. This is used for tent ropes, bridge building, etc.

A braided rope, such as clothesline or sash cord is made of strands of cotton or other material, interwoven in a complicated pattern. This type of rope is soft and flexible.

Whipping Rope

Before you have handled rope very long, you will discover one thing. Whether the rope is laid, or braided, the ends will ravel unless they are "whipped."

Use strong twine or cotton fishline. For a rope one-half inch in diameter, cut a three foot piece of twine.

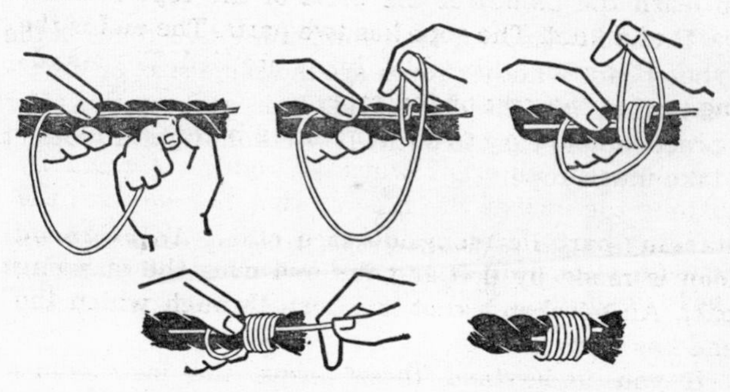

Make a loop of a 3 foot length of twine and place at end of rope. Wrap twine lightly around rope, starting ¼" from end of rope. When length of whipping equals diameter of rope pull ends of twine hard to tighten whipping. Trim twine close to whipping.

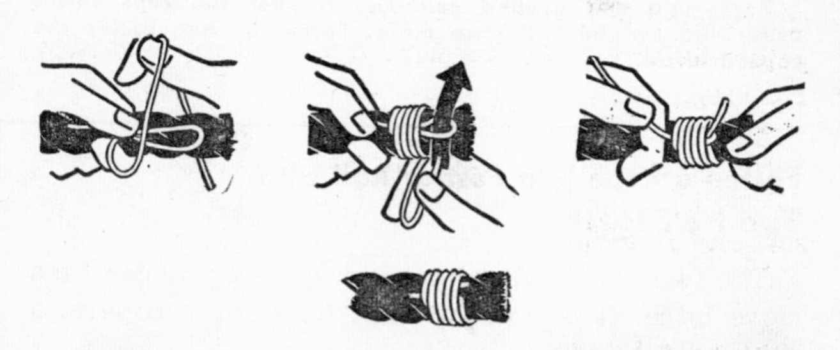

Another way to whip. Form a bight in end of piece of twine, and lay it ¼" from end of rope. Wrap other end of twine around rope and loop until whipping equals diameter of rope. Place end of twine through loop. Pull loop under whipping. Trim loose end.

Join Two Ropes with a Sheetbend

Probably the best knot for joining two ropes is the sheetbend. Whether ropes are the same size, or different sizes, use the sheetbend. It is easy to tie, after practice; and easy to untie. It will hold tight. It doesn't take much rope.

Form a bight in heavier rope. Bring up other rope end through bight, twist it over and under bight, then bring it under itself.

Attach a Rope to a Post or Rail with a Clove Hitch

A clove hitch is a useful knot. It is easy to tie and untie. It will hold, even on a slick pole, because the rope pulls against itself. Most lashings start with a clove hitch.

Pass rope end around rail. Lay it over the rope itself. Bring end around rail once more. Carry the end under the rope itself.

Fasten a Rope to a Post or Rail with Two Half Hitches

The two half hitches knot is easy once you can tie a clove hitch. It is a useful knot for tying a rope to a ring, pole or rail.

Pass the rope around the rail or through the ring. Carry the rope end over and under its own standing part, and through the loop thus formed. Repeat the process.

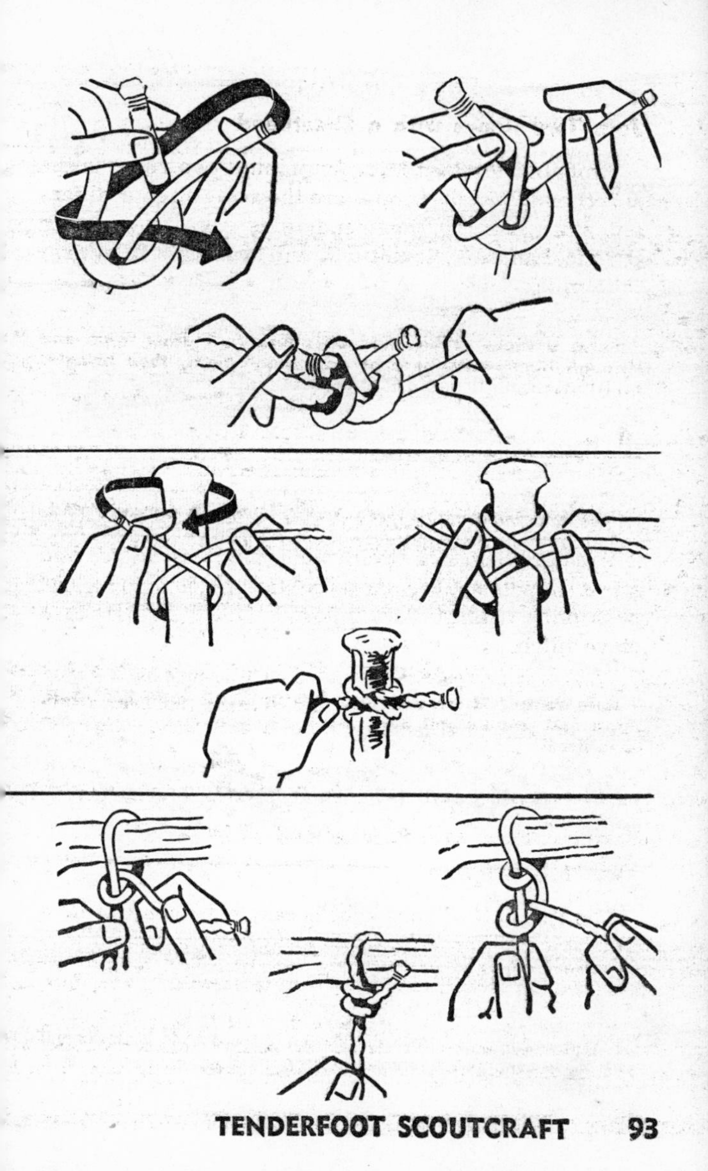

Fasten One End of a Rope Around Your Waist with a Bowline

Another useful knot is the bowline. With this knot, you have a loop that will not slip. It is important as a rescue knot in fires, mountain climbing, and boating accidents. It can also be used to tie a rope to a pole or for joining ropes. Tie a bowline in the end of one rope; slip the end of the second rope through the loop of the first bowline, and tie a bowline with the second rope end.

This is one knot that you should be able to tie blindfolded, with your right hand only, with your left hand only, and around someone else. Practice until you can tie it quickly and easily.

Place end on standing part. With twist of hand carry end around through the loop formed. Bring the end around the standing part and down through the loop.

Timber Hitch

The timber hitch is used for hauling logs and for starting a diagonal lashing.

Pass end of rope under and around log. Carry end under and over standing part. Twist the end around its own part a few times.

Tautline Hitch (with Stopper)

The tautline hitch forms a loop which will not slip when rope is taut, but will slip when tension is released. It is a useful knot for tying tent guy lines to pegs.

Tied the same as two half hitches, except that there is an extra turn around the standing part, in the direction of the strain.

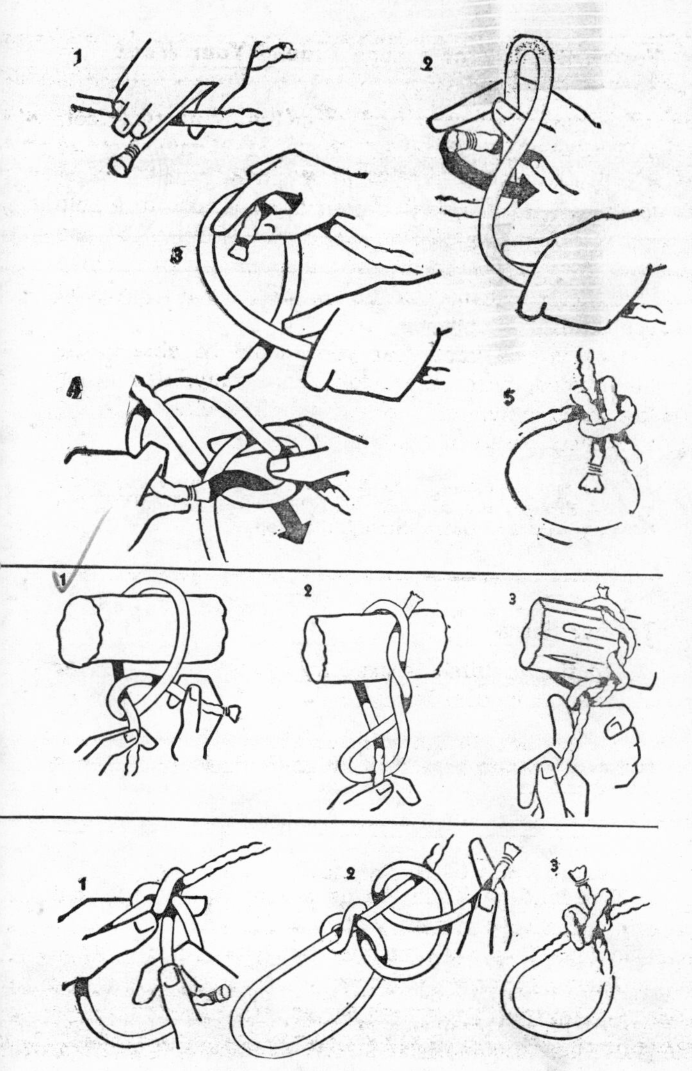
1
2
3
4
5
1
2
3
1
2
3

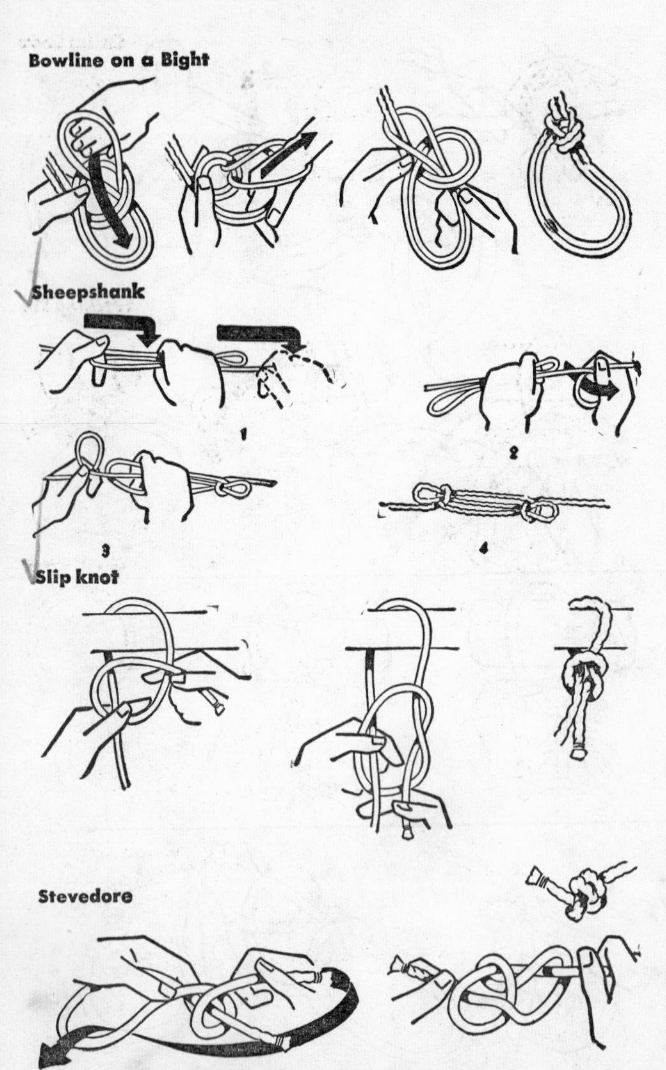
Bowline on a Bight
Sheepshank
1
2
3
4
Slip knot
Stevedore

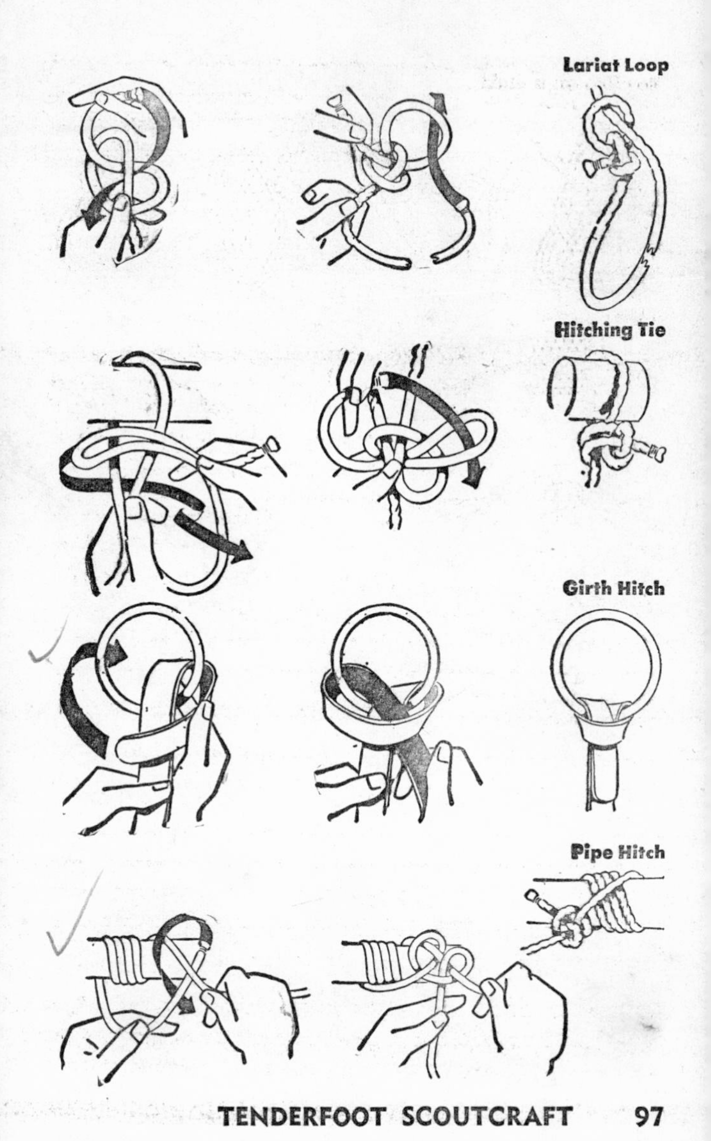
Lariat Loop
Hitching Tie
Girth Hitch
Pipe Hitch

THE CONSTITUTION OF THE UNITED STATES protects you:

- It is the agreement under which people in the United States live.

- It is the oldest federal constitution in existence.

- It is the basis for living in a free country.

- Called by William E. Gladstone, a prime minister of England,

"...the most wonderful work ever struck off at a given time by the brain and purpose of man."

THE SCOUTING TRAIL

PART II

CLIMBING THE TRAIL

CHAPTER 7

Did you ever climb a trail up a high mountain? As you struggled up you looked forward to the big thrill of reaching the peak. When you reached the very top, how glad you were to be there! You could look for miles over valleys and mountains. The cooling winds made the hard climb to the top worth while. There, soaring in the clouds was an eagle, making use of every wind current to float aloft. Wasn't that a thrill you will never forget?

Climbing the trail to Eagle Rank is like climbing a mountain. When you become a Tenderfoot Scout, you have already climbed the first steep part of the trail. In learning about the ideals of Scouting, taking part in Patrol, Troop and community activities, and in learning a few simple skills, you have opened the door to wider opportunities and outdoor adventures.

Requirements are Part of the Game

There may be a few steep places ahead, but when you think of the good times along the way and the final thrill of reaching the top, you work all the harder to be a real Scout and to achieve the goal of Eagle.

Scout Requirements are not tests to pass as in school. They are part of the adventure of Scouting. They are projects to help you become a better hiker and camper, and a better citizen of your community and your country.

How to Use this Book

As you read the requirements in Chapter 8, you see that they are divided into three parts, I—Scout Spirit, II—Scout Participation and III—Scoutcraft. This has been done to make them easier for you to understand. Naturally, while you are learning your Scoutcraft in your Patrol and Troop, you are growing in your Scout character and Scout participation. You have a better understanding of what it means to live up to the Scout Oath and Law, and to practice the ideals of Scouting. You are a better Scout citizen, and realize better your heritage as a citizen as discussed in Chapter 9.

Naturally, too, as you grow older and learn more Scoutcraft, your record of "Scout Participation" increases. You are able to do more things for your Patrol and Troop and others in your home and community. This is discussed in Chapter 10. During the time it takes you to become Second Class and then First Class, your record should become more impressive all the time. This "record" is not something put down in writing, but something that you make day by day, by your actions as a Scout. Your leaders and your fellow Scouts see that you are trying, and will judge from your own effort, whether you deserve the honor of advancement.

Read, Then Act.

So in reading Chapters 9 and 10, which deal with the first two parts of your Second and First Class Requirements, remember that it is what you are and what you do that count. Take these requirements seriously for they are a part of your climb up the trail.

Practice Makes You Better

You can hardly help advancing in rank if you take an active part in a good Troop program. The game of Scouting is like any game that you play. The more you practice the better you are at playing that game. And the more fun it is.

During Patrol and Troop meetings you will practice such skills as fire building, cooking, tent pitching, stalking, sending a message in code, and using your compass. Then you go hiking and camping and do these things out in the woods or fields. When you can do them well, and prove your skill, you have climbed further along the trail of Scouting.

How You Advance

At last the time comes when your Scoutmaster feels you are qualified to receive the Second Class badge, or ready to be recognized as a First Class Scout. This means that you have tried to live up to the Oath and Law, and have a good record of teamwork in your Patrol and Troop, and that you really do know how to do the things you have been practicing. You have proved it to the satisfaction of your Troop Leaders. Your Scoutmaster tells you to report at a certain time to your Board of Review.

Awards are made at a Court of Honor

The men on the Board of Review ask you about your Scout experience, and talk to you about what you have done in your Scout Requirements and your service in your Patrol and Troop. They ask you questions to make sure you are trying to live up to the Scout Oath and Law every day. If they feel that your record is satisfactory, they approve it.

You will get your Second Class or First Class Badge at a Court of Honor. This will probably be a public ceremony, with your parents and Scoutmaster and members of your Troop there to see the honor conferred upon you. You should wear the badge of your new rank proudly on your uniform. You have climbed part way up the trail, and are ready to start climbing higher.*

---

* To learn more about your Board of Review and Court of Honor, read Chapter 26.

SECOND CLASS REQUIREMENTS

(Requirement Index in front of book)

CHAPTER 8

To become a SECOND CLASS SCOUT, you do the following:

I. **SCOUT SPIRIT**—While a Tenderfoot Scout, satisfy your Scout Leaders that you do your best, in your everyday life, to live up to:

1. The Scout Oath or Promise.
2. The Scout Law.
3. The Scout Motto.
4. The Scout Slogan.

(Your Troop leaders, both the boy and man leaders, will decide whether you have done your best to live up to the Spirit of Scouting. They will know after watching your actions and your behavior. Your Scoutmaster may want to talk with your parents, teachers, religious leader, and others. Work on your own Church or Synagogue religious award will demonstrate your Scout Spirit.)

II. **SCOUT PARTICIPATION**—While a Tenderfoot Scout, show to the satisfaction of your Scout Leaders that you:

1. Work actively in Patrol and Troop meetings, outdoor activities and service projects.

(Your actions and behavior while a Tenderfoot Scout are important. Troop and Patrol records will show your attendance. Statements of your Troop Leaders will show how actively you have taken part.)

2. Do your share in helping in your home, your school, your church and your community.

(Your Scoutmaster may check with your parents, your teachers and your religious leaders to see if you have been helpful, in the spirit of the Daily Good Turn.)

3. **Take care of things that belong to you, the property of others, and your country's natural resources.**

(A check with your leaders and your parents will show whether you have met this requirement, taking proper care of your personal belongings, protecting other people's property, and helping protect wildlife and forests.)

4. **Maintain a personal savings plan (such as regular payments into a savings account or into a savings project sponsored by your family or Troop).**

(The regular practice of thrift counts more than the amount. The amount may be in the form of a savings bank account, savings stamps or bonds, or insurance. Regular payments into a family savings project or a Troop project such as for camp, uniform, equipment, will be accepted.)

III. SCOUTCRAFT

1. PREPARE FOR SCOUT HIKING

a. *Clothing and Equipment*—Present yourself for inspection suitably clothed for the locality, season and the weather, and equipped for a five-mile hike.

(Clothing will depend upon the time of year; equipment upon the type of hike and the place. Your Troop Leaders will give you that information.)

b. *Hiking Methods*—Tell the safety precautions to take on the highway and crosscountry for day and night hiking. Show correct way of walking and proper care of feet. Demonstrate at least six Silent Scout Signals for formations and field work. Demonstrate how to purify water for drinking. Explain how to make a one-man latrine. Identify local plants that

may cause skin poisoning. Tell what to do if lost.

("Tell" and "explain" mean just that. Using your own words, explain how to do these things. "Show" and "demonstrate" mean to *do* those things. "Identify" means to recognize from pictures or in nature.)

c. ***First Aid***—Demonstrate artificial respiration. Demonstrate first aid for shock and fainting and, on yourself, for the following: arterial bleeding of arm and leg, common cuts and scratches, bites of insects and chiggers and ticks, burns and scalds, sunburn, blister on heel, skin poisoning from poison plants, objects in eye, sprained ankle.

(You must actually demonstrate first aid for each item. Use proper first aid materials where necessary, and practice on yourself.)

2. FIND YOUR WAY

a. ***Compass***—Explain how a compass works and give its eight principal points. Set a compass and take a degree reading with it.

(Tell in your own words, how earth's magnetism attracts the compass. Recite the principal points. Using a compass, actually take a degree reading.)

b. ***Measuring***—Determine the length of your step. Walk a course for which you must take three compass degree readings and measure three distances with your step. OR Lay out, in this manner, and stake a four-acre tract of land.

(These are all things that you must actually do.)

c. ***Map Reading***—In the field, orient a map (preferably a topographic map) and follow a route far enough to prove that you know how to use the map. Read at least ten different conventional signs on a map, including contour lines.

(This is a project that you must complete, to show that you can use a map.)

3. COOK A MEAL IN THE OPEN

(The four parts of this requirement should be met in the order given. You may sharpen your knife and axe ahead of time, but you should do the rest of the requirements at one time, in camp or on a hike.)

a. *Preparing Fire Wood*—Sharpen a knife and an axe, and use these sharpened tools to prepare kindling and fuel.

(Prepare enough wood to cook your meal.)

b. *Fire Building*—Locate and prepare a suitable fire site. Lay and light a fire (this should normally take not more than two matches). Keep the fire going for cooking a meal.

(Clear fire site. When dry wood is used, two matches should be sufficient.)

c. *Hike Cooking*—Cook a meal from raw meat (or fish or poultry) and at least one raw vegetable.

(You have your choice of cooking your meal without utensils as kabob, on broiler or in the ground, or using utensils stewing, frying, baking.)

d. *Clean-up*—Dispose of garbage in proper manner. Clean utensils, Put out fire. Clean up the site thoroughly.

(Garbage should be burned: utensils cleaned in hot water. Put out fire by sprinkling water on it. Clean site so that it is almost impossible to find signs of the fire and camp.)

4. BE OBSERVANT

a. *Observation*—Do ONE of the following:

TRACKING. Follow the track of a person or an animal in soft ground or snow for ¼ mile. reading the main meaning of the track. OR

TRAILING. Follow a track made with trail signs for ½ mile. OR

STALKING. Follow another Scout, who knows that you are stalking him, for a distance of ½ mile, without being seen by him.

b. *Wild Life*—Find evidence, in natural surroundings, of at least six different kinds of wild mammals, birds, reptiles or fish. Identify them.

(The simplest "evidence" is the discovery of the animal itself. Other evidence: tracks, burrows, nests, feathers, skulls, and "pellets", snake skins, turtle eggs, etc. Name the animal from the evidence discovered.)

5. TAKE A HIKE

The Second Class Hike*—After you have done the above, prove yourself a SCOUT HIKER by taking a hike, properly clothed and equipped, with your Patrol (or, if this is impossible, with at least one companion approved by your Scoutmaster). On the hike, cover a route of a total distance of not less than five miles, indicated on a map or a map sketch, show correct hike style and highway safety, cook a meal, clean up, and return in good condition.

(This is the *last* requirement to meet in working for Second Class. It is a separate hike, taken after you have proved your Scoutcraft ability on previous hikes. The "one companion" may be a junior leader, a fellow who has already become Second Class, or your own father. The hike should cover all the activities of a real hike as listed.)

*NOTE on the SECOND CLASS HIKE
If a physician certifies that the Scout's physical condition for an indeterminable time does not permit the Second Class Hike, the Advancement Committee of the Local Council may authorize the following substitution for the hike: The requirements for any one *"outdoor"* Merit Badge (Selected from the NATURE or CONSERVATION groups) which the Scout is capable of meeting. *In EACH individual case, application for a substitution must be made in advance by the Scoutmaster to the Advancement Committee and the specific substitution must be approved in writing by the Committee, after thorough review.*

FIRST CLASS REQUIREMENTS

(Requirement Index in front of book)

To become a FIRST CLASS SCOUT, you do the following:

I. **SCOUT SPIRIT**—While a Second Class Scout, satisfy your Scout leaders that you do your best in your everyday life, to live up to:

1. The Scout Oath or Promise.
2. The Scout Law.
3. The Scout Motto.
4. The Scout Slogan.

II. **SCOUT PARTICIPATION**—While a Second Class Scout, show to the satisfaction of your Scout leaders that you:

1. Work actively in Patrol and Troop meetings, outdoor activities and service projects.
2. Do your share in helping in your home, your school, your church and your community.
3. Take care of things that belong to you, the property of others, and your country's natural resources.

4. Maintain a personal savings plan (such as regular payments into a savings account or into a savings project sponsored by your family or Troop.

(As for Second Class, your Troop Leaders will decide whether you are trying to live up to the rules of the game of Scouting in your everyday life. Having watched your actions and behavior while you were a Second Class Scout, they can tell if you are doing your best. A check with your parents, teachers and church leaders will show to what extent you share in home, school and church duties; whether you take care of the things that belong to you and others, and whether you make a regular practice of thrift.)

III. SCOUTCRAFT

1. PREPARE FOR SCOUT CAMPING

a. ***Clothing and Equipment***—Present yourself for inspection suitably clothed for the locality, season and the weather, and equipped and packed for an overnight camp.

(Equipment may be packed in a knapsack, pack basket or pack frame, or in an improvised pack to carry on the back. Your equipment and clothing should include all things you will need in camp, for the time of year in which you are camping.)

b. ***Health Protection***—Explain methods used in camp for care of food and drinking water, fire protection and waste disposal.

(You must show that you know how to do these things, so you will be able to do them in camp.)

c. ***First Aid***—Give artificial respiration for three minutes. Explain danger of taking laxative for pain in stomach. Improvise a sterile dressing. Use triangular bandage for arm sling and as binder for wounds on head, hand, knee and foot. Demonstrate first aid for one problem from each of the following groups (problems to be chosen by your leader after you have trained for all of them):

Arterial Bleeding from face, throat, arm, leg.

Shock, Heat Exhaustion, Sunstroke, Frostbite, Internal Poisoning.

Puncture Wounds from splinter, nail, fish hook, dog bite, poisonous snake bite.

Fracture of collarbone, upper arm, forearm, lower leg.

Explain under what circumstances a person should or should not be moved. Improvise a stretcher and, with helpers under your direction, transport a presumably unconscious person.

(Read Chapter 20 before taking part in Patrol or Troop first aid problems. Practice all these problems so that you can do them on *yourself*, if possible, and on someone else. After you have trained in all problems, your leader will ask you to demonstrate first aid on a few problems from the groups described in the requirement. You will not know what these problems are ahead of time.)

2. GET THE LAY OF THE LAND

a. ***Directions***—Lay out on the ground a true north-south line with the help of the sun by day and the North Star by night, and a magnetic north-south line, using a compass.

(The line may be scratched on the ground, or may be a pole laid in the proper direction. You should have a general idea of the difference between true North and Magnetic North.)

b. ***Measuring***—With simple means and using your own personal measurements, determine a height you cannot reach (such as a tree) and a width you cannot walk (such as a river or a canyon).

("Simple means" may involve such things as small sticks, rustic poles or stakes driven in the ground. "Personal measurements" may be the length of your step, span of your hand, width of your thumb, or length of your reach.)

c. *Map Sketching*—Select a site suitable for a Patrol camp and make a map sketch for laying it out. Make a map sketch by which someone unfamiliar with your camp location can find his way to it over a distance of at least two miles.

(Map sketch of camp should use proper conventional signs for natural features with tents, fireplaces and other camp features, indicated by simple signs. The map need not be drawn to exact scale.

The two mile map sketch may be made from memory, after you have been over the route. *It is not a map*, but a sketch, and specific distances and compass degrees are not necessary. The main features will be landmarks that show where turns are made, types of roads or trails and other marks to show how to reach the campsite. Draw a North arrow to show the general lay of the land.)

3. LIVE IN CAMP

a. *Camp Making*—Sharpen an axe and use it for cutting light wood into tent pegs. Locate a tent site and pitch a tent, fastening the guy line with a taut-line hitch. Prepare a comfortable ground bed. Improvise a piece of camp equipment requiring lashings.

(A ground bed may be made of grass, leaves or boughs; or may be a piece of ground cleared and smoothed, with hip and shoulder holes scooped out, and covered with a waterproof ground cloth. Improvised camp equipment, using lashings, may be such things as camp broom or rake, fire crane, table, kitchen rack, or wash stand.)

b. *Wood Lore*—Find and identify ten different trees or shrubs. Tell their uses.

("Uses" may be suitability for fuel, poles for engineering, wood for tool handles, edible parts, food for animals, shelter for animals, or use in soil control. You may identify ten trees only, or ten shrubs only, or a combination of trees and shrubs totaling ten in all.)

4. COOK YOUR MEALS

a. *Camp Cookery*—Prepare in the open, for yourself and a companion, from raw ingredients, a complete breakfast of fruit, hot cereal and bacon-and-eggs (or griddle cakes); and a complete dinner of meat (or fish or poultry), vegetable, dessert and bread (or biscuits, or twist baked on a stick).

(Second Class cooking provides for an individual meal and First Class asks you to cook for another fellow. Breakfast may be prepared on one trip, dinner on another. The dishes are to be served as a complete meal, in their proper order. Fruit may be served raw. Dessert for dinner must be a cooked dessert, such as stewed fruit or pudding. Bread may be cooked in a reflector oven, pan, Dutch oven, or on a thick stick.)

b. *Edible Wild Plants*—Find and identify four different edible wild greens, roots or fruits.

(Greens range from watercress to dandelion leaves; roots from cattail to Indian cucumber; fruits from wild grape and numerous berries, to a great variety of nuts. Even in winter snow country, you should have little trouble finding edible plants. Certain lichens and tree bark. It is not necessary to collect and cook the plants, but you will probably want to try it.)

5. GO SWIMMING

Swimming—Tell what precautions must be taken for a safe swim. Jump feet first into water over your head in depth. Swim fifty yards. During the swim, stop, make a sharp turn, level off and resume swimming.**

(By precautions are meant: 1. Have medical examination and follow doctor's orders; 2. Know your swimming ability and stick to the swimming place that fits your skill; 3. Always swim with a buddy; 4. Wait two hours after a meal; 5. Follow all rules and orders given by waterfront directors; 6. Never dive into unknown water, never take a dare to show off in the water, and never swim long distances, unless someone goes along in a boat.

6. GET A MESSAGE THROUGH

Morse Signaling—Know the International Morse Code, including necessary procedure signals. Using that code, send and receive, by any suitable means, a message of 20 words (100 letters), over a distance of at least 100 yards.

Morse Signaling— Suitable means are flags, blinker or sound device. No speed is required. No more than 5 errors are permitted, and none that destroy the sense of the message. Procedure signals include: For sending: Attention, Error, End of Word, End of Sentence, End of Message. For receiving: Go ahead, Repeat, Word received, Message received.

7. GO CAMPING

***The First Class Camp*—After you have done the above, prove yourself a SCOUT CAMPER by camping, properly clothed and equipped, on a suitable camp site for not less than twenty-four hours with your Patrol (or, if this is impossible, with at least one companion approved by your Scoutmaster). During this camp, cook at least one hot meal, sleep in a tent or improvised shelter or under the stars, keep camp clean and safe, and leave camp site in good condition.**

(This requirement must come last. It is a separate camp, taken after you have proved your Scoutcraft ability on previous hikes and camps. The companion may be a junior leader, a First Class Scout, or your father. The camp must include all the activities listed.)

* NOTE on the FIRST CLASS SWIMMING REQUIREMENTS

Under certain very exceptional conditions, where the climate keeps the water cold the year round, and/or where there are no suitable and accessible places within a reasonable traveling distance to swim at any time during the year, or in cases where a physician certifies that the Scout's physical condition for an indeterminable time does not permit swimming, the Advancement Committee of the Local Council may authorize a substitution for the First Class Swim (as indicated on the "Application For Substitution For Basic Scout Requirements," Cat. No. 4434). *In EACH individual case, application for a substitution must be made in advance by the Scoutmaster to the Advancement Committee on the special standard form provided for this purpose, and the specific substitution must be approved in writing by the Committee, after thorough review.*

THE STAR-SPANGLED BANNER

O, say, can you see, by the dawn's early light,
What so proudly we hail'd at the twilight's last gleaming,
Whose broad stripes and bright stars, thro' the perilous fight,
O'er the ramparts we watch'd, were so gallantly streaming?
And the rockets' red glare, the bombs bursting in air,
Gave proof thro' the night that our flag was still there.
O, say, does that Star-Spangled Banner yet wave
O'er the land of the free and the home of the brave?

On the shore dimly seen thro' the mists of the deep,
Where the foe's haughty host in dread silence reposes,
What is that which the breeze, o'er the towering steep,
As it fitfully blows, half conceals, half discloses?
Now it catches the gleam of the morning's first beam,
In full glory reflected now shines on the stream.
'Tis the Star-Spangled Banner, oh, long may it wave
O'er the land of the free and the home of the brave!

Oh, thus be it ever when freemen shall stand
Between their loved homes and the war's desolation!
Blest with vict'ry and peace, may the heav'n-rescued land
Praise the pow'r that hath made and preserv'd us a nation!
Then conquer we must, when our cause it is just,
And this be our motto: "In God is our Trust."
And the Star-Spangled Banner in triumph shall wave,
O'er the land of the free and the home of the brave.

—Francis Scott Key

THE BILL OF RIGHTS . . .

(first ten amendments to the Constitution)

. . . protects you against the government's possible abuse of power and assures you:

- Freedom of religion
- Freedom of the press
- Freedom of speech
- Freedom of assembly
- Right to petition (right to give your point of view to government officials)
- Right to a jury trial
- Right to hold public meetings
- Right not to have your house searched without a warrant
- Right not to have to testify against oneself

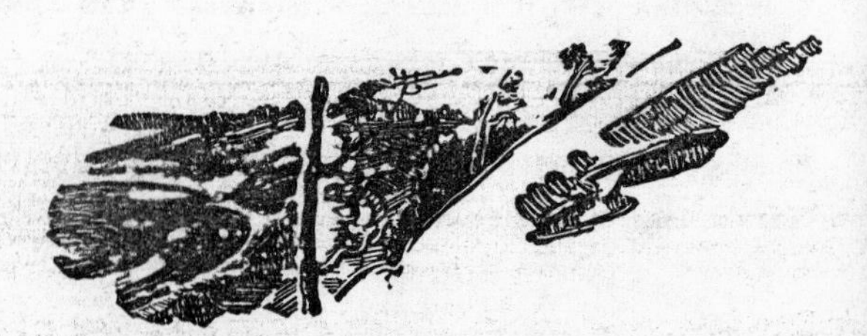

PLAYING THE GAME OF SCOUTING

PART III

SCOUT SPIRIT AND CITIZENSHIP

CHAPTER 9

People in every age and every race have had their codes of Honor. The Laws of Moses were observed centuries before Christ. The citizens of ancient Athens, the followers of Christ, the Incas in Peru, the Knights of the Middle Ages, the American Indians, the Pilgrim Fathers, all were guided by their codes as you are guided by the Scout code today.

Athenian Oath

One of the famous codes was developed about three hundred years before Christ. As a Scout you ought to know about it, because it is so famous that you often see references to it today. It was the Athenian Oath which the young men took in ancient Athens, when they became seventeen years of age.

THE ATHENIAN OATH

"We will never bring disgrace on this, our city, by an act of dishonesty or cowardice.

"We will fight for the ideals and Sacred Things of the city both alone and with many.

"We will revere and obey the City's laws, and will do our best to incite a like reverence and respect in those about us who are prone to annul them or set them at naught. We will strive increasingly to quicken the public's sense of civic duty.

"Thus in all these ways we will transmit this city, not only not less, but greater, better and more beautiful than it was transmitted to us."

The Scout Code

Your Scout code includes the ideals of the Athenian Oath and of other splendid codes that have gone before you. It has in it some principles from the Mayflower Compact, an agreement drawn up by the Pilgrims after they landed in Plymouth. It includes some of the ideals in the Declaration of Independence. In many ways it resembles the Knight's code to which the Knights pledged their honor in the Middle Ages. It is your Code as a Boy Scout in this Twentieth Century, in the United States of America.

Living Your Scout Code

The purpose of the other famous codes of history was to help the individual grow into a better man and a better citizen. That is the purpose of your Scout code. Before you became a Tenderfoot, you learned what the Scout Oath and Law, the Motto and Slogan mean. Now as a Scout, you have an opportunity to practice them and, with your Scoutcraft skills you can be a helpful Scout citizen.

Men of all ages had their codes of honor

Your American Heritage

As a Scout citizen you have the greatest heritage ever given to anyone on the face of the earth. Every day you enjoy many things that you have done nothing to earn. You know of some of them, provided for through the Declaration of Independence, the Constitution, and the Bill of Rights. You should know more about them. (See *Citizenship* Merit Badge pamphlet.)

Washington's soldiers, their feet frozen and bleeding in the snow at Valley Forge, bought freedom for you. Since then thousands of men and women have given their lives to help keep it. Men faced death at Anzio beach and Guadalcanal and on other battlefields in Europe and the Pacific, helping to preserve our democratic way of life.

What Others Have Done for You

Your heritage has not been won in battles alone. The electric light, the telephone, the many advantages you enjoy are possible because of someone's hard work and sacrifice—for you.

The school you attend was built and is maintained by taxpayers so that you may have a better chance.

Your church or synagogue was built and is at work to help you. Your health is safeguarded through the efforts of thousands of citizens. Through the centuries others have searched for knowledge in order to protect you.

Libraries, museums, and other institutions are maintained for your benefit. Scouting experiences are available to you because of the unselfish service of many people eager to help boys.

America — Land of Opportunity

This country is today the unbelievable dream of millions of suffering people in other lands. Here are luxuries unheard of by them that you accept as a matter of course. Here are freedoms of which they do not know the meaning. The American people speak as they think, worship as they choose, work where they wish, and publish and read what they select.

Here is opportunity beyond belief. There is nothing to which you may not aspire. Any boy can grow up

The Mayflower Compact is part of our heritage

to be a statesman or cabinet member; the sons of immigrants have headed some of the largest business enterprises. A railsplitter became President.

This is something of your heritage, bought for you by the heroism and sacrifice of other people who went before you. As a citizen of the United States of America, it is yours to use rightly now and to transmit to those who come after you.

The Opportunity to Work

Work for the satisfaction of accomplishment, and self-respect, is the measure of the greatness of a person or a nation. This country was originally settled by men of toil. The early American pioneers worked hard, long hours to win this Continent. The Western pioneers, braving the desert in their covered wagons worked hard. Our country was settled by workers and brought to its high place among the nations of the world by workers.

We hear a lot of talk these days about opportunities for leisure, but very little about the glory of work. Never forget that men who built America were workers—men whose shoulders grew bent by farming the stubborn soil of New England, men who wiped the sweat from their brows as they labored to build a railroad across the desert, needleworkers and small traders who toiled long hours into the night, seamen who sailed American clipper ships to the far corners of the earth. These and many like them left for us a rich heritage of a high standard of living in a land of freedom.

The priceless heritage of America is the privilege of work. America is the land of opportunity—the opportunity to work and achieve a goal.

DO YOUR PART

CHAPTER 10

No Boy Scout needs to wait until he reaches voting age to be a participating citizen. The first part of the Advancement Requirements is concerned with the Scout code and the Scout's individual character. The second part deals with your helpfulness to others, and your participation in the lives of others. This is part of your future life as a citizen of your country, and of your life as a Scout.

You Are a Scout Citizen Now

Right now there are hundreds of chances for you to take hold and do your part. No doubt you hope to do big and useful things some day. Don't forget the little things right here and now. Begin in your Patrol, Troop, home, church and community.

In Your Patrol

You do your part in the Patrol at meetings, hikes and camping trips. You may be selected for a Patrol job: such as Patrol Leader or Assistant, Scribe, Treasurer, Cheer Leader, or Hikemaster; or may help the Scout who has one of these jobs.

Patrol meetings may be held at your home because you have a good place to meet. You may know where a Patrol Good Turn is needed, and help to carry it through. You may think of a new kind of hike or camp, or a new place to go. You get ideas for a Patrol project or demonstration to make the meeting a success, such as a new opening or closing ceremony or a new game.

Your part in the Patrol is to work cheerfully and hard with the other Scouts in what the Patrol decides to do. Most Patrol activities are decided upon by all the members of the Patrol. You as a part of this democratic group will cooperate. If your ideas are not followed the first time, do not give up. Keep thinking up new ideas and projects.

Many Patrols have dues to buy equipment: tents, cook kits, signal flags, Patrol flags, and the like. Earn the money needed to pay your own way in the Patrol. Help make equipment you do not buy.

When you have learned a few Scouting skills you may find that you can help your Patrol Leader train the new Scouts in your Patrol. This will help you too, for there is nothing like teaching others to help you learn a subject yourself.

Let us suppose, for example, that your Troop program theme for a month is Exploration, that is, use of compass, map reading, map sketching, and using stars to find direction. In Patrol meetings you may show younger Scouts how to use their compasses to find their way and to follow a map.

Then you may get an idea for a Patrol Exploration Hike. You work out the details for the hike, get the

Help to make your Patrol the best in the Troop

maps, talk to your Patrol Leader and help him lead the Patrol on such a wilderness hike.

Other Scout Skills—first aid, nature, signaling, or cooking may suggest ideas to you for unusual projects.

You do your part in the Patrol when you do your best to live up to the Oath or Promise, the Scout Law, and the Motto and Slogan. This makes you a better Scout yourself, and you set an example for others. When they see that you are living up to the spirit of Scouting, you help them to be better Patrol members.

In Your Troop

You take part in your Troop in the same way. You come to meetings promptly. You are careful of the equipment in your meeting room and of the building where the Troop meets.

A Den Chief helps younger boys enjoy Cub Scouting

You help the Scoutmaster and other Troop leaders as they need you. You pay dues promptly. You make the Scoutmaster feel that you are a Scout he can count on for cheerful cooperation and to do the right thing at the right time.

If it rains on the day when the field trip was planned, you are the Scout who shows up promptly with a smile, just as if the sun shone. If no one wants the job of delivering notices on Saturday afternoon, you help the Scoutmaster by volunteering, and you are such a good Scout about it that some of the other Scouts volunteer too. Don't be afraid to do more than your share. If you do it in the right way, you'll have company.

Be a Den Chief if there is a Cub Scout Den which needs one. That is a fine way to do your part.

In School

In school, you stand out because you are a Boy Scout. Teachers as well as other boys are going to judge Scouting by the way you act. The good name of Scouting is in your keeping. You keep your promise to be mentally awake by punctual attendance and by not neglecting your studies. This means doing your best, not just sliding through.

Your work in Scouting often helps you in school. Surveys made in schools in all parts of the country have shown that the big majority of student offices were filled by Scouts. The majority of school athletes are Scouts too. Scout training in leadership and character seems to make boys stand out, so that their schoolmates respect them.

Teachers call on Scouts to help in safety work, first aid demonstrations, displaying the school Flag, leading games and athletics, and in other forms of skill and leadership. Most Scouts have served modestly and effectively in such jobs. You too can do your part.

In Your Church

Doing your part in your church starts with knowing the teachings and ideals of your religion. But then you must live up to your belief in your everyday life.

Regular attendance and active participation in religious services and other activities are important. Take an active part in your church or synagogue. Help out whenever you can, set a good example for younger members. Leadership experience in Scouting helps you to lead church clubs and other groups.

By doing your duty to God, by living up to the Twelfth point of the Law, and by taking part in church activities you are helping your church.

Scoutcraft helps you do good turns

In Your Home

Of course, in your home you live up to your promise to help other people at all times. Besides your regular home duties, you do things which you were not asked to do, but which you know are needed.

Your Scout skills are useful. Your knowledge of when and how to display the Flag, is important in your home and in your community. If you know your knots, you can find many occasions to use them. Helping your mother put up a clothesline, tying up packages for mailing or storage; putting up a swing for a younger brother or sister or a neighbor; these are some uses for knots around the home. If you live on a farm, you know of many other uses for rope and knot-tying.

You can easily see the value of knowing how to get in touch with a doctor and hospital, how to report a fire, and how to call the police or sheriff. Your first aid skill is useful in the home too, for more accidents happen at home than anywhere else. Your knowledge of safety and accident hazards make you a useful member of the household.

In Your Community

Because you are a Scout, people call on you for help in many community projects. Fire Prevention Week, Arbor Day, Memorial Day, Independence Day, Flag Day activities, and many other community improvement projects need Scout help. There are many other important ways you can find to help.

Take Care of the Property of Others

Every day you use things that belong to other people. Perhaps your school loans you books, either textbooks or library books. It is your duty to take good care of them.

Displaying the flag correctly is practicing citizenship

Treat public buildings such as your school and museums, with the same respect as you would your own. The streets and highways are maintained for your use; do not litter or deface them. You as a citizen own a share in public property. Guard it and care for it.

Your Country's Natural Resources

America's natural resources are a part of your heritage. The mountains, forest, streams, with the wild animals, the trees and plants and bird life, all belong to you, and it is your duty as a Scout and a citizen to help protect them.

Read the section on Conservation in Chapter 12, and you will realize how important it is for all Americans to help in the wise use of natural resources.

Two things that are important in conservation are included in the Tenderfoot Requirements. They are: (1) Be sure that you take all precautions, before you build a fire outdoors. In that way you can help guard against forest fires. (2) Help protect trees, by not hacking them with axes, carving them with knives, and peeling off bark. Help to show other Scouts how that is harmful to the tree.

Protect wild flowers and wild life. On a hike if you find wild flowers, help to protect them by not picking them, and by not trampling them down. If you find a bird nest, and think it would make a suitable decoration for your Patrol Den, be sure that the bird has moved out. In the spring or summer, let nests alone. In the late fall or winter, the birds are not using them. If you find a nest with eggs in it, move away as quickly as possible. Do not disturb the shrubbery around the nest. If you stay near the nest too long, you may frighten the parent away.

OUTDOOR CODE

As an American, I will do my best to:

Be Clean in My Outdoor Manners

I will treat the outdoors as a heritage to be improved for our greater enjoyment. I will keep my trash and garbage out of America's waters, fields, woods, and roadways.

Be Careful with Fire

I will prevent wild fire. I will build my fire in a safe place and be sure it is out before I leave.

Be Considerate in the Outdoors

I will treat public and private property with respect. I will remember that use of the outdoors is a privilege I can lose by abuse.

Be Conservation-Minded

I will learn how to practice good conservation of soil, waters, forests, minerals, grasslands, and wildlife; and I will urge others to do the same. I will use sportsmanlike methods in all my outdoor activities.

Help Conserve Natural Resources

Take an interest in conservation all over the United States. You may think that soil erosion, floods, or forest fires thousands of miles away have little effect on you. But they affect you just as surely as if they happened in your community. The need for conservation of natural resources is a serious problem facing America today. It is something that every citizen should understand. You can do your part by reading a good book on conservation (see Bibliography in this Handbook) and then by taking an active part in helping to save America's resources. You can probably find a good book in your school or public library.

Maintain a Savings Plan

Many of the habits that you are starting to form now, both good and bad, will last the rest of your life. You will have a much easier time later on if your habits formed now are good ones. A good habit for you to begin is to be careful with your money.

A savings plan does not mean that you are stingy or selfish. It means developing a habit of saving, managing a budget, saving towards something you want or may need in the future.

If possible, maintain your own savings account in a bank or public savings institution. Frequently it is possible to deposit money in a bank savings account through your school.

You may find it better to give the money to your parents, who will put it in the bank for you.

If your Troop has a savings fund for camp or uniforms in which Scouts deposit a little money each week, you can meet your Thrift requirement in this way.

Payments on bonds, insurance or savings stamps are also acceptable for this requirement.

In any case, however, you must show your Scoutmaster or other leader actual evidence of how you are meeting this requirement, your regular payments, and any other information he requests.

Your Scout Participation

This chapter has suggested some of the ways in which you as a Scout citizen may do your part. Of course, you will find many others. Only you will know how wholeheartedly you have done your part.

You are an American—do your part

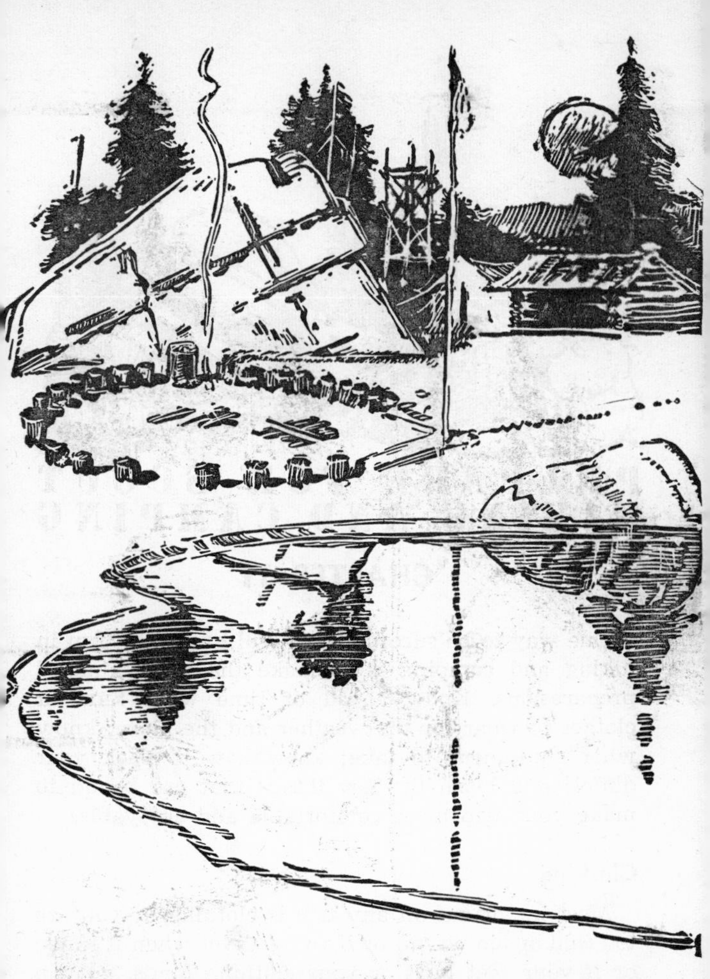

SCOUTING SKILLS

PART IV

PREPARE FOR SCOUT HIKING AND CAMPING

CHAPTER 11

One way to be sure that you will have most fun in hiking and camping is to make the right kind of preparations. Know ahead of time what kind of clothes to wear for the weather and the place; know what equipment to take; know how to pack your duffel; and learn the few things that are bound to make your trip more comfortable and enjoyable.

Clothing

Most important on any trip is clothing. If you are too cold or too warm; or if you get wet when it rains; or if your feet hurt or your clothing binds, no trip will be much fun. So here are a few general rules about clothing. First, your clothing should be tough and strong enough to protect you from snags, rocks, or brush. It should be selected for the place and the weather. It should fit loosely enough to allow easy movement of arms and legs, and should not bind or pinch and cut off blood circulation.

Now, here are a few clothing rules for definite kinds of weather.

Warm Weather Clothing

Starting at the ground and working up, your shoes come first. Every outdoorsman needs to keep his feet in tip-top shape. Shoes should be sturdy with thick soles, to protect your feet, and provide the support that will help you from getting tired. Your shoes should be well broken in before you start on a hike, and should not be tight.

You will find that light weight wool socks are best for long hikes. Many outdoorsmen prefer two pairs of lightweight wool socks. Two pairs prevent friction that might otherwise cause blisters, and wool socks absorb perspiration and help keep your feet dry. Damp socks will soften your feet and may cause blisters or sore spots. If you find that you are most comfortable walking in two pairs of socks, be sure your shoes are large enough. It is better to wear only one pair than to wear two pairs and have your shoes fit too snugly.

For some regions light-weight wool underclothing is cooler than cotton. It absorbs perspiration and evaporates it faster than cotton. Then too, if evenings are cool, as they are in mountainous or desert country, light woolen underclothing keeps you warm. In many sections of the country the days may be hot, but when the sun goes down it gets quite cold.

In most places, your Scout uniform is adequate for outside clothing. The long-sleeved shirt and long trousers are loose fitting and comfortable for hiking. They protect you from brambles and snags and from the rays of the sun. But if the evenings are cold, you may need a long-sleeved woolen shirt or sweater.

In many places short-sleeved shirts and Scout shorts are ideal summer clothing.

In addition, you need a poncho or slicker in case it rains. In some places during the summer it never rains. But in other localities, showers come up and blow over quite quickly—or last for a day or two. It is always best to be prepared for any weather.

Many outdoorsmen like a well broken-in, wide-brimmed hat, such as the Scout Hat. They say it protects the eyes from the sun and keeps rain from dribbling down their necks. Others prefer a ski-type or baseball-type hat. This protects the eyes and is cool to wear. Others may not wear a hat, but carry an old hat in their pack in case they need it. Your choice depends upon preference and the place you are going.

Cold Weather Clothing

There are three basic principles for keeping warm in cold weather, and if you follow those rules, you can camp comfortably in cold weather.

First, wear layers of clothing—that is, wear two light woolen shirts, instead of one heavy one; two or three pairs of light woolen socks instead of one heavy pair. The reason for this is that the dead air spaces between the layers of clothing act as insulation and help keep your body heat from escaping.

Second, reduce the circulation of this dead air by wearing a water repellent, wind resistant outer garment. To keep warm, keep the wind from cutting through your outer clothing.

Third, keep dry. This means keep dry from within as well as from without. Perspiration dampens your clothing and is as cooling on your body as clothing wet from melting snow or rain. Wear outer garments that shed water; remove layers of clothing as you exercise, to avoid perspiring and getting too warm. When you stop exercising, add layers of clothing to keep from getting chilled.

Now, let's get dressed for cold weather trips.

Underwear—Light woolen underwear of the two-piece type is best, so that top or bottom may be removed without the necessity of complete disrobing. Two suits of light underwear are warmer than one because of the insulation provided by the air spaces in and between the two suits.

Socks—Two pairs of woolen socks in boots equipped with felt insoles are sufficient for even very cold weather, providing both socks and insoles are kept dry.

Socks should be worn inside the boots, and should not extend up the leg on the outside of your trousers or be turned down over the boot tops. This prevents their becoming wet from snow.

Shirts—Overdressing so that you prespire should be avoided. A person wearing a woolen shirt, and either a sweater or another wool shirt, and protected by a water repellent jacket or parka should, if carrying on normal exercise, be warm enough for even very cold weather.

Additional garments may be added, if necessary. Be sure to remove them before you become overheated and begin to perspire.

Trousers—Trousers that are water repellent (that will shed snow or rain but allow the air and moisture from inside to escape) are desirable.

Hand-Covering—Knitted mittens or gloves worn inside a water repellent over-mitten, will serve well for hand covering. Knitted gloves, if worn inside an over-mitten are warm. They have the advantage that if the over-mitten is removed, the fingers may be used without exposing them.

Parkas—The parka has advantages over most outer jackets since it is large enough to permit the free circulation of air, permitting evaporation of moisture and cooling.

If it is very cold, the parka may be secured around the waist with a cord, sash or drawstring. It can be loosened, however, to permit the escape of moisture when you are exercising.

Moist air will escape from the parka when it is loosened around the neck and air pumped through it. This is done by grasping the garment at the bottom, extending it and then bringing it back and forth in front.

Boots—Except in very cold temperatures, boots should have a waterproof foot and be large enough to accommodate inner soles and two pairs of woolen socks.

The inside of the boots will become moist from perspiration during wearing. At night, the inner soles as well as the socks should be removed and dried.

How to Wear Clothing in Cold Weather

The outer garment (jacket or parka) should be loose at the bottom. The shirt should also hang loosely except when tightened at the waist by a belt or cord.

When traveling or exercising, as you become warm, let your clothing hang free around your waist, thus permitting the circulation of air, which cools your body. If additional cooling is desirable, your coat

Don't try to dry wool or leather quickly

and shirt may be loosened at the neck. Mittens may be removed for cooling, or some garment taken off as the body becomes warmer. It can be put back on as the body cools.

The idea is, that if you chill or warm any part of your body, the other parts are also chilled or warmed.

It is important to remember that the amount of your foot gear should never be decreased, since frozen feet are particularly serious. It is difficult to tell when your feet are approaching the freezing point.

Drying Wet Clothes

Outdoorsmen say that you can tell an inexperienced hiker by his burned shoes. There is one safe way to dry clothing or shoes. Stretch a rope or vine between two trees or poles, well above and about three feet to one side of the fire. Don't try to dry wool or leather quickly. It cannot be done. Tie your shoes together by the lacings and hang them so that the heat strikes the soles. Socks or clothing may be pinned together and hung on the line. A thin bent twig placed inside your socks will help them to dry more quickly.

Hike Equipment

When an outdoorsman plans a hike, he gathers the things that he will need and then includes the things he may need. Let's make a list of equipment that you will need, and one that you may need. Such a list might be:

HIKE EQUIPMENT

Will need	*May need*
Matches in waterproof case or waterproofed matches	20 feet of cord
Pack	Fishline—hooks
Water purification tablets	Hand axe
Drinking cup	Fish lures
Cooking gear	Two bars of chocolate
Eating utensils	Scout handbook
Food in food bags	Pencils—paper
Extra socks	Small flashlight
Knife	Poncho or raincoat
Compass	Whetstone
Map	File
Candle	Camera—film
First aid kit	
Canteen	
Toilet paper	

CAMP EQUIPMENT

Will need	*May need*
Hike equipment (see above)	**Hike equipment (see above)**
Tent—ground cloth	Small shovel
Blankets—or sleeping bag	Extra candles
Pajamas	Small coil of light wire
Extra clothing	Sewing kit
Toilet kit: soap, towel, tooth paste, toothbrush, comb	*Boy Scout Songbook*
Flashlight	
Handkerchiefs	

Packs

The important thing in carrying a load is to make your pack as comfortable as possible. All heavy packs are uncomfortable to some degree. But in time, practice will strengthen your muscles and then toughen you, so that you will not mind the pack so much. Then too, a great deal of unnecessary discomfort can be avoided by a careful selection of a pack and the careful arrangement of what goes into it.

Basically, there are three types of packs, each of which you can make for yourself or buy ready-made. The type that you select should be based on your personal preference, the place where you are going, how far you have to carry the pack, and how much money or time you want to spend, buying or making one.

Knapsack—A knapsack is a large bag with shoulder straps. It is made about the width of your back and in various lengths and depths, for various size loads. Some knapsacks have pockets sewed on the

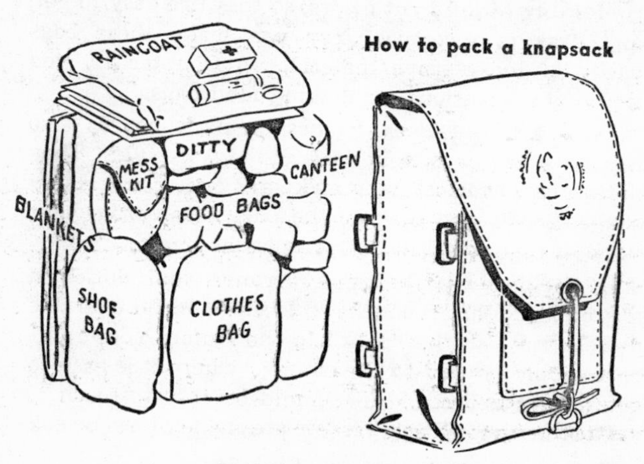

How to pack a knapsack

outside, inside or both, for small equipment. There are many different types of knapsacks planned for different purposes.

In selecting or making a knapsack, be sure that it is not too long for your body (from shoulders to belt) and that it can be adjusted to fit you with different loads.

In packing a knapsack, place blankets and other soft articles next to your back. The part of the pack that hits your back should be as wide and soft as possible. Place the hard objects on the outside.

Be sure too, to adjust the weight evenly. Place articles on the bottom that will be taken out last. Generally, your raincoat or poncho, flashlight, first aid kit and drinking cup ought to be on top. Be careful that heavy objects are so packed that they won't shift to the bottom and cause the pack to sag.

Actually, any pack is a "bag full of little bags." That is, such things as shoes, food, toilet articles—in fact any small articles—are placed in small bags preferably of different colors, so they are easy to get, and easy to recognize. You can make these bags easily of inexpensive material. In Chapter 19, you will find suggestions for making food bags.

Pack Frames—Pack frames or pack boards also can be made or bought in a variety of styles. They are designed for carrying awkward or uncomfortably shaped loads, and to keep the pack away from your back so that you will not perspire as much.

In packing a pack frame, arrange your duffel on a ground cloth, or poncho, fold the poncho over the duffel, and lash the "pack" to the frame. Your raincoat should be tied to the outside, where it is easy to get, and your first aid kit should be easy to reach.

Pack baskets—Pack baskets are made of ash or oak

strips and have shoulder straps attached. They can be made or bought, in two or three styles. Again, be sure that the basket fits you.

Ditty Bag

Almost every outdoorsman carries a "ditty bag" near the top of his pack. This is a catchall for things you may need along the trail, such things as fishline and hooks, wire, small pliers, needles and thread, cord, extra flashlight bulbs and batteries.

Tumplines

On a long hike, or with a heavy load, or in moun-

How to pack a frame (1, 2, 3, 4); and a pack basket (A, B)

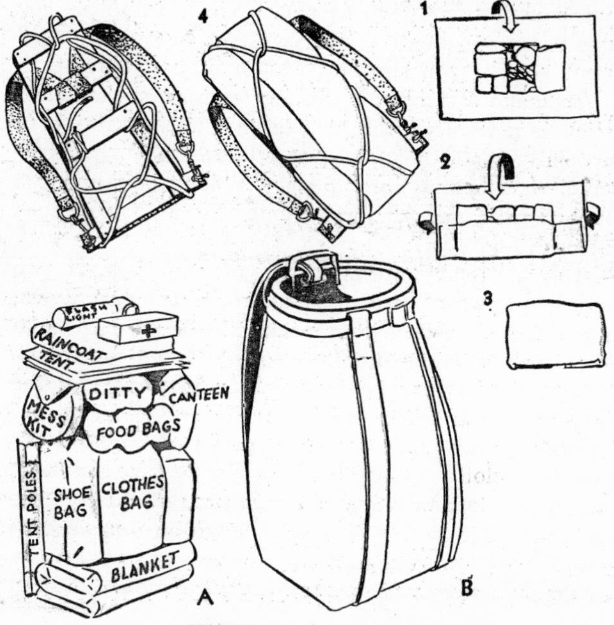

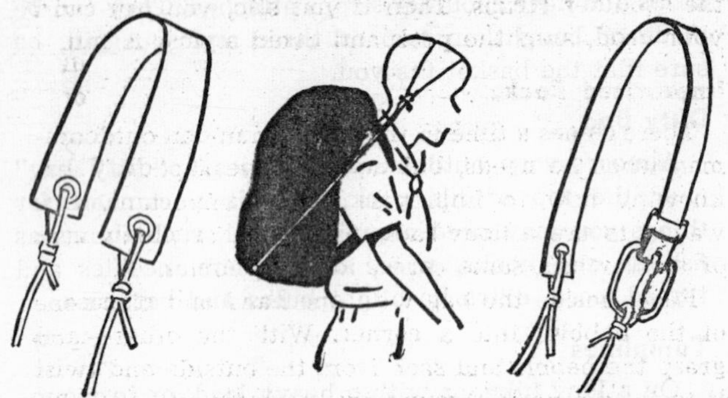

Using a tumpline, you can rest your shoulders

tainous country where walking is tricky, you may want a tumpline on your pack. With a tumpline you can rest your shoulders as you hike, or quickly shed your pack if you slip on rocks or on a steep hill.

To make a tumpline, use any soft, strong material such as a woolen sock, neckerchief or stocking, or a specially made headpiece and lines. Fold a neckerchief or stocking into a loose, oblong roll about 3 inches wide and 18 inches long. Tie a loop of cord at each end.

To the outside bottom corners of your pack, tie two strong pieces of cord or small rope. Then sit down, and after adjusting your pack, tie the cord through the loops on your tumpline, so that when the tumpline is across your head, it will support part of the weight of the pack.

Now, when your shoulders get tired, tighten the tumpline and take some of the weight on your neck and head. When your neck gets tired, loosen the tumpline and ease the weight down on your shoulders. When walking on rocks, across a narrow bridge, or on a narrow trail, use the tumpline alone, without the shoulder straps. Then if you slip, you can twist your head, shed the pack and avoid a serious fall.

Improvised Packs

There comes a time in the life of many an outdoorsman when he needs, but doesn't have a pack. Then, knowing how to improvise one is important. One way is to use a flour sack, feed sack, or pillow case or similar bag, some cord and two pebbles.

Reach inside the bag with one hand and place one of the pebbles into a corner. With the other hand grasp the pebble and sack from the outside and twist it to form a neck. Around this neck tie one end of a two and a half foot length of soft rope or twine with a clove or timber hitch. Repeat the procedure on opposite corner. Fill the bag with your duffel, taking care the soft items are so placed that they will rest against your back. Take loose ends of the rope or twine and tie firmly to the neck of the pack sack, leaving them loose enough to slip your arms through. With a little practice you can adjust this sack so that it will ride comfortably.

To keep the ropes from cutting into your shoulders, place a pad of soft cloth or grass under the ropes, where they pass over your shoulders.

A flour or grain sack may be used as a pack

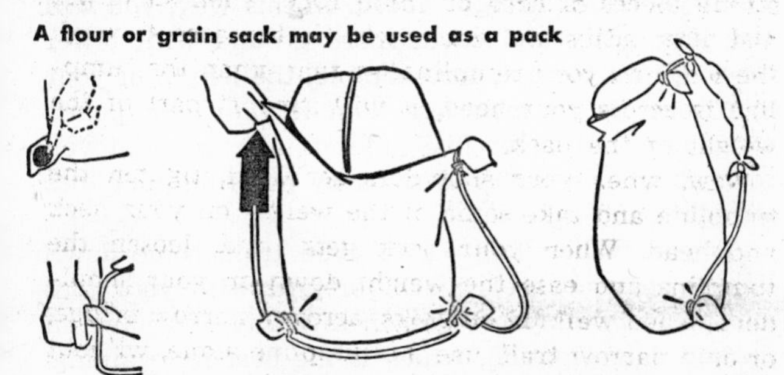

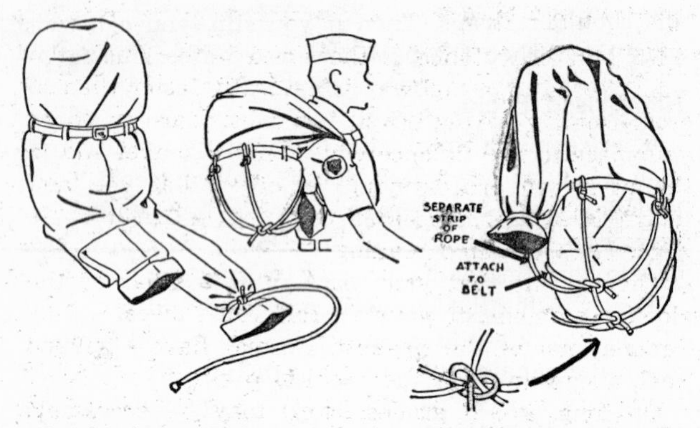

Another improvised pack is a "pants pack." The legs of your trousers or overalls act as shoulder straps and the duffel is fastened inside the waist of the pants.

How to Hike

The most important part of hiking is knowing how to walk. Probably the best rule is to walk in a way that will cover the most ground with the least effort.

Use a gait that is comfortable. Do not take too long steps or too short ones. Generally the ground over which you walk controls the length of your step. Point your toes straight ahead. In this way, you will tire less easily and cover more ground with fewer steps. If you toe out, for example, the length of your step may be an inch less than if your foot points straight ahead. Over five miles this means that you save about five hundred steps by pointing your toes straight.

As you walk along on an even trail, come down lightly on your heel, reach forward with your toes and push up off your toes. In this way you have an up and down motion, which is the best for walking.

Speed in Walking

Next in importance is the speed with which you walk. Speed on a highway is naturally faster than in cross-country hiking. First, you must learn to adapt your pace to the distance you intend to travel and to the pack you are carrying, in order that you and your Patrol will have plenty of pep left over to do a good job of camp making.

That means that your pace must fit that of the slowest member of your Patrol. The slowest member may not be the weakest. He may have a rubbed heel, a sore ankle or the heaviest pack.

On long, uphill grades, stops may be necessary. Experience has shown that short rests at reasonable intervals are better than long rests at long intervals. The main reason is that long rests allow the body to cool beyond the point of comfort. A good test for your speed is the talking test. For a long hike, the pace should never pass the mark of physical comfort or enjoyment of your surroundings. To enjoy yourself to the full, talking should be general throughout the Patrol. When the pace is too fast for conversation, it is too fast for a long hike. A steady pace maintained will usually cover more ground than a fast pace requiring numerous rest periods.

A good thing to remember on long hikes is that your spirit has much to do with how tired you seem to be. If you keep interested in the things you see and hear, sing occasionally, and look for interesting things, the miles will fly past as you hike along.

Care of the Feet

The main reason for foot trouble on hikes is that we don't walk much. Our feet get soft from lack of use.

The easiest remedy for sore feet is adhesive tape applied over a thin piece of gauze to a sore spot as soon as it is noticed. It is a good idea to apply adhesive ahead of time to spots that may get irritated.

The best aid to foot comfort is always to have a freshly washed pair of socks to put on when you reach camp and an extra pair of shoes, sneakers or moccasins. If you have bought a new pair of leather shoes, wear them as much as you can before using them on a hike so that they may take the form of your foot, and be ready to change at once to a pair of soft shoes if they begin to rub. You can wash your socks at night, and they should be dry in the morning. Toe nails should be trimmed at frequent intervals. In-growing toe nails can be dangerous; by watchfulness and trimming the nails straight across, this danger can be eliminated.

Safety on the Trail

The ABC of safety on the trail or highway is **Always Be Careful.** Most accidents are caused by recklessness or carelessness. Another reason for accidents is fatigue. After a long hike or day in the outdoors, you are bound to be tired. When you are tired, you look for the easy way to do things. Unfortunately, the easy way is not always the safe way. If you think before you act, you will generally be safe. Twisted ankles or fractured arms aren't fun any place. But they are especially bad out on the trail. So **Always Be Careful** and avoid accidents.

Safety on the highway boils down to two general rules: (1) Walk single file on the lefthand side of the road, facing traffic (if no local or state laws prohibit it). Watch for cars and get off the road when you see them coming. You may have the right of way, but if a car hits you, the injuries are just as painful as if you were wrong. Be especially careful when approaching turns in the road, crossroads or hills, where you cannot see far in front. Keep well over on the side of the road. Be sure that all Scouts in your Patrol or Troop are on the same side of the road, in single file.

(2) When hiking at night, be sure to tie a white handkerchief or other piece of white cloth around your right leg and right arm (if you hike on the left side of the road. If you must hike on the right, mark your left side with white cloth). Thus motorists coming toward you will see you easily. But even then, get off the road and let cars go by.

Remember too, that you are hiking—not hitch hiking. No Scout "thumbs" a ride, except in very exceptional circumstances. Only in an extreme emergency would you ask for a ride. Being tired is no excuse. If you start a hike, finish it hiking.

Hiking cross-country, on trails or off, the general rule is **watch your step.** It may seem easy to jump from rock to rock or hurdle over down logs. You may do it successfully many times. But, if the rock is slippery, and you fall, you have to do it only once to wish you had been more careful. You can never tell until you look what is on the other side of a log. There may be a hole or a sleeping rattler.

Watch every step you take. Be sure that when you put your foot down, the ground is solid—that no rock will twist over or soft spot swallow up your shoe in mud and ooze. If you like to swing your way down a mountain side, from tree to tree; or pull your way up using trees and shrubs for support, **be careful.** A dead branch may break off, or a shrub pull up by the roots, and what happens to you? If you are lucky, you will only fall down, but more serious things may happen.

If you watch your step and use common sense, you can go a long way toward avoiding accidents.

Purifying Drinking Water

Unless you know positively that water is safe to drink, you will always be wise to "purify" it yourself. The only way you can be sure, is to know that the water was tested by a reliable laboratory. Usually, this is not done except at established camps and campsites. Brooks, streams, springs and wells which you find in the open may be safe—and they may not. Streams may flow through a pasture; animals may use the same water you do. Or the sanitary facilities of nearby homes may drain into the water. It is always wise to do your best to be safe.

Here are two goods ways to purify water.

(1) Boil it for at least five minutes, then pour it back and forth from one clean container to another several times. The

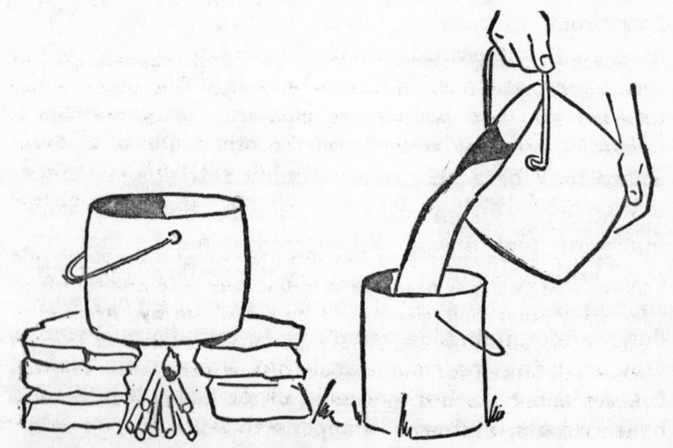

boiling kills harmful plant and animal material in the water; the pouring restores air to it so it does not taste flat.

(2) Use water purification tablets such as Halazone, that are in your Scout first aid kit or can be bought in a drugstore. The tablets should be fresh. Place two tablets in a quart of water. (Read the directions on the bottle.) Let the water stand *thirty* minutes. Shake the container occasionally during the *thirty* minute waiting period.

Latrines

A one man latrine is simply a hole scooped out of the earth, about six inches in diameter and eight inches deep, to be used once by one man. After using, the hole is filled in with the original soil, so that there is a three-inch mound. After the first rain, the soil will settle to the original ground level. Be sure that all latrines are completely filled in after use.

Latrines for a camp of a few days for several Scouts should be at least two feet deep, eight inches wide and one foot long for each Scout. The dirt should be piled nearby. After each use, a few inches of dirt should be shoveled into the latrine. When the latrine is filled to about fifteen inches from the top, shovel in all the dirt, mounding it six inches high on top. Then dig a new latrine.

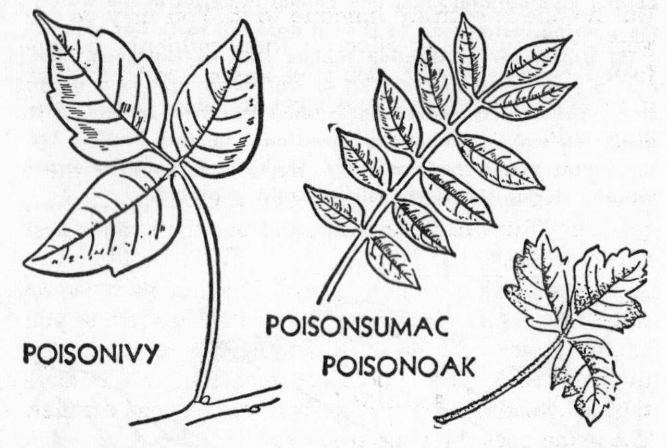

Poisonous Plants

There are three plants that most frequently cause skin poisoning: poisonivy, poisonoak and poisonsumac. Poisonivy may grow in different ways: along the ground, over logs or fences, up a tree or in shrubbery as a vine, or as a low growing bush. The leaves grow in separate groups of three. Study the illustration well so you will recognize it when you see it.

In the winter you can recognize poisonivy by the white berries and the aerial rootlets with which it clings on trees. These rootlets are wavy, but they do not have suction cups at the end such as Boston ivy or Virginia Creeper has.

Poisonsumac has drooping clusters of white berries instead of the ordinary reddish sumac fruit. Poisonsumac usually grows in wet, moist or damp places.

Individual people vary greatly in how these poisonous plants affect them. Some people are very sensitive and others seem not to be affected at all.

But no one is entirely immune to it. You may go for years without being affected, then suddenly be infected very seriously. Don't let anyone tell you that if you get it once, you won't get it again. You probably will.

If you are wise, you will learn to recognize these plants and avoid them. But if you should be affected, read the "First Aid" Chapter, and use the proper first aid remedies.

It may be that you have to walk through it, or do walk through it without realizing it. Then when you handle your shoes or trousers, the oily poison from the crushed leaves will infect you. You can remove the oil by sponging your shoes off with a good cleaner. The same goes for your trousers.

What to Do if Lost

The best thing, of course, is not to get lost. One way to avoid it is first to get acquainted with the country where you camp. Make yourself a small pocket map showing the essential landmarks around camp so that you can find your way back.

One excellent method to help you find your way back to camp from a hike is to establish a base line at right angles to your hike direction. This base line might be a river, stream, ridge, rock cliff or line of marked trees or shrubs.

Become acquainted with this base line by exploring it for three miles in each direction from camp. Memorize outstanding features, so that you will know on which side of camp you are. Let's imagine that you have camped on a stream. You have explored the stream for three miles above and three miles below camp. Then, let's imagine that you go on a hike to the west. Coming back, you may get off the course

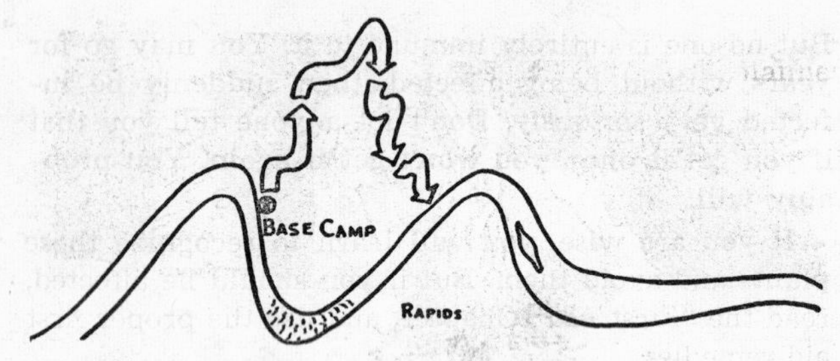

Establish a base line and get to know it

a little, but you come to the stream. By looking around, you know where you are in relation to camp, and follow the stream back home.

But there may come a time when you are temporarily "bumfuzzled" and don't know where the camp is. Here are a few things to do.

Sit down on a rock, or under a tree, and think the whole thing over. In fact it's a good time to think of a few funny stories. In other words calm down, and don't be afraid. If you let your imagination run away, you will run away, and probably run in a circle and come right back to where you started. On top of that, in running, you may fall down and get hurt.

Here are a few things to think about: Which way is north? Look at your compass, at the shadows, or use your watch. That may help you.

After thinking for a while, mark a small tree on four sides so you can see it from one hundreed feet away. Then walk straight out for seventy-five to one hundred feet, and swing in a circle with the marked tree as the center. Study the ground and look for landmarks or signs of a trail, or camp. If you do not find such a landmark and have decided which way camp is, you have a decision to make: whether to stay where you are until someone finds you; to

At night build a windbreak and a fire

stay all night and start out the first thing in the morning; or to start out immediately for camp.

If darkness is only two hours or less away, and you know camp is a long way off, stay where you are. Find a windbreak—either a rock, down log, or cliff. Build a fire for heat and sit between the fire and the windbreak.

Be sure you clear the fire site first though, and have a good supply of small sticks and larger fuel on hand to keep the fire going all night.

There are two reasons for this fire. It will be cheerful and keep you warm. It may attract the attention of searchers or forest wardens.

Before you start out, whether it is immediately after the waiting period, or the next morning, write a note if possible (pencil and paper, charcoal on bark) and fasten it with pegs to your marked tree. Give your name, which way you went, and the date.

Then select a landmark in the direction you want to go. Walk toward it, marking your trail, by breaking down small shrubs or by leaving trail markers. When you arrive at your first landmark, pick a second one that lines up with the marked tree and the

A smoke signal or a bright fire may bring help

first landmark. This is called "bee-lining" your way. Only in this way, or by taking sights with your compass, can you travel in a straight line.

If you cannot decide which way to go, a smoke signal might attract attention. Clear a fire site and build a fire. Then throw green wood, ferns, grass or live brush on top, and a dense smoke will result. But don't let the fire get out of control and don't neglect to put it out. If it spread and started a forest fire, you would be in a worse jam than before.

You may have heard that if you get lost in snow or cold weather, you must keep moving. Don't you believe it. Dr. Vilhjalmur Stefansson, who has spent many years in the Arctic says:

". . . The principles to remember are: Don't keep moving—keep still. Keep your clothes dry. Sleep as much as you can—because it saves energy and passes time."

If you try to keep awake you use up energy that keeps you warm. If you walk around, your perspiration makes your clothing wet. Then you feel colder still. Find a windbreak and build a fire.

In snow it may be easier to find your way out, if you can follow your own steps backward. You may be able to back track on your footprints.

Care of Food

Camp food may be divided into three groups as far as care is concerned: (1) fresh milk and meat which must be kept at a temperature lower than 50°, to avoid loss by spoiling; (2) some vegetables, butter, and some processed meats which must be kept cool, or they will spoil; (3) dried or canned foods, or fresh foods which will keep at air temperature.

In addition, any food, unless canned or securely wrapped, may attract ants and flies. The camper's job is to care for food so that it will not spoil or become infested with animal pests.

Unless you can take ice to camp, it is best not to use fresh meat and milk. Use canned or processed meats and dried milk.

Foods that need to be kept cool can be kept in a cool, shaded place, and protected from ants and flies.

All food that is not canned or wrapped in wax paper, as well as cooking and eating utensils, should

Store food and water in a clean, safe place

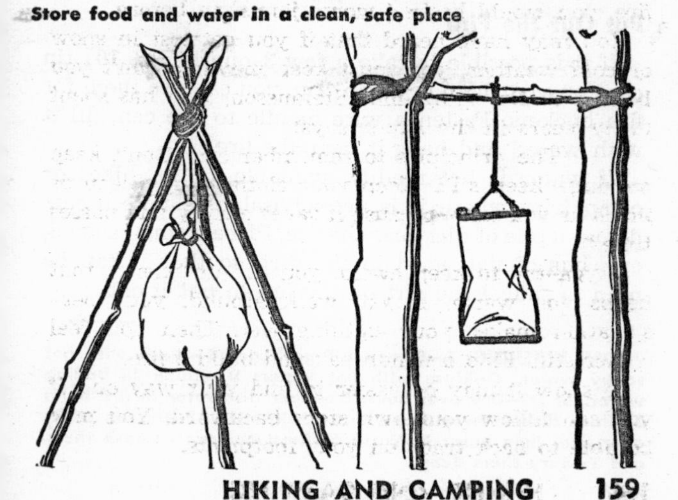

be stored in racks or bags hung from trees or tripods, where animal pests cannot touch them.

Water may be kept sweet and cool, if stored in a desert water bag suspended from a tripod or tree limb. If canteens are used, keep the cloth cover wet. This will keep the water cooler than air temperature. If water is stored in other containers, be sure that the containers are covered, to keep insects and animals out.

Waste Disposal

All garbage and rubbish should be burned. Tin cans should be burned out, smashed flat and buried. Bottles may be washed out and buried.

The cooking fire may be used to burn garbage. Place a row of fingersized sticks across the fire, and place the garbage on top. The coals will dry the garbage. Then a little more fuel added to the fire will burn the sticks and the garbage.

Put Out the Fire

If it is possible to take a few 3-quart (No. 10) tin cans on your hike or camp trip, you can use them for fire buckets. Fasten a wire handle to the can, fill it with water, and hang it near the fire.

If water is not readily available, or on hikes or camp trips where it is not advisable to take a can, dig up a pile of dirt near the fire. Place a small shovel, or piece of flat wood in the dirt, so that it can be used to shovel the dirt on the fire to put it out.

⟶

DISH WASHING: A—Scrape off garbage; B—Wash with hot soapy water; C—Rinse with hot water; D1—Dunk in boiling water, or D2—Dry over heat; B2—Pour dishwater in fire hole; E—Store dishes away from flies. GARBAGE: A2—Dry on sticks over fire, then burn; X—Wash or burn out cans, smash them, and Y—Bury them deep.

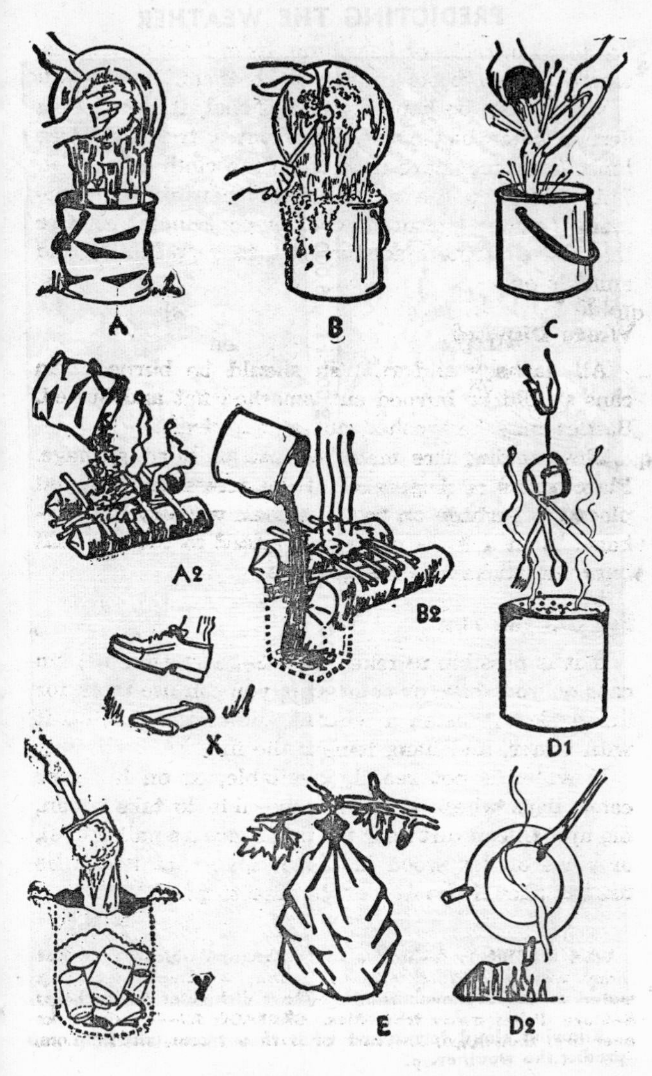
A
B
C
A2
B2
D1
X
Y
E
D2

PREDICTING THE WEATHER

Knowing cloud forms and what they mean will help you predict the weather.

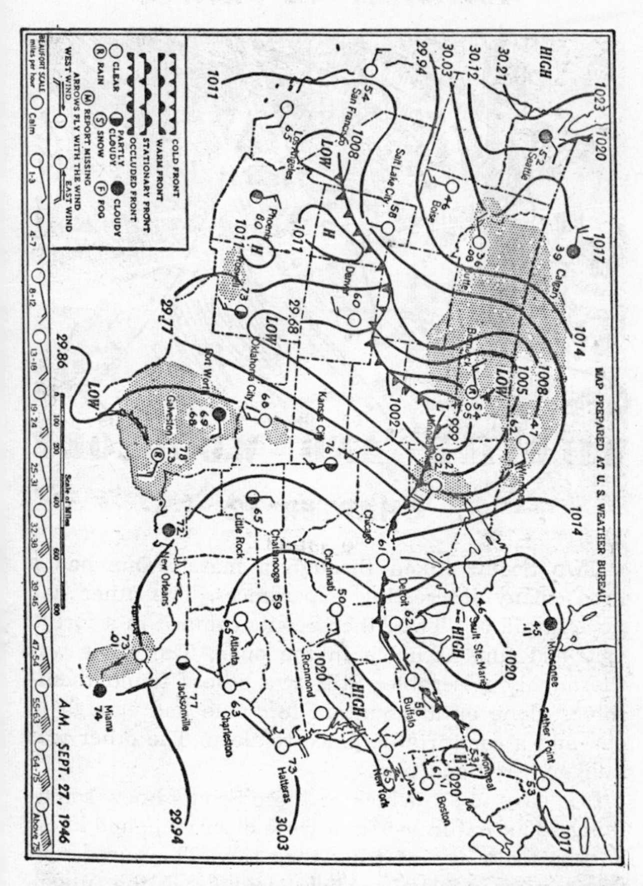

Weather maps are published daily by the Weather Bureau and in many papers. They help you predict the weather. Figure beside Station Circle indicates correct temperature (Fahrenheit). Cold front: a boundary line between cold air and warmer air, usually moving southward and eastward. Warm front: a boundary between warm air and colder air usually northward and eastward. Stationary front: an air mass boundary which shows little or no movement. Occluded front: a line along which warm air has been lifted from the earth's surface. This often causes precipitation along the front. Winds are counter-clockwise toward the center of low-pressure systems, and clockwise outward from high-pressure areas.

WILDLIFE AND WOODLORE

CHAPTER 12

Two Scouts hiked through a marsh. One had a great many interesting experiences. The other had none at all. . . . Two other Scouts camped in a forest. One had fun, at home in the open. The other was thoroughly miserable. Still two others found themselves alone on a mountain top. One had enough to eat, and a comfortable place to sleep. The other was hungry, tired and cold.

It is easy to see which of these Scouts knew something about nature—which were observing, and knew how to make use of what they saw. The purpose of this section is to help every Scout know the fundamentals of nature—so that he may have more fun in the open, and train himself to be at home in the out-of-doors.

For nature makes the rules of the game she plays, and to win, Scouts must play according to those rules, not their own. It is much easier to know where and when to see an osprey diving, trillium in bloom, or a beaver building a dam—than to try to make these creatures do those things at any desired time.

Just as every Scout has a community in which he lives, so has every animal—insect, fish, reptile, bird or mammal. Naturalists call these communities "habitats." Think for a minute now, of the different kinds of habitats or communities where animals are found! Would not almost every one of them fit into one of these groups: (1) Water, (2) Marshes or Swamps, (3) Grasslands or Prairies, (4) Forests or Woods, (5) Deserts or Seashores, (6) Mountain Tops? Would not any place where the Scout might find himself, fit into one of these groups?

Think too, of what it is that makes a habitat what it is. Is it animal life found there, or is it plant life? Is it the herons, ducks, and muskrats that make a marsh, or is it the cattails, sedges, or wild rice? Is it the tiny warblers, black bears, squirrels and porcupines that make a forest, or is it the oaks, hickories, spruces or pines? Habitats are made up of all living things in them, plus conditions such as land, water, air, light and temperature.

Animals Depend on Plants

Wild animals, all the way from the tiniest plant lice up to an enormous brown bear, all depend upon plants, either directly or indirectly for food. Plant lice, as the name implies live on rose bushes, garden peas, or other plants. Ants and ladybird beetles eat the tiny lice. Flickers or robins may eat the ants or beetles. Minks or hawks may eat the robins or flickers. So the minks or hawks which are meat eating, or carnivorous animals, are dependent on plants.

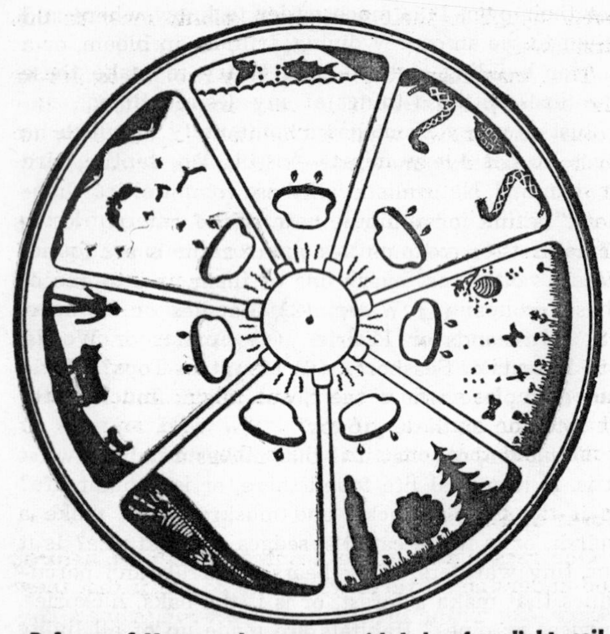

Balance of Nature—plants grow with help of sunlight, soil, water and air. Insects, reptiles, fish, birds and mammals all live together, dependent upon plants and each other. Plant and animal remains, plus rocks and minerals, make up the soil in which plants grow. So the circle goes around.

On the water plants and algae that grow in common streams, live tiny, almost invisible animals called protozoans. These protozoans are eaten by larger animals. These then, are eaten by insect larvae that live in the water. Minnows and other small fish eat the larvae, and in turn are eaten by larger fish, such as salmon. Finally along comes a bear, or a bald eagle, and catches a salmon for its meal. Thus even one of the largest mammals and one of the largest birds in North America, is dependent upon plants, even though in their food chain, plants must be the first link.

That may seem like a long way around to get to the main point. But it is very important, for the Scout who knows what a "habitat" is, and how to make use of this knowledge, will be the Scout who is thoroughly at home in the out-of-doors. Whether your nature adventures take the form of hiking through the woods or swamps for the sheer joy of hearing warblers singing, or seeing muskrats building their homes, or camping in the wilds of a desert or prairie—or even if some day you were marooned on a mountain top or in a jungle—you will have more fun, be much happier, and have a much better chance for survival, if you know wild animals at home, and the homes in which they hide.

Cover or Shelter

One reason why some Scouts see little in nature, and understand little of what they do see, is that they look in the wrong places, or at the wrong times. The observing Scout will soon learn to associate certain animals with certain kinds of plants or habitats. He will learn what types of shelter different animals prefer, and what they eat. He knows already that rabbits do not make their homes in tree tops as squirrels do, and that squirrels do not feed on fish the way otters do. When he wants to find squirrels he looks in treetops, or under nut-bearing trees. When he wants to find kingfishers, he looks along streams or ponds where those birds find their food. If he wants to find beetles or snakes, he looks under rocks, inside logs or in the grass. If he wants to find trout, bass or clams, he looks in streams, ponds, or along the seashore. He soon learns that every animal has a home, and

All animals depend directly or indirectly on plant life for food. Even fish-eating birds eat animals, which eat smaller animals which eat even smaller animals, which eat plants.

that the easiest way to see that animal is to go to its home.

When he wants to learn about trees or shrubs, birds or mammals, he goes to one habitat, knowing in advance what he may find there, for identifying different kinds of birds, is largely the process of elimination. Knowing what the birds are not, is easier at first than knowing what they are. For example, a Scout walking through a forest could immediately eliminate a great many families of birds. He would forget about geese, sandpipers, gulls, rails, most of the sparrows, many of the swallows, and a few others. He would concentrate on woodpeckers, thrushes, warblers, some of the hawks, owls, tanagers, and such typical birds of the woods. The same principle applies to mammals and trees, and to all other habitats.

The observing Scout will also take a lesson from the animals he sees. For Scouts like the birds and mammals, must have shelter to lead a comfortable life.

When rain or the blazing sun beats down, animals react very differently. Deer huddle around the base of a tree, where the needles or leaves keep off the rain. Woodchucks or marmots dive for a stone wall, or the shelter of rocks. Bobcats, or mountain lions crawl into caves, or under the overhang of a rocky ledge. Rabbits jump into a dense thicket, or down a hole. Squirrels and owls seek out their nests in a hollow tree. Snakes slither into a log—and beetles crawl under rocks or leaves—all to stay there till the weather is better for them.

The Scout will remember these things and, if he is caught in the open without shelter, he will take a lesson from them. He will build a lean-to of boughs or branches, a cabin of logs, or an improvised shelter in the lee of a rock or ledge. He may even dig a "fox-hole" and cover it with layers of grass or reeds.

Time and Temperature

So far you have seen why "place" is so important in observing and understanding nature. The second important factor is time. Every Scout knows that there are times when it is hot and times when it is cold; times when the wind is strong and times when it is calm. He also knows what he can do to make himself comfortable during these times. In a similar way, animals react to temperature and wind changes. You would not expect to find butterflies or wood warblers on a cold winter day. Nor would you look for snowy owls in the United States in mid-July. Some animals prefer heat, others the cold. The Scout who is successful in his nature adventuring, comes to know these preferences. The more successful fishermen carry a thermometer and consider it as important as their rod or plug. Some will not even bother to fish, if the temperature is not just right. They know that fish react to temperature changes, and feed only at certain temperatures. No matter how tempting the plug, or how appetizing the bait, generally speaking the temperature and other conditions must be right, or fish will not feed.

Any Scout who has earned his Bird Study Merit Badge knows that some birds are best observed in the early morning, before the sun is up too high. This is partly because these birds feed after a night without food, but also because during the heat of day they are less active. But the Scout who looks for turtles or snakes, knows that these animals are apt to be found most frequently sunning themselves on logs or rocks. Scouts will find, too, that some animals are more active at night. The best time to listen for owls, spring peepers, or whip-poor-wills is after dark.

When a Scout is at home, he knows how to control the temperature—but does he know what to do in the open? Very probably, if he uses his knowledge of nature.

Scouts Can Learn from Animals

From the turtle, or snake, he learns that rocks hold the heat of the sun—so to get warm, he looks for a large sheltered rock that will reflect the sun's heat. He learns that breezes blow across hilltops, so to cool off, he may stand or camp in such a spot. From the beetles or deer, he learns that the leaves or needles of trees, or the tall grass on a prairie will shelter him from the heat of the sun.

He soon learns that some trees furnish wood that is better for fire building than others. He finds that soft wood from some of the pines is better for kindling, and that hard woods are better for heat or cooking.

The Scout naturalist will learn all of these things for himself, and remember them. These lessons will pay him well, as he hikes or camps in the open. He will find that nature is a skill to learn, as are first aid, signaling, knot tying or compass. For a knowledge of nature will help him as he camps, and may save his life if he is ever lost or marooned in the wild.

Food

As every Scout knows, animals must eat. Some may eat plant life, others will eat other animals. Some may eat both plants and animals. Knowledge of what animals eat, will help the Scout in his nature observations. If he wants to find bees or butterflies, for example, it is easier to find a flower that provides these insects with nectar, than to dash wildly through the woods or fields looking for the insects. If he wants to watch sandpipers, he will go to the edge of a lake, bay or ocean, where these birds find the tiny shellfish they feed on. If he wants to find mice, he will look in the grass, or woods, where these small mammals find the roots and shoots they prefer.

The Scout naturalist may be interested in tracing food chains, as they are called. Reference has been made to a simple chain from underwater plants to the brown bear. Every Scout, after reading this nature section, will be able to find what many common animals eat, from the tiniest bug up to the largest mammal found in his area.

Just as animals live on natural foods, so can Scouts, if they find it necessary. There are many edible plants in any natural habitat, and animals too, that may be caught and eaten. No good Scout will kill or hurt any living creature needlessly. But in an emergency, the Scout who understands the habitat in which he

ANIMAL HOMES

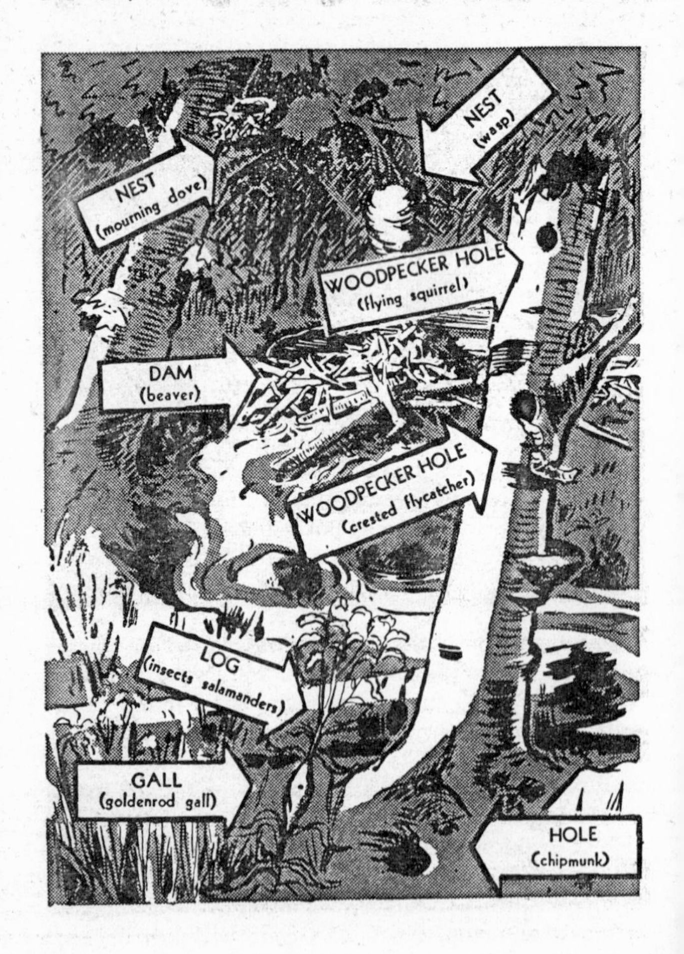

AND SIGNS •

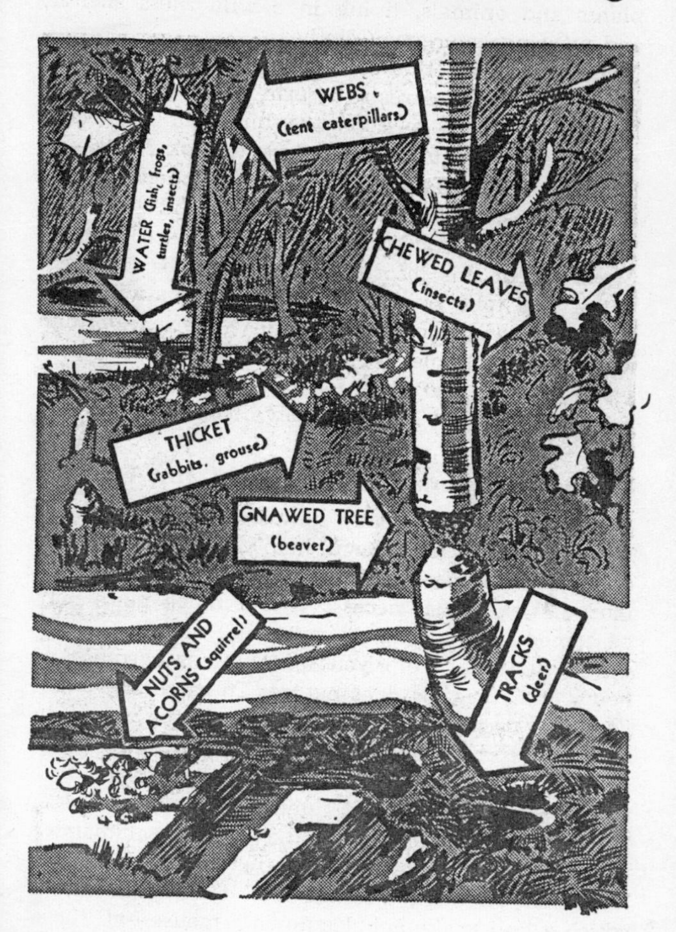
WEBS
(tent caterpillars)
WATER (fish, frogs, turtles, insects)
CHEWED LEAVES
(insects)
THICKET
(rabbits, grouse)
GNAWED TREE
(beaver)
NUTS AND ACORNS (squirrel)
TRACKS
(deer)

finds himself, may get along very well on native plants and animals, living in a wilderness shelter, and wearing emergency clothes.

Other pages of this section are devoted to water, marshes, prairies, forests, deserts, and mountaintops. In each of these sections are hints for the Scout naturalist—what to look for, how to look for it, and how to understand what he sees. Included too, are hints for making shelters, finding food and water and living as comfortably as possible in each kind of place. All of this information may not be required, but if you take some of these hints you will have more fun and more interesting experiences than would seem possible. For all the men who wrote these sections found nature interesting enough, and important enough, to make it their life's work.

Nature Adventuring Is More Than Just Fun

You have seen already how a knowledge of the fundamentals of nature will help you have fun in the open, help you be a better camper and help you find food and shelter if necessary. But much more may be gained from nature adventuring.

Few activities help you learn the importance of being observing, as does nature. To catch the quick flash of a deer's tail as it disappears in the woods, to see the muskrat before it dives for the opening of its house, to see a tiny warbler flitting about the tree tops—or a mountain goat jump from ledge to ledge, to see a hawk soaring high in the sky, or a salamander disappear under a rock, to see the flash of blue as a kingfisher dives for a minnow, or the rapidity with which a bull snake gobbles down a mouse—all these take keen eyes. To hear the whistle of a woodchuck, the faraway hoot of an owl, the chatter of a squirrel, the warning of timber rattlers, the beautiful song of a winter wren—all these take trained ears.

Many a present-day biologist, physicist, wildlife or soil technician, forester, conservationist and science teacher got his start as a Boy Scout naturalist. And many of the best contributions to natural science were made by people who watched birds, bugs and other animals just for the fun of it. What you do now in the field of nature, may be the beginning of a life work, or the start of a lifelong hobby.

Every Scout has heard the word "conservation," applied most frequently to natural resources,—minerals, soil, trees and wildlife. Conservation will mean more if you know something of the fundamentals of how nature works.

One thing a Scout naturalist learns is, that it is not safe to jump to conclusions. Just because some hawks or owls on a few occasions eat chickens, is no reason to condemn all hawks and owls. These birds destroy vast numbers of mice and insects. Skunks may raid hen houses, but a great many more skunks eat grubs, and other insects. Deer may carry ticks that are injurious to cattle, but they also provide food for mountain lions, that would otherwise feed on cattle or sheep. Coyotes and foxes may be detrimental to man's interests in some cases, but many more of them eat gophers and mice.

Nature teaches you that there is a definite plan, along which she works, and that almost any conflict between nature and man happens because man upsets that plan. The more you see of nature, the more you will be amazed at how this plan works.

SCOUTING IN BOGS AND MARSHES

Ever since the days of the "will o' the wisp," bogs and marshes have held a lure for the adventurous. In recent years many things have been discovered about swamplands. Many marshes have been brought under cultivation. They are the most productive spots on earth. It would be a mistake, however, to drain all bogs. Bogs are "islands" of wild life. They afford rare plants like the fringed orchid, and interesting animals like the marsh wren. Some marshes must be preserved as objects to study, as well as for recreational purposes. Such a habitat group cannot be brought to the museum. Bogs and marshes are living museums. They offer one of the most adventurous trips that a Scout can take. Every Scout should go bog trotting once and having tried one, he will hardly wait for other such trips.

A Profile of a Swamp

The glacier which once covered much of the northern United States left a plowed landscape. If the area to be visited is a northern one, we are concerned with the return of vegetation to the low wet lands, to kettle holes, and to shallowing lake basins. In any case, the invading plants have been contributing their remains to the filling of the lowland. Peat-forming plants displace one another in sequence, and give rise to different layers of peat. Aquatic and marsh plants, and the forest give rise to sedimentary, fibrous, and woody peat. Aquatic vegetation is in the open water, marsh vegetation borders it, and then comes the swamp forest.

The underlying stratum or "hard pan" bottom of the bog-bordered lake lies a few inches to many feet below the surface water. You may wish to tie poles end to end and force them through the brown soup "false bottom." Bog probing is lots of fun and it will give you a basis on which to estimate the depth of the true bottom. The cross section of the area should extend from upland to upland. The area will probably be saucer-shaped. The slope of the hillsides toward the bog will also give an idea of the slope of the basin.

Some Scouts may be interested in making a collection of peats and other bog products, placing them in bottles for future examination.

Marsh gas or methane often bubbles up through the ooze. It forms where organic matter decays in the absence of oxygen. The spontaneous combustion of marsh gas may account for some "will o' the wisp" stories. Some chemistry teacher may help you naturalists to demonstrate this with a test tube. He may allow you to sniff hydrogen sulphide so that you will recognize it at the marsh. Some think that the odor resembles rotten eggs.

Dry out and bale a wad of brown peat. Burn it in the "lab" or at the Troop meeting. Why is it a good fuel? Why is it not used more in this country? Drainage lowers the ground water for truck crops like cranberries. Why is a dried-out peat bog a serious fire hazard? Any Scout may think of some more experiments.

Plants of the Area

The glacial invasion destroyed the plants that did not migrate south of the glacial field. As the Arctic climate retreated the plants migrated north. Whether the area you are visiting is in glaciated region or not, it is passing through stages of plant migration, such as water vegetation, marsh-meadow, swamp-forest, and climax forest. It is always an interesting "movie." A Patrol can select as a project a study of these plants, but probably it is best to list the significant species. There are 250 species of sphagnum moss at least.

Scouts should understand that every bog or meadow is in a stage of change. It even varies considerably from one summer to another. Let us try to picture one of the oldest swamp "movies." Vegetation which built the coal-forming peat beds occupied swamp land. Gigantic ferns and horse-tails, or scouring rushes and club mosses, were the most conspicuous. To pass from peat to lignite, to bituminous, to anthracite and then to transparent diamonds, one of the hardest of minerals, or to opaque graphite, one of the softest of minerals, was a long, long story. There was no human eye to see it take place. But the evidence tells the story. Coal seams 10 feet thick

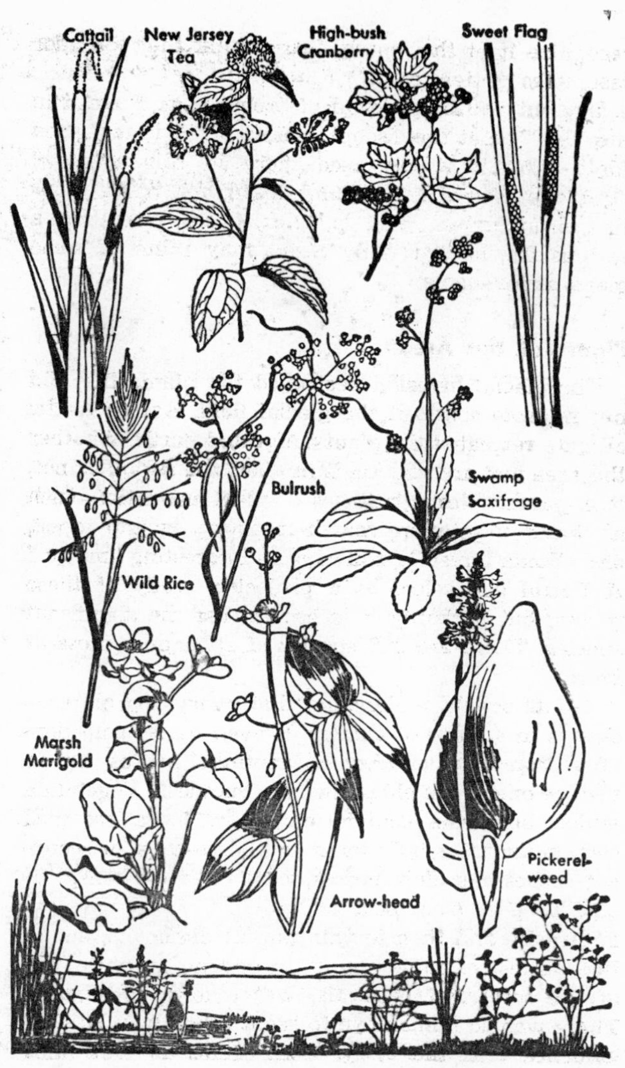
Cattail
New Jersey Tea
High-bush Cranberry
Sweet Flag
Bulrush
Swamp Saxifrage
Wild Rice
Marsh Marigold
Arrow-head
Pickerel-weed

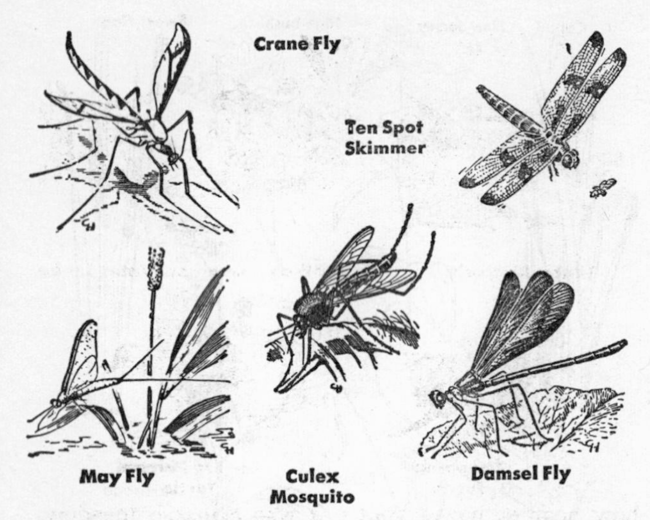

represent peat beds 50 feet in thickness. Large coal seems are 50 feet thick. Carboniferous strata are 2 miles thick. Some geologists estimate that it took 300 million years to form.

Flowers and seeds have developed since the coal age. That may have taken another 100 million years! To visit a nearby bog or marsh area where the rarest creations of orchids, ferns, and heath shrubs are found is like going to another country. The same biological orderliness that has occurred down through eons of time can be seen occurring at the bog or marsh. The human eye can see this, if it is an observing eye.

Sod forming plants, like grasses and sedges, live in the meadow. The tussock formers make tufts that can stand the stress of high water and wind. The Scout may cut a sedge tussock (*Carex stricta*) or dig out a royal fern tussock. Sedge tussocks in a pasture show

how near or how recently it was a marsh meadow. Tussocks are less than a foot in diameter. The Indians used them for stepping stones in wet seasons. Try it!

The mat formers are the cattails and sedges. You never see cattails in open dry fields. Their structure limits them to swamps. Their wind-borne seeds do not take long to populate an open swamp.

We have already seen that sphagnum is a peat former. If you pick a single strand of sphagnum, you can see that it has green growing leaves at the tip. The lower end is dead and forming peat. The part between acts like a wick and draws the water up above the general water level. If you squeeze a handful of sphagnum, you will see what a great water holding capacity it has. If you step on the sphagnum, you can see how the mat rises again. That is indeed remarkable since the sphagnum is too weak to stand alone. Sphagnum is soft and absorbent. It was used as absorbent cotton in the first World War.

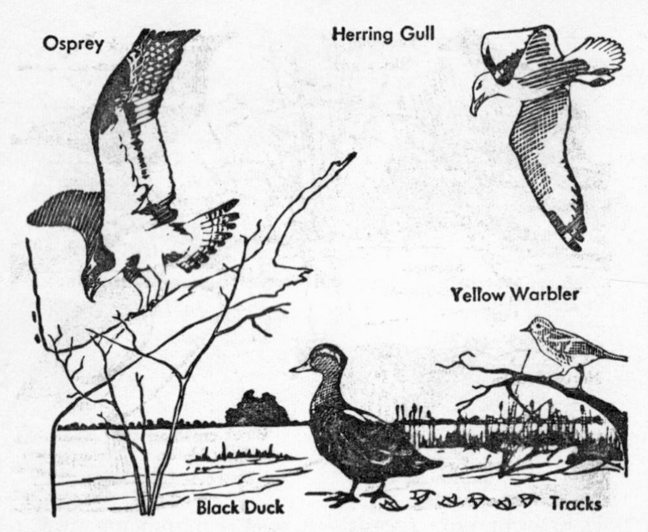

In the same way that we associate pumpkins with corn, there are certain plants that we associate with sphagnum moss. Two of the most famous are the insect catching plants, the pitcher plants and the sundews. The pitcher-shaped leaves hold water in which the insects drown. The sundews have sticky leaves which fold on the insect.

Associated with these may be a scattering of cotton grass, and cranberry. In June you look for arethusa, in July for calopogon, and in August for the fringed orchid. The group of plants that grow in the sphagnum is known as a **sphagnum association.**

The next plant group is the marsh-shrub association. Sweet gale, red osier dogwood, mountain holly, wild raisin, black chokeberry, and high bush blueberry are typical shrubs in this group. Alder thickets, willow flats, and mangrove swamps belong to this group. At a bog the sheep laurel, New Jersey tea,

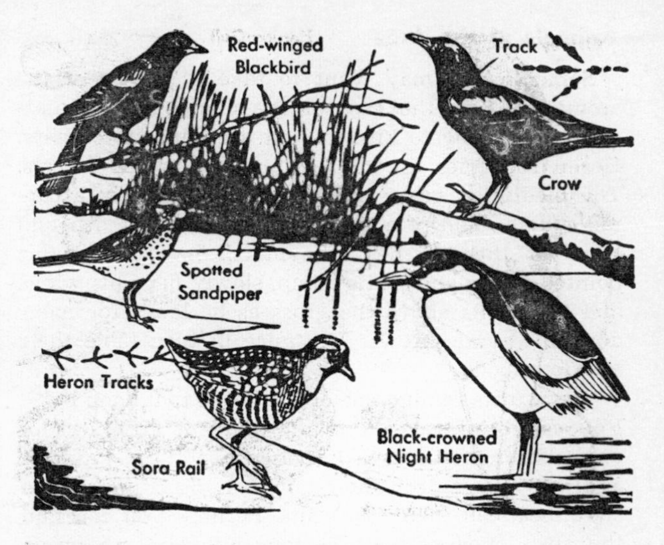

and leather leaf are usually in the front ranks marching onto the sphagnum. Sample sprays of shrubs can be neatly cut, labeled and stood in bottles of water at the Troop room.

The shrub zone is the place for the "Bog Jounce." Select a spot about 50-100 feet from a lone, large pine or red maple that has ventured amongst the shrubs. Have the Scouts gather in a group. They say"Oompah, oompah," bending their knees on the "oomp" and straightening them on the "pah." By united effort they try to jounce the pine. Since they are standing on a mat that has been woven over an ancient lake the chances of jouncing the tree are excellent.

The swamp-forest association may be the red maple, elm, and black ash. In New Jersey the forest may shelter a rhododendron thicket. Northern trees give way to the cypress in the coastal plain swamps.

Animals of the Area

Some Scouts may want to take a survey of the animals. As in the case of the plants, the animals differ according to kind of wet area and its climate. Heron rookeries are to be found in swamp-forests. The piedbilled grebe builds a floating nest in a cattail marsh. The sora rail eats insects, shell fish and seeds of the marshes. The marsh hawk, with his pointed wings and white rump, slowly flaps his wings and then sails above the grass as he looks for meadow mice and shrews. The mice in turn have their meadow foods.

These facts remind one of the house that Jack built. You can best travel a marsh and get evidences of animals when the area is frozen over. The muskrat and deermouse drop their tails leaving a line in the snow between their footprints. Perhaps you can find the abandoned nest of the long-billed marsh wren. It is five to six inches in diameter and globular in shape. You should look for it two or three feet from the ground in the cattails or reed grass. The doorway is on the side. The white-footed mouse may have lined the nest with cattail floss. The story then might run like this. This is the house that Jennie built. This is the cattail that grew the floss, that the deerfoot used to make snug and warm, the globular house that Jennie built. This is the marsh hawk—well, you can finish it as a surprise for the Troop meeting.

If you choose to visit the marsh or meadow at nesting time, you might enjoy using a flushing pole. It is a long light pole held by a rope, tied at each of the ends. Two Scouts march slowly along swishing the top of the vegetation. The other members of the Patrol act as "spotters." The pole may flush a bittern, a marsh hawk, or a marsh wren. The flushers then

Beaver and Tracks

Muskrat and Tracks

stand stock still and the spotters try to find the nest. Of course they do not disturb the nest or its contents, and linger only long enough to get a description.

The most important marsh mammal is the muskrat. He prefers the lakeside of the marsh where he can go fishing for mollusca and crayfish. He is not a rat and neither is he a rabbit, although he is sometimes called a "marsh rabbit." The muskrat is edible. His house is built in late summer. It is made of sod, roots, and stems cemented with mud. The wall is about six inches thick. The bedroom is in the upper chamber. The lower chamber consists of runways which lead into deep water. On cold days muskrats sleep. Sometimes one can see them swimming under the ice. Scouts prefer to protect wild animals and will see that the muskrat's house is not disturbed. Comstock's *Handbook of Nature Study* has a diagram of a muskrat house which might be copied on a large piece of brown paper, so that a member of the Patrol can tell the Troop about the muskrat home.

No two marsh areas present the same animals. We must not forget that mosquitoes, crane flies, and midges are animals as are beautiful butterflies, mussels, and crayfish. It would be a "dead patrol" that could not find enough animals or traces of enough animals; so that every Scout could make a complete report about one.

Marsh Management

About 1931 the duck population of North America reached its lowest point. Investigation showed that wholesale drainage of swamps for proposed agricultural use, had deprived innumerable waterfowl of effective and necessary breeding grounds. Originally many of these marshes had been created by the damming of small streams by beavers. But the beavers had been trapped out and their dams rotted with time. The result was that the water level was lowered and the marshlands decreased.

Steps were taken to restore many of the marsh areas. Lands were bought by the government. Semi permanent dams were built; the marshes reappeared, and the ducks multiplied. Muskrats found food and shelter where there had been none. The whole economics of the marsh had again been converted into a productive unit.

Since marshes can be managed, it is best to know what products are desired. Under suitable management, it is possible to get the desired results—food and shelter for birds and mammals useful to man.

GRASSLAND SCOUTING

It is fun to read about the great grass-covered prairies in Central North America that once supported enormous herds of bison; about the great fires that swept over them seasonally; the sudden blizzards of winter. Some Scouts may even wish that they might have lived in those days. But those who know grasslands of the present, would not wish to turn the calendar back. There is reason to believe that better future civilization depends on the ability of mankind to understand these important parts of the land in which we live.

The grassland probably most familiar to the average Scout is the front lawn over which he regularly pushes a lawn mower. He may also have seen grassy weed patches in vacant lots and pastures, meadows or great open prairie lands. There is not, probably, a foot of such land anywhere that does not contain something really worth looking at.

Grasslands are usually open stretches, free from

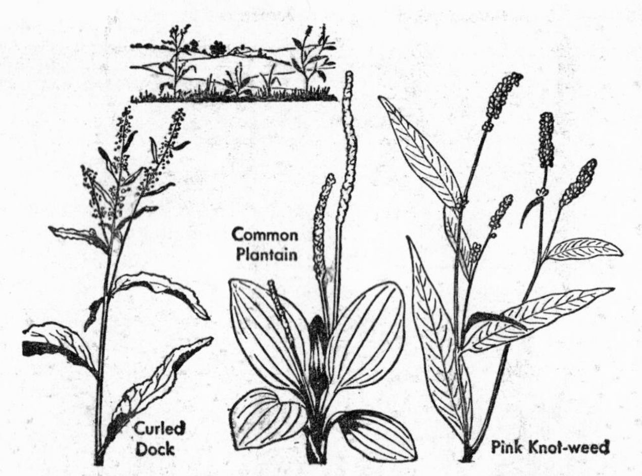

large trees or shrubs, exposed to wind, rain and sun, and yet covered by mats of plants that hug the ground closely. Except in dry weather, they are almost wholly green. The plants and the relatively hard ground beneath, give a firm footing. Over such areas run animals that can beat all others. On such grounds Scouts play baseball and football. It is the sort of ground that produced our Wild West with its cow-punchers and its feather-decked horse-back-riding Plains Indians. In other words, it long has been and always will be a fine kind of country.

Shelter in Grasslands

Open stretches of grasslands bordered by areas of taller plants offer ideal conditions for many kinds of wildlife. People who want to conserve wildlife, plant shrubby fence rows and field borders where quail, pheasants and rabbits can find shelter. These shrubby borders serve also as nesting areas for bumblebees and other insects that are necessary for the produc-

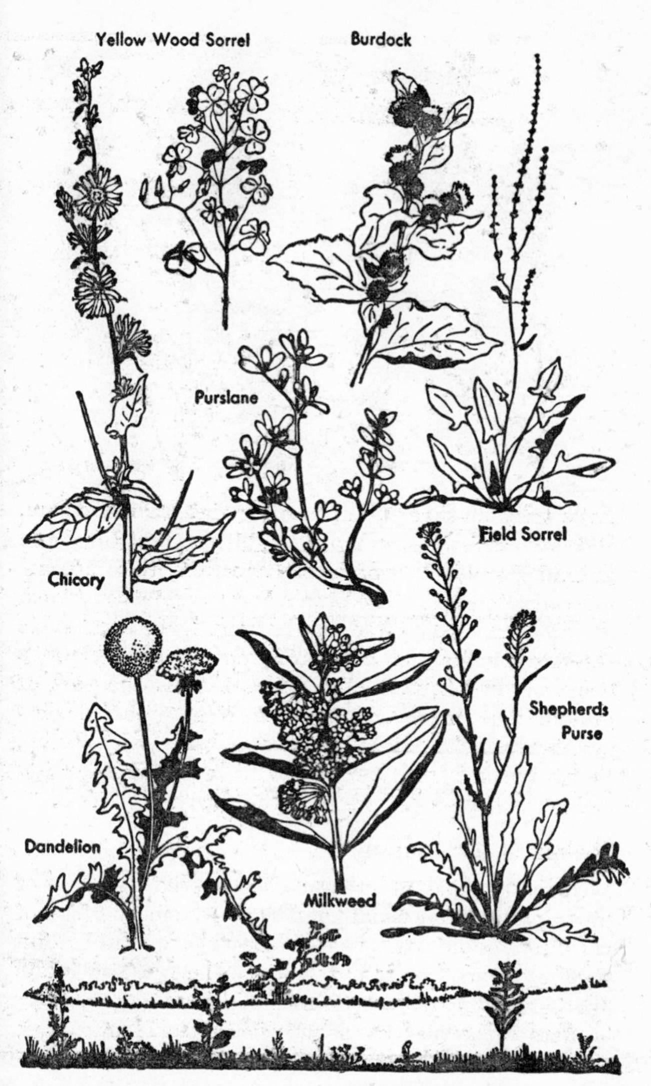
Yellow Wood Sorrel
Burdock
Purslane
Field Sorrel
Chicory
Shepherds
Purse
Dandelion
Milkweed

Garter Snake

Common Milk Snake

Fowler's Toad

Red-bellied Snake

tion of seeds, in such plants as the clovers and alfalfa.

Some animals of grasslands do not need tall plants for shelter. Animals such as the ground squirrels, gophers, badgers, marmots and woodchucks get perfect shelter by digging holes under the grasses. When danger approaches, all they have to do is to dive into these "fox-holes" of their own. Even in your front lawn animals escape into holes. Take a flashlight some warm, wet summer night and walk slowly across your yard. If you are careful, you may see earthworms or "night-crawlers" stretched out feeding, or calling on other earthworms.

If you look carefully through most grasslands, you will find that the earth is peppered with small holes. Those made by earthworms are usually marked by earth pellets that passed through the bodies of the worms. Other holes may be marked by little mounds of fine earth piled into hills with a hole at the top. Some of these may have been made by ants. Other holes made by the immature ant-lion

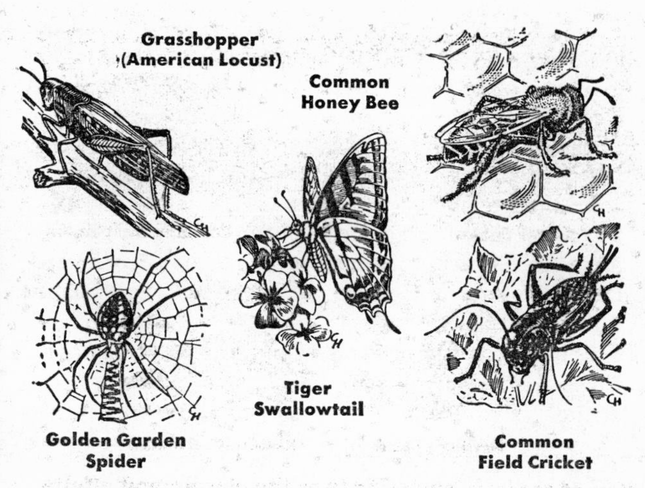

or "doodle-bug," are pits shaped like cones with their points turned down. The holes serve as traps for ants which slide down to the ant-lion, waiting at the bottom of the pit for a meal. If you lie for a quarter of an hour on a dry lawn with your face to the ground, you will be surprised at the large numbers of little animals that have found shelter in these "grassroot jungles." Spiders string their webs among the grasstops. Grasshoppers hide on the sides of grass blades opposite him and down among the grassroots all sorts of creatures crawl, burrow and squirm.

Scouts likely to stalk animals or birds on grasslands learn to crawl on their elbows keeping their bodies close to the ground. They learn to camouflage their heads and backs with grassy materials, and move only when the wind is disturbing the grass so that their own movements are less conspicuous.

The amount of available shelter in grasslands varies considerably through the year. In the summer when the grass is high, many animals can find all the shelter they need. In the winter, snow may provide ample shelter for mice that can feed on the grass close to the ground. In the spring, however, there may be relatively little shelter and mice, the worst animal pests of grasslands, are relatively unprotected from their enemies, the foxes, weasels and hawks. At this very time hawks are likely to appear in greatest abundance, during their spring migration northward. Campaigns to hunt these useful animals are wholly unwise.

Shelter for humans on open grasslands is sometimes a serious problem. In summer, there is little shelter from the sun and rain, and in winter less from the driving snow and wind. During dry seasons, grass fires may prove a serious hazard.

Good, as well as relatively permanent shelters for man and domestic animals, are made by using "building blocks" cut from sod. These sod shelters may be warmer in winter than log cabins, since they are likely to be more wind proof. Given suitable snow, men may make winter shelters of snow blocks, and thatches may be made from bundles of grass.

The important food to be found in grasslands is the grass itself. If ranchers wish to raise sheep for wool or mutton; cows, for milk or butter or beef; or horses, for labor, then grass must grow in the greatest possible abundance. So far as man's interests are concerned, anything that destroys grass without itself being useful, is unwelcome. Grasshoppers, crickets, mice, gophers, woodchucks and rabbits that live largely on grassland plants are, for the most part, man's enemies, though the rabbits may supply some food and sport in return for the plants they eat. Hawks that soar over the fields; coyotes, foxes and weasels that catch small grass eaters by running them down or pouncing on them; such snakes as the bull snake, and milk snake that eats gophers and mice; the green snake that eats insects; the red-bellied snake that eats slugs; and the meadow frogs and toads that feed on all sorts of grass-eating insects; all these are distinctly useful to man. Even skunks must be considered worthy of protection, since they not only catch mice and grasshoppers but dig under the surface of the ground to catch white grubs and other enemies of plants.

The animals of the open grasslands are past masters at concealing themselves by remaining motionless when danger threatens. Most of them have excellent eyesight and can detect danger by sight farther than can man. Most of the larger grass-eaters like the antelope, jack-rabbits, horses and cattle have relatively large ears that can be directed towards suspected sound more readily than with the animal eaters.

Emergency Food

Most animals of grasslands are of value as food to man. In an emergency, woodchucks and gophers may be captured by laying nooses at the entrances of their burrows. (In some states, woodchucks are protected by law.) These nooses may be drawn shut by the animals as they enter or leave the burrow or by means of a long string held by a distant watcher. There is no reason why a Scout should try to catch these animals unless he is lost and desperately in need of food. Campaigns to control woodchucks and gophers by the use of poison foods or gases are usually unwise because the poison may destroy valuable fur-bearers.

Many of the plants of grasslands are of direct value as food to man, but the kinds found in different parts of the country vary so greatly that it is difficult to draw up a satisfactory list. Dandelions, abundant in most lawns make excellent greens. Both the flowers and the young shoots of milkweed are edible, the flowers eaten raw and the shoots cooked like asparagus. Jerusalem artichokes, a kind of wild sunflower, produce delicious underground parts that may be eaten raw or cooked. Many other field plants have large underground parts that are useful to man as food. Most species of grass yield edible parts at the base of each joint.

Grasslands Hold Water

In the ideal grasslands, there is less likelihood of flood than in most cultivated lands. Streams arising from lands in which the sod has long been established are usually clear and relatively cool, and maintain a relatively uniform flow. This means that the nearby lands are not being robbed of valuable topsoil, that the lower stretches of the streams may be used for a longer period for power, drinking, or navigation.

How grasslands help hold water, may be seen on almost any lawn. If you dig into the lawn, you will find that some of the plants, like dandelions and clover have long, deep root systems, while many of the grasses have densely matted relatively shallow roots. In the dry season, the deep rooted plants remain green, in part because they can get water no longer available to the shallow-rooted plants.

In the Southwest, the Indians have been known to catch, dry and roast such insects as the locust and use them either directly or in a ground form as food.

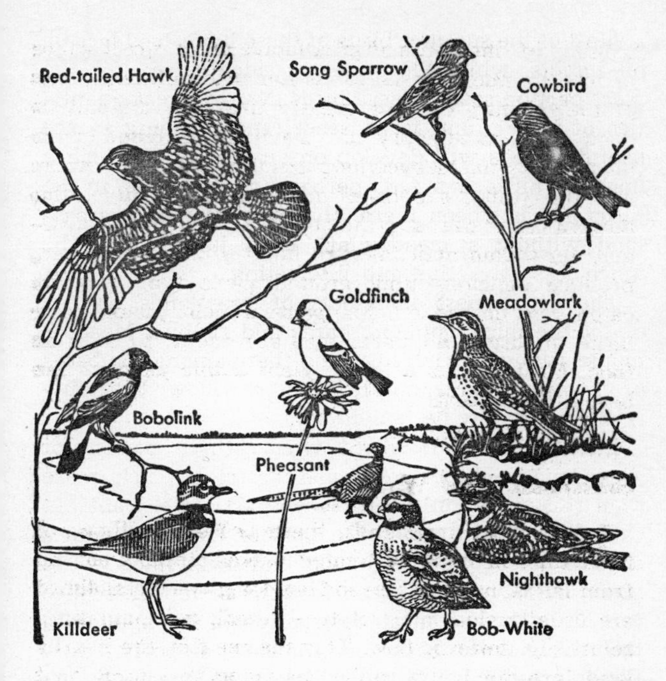

Army men trained to survive under severe conditions, are taught to use as food the grubs of some beetles that feed on the roots of grasses. They also are shown how to roast grasshoppers and cicadas.

Grasslands at Their Best

To many persons no type of country is more attractive than a good grass country. It is the place where some of our finest song birds are found. Meadowlarks, dickcissels, quail and song sparrows are found almost everywhere in good grass country. In the winter the places of some of them are taken by juncos, tree sparrows, snow buntings and redpolls.

Most of the summer birds of these lands feed largely on insects, while the winter residents feed for the most part on seeds. These birds destroy great quantities of insects and weed seeds, and in doing so are useful. Weeds will develop on an area over which a flock of birds has fed, perhaps as much as if the birds had not been there. However, to man a grassland without a meadowlark or a junco would be much less attractive and interesting.

The commonest mammals of grasslands are no doubt the mice, gophers, hares and rabbits. Meadow mouse runways wind here and there among the bases of grassland plants, and if these are followed carefully the nests may be found.

Each mouse eats about twenty-three pounds of green material per year and destroys much more than this, since only the choice parts of a plant are eaten. If it were not for a host of natural enemies such as weasels, foxes, hawks and owls, mice would probably leave little green food for man. While mice are probably the most destructive of all mammals, they serve as the basic food for many important furbearing animals. Coyotes, foxes and weasels are tremendously valuable in keeping these vermin in check and thereby saving plants that may provide food for cattle, sheep and horses that give us food, clothing and work. One of the biggest problems that will face America for many years to come, will be the production of food. This food—grains and meat-producing animals—must come from the grasslands. These grasslands will produce all the necessary food only if more people know how to manage them. Nature adventuring in grassland areas is a fine start in this direction. You will have fun—and you may make discoveries that will contribute to a better civilization.

Mountain Lion
Bobcat
Mule Deer
Antelope
Bison

FORESTS - TREES AND ANIMALS

Eons and eons ago, when the earth was young, all life, both animal and plant lived in the water. Just rock and water, that is all there was; there were no soil, no grass, no trees; no animals as we know them today. What brought about the changes? And how do we know what happened so many, many years ago?

Certainly no one living now can say he saw what happened. That is impossible. The things that happened then are still happening now, and if we look in the right place, we can see the drama unfolding before our astonished eyes. Here is one way a forest may be born.

The Beginning of a Hardwood Forest

A sandbar is built up in the river by high water, till it protrudes above the surface at low water, and appears as dry land for a large part of the year.

Only during the spring rise is it completely submerged. The stream has also brought down silt eroded from the highlands, to add fertility to the sandbar. It also has brought down the light seed of the cottonwood and the willow. They lodged on the sandbar. They found the seedbed good, and in two or three days they have covered the sandbar with fast growing seedlings.

Along with the willow and cottonwood, have come other seeds, but they are slower to germinate. And they are not able to endure flooding for long periods.

The next spring the river rises as usual and floods the sandbar and all the river bottom for several weeks. When the floods go down, only the willow and the cottonwoods remain alive. The others have all been killed, smothered by the water. The willow and cottonwood grow with great speed. Year after year their leaves fall down to mingle with the new sand and silt added by the last spring's flood. Year after year the leaves and the silt help to build the sandbar higher.

At last the sandbar is built so high that it is flooded only by exceptionally high water, and only for shorter periods, at longer and longer intervals. The cottonwoods and willows are no longer the only trees that can grow there, but they do not prevent other species from coming in under them. These new trees need plenty of light and are unable to grow in very dense stands. Other trees, such as box elder, soft maple, ash and elm, which can stand more shade grow under the cottonwoods and willows.

This new type continues to build up the soil with its leaves even faster than its predecessors. Earth worms help the fungi and bacteria to decompose the leaves and wood, and mix them with the soil.

But the succession is not yet complete. The still more tolerant oaks, basswood, hickories, and beech gradually invade and supersede the others. They come slowly, because their seeds are heavy and cannot be blown by the wind. They can only roll for short distances, or be carried in by undependable and absent-minded squirrels and chipmunks. who bury them and forget where. But once established, they grow under the others and replace them, to complete another stage in the succession.

Even that is not the end. This type is gradually invaded by maples, beech, basswood and yellow birch which are known as the "climax type," because they are the last to come in.

These are the changes that may take place when nothing interferes with the succession. The forest requires many years for completion. Often it is delayed and set back by fire, windstorm, insect and fungi epidemics, and may be many centuries in reaching the climax.

In a somewhat similar way and in other ways, too, forest types were developed in the different regions, according to the species that were hardy in each region.

For convenience we are going to divide the whole United States into forest regions based on the species that dominate each one.

White Pine Forests

The region of the white pine comes first historically. It extended from Maine to Minnesota, occupied most of New England and the Appalachian Mountains to Georgia.

Usually the forests differ in different parts of the same "region." This is caused by difference in

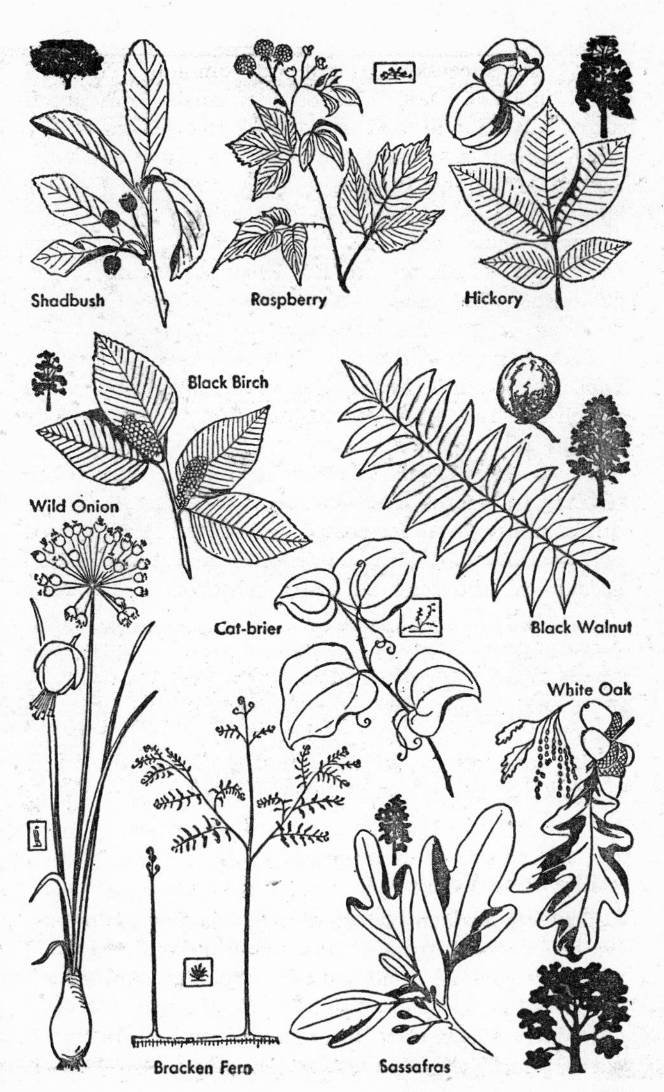
Shadbush
Raspberry
Hickory
Black Birch
Wild Onion
Black Walnut
Cat-brier
White Oak
Bracken Fern
Sassafras

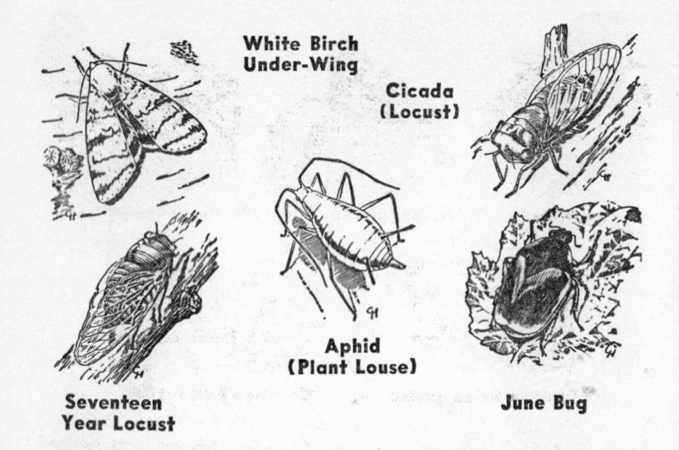

topography, in altitude, in soil and water content or in temperature. Thus in the white pine region there are at least four distinctive types: the **northern hardwoods,** made up of beech, birch and maple; the **central hardwoods,** largely oaks and hickories with many elms, ashes, basswood, maples, walnuts and other species scattered through them; the **spruce-balsam forests** of the higher and northern country; the **swamps.** (In this description the term "hardwood" refers to all the broadleafed species; and "softwood" to all cone-bearing trees, regardless of the structure or hardness of the wood.) In the original forest, white pine was mixed all through the central hardwood forest, and with the northern hardwoods along the lower edge of that type. In addition there were spruce and cedar swamps.

The northern hardwood type is found to the northward and on the mountain slopes above 1,000 feet. This is the hardwood-climax forest of the region, and it gradually gives way in the north and up the slopes,

Coral Snake

Timber Rattlesnake

Northern Copperhead

Spotted Salamander

Common Box Turtle

to a greater and greater mixture of spruce, till the pure spruce-balsam-birch forest is reached.

It may be said that roughly the southern hardwood forest is the home of the deer, and the northern hardwood-spruce-balsam forest is the home of the moose.

These same types of forests, with certain local changes, extend all the way across the northern tier of states to Minnesota, and down the Appalachian Mountains to Georgia. The white pine gradually gives way to a mixture of white pine and Norway pine to the westward, and the swamps increase in area.

As the climate grows more severe toward the interior of the continent, many of the more tender species drop out. Thus such common species of the eastern forest as beech and tulip tree, with many others, are entirely lacking in the Minnesota forest.

The whole southeastern quarter of the country is divided into three great divisions: The Appalachian Mountains, the Piedmont Plateau, and the Coastal Plain.

The mountains are covered with much the same

types of forest as are found in the Northeast. They are considerably enriched by the addition of many southern species but the framework of the types is much the same.

Oak and Hickory Forests

Forests of the Piedmont Plateau are for the most part oak and hickory, with varying mixtures of red gum, tulip poplar and shortleaf pine. The forest itself has been largely cleared away, with the exception of the farm woodlots. There are few areas of unbroken forest.

For centuries the Coastal Plain rose slowly from the sea and vast sections of the ocean bottom became dry land, great flat, sandy plains. It follows the coast beginning with a strip a few miles wide in New Jersey, widening to 150 miles in North Carolina, and all the way across the Gulf Coast in varying widths to Mexico.

It is known as the "southern pine belt," and four species of pines with such strange names as: longleaf, shortleaf, loblolly and slash, make up the great bulk of the stand throughout the type.

There are still wild turkeys, deer and many wild razorback hogs hanging around in the hardwood bottom lands that are scattered through the Plains. The deer are the same species found in the North, but they are much smaller. The bob-white quail is an important game bird.

Still another type of forest is found in the swamps. These southern swamps differ greatly from the swamps of the North, which are nearly always peat formations.

There is seldom any peat in the southern swamp; it is simply overflow land on which the water stands,

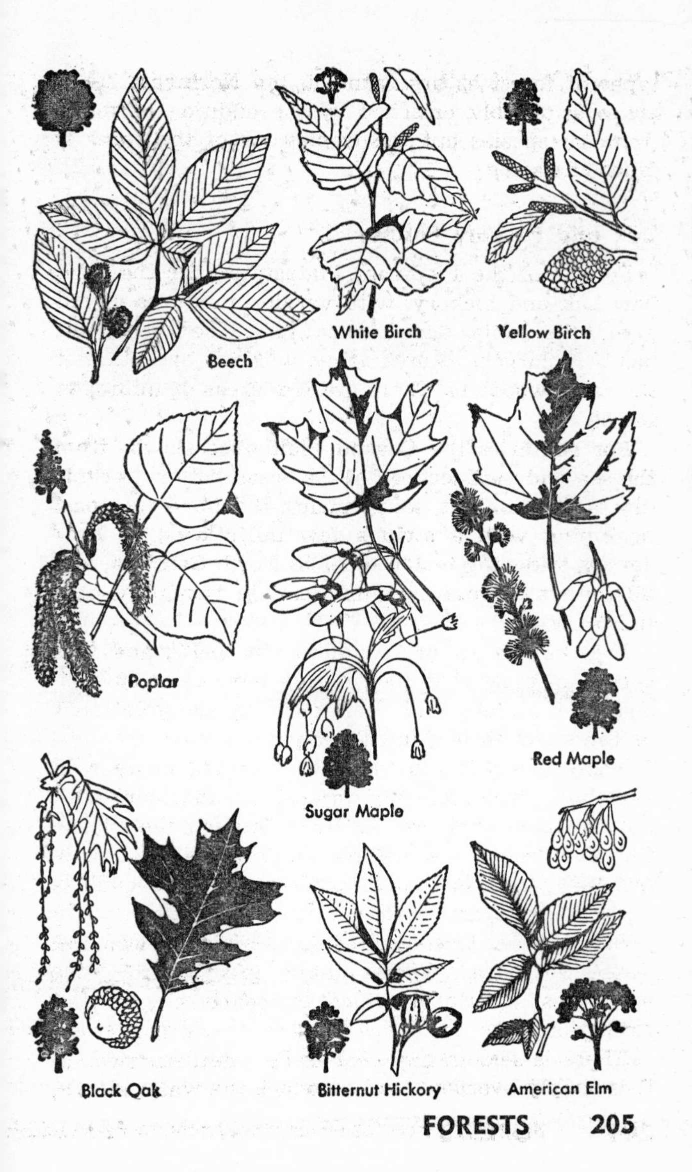
Beech
White Birch
Yellow Birch
Poplar
Sugar Maple
Red Maple
Black Oak
Bitternut Hickory
American Elm

six inches, two feet, ten feet deep, for all or a large part of the year. The depth of the water in the swamps depends entirely upon the height of the water in the river. The bottom of these so-called swamps is usually sand and nearly always solid.

There are only two species of trees that grow commonly in swamps that are flooded the year round, the bald cypress and the tupelo gum.

Animals of the Forests

Probably the easiest way to get to know animals is to know the types of forests in which they make their homes. The Scout who knows the plant and animal associations is the one who will have the most interesting experiences in the woods.

The largest mammals of the forest are deer, elk, moose and bear. Deer are found in most of the forests of North America.

But the largest are not necessarily the most interesting animals. Many of the smaller ones occur more abundantly, and probably are more easily seen and observed. Every Scout has seen squirrels and rabbits, and knows something about them. But raccoons also range throughout the forests of every eastern state. Opossums too, live over a wide range, as do beavers, which are found near waterways where they make their homes. Bobcats and foxes are animals of the forests. although they are rather difficult to find.

Outnumbering all other mammals are the rats, mice, shrews and bats found in wooded areas.

These small mammals are often overlooked, in the search for the larger ones, but they are still a part of the forest habitat, and play an important part in it. For bats eat the insects that fly over forests, while shrews and moles feed on the insects that live in the

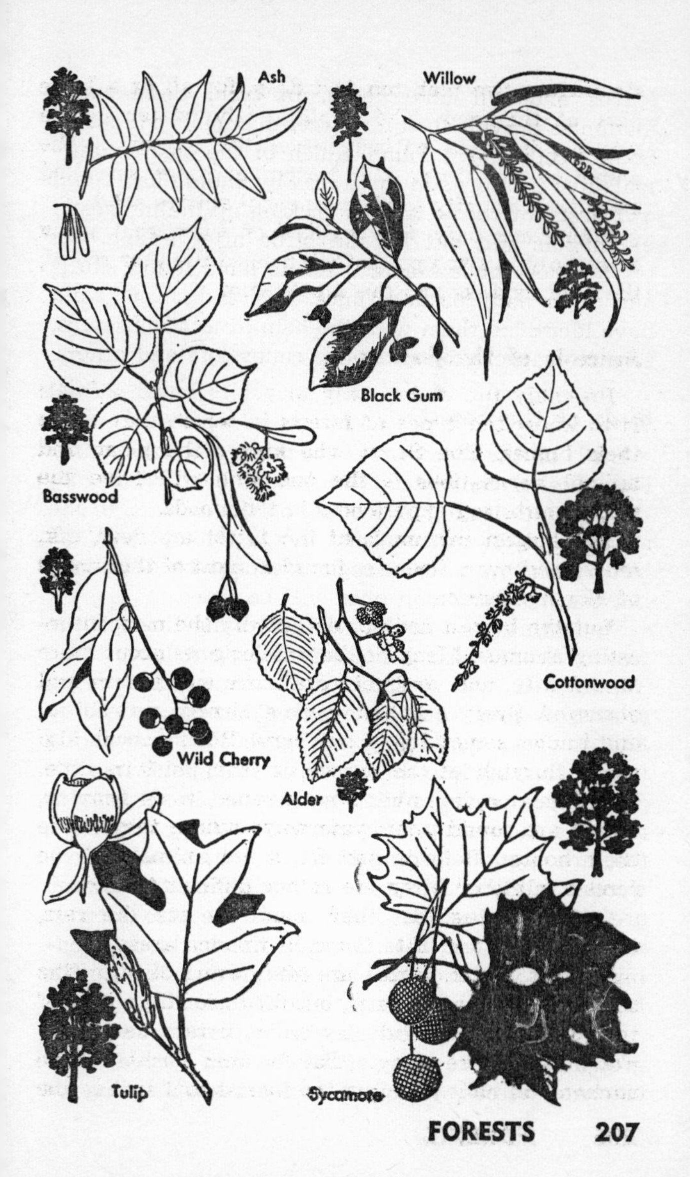
Ash
Willow
Black Gum
Basswood
Cottonwood
Wild Cherry
Alder
Tulip
Sycamore

leaves and soil underneath. In turn, these small mammals provide food for larger mammals and birds. Some Scouts have found which of the smaller animals live in forests in their area by finding hawk and owl nests, or roosts, and by picking up the indigestible pellets spit out by the birds after eating. On taking these pellets apart, Scouts have found skulls and other bony parts of mice, rats, and shrews, and have identified them with the help of local museums, science teachers, Merit Badge counselors and others.

Birds of the Forest

Birds on the forest areas are many and interesting. For sake of convenience they will be divided into those found nesting or feeding on the ground, in the shrubs and lower trees, and in the treetops. All the birds found in wooded regions cannot be described, but the most common ones will be listed.

Many times, no doubt, while walking through the woods, Scouts hear a noise in the dead leaves . . . Thinking it was a squirrel or chipmunk burying acorns, or pine cones, they have been surprised to find towhees scratching for grub. When walking from a clearing into the woods, or from fields into the denser trees, many a hiker has jumped in surprise, as a grouse flushed up and noisily flew away. Towhees, too, are ground-feeding birds, and in some regions woodcock. Other birds found feeding on the ground are the thrushes, but these birds are also seen in shrubs and lower trees. Some of the warblers, ovenbirds and water thrushes, are ground birds. The latter are always near streams or brooks.

Birds commonly seen in shrubs, bushes and low-growing trees are many of the common warblers, flycatchers, vireos, tanagers, and orioles. Feeding on

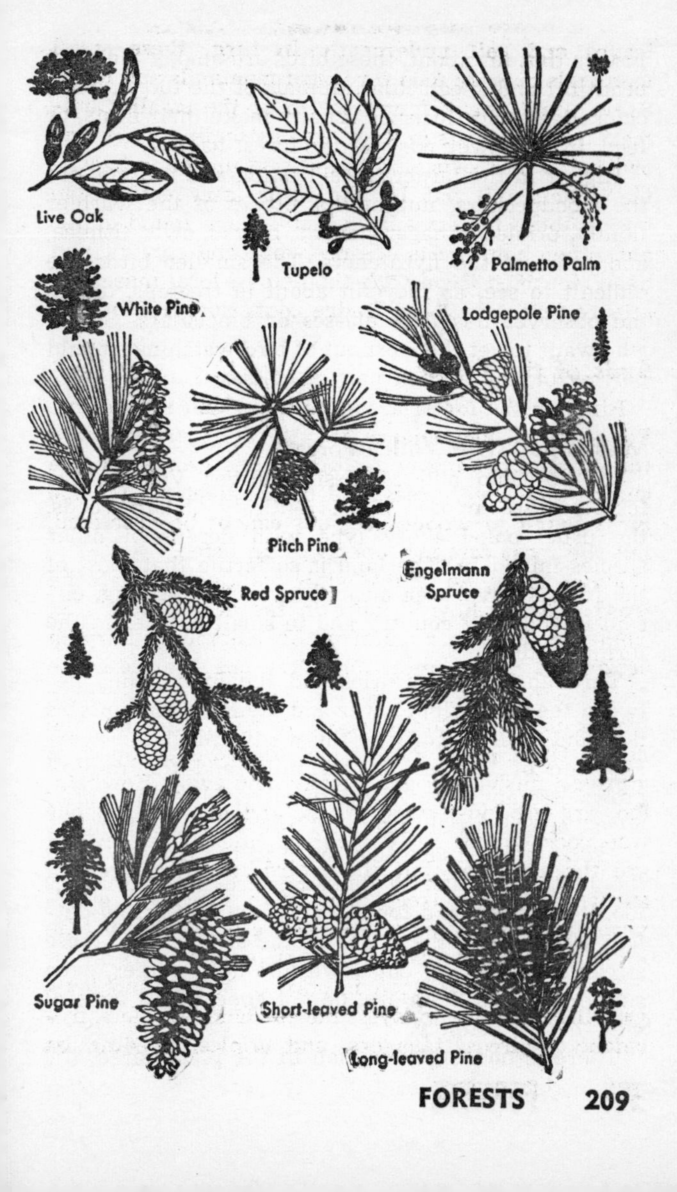
Live Oak
Tupelo
Palmetto Palm
White Pine
Lodgepole Pine
Pitch Pine
Red Spruce
Engelmann
Spruce
Sugar Pine
Short-leaved Pine
Long-leaved Pine

insects that flit about, these birds are among the most beautiful and spectacular animals of the forest. Jays, chickadees, and thrushes usually make their nests, or feed, in the lower parts of the forest habitat.

Higher in the larger trees, nesting and feeding, are the woodpeckers, nuthatches, others of the warbler family, orioles, tanagers, crows, hawks, owls, titmice, and some of the flycatchers. The smaller birds are difficult to see, as they flit about in treetops, unless the observer has field glasses or binoculars. Scouts who want to get the most out of bird watching, should borrow or buy a good pair of glasses.

Mississippi River Valley Forests

In the Ohio and Mississippi River Valleys, the forests are composed almost entirely of hardwoods, the usual oak-hickory type with dozens of other species mixed in. The land is so fertile that most of the forests have been cleared away for farming, except in the hilly country and in small patches in the farm woodlots.

Throughout the prairies and the high plains between the Mississippi River and the Rocky Mountains the land rises steadily to the westward at the average rate of ten feet to the mile, and the rainfall grows less and less. About twenty inches of rainfall a year are required to support a forest in the temperate zone, about twice that much in the tropics. From the 100th meridian to the westward, the climate is too dry to support a forest, except in the narrow bottom lands along the edges of the streams. As these streams are usually cut down into deep gorges, even such forests as there are, do not appear in a general view of the country.

There is one big exception in the plains area, the

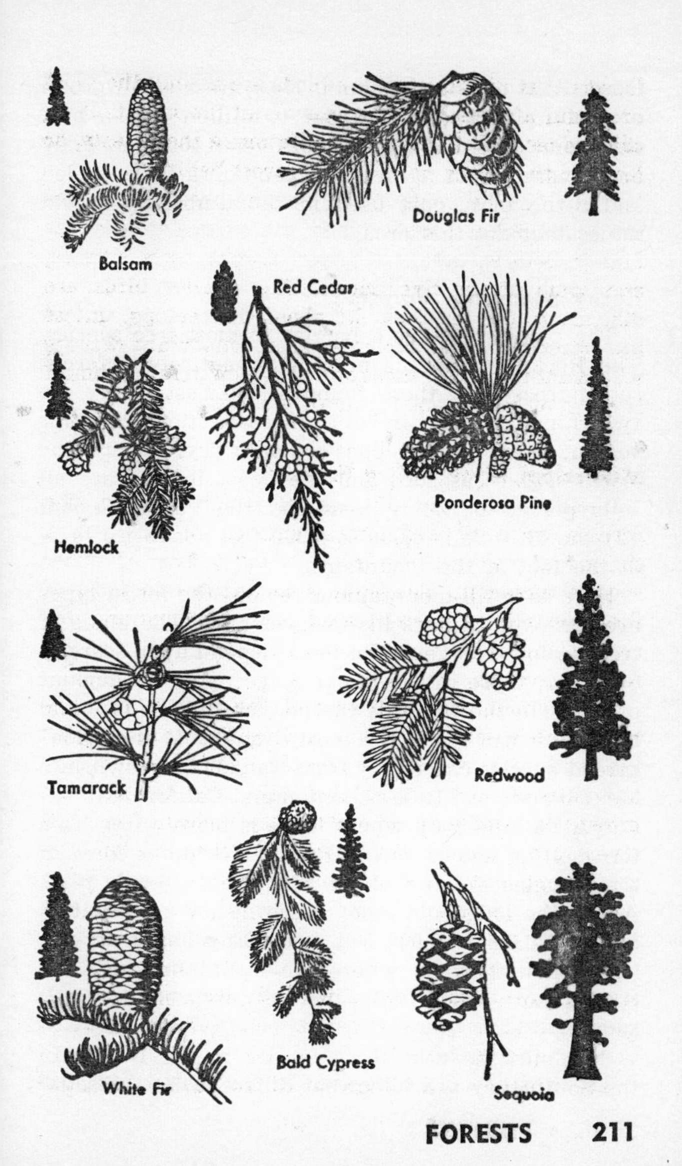
Balsam
Douglas Fir
Red Cedar
Ponderosa Pine
Hemlock
Tamarack
Redwood
Bald Cypress
White Fir
Sequoia

Black Hills of South Dakota. They are a small group of mountains covering about a million and a half acres and reaching a height of over 8,000 feet. They are covered with a forest of ponderosa pine, which is for the most part used in the timbering of old mines that dot this area.

Rocky Mountain Forests

The plains serve as a barrier to most tree species. The Rocky Mountains present an entirely different set of trees from those found in the East. There are two things to keep in mind in connection with this region: (1) the East slopes are very dry, because the Rockies, the Cascades and the Coast Ranges are all interspersed between them and the Pacific Ocean; (2) the altitude is 4,000 to 5,000 feet above sea level at the foot of the mountains.

Here as in all mountainous regions the forest types are arranged in tiers like a layer cake. The kinds of trees in lower edge of the layer depend upon scarcity of water, those in the upper ledge upon the amount of frost. In the foothills the ponderosa pine is found because it can stand the most drought. It is a widespread species extending from Canada far down into Mexico and west to Washington and California.

A little higher up where there is more water from the melting snows, is the Rocky Mountains form of the Douglas fir, and above that the lodgepole pine. Above the lodgepole pine, which means an elevation of about 8,000 to 9,000 feet, is the Engelmann spruce, and above that, up where the mountain goats and the big-horn sheep begin, there is only a scrub alpine growth.

Such are the east slope forests in the North. In the South they are somewhat different. To the south

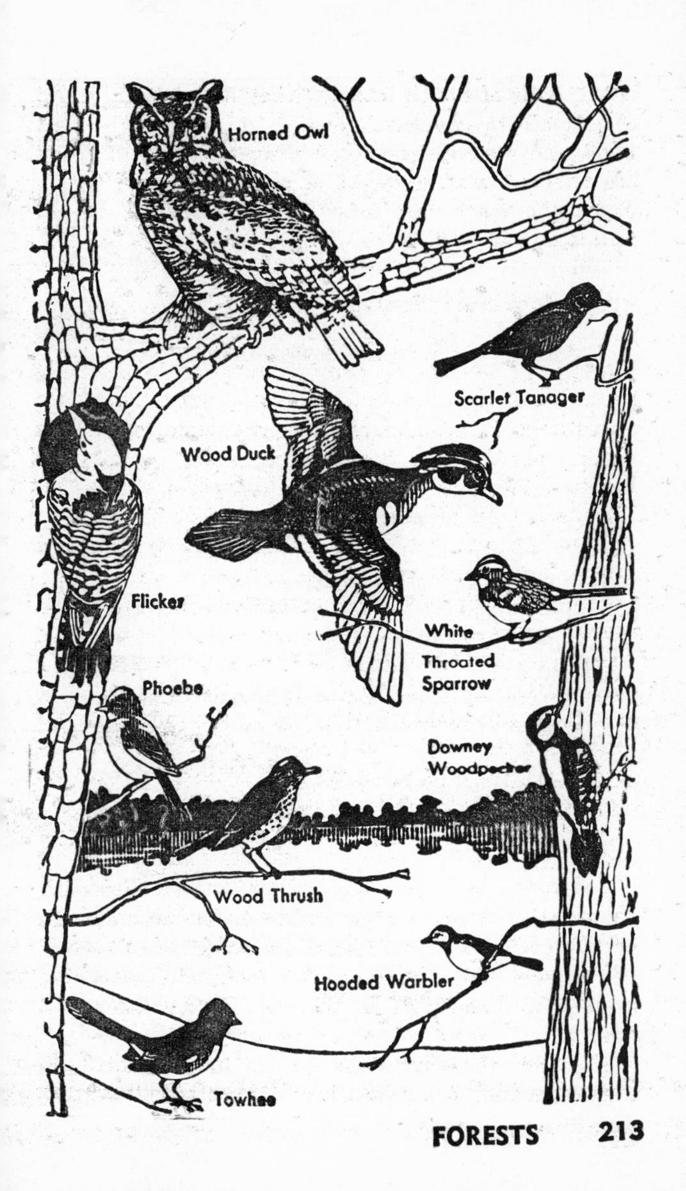
Horned Owl
Scarlet Tanager
Wood Duck
Flicker
White
Throated
Sparrow
Phoebe
Downey
Woodpecker
Wood Thrush
Hooded Warbler
Towhee

the species climb higher up the slopes to try to maintain the same climatic conditions, because in the matter of temperature, about 300 to 500 feet in altitude is roughly equivalent to one degree of latitude. One can start at the equator and travel to Arctic climate just as surely and far more quickly by climbing the mountains, as one can by traveling north to the Arctic circle. For this reason some of the species are pushed off the top of the mountains in Colorado, and the ponderosa pine, which grows only in the foothills in the north, extends clear to the top of the mountains in New Mexico.

On the west slope of the Rockies the types are more varied. There is a little more moisture and consequently a greater variety of tree species.

In the more moist areas at low altitudes, the ponderosa pine mixes with the Douglas fir, and mixtures of Douglas fir and western larch occupy large areas. Western hemlock, western red cedar and the lowland white fir, species seldom seen on the east slope, sneak in under the other species to form the climax type. And in a moist spot in northern Idaho, lapping over a little into western Montana and eastern Washington, the western white pine is found, the most valuable species in the region.

Cascade Forests

The forests on the eastern slopes of the Cascades are very much like those on the eastern slopes of the Rockies. But over the ridges on the western slopes, oh, what a change! Here on these high mountains exposed to the moist winds from the Pacific is the heaviest rainfall in all our nation. Here are the Douglas fir and the western hemlock spread over the whole mountain slopes. They form the heaviest forest

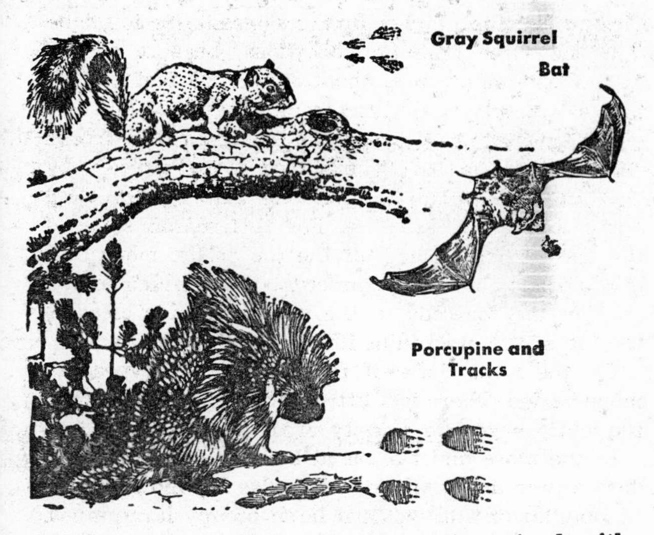

in the world. There are other species mixed with them, such as the western red cedar, western larch, and the true fir; but the great bulk of the forest is Douglas fir. At the present time, there is more Douglas fir than all the other conifers in the whole country put together. This type extends all over the west slopes of the Cascades and Coast Range throughout Washington and Oregon.

Far down on the western slope of the Coast Range, next to the sea in the land of almost perpetual fog, there is a narrow strip of Sitka spruce and western hemlock.

South of the Douglas fir forest, across the line in California, everything changes, because the rainfall is less. Instead of the northern fir-hemlock forest, everything is pine. Both the eastern and western slopes of the Sierras are covered with ponderosa pine, pure on the east slopes; mixed with sugar pine, incense cedar and a sprinkling of other species on the west slopes. This type covers a tremendous area.

Just as the Sitka spruce occupies the fog belt in Washington, so the redwoods occupy the fog belt in California. Strange to say this species refuses to live outside of the fog belt. It is a magnificent forest of great trees growing from twelve to fifteen feet in diameter; some of them hundreds and even thousands of years old. But they must not be confused with the famous "Big Trees" of California. That is another species of the same family occurring farther inland in small groves.

Such are the general characteristics of the different forest regions. Of course there are a great many local variations in that vast area of 700 million acres, and a great many subtypes that cannot be described here.

Wood is undoubtedly important, but the forests do something else for us in addition to supplying us with wood. On steep slopes everywhere they hold the soil in place and prevent the ravages of erosion.

Our forests also offer recreation areas for our overworked people. More and more people seek the restful calm of the forest every year. Records show that over 30 million people visited National Forests alone last year. Other millions visited the forests of the National Parks and picnicked in the local woods.

At one time, in fact for many years, the people of America thought that all the forests in the country would be cleared away someday to make way for farms. Everything was cleared as they came to it, and very little attention was paid to soil. That was a mistaken idea. Much land was cleared that should have been left in forest, for forests will grow well on land so poor that it will not pay in farms.

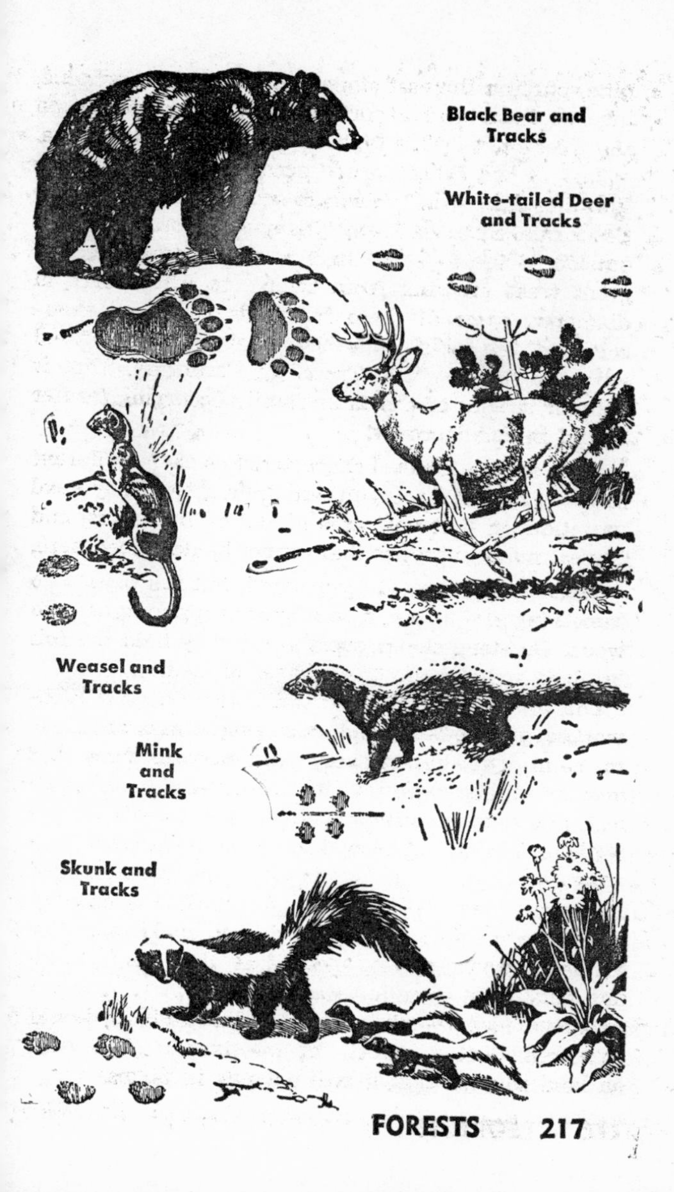
Black Bear and Tracks
White-tailed Deer and Tracks
Weasel and Tracks
Mink and Tracks
Skunk and Tracks

DESERT LIVING

Most Scouts think of deserts as uninhabitable places where plants and animals cannot survive; where men die of thirst under a scorching sun; where the temperature is always in the hundreds. But the Scout who knows something of the secrets of the desert, knows that these are not necessarily so. For the Scout, the desert may provide many nature adventures; and he will know how to survive, should he be lost or marooned.

Generally the term "desert" is applied to those areas where plants do not thrive, either because of cold or dryness. The cold deserts are high mountain ice fields; the drought deserts are sunny, hot and dry. In the United States, there are five types of deserts.

(1) Cold deserts, which occupy a very small area, since they are confined to high mountain tops.

(2) The Northern Desert-Shrub or Sagebrush Desert, which is the desert portion of Washington, Ore-

gon, Northeastern California, Idaho, Montana, Wyoming, Utah and Colorado, and all but the southern part of Nevada and Northern Arizona and New Mexico.

(3) The Southern Desert-Shrub or Creosotebush Desert, which is characterized by the Mojave Desert of Southern California, and occupies regions in Arizona, Texas and southern Nevada.

(4) The Desert Grass Savanna, or Mesquite Grasslands, which occupy parts of southwest Texas, New Mexico, Arizona and nearby areas.

(5) The Salt Desert-Shrub or Greasewood Desert, which is characterized by wet salty soil, where only plants that adapt themselves to this soil, grow.

How Desert Plants and Animals Live

These drought deserts are inhabited by those plants and animals which have developed the greatest adjustment to their environment. No plant or animal can grow without water, for it is only in solution that foods and gases can pass through the cells of the plant or the tissues of animal or man. Therefore, an active plant or animal must be provided with water. In growing plants, a stream of water passes constantly from moist soil into the plant, and over or through its cells into the air.

How then can plants or animals live in a drought desert? Plants succeed in the desert by one or more of the following methods:

(1) Drought escaping. These plants lie in the soil as dried seeds until the rains moisten them. They germinate and grow rapidly, and in as short a time as six weeks have produced a new crop of seeds.

(2) Drought avoiding. Such plants are those that conserve the available water. They accomplish this

by growing during the most favorable season of the year, by remaining small in size and by wide spacing. Much of the plant may grow under ground where it is protected from hot and dry winds.

(3) Drought enduring. These plants generally are drought escaping plants, but since they are perennials they drop their leaves, stop growing and remain in a dormant condition until moisture is again available.

(4) Drought resisting. This term can be applied only to plants such as the succulents, which absorb water rapidly during rains and store it in their fleshy leaves, stems or roots. This stored water can be used by the growing parts of the plant for weeks or months after water has ceased to be available in the soil.

Animals, like plants, must have water if they are to grow. One may separate desert animals into four groups.

(1) Drought escaping animals. These live actively when the summer annuals or winter annuals cover the surface of the southern desert.

(2) Drought avoiding animals, which avoid drought by staying in burrows or in the shade during the day, coming out only at night or when conditions are not extreme. Few animals are seen on the southern desert in midday.

(3) Drought enduring animals. Some animals are able to endure drought by remaining relatively inactive in burrows or buried in the soil during the unfavorable seasons of the year.

(4) Drought resisting animals. Drought resistance is shown by animals which obtain water from the food they eat. Many animals find water in the juices of plants and insects, or other animal food.

Giant Cactus
Joshua
Mesquite
Sotol
Mescal
Creosotebush
Yucca
Sagebrush
Prickly Pear
Hedgehog Cactus

Northern Deserts

The Northern Desert-Shrub or Sagebrush Desert is characterized by a scattered growth of deciduous shrubs, all of which have small leaves, usually of light or silvery color. The plants are woody and sometimes resemble a miniature forest. In the denser areas the plants almost cover the ground, but generally they are widely and rather evenly spaced.

Sagebrush forms by far the most important plant community. The plants are often in a pure stand, vary from 2 to 7 feet in height and resemble a miniature forest in which the crowns do not touch each other.

The chief annuals are the weeds of European origin, Russian thistle, downy brome grass and filaree, all of value as forage plants.

Southern Deserts

The Southern Desert is characterized by the scattered even growth of evergreen shrubs and by many scattered trees and succulent plants.

Creosotebush extends over enormous areas. It is comparable to sagebrush in the Northern Desert. The great expanses of desert plains are occupied by a nearly pure stand. The shrub is widely spaced, with branches from the crown. The leaves are small and lacquered and the plant is a dark greenish brown, changing to yellowish when in flower, and somewhat more ashen when in fruit.

Creosotebush varies from 1 foot to 15 feet in height, depending upon the favorableness of the site.

At higher elevations the Yucca-cactus type is one of the most interesting and varied of all the desert types. Here are many interesting plants such as the

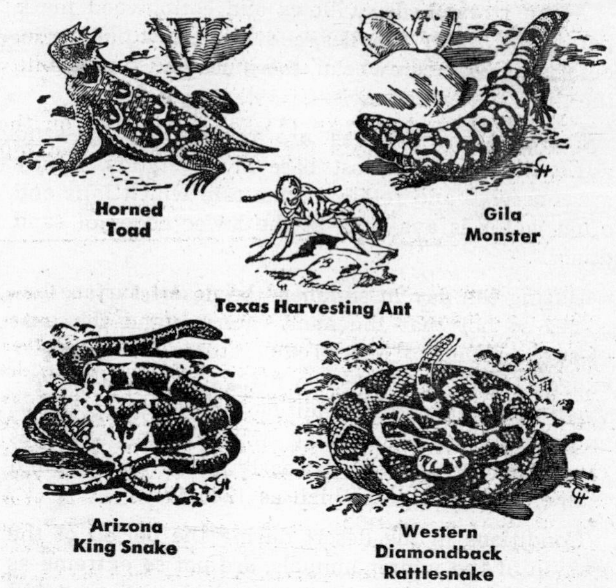
Horned Toad
Gila Monster
Texas Harvesting Ant
Arizona King Snake
Western Diamondback Rattlesnake

blue paloverde, a lemon color when in flower, and ocotillo, whose flower adds a brilliant red to the landscape and bur sage which furnishes a gray tone to the plant cover.

Here also the cacti are often prominent, the cholla forming minature forests. Dense stands of the Saguaro occur in Arizona and a few plants extend into parts of California. It is the largest and most striking cactus in this country, sometimes reaching a height of 35 feet; the single stems fluted like Greek columns, bearing clusters of nearly white flowers on the tips and producing a crop of luscious fruit of scarlet color, which bursts open to expose a pulp which has a taste like that of a watermelon. Many a traveler has found water in the cactus.

Along streambeds, willows and cottonwood mark permanent water supplies, and the yellow paloverde, desert willows, screwbean, mesquite and tesota, line the drier water channels.

Extreme desert areas are represented by sand dunes sometimes almost bare of vegetation. Sandy areas receive and retain all the rain which falls and often water is available at the lower edges of sand dunes.

During the day in summer, the desert surface becomes so hot that the hand cannot stand the heat of surface sand or rock. Temperatures are generally exaggerated, but there are many days in the year when the atmospheric conditions are usually pleasant and the dry air invigorating. Minimum temperatures range from about 0° F. to nearly frost free. The high temperatures range as high as 120°-125°.

Conditions in the desert during the period of the growth of the winter annuals, are not so extreme as they are during the growing season in the great fall and spring wheat sections of the Midwest. If the Scout wishes to study the desert, he should visit it during periods of extreme temperatures as well as during the favorable seasons. At no time is it uninteresting.

Desert Animals

In the Northern Desert, conditions of temperature are not extreme, and the traveler can go longer without water than in the Southern Desert. Animals of this desert include the mule deer, the antelope and the elk.

Smaller animals commonly found are the black-tailed jack rabbit, the cottontail, the badger, the

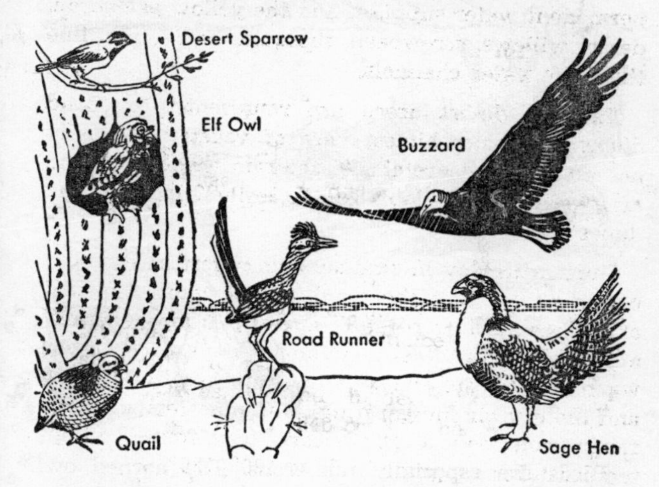

coyote and desert fox, several skunks, the little speckled and grey ground squirrels, the antelope squirrel, desert woodrat and pocket gophers. Here are found also the desert gopher snake, the western striped racer, the rattle snake, the sagebrush swift, the desert whitetailed lizard and the horned toads.

The sage hen, the largest of the grouse family, the desert horned lark, the white rumped shrike, sage thrasher, sage wren, sage and brown sparrow, are a few of the many birds which occupy the area.

The Southern Desert is much more varied and has a greater variety of animals. This desert is the home of the Mexican mule deer in southern Arizona and the burro deer along the Colorado river. The wild pig, peccary or javelina runs in bands; reaches a height of 2 feet; is aggressive and active and ranges across the southern portion of this desert. Here are found the coyote and the west Texas red wolf.

Peccary

Badger

Birds are especially numerous. The horned owl often uses the forks of the Saguaro for its nest, and the tiny elf owl, with a body the size of an English sparrow, nests in the abandoned woodpecker holes in the same plant.

Quail and doves nest in the southern part, turkey vultures are found throughout, and many hawks migrate over the desert. Ducks and geese are found during migration. Many species of humming birds, flickers and woodpeckers nest there, as do road runners.

The desert and semi-desert area is probably the center of the world's rattlesnake population, although rattlesnakes do extend into every state in the Union except Maine. The desert diamond rattlesnake is the largest, most common and most dangerous in the Southern Desert area. A remarkable snake is the white rattlesnake of southwestern Arizona, so white that it is not noticed until it moves. Of great interest

is the small horned rattlesnake, known as the sidewinder.

The Arizona king snake is a beautiful snake which feeds sometimes on rattlesnakes. The gopher snake is harmless, but feeds largely on small rodents, and is found in both the Northern and Southern Deserts.

Most active are the lizards, such as the collard lizard, a foot in length, dashing across open spaces at lightning speed and into its hole, in spite of efforts to head it off. The leopard lizard is similar in habits. Horned lizards, called horned toads, are harmless lizards, with short flattened bodies. They make very attractive pets.

Insects and spiders are of special interest. The tarantula may be seen mostly at night, and especially after a shower, moving slowly along. Centipedes of large size, and scorpions are common. You should not handle tarantulas, scorpions or centipedes. Termites, or white ants, cover pieces of dead vegetation with soil, and under this protection eat the wood. In the tropics they are eaten by man and other animals. Here are grasshoppers and other insects.

After a light summer rain, many animals which would otherwise be entirely overlooked, may be seen at night with a flashlight.

The Scout who travels in the desert should be amply supplied with water and should drink freely. If lost, you should rest during the day and travel only at night. In sleeping in the desert, the soil will cool off rapidly. To insure warmth at night, a blanket should be spread on the hot surface and left there.

Fuel is usually readily available in the Northern and Southern Deserts, and many of the bushes ignite readily, even though still growing. Food is more available in the Southern than in the Northern Desert. Many animals are edible. Plants during the growing season in the Northern Desert are not as varied as might be desired. Russian thistle, filaree, mustards, lamb's quarters, purslane, amaranths, salt bushes, and many other fresh green plants can be used as spinach. In the Southern Desert the spider-worts, the flowers and soft parts of yuccas and agaves, the fruits of hackberry, desert-thorn cacti (especially the strawberry, saguaro, organpipe, and prickly pear) buckthorn, buffaloberry and most tree fruits, can be eaten. Young shoots of cacti, roots of nightblooming cereus and of hogpotato and many other plants, can be eaten. Seeds of most grasses are eaten by the Indians.

There is little reason to starve or die of thirst in the desert if there are growing plants or animals. Alkali water can be made harmless by leaching it through sand or soil from areas not saturated with salt.

Antelope
Coyote
Fore
Hind
Woodchuck
Fore
Hind
Mouse
Kit Fox
Prairie Dog
Fore

CONSERVATION FOR SCOUTS

Every Scout has heard the word "conservation." There are Merit Badges related to conservation and a special award — the Hornaday Award* — for Scouts and Scouters who make positive contributions to conservation. In recent years shortages of several natural resources — minerals, some kinds of timber, some kinds of birds and animals — and an increase in dust storms, floods, bog fires, and forest fires have made conservation part of America's conversation. But how many Scouts really know what conservation means, what it implies, and what they can do about it?

Two Scouts, brothers, living on a farm several years ago, learned one of the secrets of conservation. But they learned it the hard way.

On the farm on which these Scouts lived, there was a marsh. And in this marsh, for as long as the boys could remember, were several duck nests. Each

**See page 446.*

spring, the boys had a contest to see which would be the first to find the down-filled nest and ten to fourteen eggs. They took their Patrols out to the marsh, to show them the young ducks swimming in formation behind the beautifully colored adult ducks. All summer they watched the young ducks grow, and when fall came, they dreaded the day when the ducks, young and old would jump from the marsh water to join other ducks, as they flew their age-old route to the South. During the winter they anxiously awaited the ducks' return to nest again, and teach newly hatched ducks to swim, eat wild rice, and fly.

But one summer they made a startling discovery. There were not as many ducks as usual. The next summer, there were fewer still, and finally there were none at all. The Scouts were broken-hearted. From earliest boyhood, the ducks had been a chief interest —but now they were gone . . . what had happened? They decided to ask their friend, the Game Warden.

He visited the farm. He came several times. Finally he asked them a question. It seemed a strange question to the boys. The Game Warden asked them what had happened to all the skunks which had formerly lived around the marsh.

The boys answered that they had trapped the skunks. They wanted new bicycles to ride to school. Skunk pelts brought good prices and the boys had been successful in their trapping efforts. Only one or two pairs of skunks remained in the entire marsh.

That, the Warden answered, is what happened to the ducks. The boys were more bewildered than ever. What did skunks have to do with the ducks?

Skunks, Ducks and Turtles

The Warden answered their question. Besides skunks and ducks, snapping turtles also, lived in the marsh. And snapping turtles eat young ducks. But skunks eat snapping turtle eggs. So by trapping the skunks, the Scouts had helped the turtles to increase. The result was fewer and fewer ducks. He suggested that the boys give the skunks a chance to increase, so that more turtle eggs would be eaten. This they did, and a few years later, the ducks came back to the marsh.

But the Warden went on to explain that the skunks could still be trapped. He pointed out that every year the skunks raised young, which in turn would reproduce more skunks. As soon as the skunk population had built up to sufficient numbers, the boys might safely trap skunks again. But they must be careful to leave a sufficient number—breeding stock as wild life experts call it—to reproduce every year. The surplus skunks could be taken.

In this way, the Scouts learned one of the secrets of conservation—interrelationship. They learned that skunks, turtles and ducks are all related, through a food chain. In the same way, other animals—all the way from the smallest microscopic life, to the largest birds and mammals—are related. The Scouts learned too, a good definition of the word conservation. **Conservation is the wise use of natural resources—minerals, soil, plants and animals—so that these resources will continue to serve the greatest number of people, to the fullest advantage.** They saw that conservation means the setting up of a practical plan under which all the people may share in the use and enjoyment of the natural resources of a country.

Renewable and Non-Renewable Resources

When the first white men came to America, they found vast amounts of natural resources of tremendous value. Forests covered a large part of the nation; later gas, oil and minerals were found in unbelievable amounts. There was a great abundance of very fertile soil. Forests, prairies, streams and rivers abounded with wildlife. So vast were these resources, that it seemed that they could never be used up. So forests were destroyed to make way for farmland. Grasslands and prairies were plowed and harrowed. Minerals and oil were used in great quantities to supply a young industrial nation. Almost every river became the scene of factories, mills and power companies. Mammals and birds were slaughtered for food, sport, and because they competed with man's interests.

Within a short time, the results were obvious. Floods caused millions of dollars damage yearly. The very fertile soil washed away, or blew up in great clouds. The seemingly inexhaustible oil and minerals showed signs of depletion. Rivers were filled with silt, from eroding farms, and wastes from factories. Many of them were made unfit for fish. Several species of birds disappeared, and some mammals seemed on the verge of going. Future timber shortages were predicted. In short, Americans soon came to realize that some sort of a conservation program must be set up, if future Americans, as well as present, were to share in the resources that are the heritage of every American.

Conservation experts place all natural resources in two broad groups—those which are renewable, and those which are non-renewable. Into the first group, go forests, grasslands, other plant life, and animals.

Since these resources are all living things, they may be regrown and restored under a carefully worked plan. Into the second group, go minerals, oil, natural gas, and soil. The fertility of soil may be built up over a period of time, but the soil itself, once it washes down a river, or blows away on the wind, would take ages to rebuild without management. And oil, gas and minerals, once they are gone, can never be replaced.

The job of the conservationist then is to help restore the plants and animals that have been used up, and to control their future use, so that the supply will never be exhausted. The conservationist must plan the use of minerals, oil and gas, so that these resources are put to a use that will benefit the greatest number of people, while conserving the supply; so that future generations may also benefit from them. Conservationists must also manage soil resources, so that the soil is no longer lost through erosion, but is built up in fertility and will continue to produce.

The Ninth Point of the Scout Law, is every Scout's promise to help America conserve her natural resources. For, if these resources are to be saved, and used for the greatest good, every Scout, every American must be thrifty.

What Scouts Can Do!

Probably the first step for the Scout is that he understand a few basic principles upon which most conservation projects are based. A few pages back it was shown that in general, the country is made up of certain habitats—or homes—in which plants and animals live, each dependent for life on other plants or animals. Some scientists call this interdependence, or interrelationship, the "Web of Life." Others call it the "Balance of Nature." But by whichever name it is known, it is an important factor in conservation.

Many conservation problems have arisen, in this country, because unthinkingly man has upset this balance—or broken one strand in the web.

The ivory-billed woodpecker is on the verge of extinction, not because it was hunted, but because the forest areas in which it nested were cut for timber. White-tailed deer, on the other hand, have increased so rapidly in some sections, as to cause almost a serious problem, all because they have adapted themselves more readily to living on or near farmland, than in forests. Certain species of fish have been wiped out of some rivers, not because they were caught with rod and reel, but because eroding soil, or factory waste in the water, cut off light from the plants that fed the smaller fish that the larger fish eat. Countless other examples could be given. But these are enough to prove the point.

This leads naturally, to the second basic rule of conservation, that before any project is undertaken, all sides of the question must be considered. All possible outcomes should be predicted, as far as possible, so that the project will produce the greatest good for the greatest number of people.

If for example, a marsh is to be drained for agricultural purposes, or to destroy mosquitoes that annoy the people of nearby towns, the other outcomes of this drainage should also be studied. The soil of the marsh will change in character, so different plants will grow; the men who enjoyed duck hunting will have to go elsewhere; the Scouts who took nature walks will have to look for other places; the women's wildflower club will have to go elsewhere in search of interesting plants; the boys who caught crabs may

A soil erosion demonstration for Cub Scouts

have to look elsewhere; muskrat trappers will lose part of their yearly income; if the marsh had peat formations, it will constantly be under threat of fire —all of these may happen, if the marsh is drained. The state or county agency undertaking the project should study all possible outcomes, and consider their relative importance. Other mosquito control methods are possible, but far more costly. The county or state agency that undertakes this project, should look at all sides of the question.

Every Scout who sincerely wants to contribute to the conservation of America's resources should understand this point. No conservation project, worthy of the name, is ever undertaken, except after careful study, and careful consideration of all possible outcomes.

Soil

There are a great many things Scouts can do to help in conservation, starting with soil conservation.

As every Scout knows, good fertile soil is absolutely essential to the future of America. Without it, no crops can be produced, no cows, sheep, pigs, poultry or game raised. So the logical start for the Scout conservationist is with the soil. If a Scout has a garden or a lawn or a farm, he may see to it that the soil is maintaining its fertility and abundance. He will see to it that methods are used that prevent erosion, by wind or rain. He may see to it that crops are planted that help the soil to continue to produce. In Merit Badge Shows and Troop Displays he may exhibit projects that show how erosion may be prevented. He may obtain all the information and details he needs from his County or Extension Agricultural Agent, or from **The Soil Conservation Service, Washington, D. C.**

Water

A second field in which the Scout conservationist may work is water. Every Scout likes to fish. What Scout's mouth doesn't water at the thought of a fresh trout frying over a camp fire, as the sun goes down in the West? These fish are possible only as long as water is fit to produce them, and water filled with silt from eroding uplands, or the pollution from industrial plants, will not produce fish. Over-fished streams are just as bad.

The Scout may watch the water. If silt and dirt are the cause of poor fishing, he may look for the cause, and report it to his local State Conservation Commission. He may, with his Troop, offer to set out trees, or other plants on the land from which this dirt comes. For trees and grass will hold back the soil, and result in clearer streams, and finer fishing. If over-fishing is the cause, he and his Patrol or

Dams form feeding and resting places for fish

Troop may offer their help to the Game Warden or Conservation Commission—in planting fingerlings, or in building a series of dams that provide fish with feeding and resting places.

Exhibits in the form of aquaria may be made up, showing food chains for the fish in his locality. He may find what type of plant is the base of the food chain, and what fish eat it—fish that in turn provide food for the fish he wants to catch. Any Scout wanting more suggestions, may write, through his Scoutmaster, to his State Conservation Commission, in the State Capitol, or to the Fish and Wildlife Service, Washington 25, D. C.

Trees

A third conservation field in which Scouts may work is that of trees and plant life. Millions of trees yearly, are planted by Scouts. But millions more are waiting to be planted. If Scouts have no place of their own where nut bearing trees, spruces or pines can be planted, they may offer the services of their Troop to their local County or State Conservation Agencies. Through their Local Council Scout Office, they may find the addresses of these agencies which can always use more help in planting trees—either for soil control, food for wildlife or for future cutting for timber. Many Troop Camps, and Council Camps have taken advantage of the low cost at which trees may be obtained from State Conservation Departments to plant trees at their camps. Commercial timber growers will welcome the aid of Scouts who want to help America replace the trees used up at so tremendous a rate during the war.

But tree planting is not the only way in which Scouts may help preserve America's forests. Scouts are always careful to prevent forest fires, by always keeping their camp fires under control, and by putting them out just as carefully when they leave a campsite. Scouts in forest areas may learn forest fire fighting methods from local wardens or conservation agencies, and be prepared at all times to assist in putting out forest fires. They will immediately report any fire they see to the proper authorities. During the dry seasons, they may offer their services, through their Scoutmaster, as lookouts and forest rangers.

For further information get in touch with local County or State Conservation Departments, in their county seat, or state capitol.

Wildlife

The fourth field of conservation in which Scouts may work is Wildlife. As in the other three fields,

Planting trees helps provide forests for tomorrow

there are many things that can be done. Most important of all, probably is showing the townspeople the value of wildlife.

A Troop, or Patrol may build a nature trail. The purpose of such a trail is to show what the Scout already knows, that plants and animals live in a definite habitat, or home, where they live in a relationship to each other. Trees would be labeled, telling what kinds of birds or mammals nested in them, or fed on them. Bird pictures could be shown, telling what the bird eats. Scouts will have many more ideas, or they may write to **The National Audubon Society, 1000 Fifth Avenue, New York 28, N. Y.**, or **The American Museum of Natural History, New York 24, N. Y.**, for pamphlets on how to build nature trails, or nature museums.

Scouts may do much in their communities in other ways too. They may take school children, service clubs, garden clubs or other organizations on nature hikes, explaining to them the habitats through which they hike. They may figure out food chains of the animals in their area, and make up exhibits for schools, clubs and Troop displays. If there is a local campaign to destroy all hawks, owls, coyotes or other animals, they may find out all they can about these animals, and make up window displays, showing why they should not be completely wiped out. They may find an owl roost, for example, and collect the pellets they find underneath. Then when they take these pellets apart, they can show exactly what the owl has eaten.

Scouts may also help wildlife planting trees and shrubs that produce food and shelter. Nut-bearing trees provide food for many animals, including man. The Audubon Society, the Fish and Wildlife Service, and any State Agricultural College will help in deciding what other trees may be planted.

Scouts, already in large numbers, feed birds and game animals, and provide watering places. But much more can be done. Birds also need dirt piles in which to dust themselves—and more food and water during the winter. Birdhouses have long been a Scout project but more can be built and set out.

There are many more projects Scouts may undertake—too many to list here. The serious Scout will use his imagination, and his knowledge, in looking for conservation work to do. He will remember what he has learned—that one of the secrets of conservation is the web of life; that the other is careful study of all possible outcomes of his project, so that it will result in the greatest good for the largest number of people. He will remember that conservation means the wise use of natural resources, for the greatest benefit to mankind.

Many Scouts help fight forest fires

Conservation Agencies

There are several nation-wide organizations that give all of their attention to conservation — of soil, forests and wildlife. These organizations are prepared to help Scouts in their conservation work.

The U.S. Forest Service, Washington, D. C., is concerned with the conservation of natural forest areas throughout the country.

The Soil Conservation Service, Washington, D. C., is chiefly concerned with saving the soil. It directs erosion control activities and practices.

The Fish and Wildlife Service, Washington, D. C., deals with wildlife problems.

The National Parks Service, Washington, D. C., is concerned with setting up National Parks, for the conservation of trees, plants, birds and mammals within the parks.

Any Scout writing to his State Conservation Commission may obtain a list of conservation booklets.

Conservation on the Hike and in Camp

If you camp in Federal, State or local parks remember it is forbidden to use *any* but dead, down trees. On private property many owners permit only dead wood to be used. But many Scouts camp in areas where there is no control over cutting wood but the Scout's own conscience.

Find out before you go, what you may cut. If you are asked not to cut live wood, *don't do it.* The reputation of the Boy Scouts of America rests on your shoulders.

If you find you are permitted to cut a little green wood, follow these general rules.

1. Carefully estimate the exact amount of wood you will need, the number of poles, and the length. Do not cut more wood than you absolutely need.

2. Look around for saplings, clumps of three or four growing together. Do not cut a tree unless there are no saplings, then choose the tree that is the least healthy and attractive.

3. Cut only one from a clump of three, or two from a clump of four. Cut low to the ground—almost at ground level. Cut the least healthy tree of the clump.

4. After trimming off branches, cut up the branches and scatter them around. Be sure they lie flat on the ground so that they will rot quickly and not be a fire hazard. Do not pile up branches and leave them in the woods.

5. In almost any forest area there are two or more groups of trees—those which will grow into the climax forest, and those which will grow for a few years, and then die. You can usually tell the best trees in the area, leave them. Cut only the less desirable trees. Many times you will find a less desirable kind crowding out one of the more desirable trees.

In the East, a soft maple might be crowding a hickory or oak. Cut the maple if you absolutely need a pole. In the West, if an aspen crowds a young pine, cut the aspen. Use the least desirable tree always.

6. In wilderness areas where making bough beds is possible, do not cut down a tree to get boughs. Instead, trim the lower branches of several trees close to the trunk. Use the tips of these branches to make the bed.

Breaking Camp

When breaking camp, here are a few rules, which are good conservation practices:

1. If you have made a ground bed of boughs, leaves, or grass, scatter the material so it will decay quickly.

2. Fill in all ditches and holes, and cover all places where sod has been removed. In many places soil erosion occurs quite soon if patches of bare ground, or ditches are left exposed to wind and rain.

3. Be sure that all paper is burned, and all tin cans or bottles are cleaned out, smashed and buried. Many animals have died cruelly because they wedged their heads in cans or jars and could not get them out.

4. If you are coming back to the campsite again, stack your unused fire wood, poles, and stakes in an open place. Use them the next time.

5. Be sure that all fires are out. If you can stir up the ashes with your bare hand, the fire is out.

6. Be sure all garbage has been burned. Unburned garbage attracts flies and other undesirable animals, that will make the campsite useless for you or others for a long time to come. Many animals can dig up buried garbage, and expose it to flies and other pests.

7. Leave the campsite better than you found it.

TRACKING AND · STALKING

CHAPTER 13

If you have ever tried to track and stalk wild animals, you know that it takes real skill and a good knowledge of woodlore. Animals are always on the alert and their keen senses of smell, hearing or sight warn them of danger long before you see them. But with a little preparation and practice, any Scout can learn to follow animals and get close enough to them to find out how they live.

To be successful in tracking and stalking, you need to know four things: something about the animals themselves; how to find their tracks or other signs; how to follow those tracks; how to stalk so that you can get close enough for a good look.

You can find out a great deal about animals, where and how they live, by reading Chapter 12 on Nature Adventuring. Read that chapter first. Then study the pictures of tracks, so that you know what they look like. Then practice careful observation, tracking and stalking. It will not be long before you can read the signs in the woods as did the Indians and early American scouts before you.

Observation

Careful observation is important. This means knowing how to look for natural signs, as well as when and where. More than that, it means understanding the meaning of what you see. So being a detective is part of tracking too.

In camp one summer night, a few Scouts were startled half out of their beds by a weird scream that seemed to come from only a few yards away. The scream was followed by a low moan. Then came a crashing through the brush.

There was little sleep the rest of that night and at the first dim light of dawn, the Scouts went out to investigate. Except for a few broken bushes and a jumble of tracks, there was nothing to show what had happened—that is, nothing for all but one of the Scouts.

He got down on his knees and scraped a few hairs off of a rock. He looked at some prints in the soft earth. He walked off into the woods. When he came back to camp, there was a smile on his face. He told his version of what had happened.

There was a raccoon trail going to the spring where the campers got their water. That night, while a 'coon was on his way for a drink, a bear caught up with him. The 'coon saw the bear at the last moment and screamed in fright. One swipe of a huge claw and the 'coon moaned his last. Then off crashed the bear, carrying the 'coon with him.

A few hairs on a rock, a few tracks in the mud, some broken bushes, all told the mystery story.

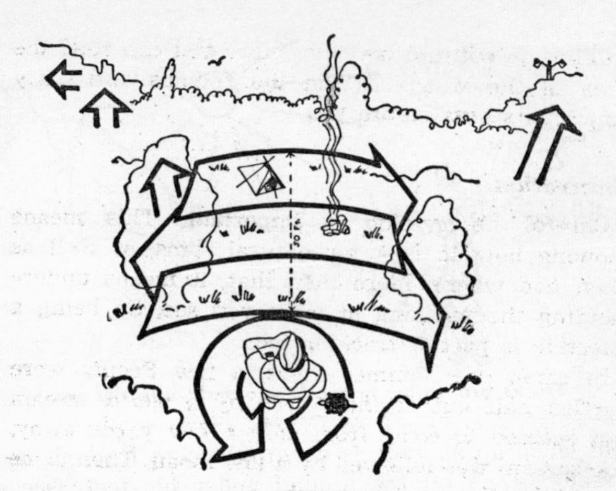

Knowing *how* to look is important in observation

Careful observation, a knowledge of woodlore, and a little "detecting" solved the mystery. One Scout knew what to look for and how to look.

How to Look

Many outdoorsmen have a definite way of "looking." As they walk along, their eyes move in semicircular rings in front of them. Drop a pebble in a still pool of water. See how the ripples run out in circles, one inside the other? A skilled observer's line of sight resembles those rings of ripples.

First he looks in an area six or eight feet in front and about ten feet wide. This ring of vision runs in a semicircle from left to right. He thoroughly observes this area, before shifting his eyes to another ring in front. He sweeps his eyes from right to left in the second ring. He continues until he is sure there is nothing for fifty feet in front worth concentrating on.

Tracks are easier to see if you walk into the sun

He looks up as well as down, glancing through the treetops, and on the ground under his feet. Occasionally he looks behind to get a different view.

If he is on the lookout for tracks, he tries to travel into the sun, because tracks are easier to see that way. Their shadows are longer and the tracks look deeper.

When he finds a track, he stops for a minute. He closely studies one track to find out what kind of animal made it. Then he looks at several tracks to try to figure out what the animal was doing. Then he carefully follows the track—if it is a fresh one, to try to catch a glimpse of the animal. If he loses the track, he stops and looks around. Perhaps the animal climbed a tree, or hid under a rock. Or perhaps it came to hard ground where tracks are difficult to see.

The tracker marks the last point where he saw the track with his handkerchief, and walks ahead twenty feet or so. Then he walks in a circle until he picks up the track again. If he is still unsuccessful, he walks in wider circles, slowly and carefully looking for further signs.

Trail Signs

A good way to practice observation is to follow trail markers set out by another Scout. Then you can lay a trail for him to follow. Look at the illustration of the different trail marks. Notice that they are either scratch marks in the dirt, or made of sticks, grass or rocks that you find in the open.

At first, use a trail that is easy to see. After a little practice, try a more difficult trail. Finally, as you become a better observer, you will be able to follow a trail which most people would miss entirely.

Another way to practice tracking is to follow a "whiffle-poof." A whiffle-poof is a piece of wood driven full of nails. Another Scout drags it over the ground and it leaves a trail that will give you excellent training in tracking.

Observation and tracking will help you find signs of an animal and follow it. Stalking is the skill that will help you get really close to the animal. Success in stalking depends upon how well you can hide yourself and how quietly you can move.

Make a whiffle-poof for good tracking practice

THIS WAY

THIS IS NOT THE WAY

THIS IS THE TRAIL

TURN RIGHT (SHORT WAY)

TURN LEFT (LONG WAY)

DANGER HELP

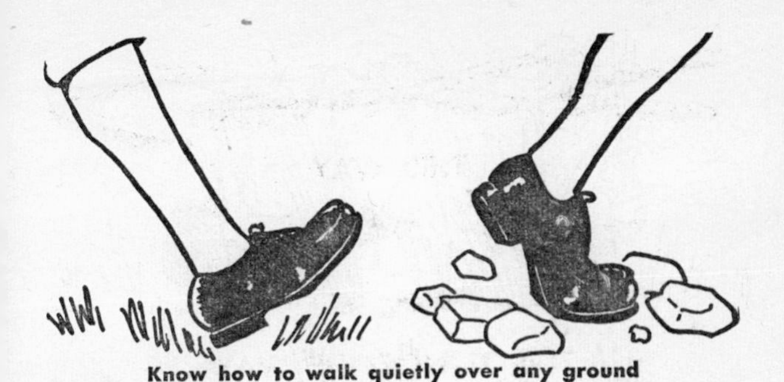

Know how to walk quietly over any ground

Move Slowly and Quietly

The first rule of stalking is to move **slowly** and **silently.** Any quick or jerky movement usually frightens the animal you are stalking. Any broken twigs or rustle of leaves gives you away, so do not make a sound.

When walking in grass or leaves step on your heel first, then bring your toe down slowly and easily. On hard or rocky ground, step on your toe first. Feel out a solid footing and then bring your heel down. In both cases, keep your balance on your back foot until the front foot is ready to bear the weight. When walking, lift your feet high, straight up, so you won't kick stones or rustle grass.

The way you move depends upon the country, and that brings up the second rule of stalking. Make use of **cover.** If walking through the woods, you can probably walk upright. If the shrubbery is low, you crouch. In grass, you crawl or creep. At all times make use of cover for concealment. Move from bush to bush, or tree to tree, or slowly through the grass. When the wind blows and rustles the grass or leaves, move on a short way, but don't move when the grass around you is motionless.

Keep low by crawling or creeping

Watch out for your **background** and your **shadow.** You may think you are perfectly concealed behind a rock or bush. But your head sticking up over the top, outlined against the sky, is not overlooked by your quarry. Look around rocks or shrubs from near the bottom. Be sure you blend into the background and do not contrast with it. Your shadow may give you away. Even the movement of your shadow frightens a bird or animal. Never stand so that your shadow is obvious. Crouch or lie down, so that your shadow is as small as possible and blends in with the shadow of a tree, rock or shrub.

The last few yards as you approach your game, you probably crawl on your belly. You can move quietly and smoothly, just by resting your weight on your toes and elbows, and by moving them only. You can also crawl by resting your weight on the insides of your legs, which you bend out sideways to make progress. You can pull yourself along by grasping grass or anything ahead of you affording a hold.

Constantly watch your quarry. At the least sign of alarm, freeze in your tracks, and don't move a muscle until the bird or animal resumes feeding or other natural activities.

A big game photographer tells how "freezing" once saved his life. He was photographing mountain goats, and for several days and nights he had stalked a fine specimen to get a picture. Finally the moment came. He was flat on his stomach on a rock, and just below on a ledge was the goat. The camera was focused. When the goat turned just a little, click, and it would be all over. But just then the photographer looked out of the corner of his eye and saw a rattle-snake not more than six inches from his bare arm. If one muscle twitched, the snake would strike. A man ten miles from camp, high on a rocky plateau, would be in a serious condition with snake venom running through his veins. Did the photographer freeze? He certainly did. Camera and goat were forgotten. He had to concentrate hard, not to twitch a muscle. For two hours, man and snake lay as they were. But finally the noonday sun was too much for the huge rattler, and it slithered off into a crevice in the rocks. "Freezing" had saved the photographer's life.

Use the Wind

The next thing to remember is the wind. Most animals depend upon their hearing and smell to warn them of danger. If the wind is blowing from you toward the animal, it will be much easier for the animal to hear or smell you. So move against the wind. If this is impossible, work yourself into a position that is crosswind from the animal. Never approach from downwind.

Plenty of Practice

Becoming a good tracker and stalker requires practice. Remember the Indians and early Pioneers lived in the wild. They had the chance to practice. They had to practice if they wanted to eat; or if they wanted to avoid their enemies and live.

You can practice on Patrol and Troop hikes, or in your back yard. Keep at it, and you will be able to watch wild animals in **their** own back yards.

Hide so that you blend into the background

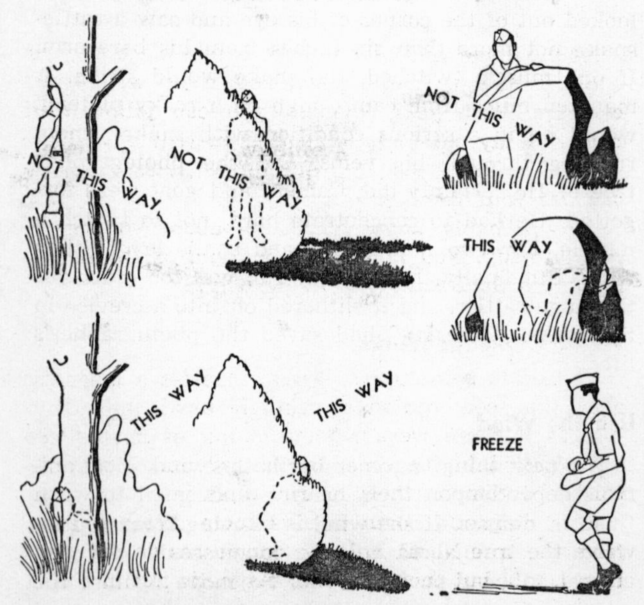

FIND YOUR WAY

CHAPTER 14

As a camper and hiker, there is one piece of your equipment you should know, and know well—your compass. With your compass, you can follow trail maps, or lay out plots of land. You will have little excuse for being lost in any kind of country, if you can use your compass correctly.

You probably know something about your compass already. You know that one end of the needle points north. But do you know why?

How a Compass Works

The earth spinning on its axis creates a magnetic attraction, centered in a **magnetic north pole.** It is just as if there were a huge chunk of magnetized iron, buried in the earth in the far north, that attracts all compass needles and dials.

This magnetic north pole is some distance away from the true North Pole. So compasses do not point true north, but they do point magnetic north.

Unless you are on a line that runs roughly from northern Wisconsin, through Cincinnati, Ohio, to Savannah, Georgia, your compass will point either east or west of true north. If you live on this line (see map on page 257) your compass will point at about true north. If you live east of the line, your compass will point west of true north. If you live west of the line, your compass will point east of true north.

This difference between true north and magnetic north is usually called "variation" or "declination."

Principal Points

Look at your compass. Whether it is a needle or dial compass, it will be marked off in principal points and in degrees.

For all practical purposes, the degree markings are the most important. But some directions are given in terms of the principal points. For example, wind directions are said to be westerly, northwesterly, or northeasterly. You may tell a friend you will meet him on the southwest corner of a street intersection. Rivers are said to run north and south, or east and west.

You should know the eight principal points: NORTH, NORTHEAST, EAST, SOUTHEAST, SOUTH, SOUTHWEST, WEST, NORTHWEST.

Degree Readings

The degree readings on the compass are used to find direction more accurately than can be done with the principal compass points. The 360 degrees of your compass dial are 360 different paths or streets that you can use in following a map, or in laying out

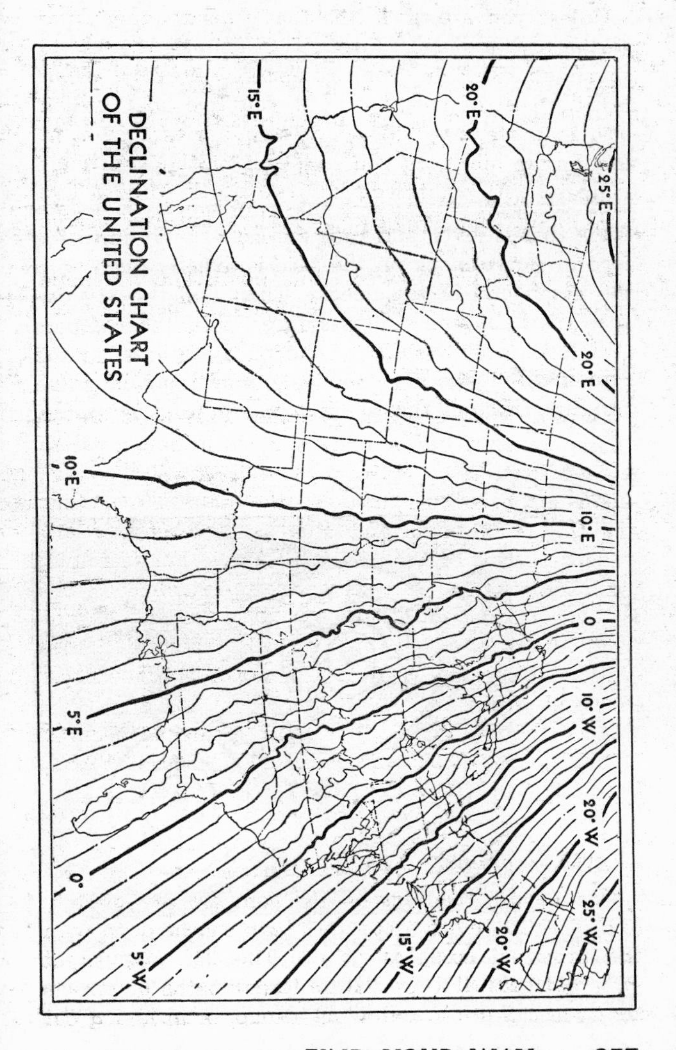
DECLINATION CHART
OF THE UNITED STATES
25°E
20°E
15°E
20°E
10°E
10°E
0
10°W
20°W
25°W
20°W
15°W
5°W
0°
5°E

a plot of ground. Any place that you want to go is located on one of these degree readings.

Now practice using your compass so that you can take degree readings with it. Suppose you wanted to find the direction of 310 degrees. How would you do it? The dial compass needs little description. The illustration shows how. But with a needle compass first, *set your compass.* That is, place it on something that is level, and turn the case slowly until the **zero** or **north** mark on the face is exactly even with the north end of the needle. Then find the 310 degree mark on the compass face. With the compass still level, and the end of the needle at rest at the zero mark on the face, sight along an imaginary line running through the pivot or center of the needle,

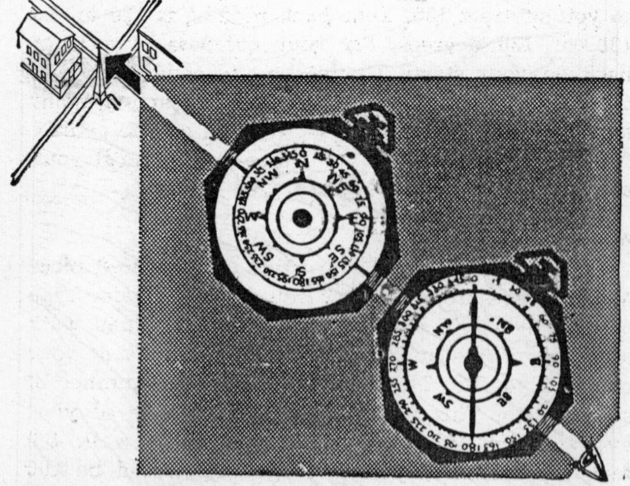

Compass at right is a needle compass which is described above. The compass at left is a dial compass. Hold it level and sight across the face, through the pivot, to the objective. The degree reading on the far side of the dial is the direction to the objective.

and the 310 degree mark. Sighting along this line, pick out a landmark such as a fence post, tree, house, or clump of grass. That landmark will be in a direction of 310 degrees from where you are standing.

Frequently, in walking through rough or hilly country, you cannot walk in a straight line. You must detour around rocks, limbs of trees, or other natural obstacles. You will be bound to get off your course. To check yourself and keep on the course, you can take a *back degree reading* on your starting point.

A general rule for taking the *back reading* is this: If the "going" reading is less than 180 degrees, add 180 degrees to it; if the "going" reading is more than 180 degrees, subtract 180 degrees from it.

In this case your "going" reading is 310 degrees, so you subtract 180. Your back reading is 310 minus 180, or 130 degrees. *Set* your compass, and sight back on your starting point, in the same way you sighted your first landmark. If your starting point is on the 130 degree reading, you are on the course. If not, walk a little to the left, or right, until your starting point is on the 130 degree reading.

Measuring Distance

With a tape measure, yardstick or measured piece of rope, measure a 200-foot course on the same type of land over which you intend to travel. Then walk over the course and back (400 feet) counting your steps as you go. Then divide 400 by the number of steps taken. This will give you the length of your average step. If it took you 160 steps to walk 400 feet, the length of your average step would be 400 ÷160 steps, or 2½ feet. (In reading about mapping in other books, you may come across the words "pace" or "stride." NOTE: Above directions are all based upon the single step.)

Suppose that you wanted to walk 630 feet. How many steps would you take? If the length of your average step is 2½ feet, you would walk 252 steps. (630÷2½ equals 252.)

It is important that you remember the length of your average step. You need it to follow a map.

This is a compass course such as you might walk, for which you would take three compass readings and measure three distances with your step.

You would be shown the starting point. Then you would be told to go 100 degrees for 165 feet, until you found a stake; then to go 195 degrees for 90 feet, to the second objective; then to go 300 degrees for 160 feet, to the end of the course.

On each leg of the course, first set your compass, then find a landmark on the required compass degree reading. Then walk toward the landmark for the required number of steps.

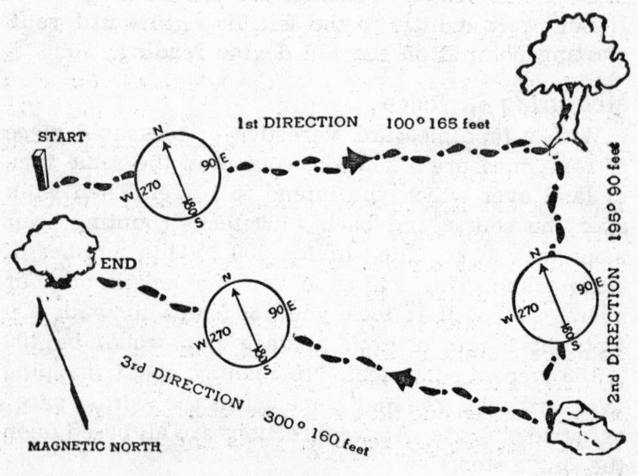

"Lay out a Four-Acre Tract . . ."

Laying out a four-acre tract of land is exactly like laying out a compass course. In fact it is easier.

First of all, remember that:

4 acres = 640 square rods.
1 rod = 16½ feet.

Remember too, the length of your average step.

Next, find out the distance along one side of the four-acre tract. Suppose, for example, that you had a woodlot in which you had to clear four acres of pasture; or a pasture in which you wanted to plough four acres for planting. Along one edge of the woodlot pasture, you fix a distance that would be one side of the four-acre tract. Suppose that this distance was 32 rods. To find the length of the other sides of the tract, divide 640 by 32. The answer is 20. Thus the tract would be 32 rods long by 20 rods wide.

In other words, after you know the length of one side, divide 640 by that distance in rods, and you will get the length of the other side.

Let's suppose that your tract is going to be 32 rods by 20 rods. First find out how many steps it takes you to walk 32 rods. If the length of your step is 2½ feet, it would take you a little more than 211 steps—211⅕ steps to be exact. (32x16½ = 528 feet. 528 feet divided by 2½ = 211⅕ steps.) How many steps would it take you to walk 20 rods? Figure it out the same way. 20 rods times 16½ feet = 330 feet. 330 feet divided by the length of **your** step equals the distance to walk.

The first step in laying out the four-acre tract is to drive a stake in the ground at your starting point, or mark a tree with paint. Then take a degree reading along the one side that you have decided upon. Write down that degree reading. Let's suppose it is 220 degrees.

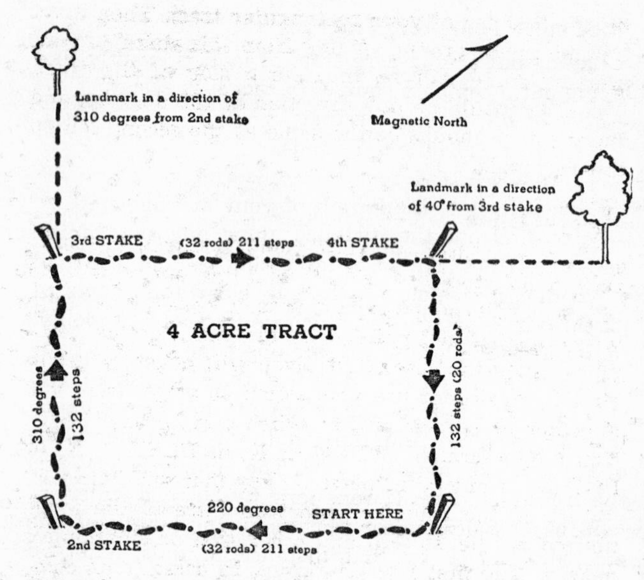

Here is an example of a four-acre tract. If your step is 2½ feet and if the tract you are laying out is 32 rods by 20 rods this would be how to do it.

The second step is to walk along the first side and measure the distance. Drive a stake in the ground at the end of the side.

Next, take a compass degree reading of 310 degrees (220 degrees plus 90 degrees), and select a landmark in that direction. Then walk in a direction of 310 degrees, toward the landmark, counting your steps for the correct distance. Then drive a stake in the ground.

Next, take a degree reading of 40 degrees. (310 plus 90.) Find a landmark in that direction and walk toward it exactly the same distance that you walked on the first leg of your rectangular tract. Then drive a stake in the ground. A line from this stake, to your starting stake will be the fourth side of the tract. This line should be in a direction of 130 degrees, and the distance should be the same as the second leg on the rectangle.

Helpful Hints

When you first get your compass check its accuracy. Then study it carefully and find out which end of the needle points north. It may be wrapped with wire, tinted blue, pointed or marked. Scratch some marking on the case so that you will never forget it. For if you do not use your compass very often, you may not be sure at a time when you need to know. You might scratch "WIRE" = N; or BLUE = N; or Pt = N; or any other personal key that will help you.

Just as the earth's magnetism attracts the magnetized needle, so will any other iron or steel object nearby. The first rule therefore, in using your compass, is "Don't use it near steel or iron." Your axe, knife, another compass, wire fences, power lines, railroads, or an automobile all should be a considerable distance away, or your needle will be attracted by them, instead of by the magnetic north pole.

MAP READING

A map and a picture of a countryside are very much alike. If you can understand the picture, you can understand the map, for a map is a picture of land; a kind of airplane view, made simple to bring out only the important details. By means of standard symbols, maps show important roads, side roads, trails, bridges, houses, churches, woods, streams, lakes—all those features that help you recognize the land when you travel over it. Pictures have a top and a bottom—so have maps. The top of most maps is north, and the bottom south. Usually there is an arrow somewhere on the map pointing toward magnetic north. There may be two arrows. One has a star, the letter N, or a full arrow point. This points true north. The other will have a half arrow point, or will be marked M N (magnetic north). You will use the half arrow point or MN when following that map with your compass.

On the map there will probably also be a key to the distance represented by the map. This is the map scale. It may be written in different ways: 1 inch = ½ mile (which means that 1 inch on the map equals one-half mile on level ground); or 1/62,500 (which means that 1 inch on the map equals 62,500 inches on level ground); or ½ ——— 0 ——— 1 (which means that each inch on the map equals one mile on level land).

You do two important things when you follow or sketch a map: you measure distance, and find direction. You measure distance with your own two feet; you find direction with your compass.

Following a Map

Suppose the map you are going to follow is a United States Geological Survey map, similar to the one in the illustration, or an air map. (You can probably get one of your own area for 20 cents from the U. S. Geological Survey, Department of Interior, Washington, D. C.) Suppose, too, that you are starting at point X, and want to lead your Patrol on a hike to point Z, which is a good place for a camp.

First of all, you orient your map. That is, aim it "true to the world" (north and south). You do this

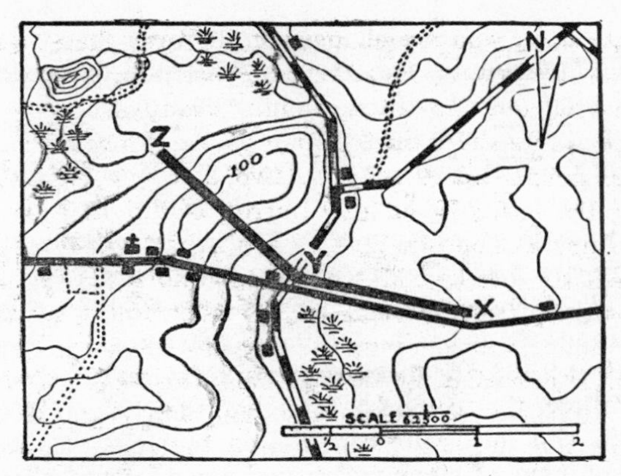

by placing your compass on the map so that the north end of the needle is at rest at the zero or N marking on the face, and at the same time parallel to the magnetic north arrow on the map. You may find this easier to do if you use a ruler, and extend the magnetic north arrow to about four inches long.

By orienting your map you know which direction you have to go in order to get toward point Z. For part of the way, you can travel by roads or trails (line X-Y), but for some of the way, you will follow your compass cross-country (line Y-Z).

You walk along roads to point Y. You then stop and orient your map as before. Then draw a pencil line from Y to Z. Place your compass on this line, so that the line runs through the center of the compass. The north end of the compass needle should be at rest at the zero or N mark on the case. Where the line which you have drawn on the map cuts the compass face on the side toward point Z, you can read the direction which you are to go. This will be the compass degree reading. It is the direction which you will go to reach point Z.

To find the distance from Y to Z, find the scale on the map. Then with a ruler, measure the distance from Y to Z, and figure the distance in miles.

On the map the distance from Y to Z is 1½ inches. The scale of the map is one mile to the inch. So the distance in miles from Y to Z is 1½. You know that there are 5,280 feet in a mile. There are 7,920 feet in 1½ inches on the map. If the length of your average step is 2½ feet, divide 7,920 by 2½ feet, and you get 3,168, the distance from Y to Z in steps.

Follow the compass direction which you found when you laid your compass on the line YZ. Walk the number of steps which you figured from Y to Z.

GET THE LAY OF THE LAND

Lay Out a North-South Line

No outdoorsman intentionally goes out without a compass. But should anything happen to his compass, he can use the sun and stars to find general directions. Neither of these methods are foolproof. At best, they give only general directions.

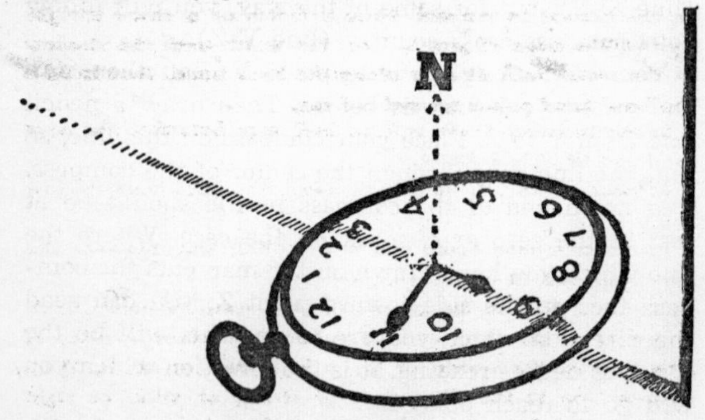

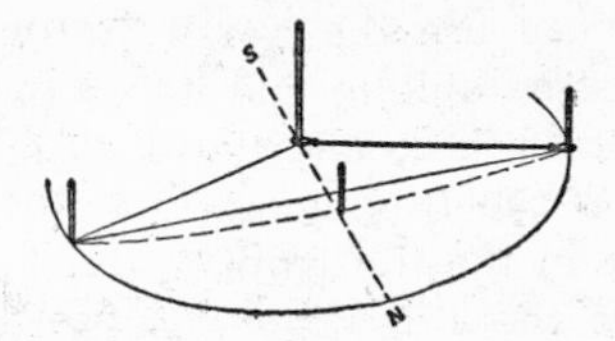

Finding North by Shadows

A staff or stick may be used to find north. Push it into the ground in direct sunlight. In the morning draw a circle with the staff as center and the length of the staff's shadow as the radius. Place a short stick at the point where the tip of the staff's shadow falls. As the sun rises the shadow will get shorter. But in the afternoon, the shadow will again touch the circle. When this happens mark the point on the circle with another short stick. The half way point between the two sticks, will be north of the staff.

Scratch a line on the ground from the bottom of the staff, to this halfway point, and you have your rough directions.

To use a watch and the sun to find north, lay the watch flat on the ground in the sun. Place a match or a straw upright against the edge of watch. Turn the watch until the shadow of the match falls directly along the hour hand, that is until the hour hand points toward the sun.

In the morning South will lie half way between the hour hand and 12 o'clock (forward).

At noon South will lie directly along the hour-hand-shadow line.

In the afternoon South will also lie half way between the hour hand and 12 o'clock (backward).

Scratch a line on the ground running south to north. Draw an arrow on the north end. Or stretch a shoelace or piece of string across the watch; or lay a long stick across it. Then, another line in the dirt, piece of string, or stick, at right angles to the first one, will run approximately east and west.

Using the North Star

Before you can use the North Star to find directions, you must be able to find it.

The easiest way is to find the Big Dipper; find the pointer stars of the Dipper; and then find the North Star as shown in the illustration.

But what if the Big Dipper is partly hidden by clouds, by trees or by a mountain? There are three other "pointers" which will help you find the North Star. The illustration shows them all.

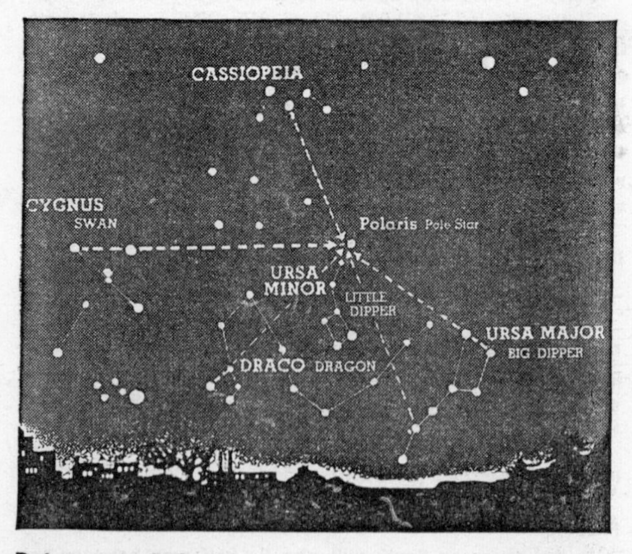

Pointers to Polaris

(1) The pointer stars of the Big Dipper (Ursa Major). (2) Through the stars furthest apart in the head of the Dragon (Draco). (3) From the double star in the middle of the Big Dipper, to the center star of Cassiopeia. (4) Through the pointer stars in the Northern Cross (part of Cygnus).

The next step is to "bring the North Star down to the ground" so you can draw a north-south line. To do that, you place a long stick in the ground. Then with a shorter stick, sight across the top of the two sticks at the North Star, exactly as if you were aiming a gun. When the tops of the two sticks and the North Star are in a direct line push the short stick into the ground.

A scratched line, a piece of string, or another stick connecting the bottom of the short sighting stick and the long sighting stick, will point north. Another line at right angles will point east and west.

Using Any Star

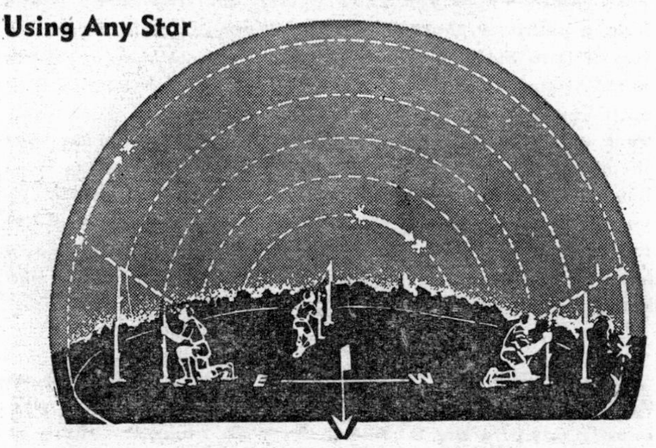

Sight the star across the tops of two sticks, as before. Watch the star for several minutes. It will seem to move. The direction in which it moves will tell you the direction you are facing.

If the star moves up, you are facing a general easterly direction. If the star moves down, you are facing a general westerly direction. If the star moves in an arc toward your left you are facing a general northerly direction.

If the star moves in a flat arc toward your right, you are facing a general southerly direction.

Determining Height and Width

There comes a time in everyone's life, and especially if you are an outdoorsman, when an ability to estimate distance accurately is important.

You are cutting down a tree. Will it fall on the tent, or won't it reach that far? How can you tell before it's too late?

Pencil Method.—Have a friend whose height you know, stand against a tree or cliff, or stand a Scout staff or other pole whose length you know against the tree or cliff. Then hold a pencil or short stick at arm's length, sight across the top of it to the top of your friend's head—or the top of the pole. At the same time move over your thumb on the stick until you sight across it to the base of the cliff. Then raise your arm and the stick, until your line of sight over your thumb hits the top of your friend's head. Note where your line of vision across the top of the stick cuts the cliff. Move your arm up again, and repeat the process. Thus you find out the *number* of many times higher the cliff is, than the known height (your friend or a pole). Multiply that *number* by the known height, to find the height of the cliff.

Step measuring.—Find a rock, tree or other landmark on the other side of the river (A). Place a stick on this side exactly opposite the landmark (B). Walk along the shore at right angles to AB. Take any number of steps—100, for example. Place a stick there (C). Continue walking for half as many steps as before—50. Place another stick here (D). At this point turn away from the river and walk at right angles to DB. When you sight stick C and landmark A in a straight line, stop. This is point E. Then DE is one half the distance across the river. Walk from D to E, and count your steps. Double the number and you have the distance across the river in steps. Multiply the number of steps by the length of your step to get the width of the river in feet.

You know that you can swim one hundred yards. But how wide is that river? Distances over water are tricky to judge. Can you do it accurately?

There are several ways to determine height and width. Know at least one. But practice different ways, so you can use them if necessary.

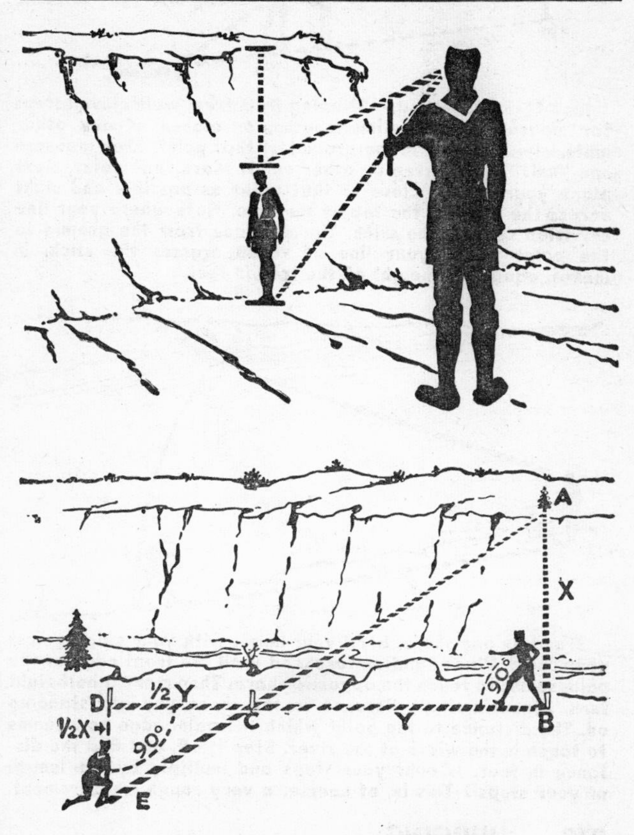

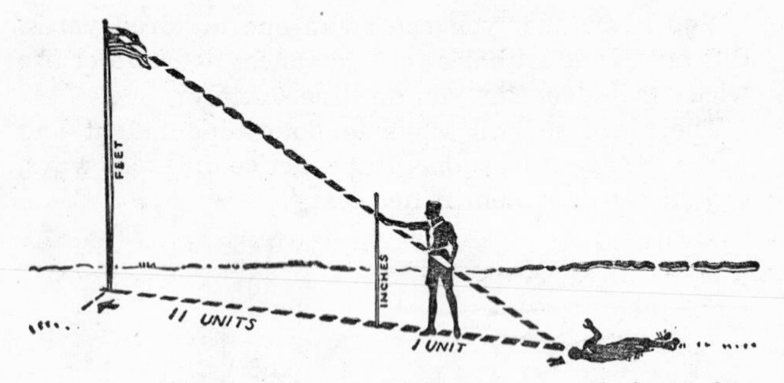

Inch-to-foot Method.—Starting from tree, walk eleven steps (or measure eleven stick lengths, or eleven of any other units.) Push a stick in the ground at that point. Then measure one "unit" more (step or other unit). Mark that point. Next place your eye as close to that point as possible and sight across the stick to the top of the tree. Note where your line of vision crosses the stick. The distance from the ground to the point where your line of vision crosses the stick, *in inches*, equals the height of the tree *in feet.*

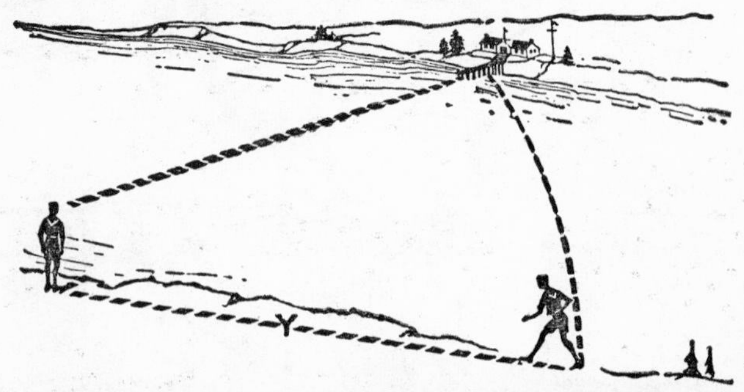

Stand on one shore, bend your head, with your chin against your chest. Place hand on forehead until the front edge of the palm seems to touch the opposite shore. Then make a half-right turn, "transferring" distance to the shore you are standing on. The distance to the point which the palm edge now seems to touch is the width of the river. Step it off, and find the distance in feet. (Count your steps and multiply by the length of your steps.) This is, of course, a very rough measurement.

Personal Measurements

You do not usually take a tape measure or yardstick with you on hikes or camp trips. But you do have a ruler with you at all times—your own personal measurements.

Here are some measurements that will be helpful to you. Get a tape measure, and fill in the blanks. Then remember them. But check up on them every six months.

My height is	............feet............inches
Height of my eyes above ground	............feet............inches
My reach up to tip of upstretched fingers	............feet............inches
My reach across, from outstretched fingertips	............feet............inches
Span of my hand, from thumb to little finger	............feet............inches
Length of my foot	............feet............inches
Length of my step	............feet............inches

Next, find a measurement for exactly one inch. It may be the length of one finger joint, or the width of your thumb. Then find exactly one foot. It may be the length of your shoe, or your arm from elbow to a point on your hand. Finally find one yard. It may be the distance from outstretched fingertip to your chin or opposite shoulder.

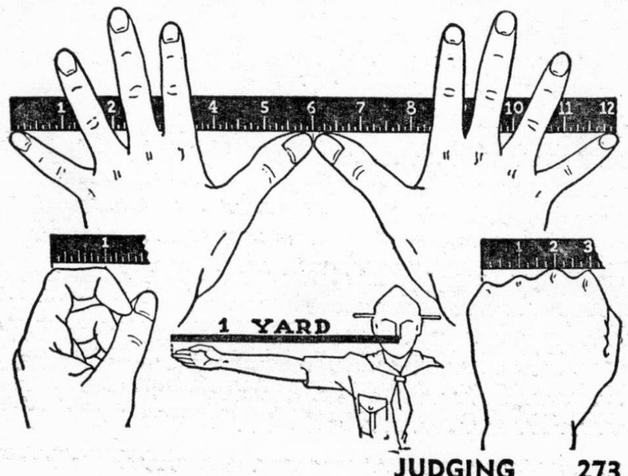

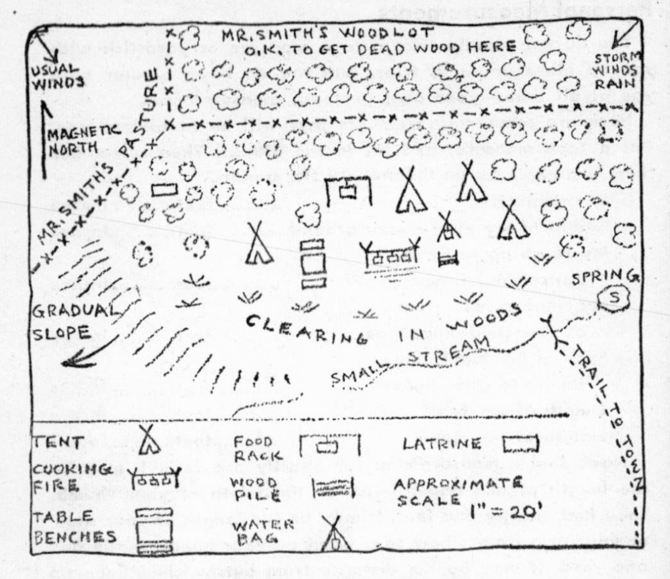

MAP SKETCHING

Sketch the Patrol Campsite

Your map sketch of the Patrol campsite should be very simple. It should show the directions from which winds blow, and the general direction the land slopes. It should show where to get wood and water. An approximate scale of about one inch to twenty feet will enable you to show how far apart tents are pitched, the distance of the latrine from camp, the distance from the spring and wood supply and the general size of the campsite.

Indicate natural features, such as trees, fences, and streams with conventional signs. Tents and camp furnishings may be drawn in simply and labeled.

The chief purpose of this sketch, is to show that

you know how to lay out a campsite so that it will be comfortable and safe.

Two-Mile Sketch

Suppose that on a hike in the woods, outside town, or summer camp, you found a good site for a Patrol overnight camp. You would want to remember how to find it again or how to show the other fellows how to find it.

As you walk back to town or camp, note the outstanding landmarks that will help you find it again. Remember the approximate distance you walk.

Then when you get back, draw a sketch of the route to the campsite. Show only the landmarks that are necessary to find the camp.

The important thing to include on the map is an easily seen landmark wherever you turn off a road-

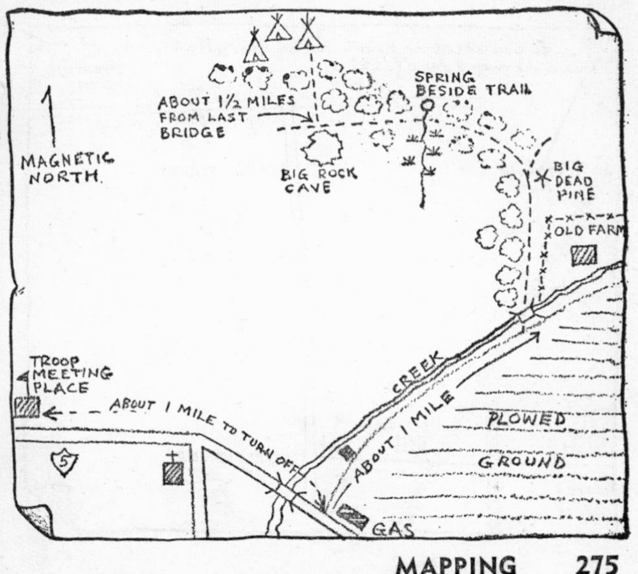

way or trail. Be sure that these landmarks are obvious, and that anyone else can find them.

On the map, indicate the general northerly direction, a wellknown starting point, and approximate distances.

Remember! This is not a detailed map with specific compass directions and distances.

This map might be sketched to show someone how to get to the hospital; a sketch to show a new friend how to find the Troop meeting place; or a sketch to show the game warden where you found an injured fawn; or a sketch to show you how to get back to camp after a hike in the woods.

The important thing is that you be able to make this sketch quickly, and accurately enough so that someone else can get where you want him to go.

The illustrations show how simple the map can be.

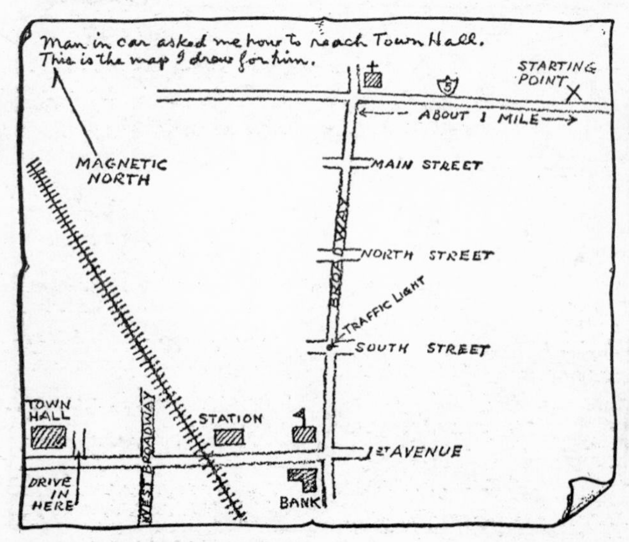

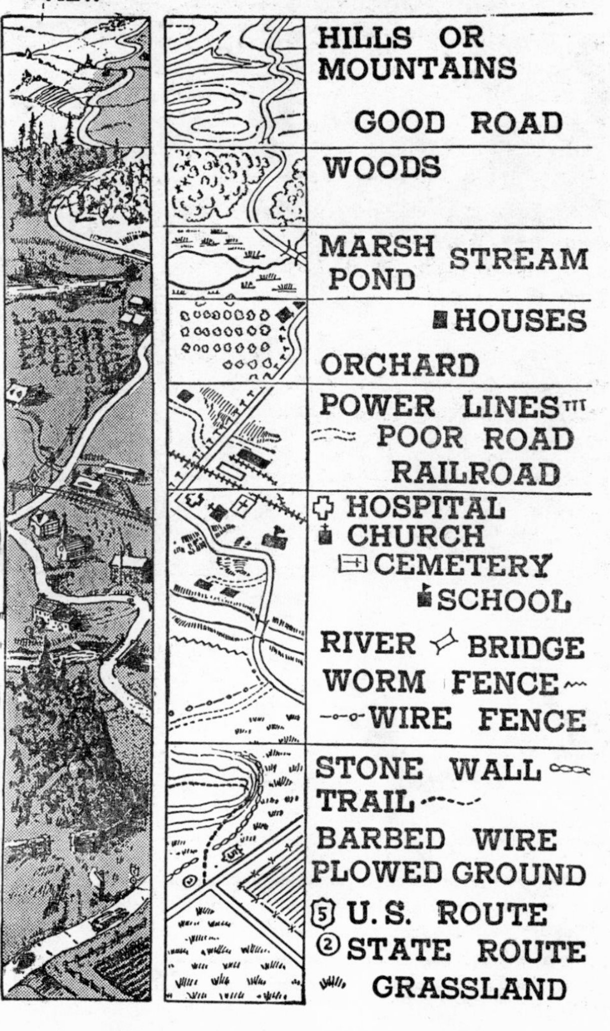

AIRPLANE VIEW
STANDARD MAP SYMBOLS
HILLS OR MOUNTAINS
GOOD ROAD
WOODS
MARSH
POND
STREAM
HOUSES
ORCHARD
POWER LINES
POOR ROAD
RAILROAD
HOSPITAL
CHURCH
CEMETERY
SCHOOL
RIVER
BRIDGE
WORM FENCE
WIRE FENCE
STONE WALL
TRAIL
BARBED WIRE
PLOWED GROUND
U.S. ROUTE
STATE ROUTE
GRASSLAND

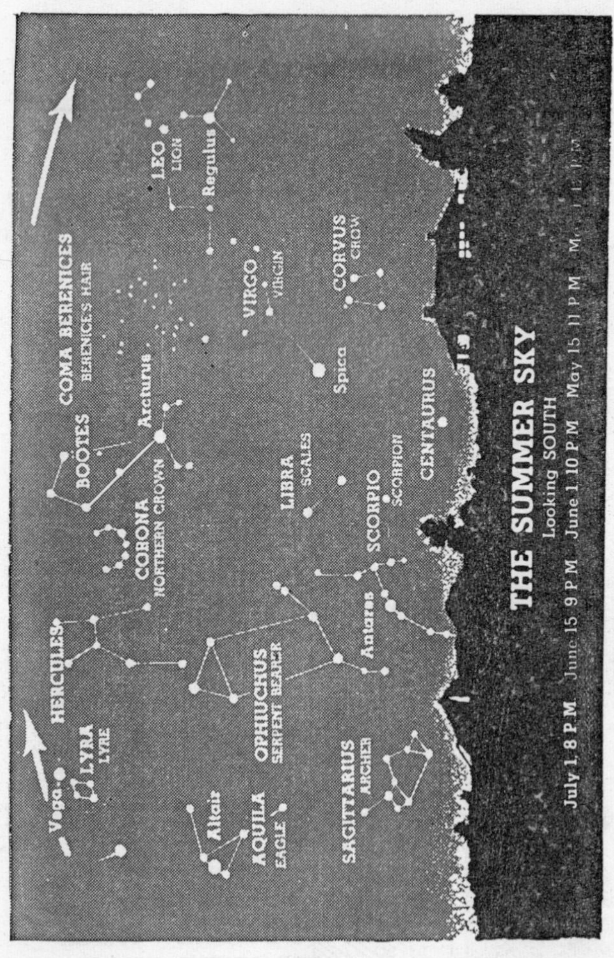

Have you ever been in a strange place at night, with no idea which direction is which? If you know a few star "friends" you need no more than a glance at the sky to get your bearings. "Oh, there's Orion coming up over there, so I'm headed east, and everything is all right." It's a good feeling!

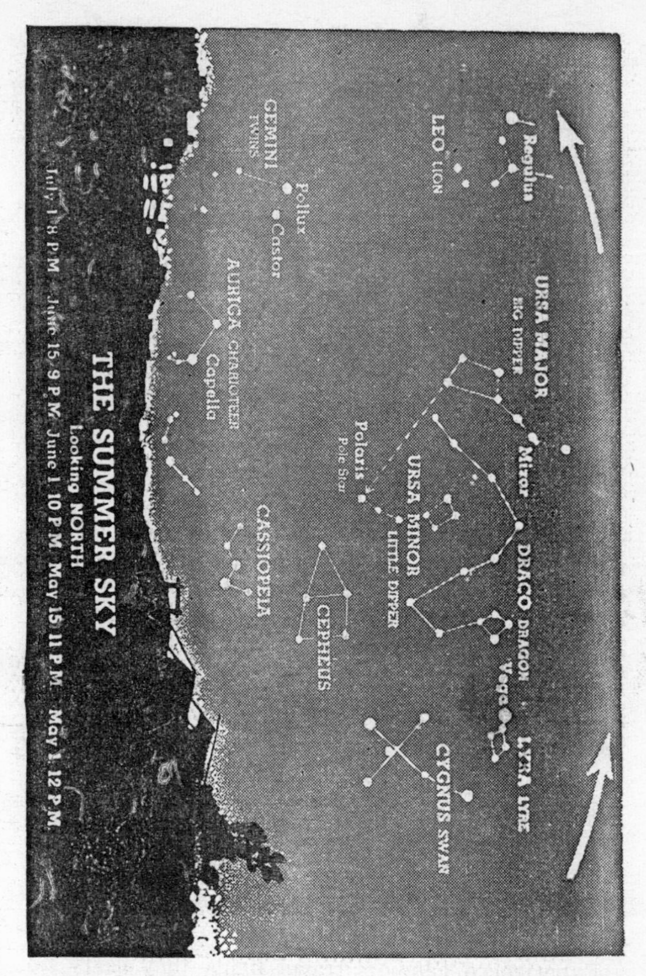

The star charts on these pages give a little idea of what the sky looks like during the summer months. If you are interested in knowing more about the stars which "cross your sky" winter and summer, you will find similar charts in the star books listed in Books to Read. It's a lot of fun to get acquainted with stars.

THE WOODSMAN'S TOOLS

CHAPTER 15

Pioneers who settled America and built homes, and cut farms and roads out of a wilderness, depended more on their axes and knives than on any other equipment except their guns. A knife and axe still are a woodsman's most useful tools.

They will help you to cut firewood, pitch a tent, make a bed, clear a trail and build camp gadgets. But you must keep them sharp and use them skillfully.

The pictures and text in this chapter can only *show* you how to use your knife and axe in the right way. To really *know* how, you must use these tools correctly on hikes and in camp. If you practice the right way from the very beginning, you will become skilled more quickly.

Experienced campers travel light—they carry no more weight than necessary. That's why the Scout belt axe and a pocket knife are best for all around Scout use. They are light and sturdy. They will do all the necessary work for general camp making.

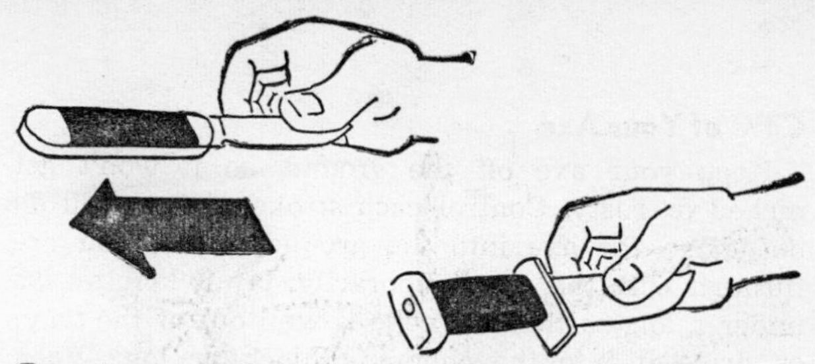

Carrying and Passing Your Knife and Axe

Carry your pocket knife closed in your pocket. If you use a sheath knife, carry it in its sheath, and be sure to wear it just back of the hip. Many outdoorsmen wear the sheath so that the lower end sticks in the right hip pocket. Several Scouts have been seriously injured by wearing a sheath on the belt in front of their body.

When passing a pocket knife to some one else, close it first or pass it as shown. When passing a sheath knife, pass it handle first.

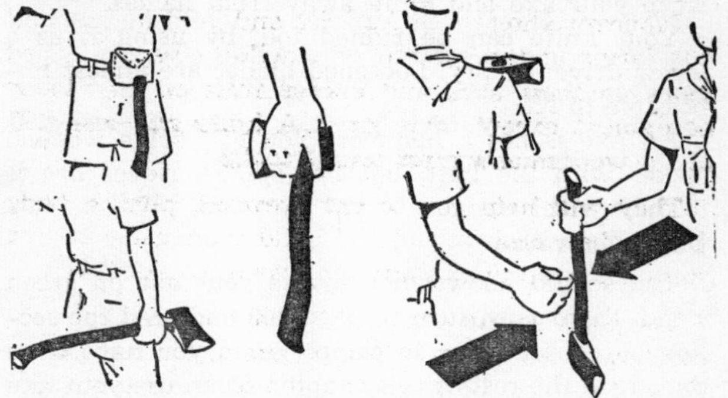

Carry an axe in a sheath in your pack or lashed to the outside. If you must carry it on your belt, wear it just back of your hip.

Carry an unsheathed axe at your side with the edge turned outward; if over your shoulder, with the edge turned away from you. Watch out for other people who may bump or rub against the edge.

If you hand your axe to some one else, pass it by the handle, with the head down and the edge outward.

Care of Your Axe

Keep your axe off the ground, so it won't get nicked or rusty. Control each stroke so that you do not drive the axe into the ground. When you are through with the axe temporarily, lay it lengthways under a log, so that the edge is well out of the way; or drive it into the chopping block or log. When through using it for a few hours, place the axe in its sheath in your tent. Don't ever leave the edge exposed so that anyone may kick it or fall on it.

Keep your axe head tight. If it has a screw wedge, keep the screw tightened. Otherwise use a hardwood wedge. You may tighten a loose head temporarily by soaking it in water for half an hour.

Fire takes the temper (hardness) out of steel. Keep your axe and knife away from flames.

Your knife can be ruined too, by using it as a screw driver or pry. Loosened blades are almost impossible to fix.

An axe is not a hammer. You can drive wooden stakes with the butt, but not spikes. Never use it to drive steel wedges.

Using Your Axe

You should know when to use your axe on green wood. Right now, turn to page 243 and read the section on conservation in camp. When you have done that, read the rest of this chapter. Then use your axe and practice whenever you can.

Like the baseball batter who stands up to the plate and keeps his eye on the ball, a skillful axeman stands squarely in front of his log and looks right at the spot where he wants his blow to fall. That is a big part of the secret of accurate chopping. Keep your eye on the ball—the spot where you are aiming each stroke of the axe.

Cut at an angle to the grain. Stand on opposite side of trunk when lopping branches.

When cutting in the woods, "clear the ground an axe-length around." An "axe-length" means the length of handle plus the length of your arm. "Around" means overhead and underneath, in front and back and on both sides. It does not mean to chop down trees in order to have a free swing at the one you want to cut. It does mean cutting bush and small branches so they will not catch your axe. Even a twig can turn axe or pull it out of your hand, so that you or someone else may be injured. Be sure there is no one standing in the line where the axe would fly if it slipped from your hand.

When cutting a sapling, bend it over at a sharp angle and cut close to the ground with a slanting stroke. Cut at an angle to the grain instead of straight across it. In trimming branches from the trunk, cut from the bottom toward the top. Do not cut into the crotch. Stand on the opposite side of the trunk.

Preparing Firewood

Hold the axe with a firm but not tense grip. Work with controlled rather than hard strokes. Control will do the job more easily and more safely than brute strength. Rest a minute if you get tired. Then you won't lose control.

When splitting dead branches or dry boards for small firewood, stand or squat close to the chopping block and use the contact method. It is much faster than free swinging and there is less chance of your being cut if your axe slips off the stick.

Place the edge of the axe against the end of the wood, so that it is parallel to the grain. Raise the wood and the axe and bring them down together on the block. Twist the wood against the axe, and the wood will usually split.

In chopping across a stick, set the blade on a slant to the grain. Raise the stick and the axe, and bring them down together on the block.

The illustrations below show this method of chopping and splitting.

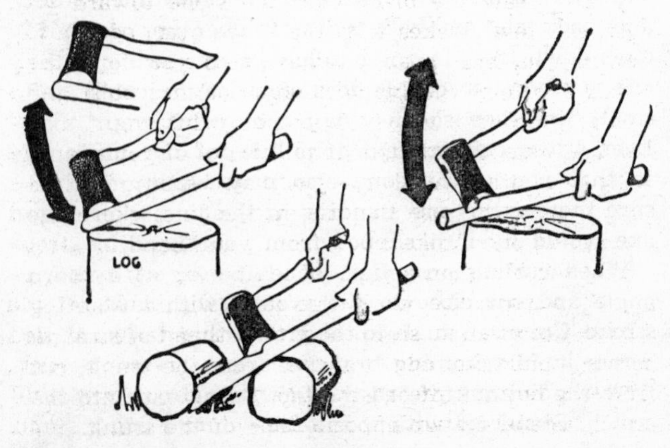

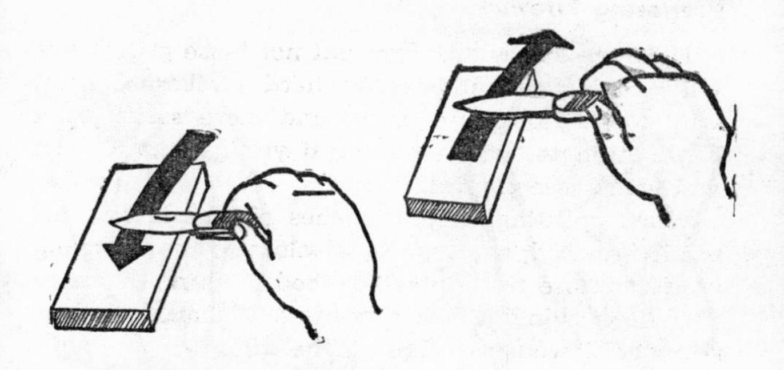

Sharpening Your Knife

Carry a combination rough and fine sharpening stone in your pack. A small, rectangular one, about four inches long is wonderful for your knife and axe. Start by using the rough side, and then the fine side. Put a few drops of oil or water on it first.

Lay the blade flat on the rough side of the stone. With the edge toward you, raise the back very slightly and draw the blade over the stone toward you. After a few strokes turn the blade over, edge away from you, and push it away from you for a few strokes. Keep the blade almost flat, or you'll get a chisel-like edge which is poor for whittling.

Continue working on one side of the blade and then the other until it begins to be sharp. Turn the stone over and use the fine side—one stroke toward you, and one stroke away from you. Finish by stropping the blade on a piece of leather or soft wood.

To remove the wire edge from the blade (if the edge becomes so sharp and thin that it has curled over) pull the edge of the blade across a stick. Sharpening a knife that is badly nicked or very dull may be started with a fine file before using a stone.

Sharpening Your Axe

Use a flat file 8–10 inches long and moderately rough. Lean the axhead against a peg driven in the ground or between a peg and a log, as pictured. Hold it steady with your foot or knee on the handle.

On a new axe only the edge needs filing. Start at the heel or toe and work to the other end. File toward and at right angles to the butt or poll (see top center of next page). Use a slightly rocking motion of the file and lift it free on return strokes. Then turn the axe around and do the other side. Finish with a sharpening stone, applying it with circular motions to both sides of the axe blade (see next page).

Before you touch the edge of an old axe, file down the fan shaped surface of the blade from a line a half inch from the edge to a point centered two inches in from the edge. Handle the file as described above but without the rocking motion. Do the same on both sides. By filing the flat of the blade and then the edge, you keep the shape of the blade so it never gets stubby and will always bite into the wood.

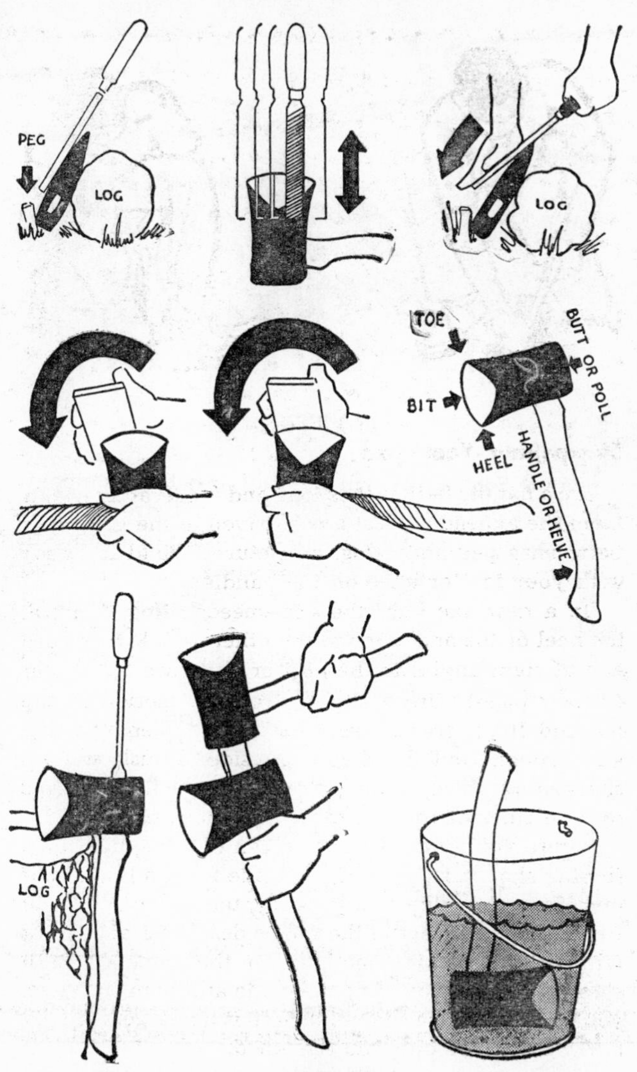
PEG
LOG
LOG
TOE
BUTT OR POLL
BIT
HEEL
HANDLE OR HELVE
LOG

FIRE BUILDING

CHAPTER 16

As a Scout, fire will be your constant companion in outdoor adventures. Whether you are on a day hike or an overnight camp, a hunting or fishing trip with Dad, or in summer camp with your Troop, camp fires will play an important part in your life. They warm you, cook your food, give you light or cast their magic spell upon you as you and your best friends gather around their glowing embers.

Finding the Place

The place to build your fire depends upon where you are, the kind of a fire you need and the weather. The nearness of wood or fuel is very important. If the weather is clear with little wind, any desirable place will do. If, however, there is rain, snow or a strong wind, try to find some natural shelter such as a rock, cliff, cave, or clump of trees or the side of a sheltered ravine.

When the place is found, scrape the ground bare of leaves, grass or any other burnable material. Take away overhanging branches which may catch fire from flying sparks.

Why a Fire Burns

Before wood will burn, it must be heated to such a temperature that it will change into a gas a little at a time. When this gas mixes with the oxygen of the air and is lit, a flame occurs and the wood is said to burn. To do this with the small flame of a match, it is necessary to have the material in extremely fine, dry pieces. Furthermore, these pieces must be very loosely arranged with a lot of air spaces.

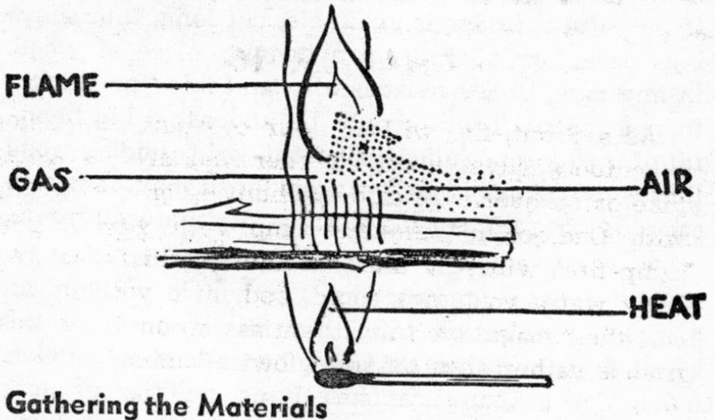

Gathering the Materials

Ballad of the Fire

"First a bunch of tinder dry as can be,
Then a little squaw wood—*dead but from a tree,*
Then some heavy firewood to make the kettle boil,
Now touch a match—then cheer and warmth reward you for your toil."

This little ballad tells exactly how to make a good fire.

Tinder is the fine material that ignites easily and produces a hot bright flame to light the fine and heavy wood. Birch bark is filled with oil and burns readily either wet or dry. The tops of dead weeds such as golden rod or wild carrot catch fire readily. The extremely fine dead branches of some trees such as hemlock take flame from a match. The bark of some of the wild grape vines and cedar trees makes excellent tinder when shredded. Some dead grasses can be used. Dry pine needles or a resin filled pine knot, burn readily. Generally dead leaves smoulder rather than burn and should **not** be used for tinder. If no natural tinder is available, cut long, thin shavings or a fuzz stick from a heavier piece of wood. In any case, tinder must be dry and fine—no thicker than a match. There should be at least a big handful of it to insure sufficient heat to light the fine wood that comes above it. In wet weather, it may be necessary to split a limb or log to get at dry material inside.

The next size of wood is often called "squaw wood." Indian squaws could gather it without an axe. It is important to gather this wood from the small dead branches on trees, because such wood is much dryer than branches lying on the ground. Branches from which the bark has fallen off burn more easily than branches with bark on them. Select squaw wood ranging from the size of a match stick to the size of your thumb. Break this wood into pieces from 12 to 24 inches in length. If small branches are not available, split some heavy limbs into fine pieces. Split wood burns more easily

If the fire is to be used to do a lot of cooking or to give light and warmth, heavy wood may be necessary. This may be cut from fallen limbs or dead trees and split to various thicknesses.

Laying the Fire

Of the many ways to lay a fire, two good methods are the tepee fire and the crisscross fire.

In the tepee fire, tinder is used as a base. Fine twigs are arranged around it to form a tepee. Split sticks are gradually increased in size and length until the fire is built to the desired size. The heavier wood is placed down wind and the fire is lit on the windward side.

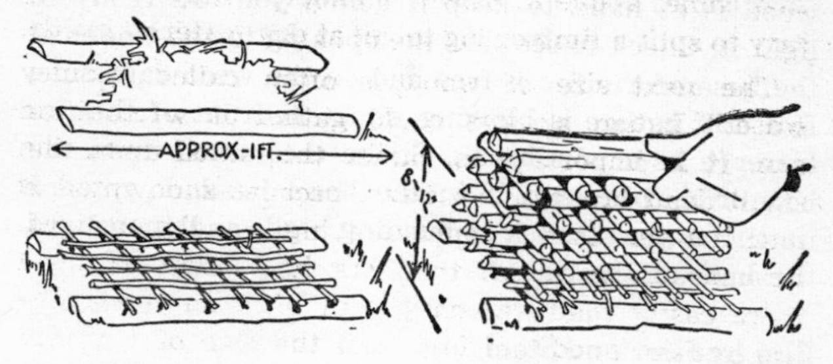

To make a crisscross fire, place two heavier pieces of wood approximately a foot long and as thick as your ankle on the ground eight or ten inches apart. Place a big handful of tinder between these sticks. Then lay fine twigs across the two heavy sticks above the tinder until the space is filled with sticks about one inch apart. Next lay slightly heavier twigs on top of the first layer at right angles to it. The third layer is of slightly heavier sticks and is placed at right angles to them. This type of fire is lit on the windward side.

TINDER KINDLING FUEL		
Tinder	*Kindling*	*Fuel*
Cedar bark, birch bark, dry pine needles, dead weed tops, milkweed and cattail floss.	Cottonwood, willow, alder, poplar, sycamore, balsam, other evergreens, soft maple.	Oaks, maples, hickories, gums, birch, beeches, elm, ash, mesquite.

The Indian is supposed to have said, "White man make-um big fire—no get-um close . . . ugh! Indian make-um small fire, get-um close, heap plenty warm . . . how!" This is a good idea. An armful of wood and a small fire are all that is needed to take care of most cooking.

Lighting the Fire

After the fire is carefully laid and a good stack of wood is at hand to keep it going, you are ready to light it. Check to see that the opening to the tinder at the base of the fire is free and on the windward side. If a stiff breeze is blowing, squat in front of the fire to serve as a windbreak. Strike the match upon the box or a rock, cup it in the hand head downward until the match stick is burning well, and then light the base of the tinder.

Fire by Flint and Steel

Our pioneer ancestors depended upon flint and steel to fire their long-barreled rifles and make their fires.

A buckskin bag containing a piece of flint, a piece of steel, some charred cloth and some tinder, were regular equipment for the men who blazed new trails through our wilderness. Today this method of making fire can be used by every Scout.

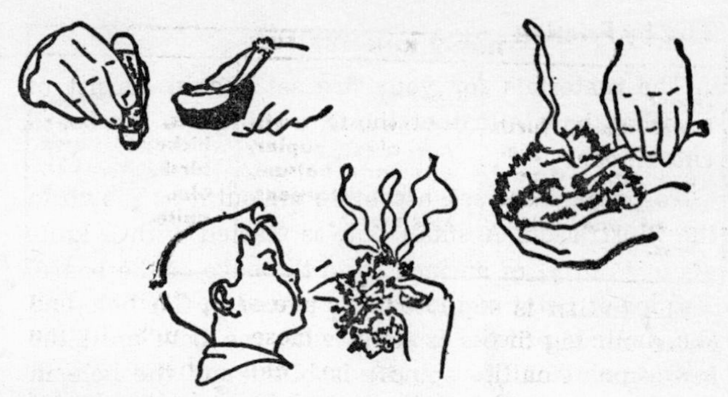

Strike spark, hold smoldering wick in tinder—and blow!

For equipment, you will need a piece of flint, or any rock harder than steel; an old file or similar piece of steel, a charred wick or some charred cloth and some tinder. The charred cloth is made as follows: set a piece of linen or outing flannel on fire; after it is burning well, smother it in an old coffee can with an air tight lid. The lid is removed when the fire has completely gone out. The black flakes of cloth will readily catch and hold a spark when needed.

To make a fire, place a handful of tinder on the ground with a few pieces of charred cloth on top of it. Place one end of the file on the tinder. The file slopes, so that when struck a glancing blow by the flint, the sparks fly downward onto the charred cloth. A little practice will determine the proper angle for the file and the part of the flint to give best results. One blow is usually sufficient to catch the spark.

As soon as the charred cloth is smouldering, cup the tinder around it and blow the whole mass into flame.

Fire by Friction

The materials for your fire set should consist of a socket, bow, a leather thong, a spindle, a fire board and tinder.

To prepare the set, assemble the outfit as shown in the illustration. A small hole is started with a knife about ½ to ¾ of an inch from the edge of the board. The lower point of the drill is placed in this hole and the drilling process is done with the bow until the lower point of the spindle is blunt and the hole in the fireboard is the diameter of the spindle. A V-shaped notch, wider at the base, is now cut from the edge of the fireboard to the center of the hole. This slot will let the hot powder, formed by drilling, fall into the nest of tinder.

To make a fire, place the tinder under the notch of the fireboard. Place your foot lengthwise on the board; hold the socket in your left hand, with your left wrist held firmly against your left leg. Press downward on the spindle to hold it in the hole in the fireboard. Make the strokes of the bow smooth, regular and the full length of the bow. When smoke begins to rise, gradually increase the pressure on the spindle and quicken the stroke until the smoke pours from the notch. This is the sign that a spark has formed in the notch.

Carefully remove the spindle. Gently blow into the notch until you see the spark. Lift the fireboard and tinder together, cup the tinder around the spark and blow gently at first and then harder as the spark grows. Remove the board only when the spark is catching hold in the tinder. Keep on blowing until the tinder bursts into flame.

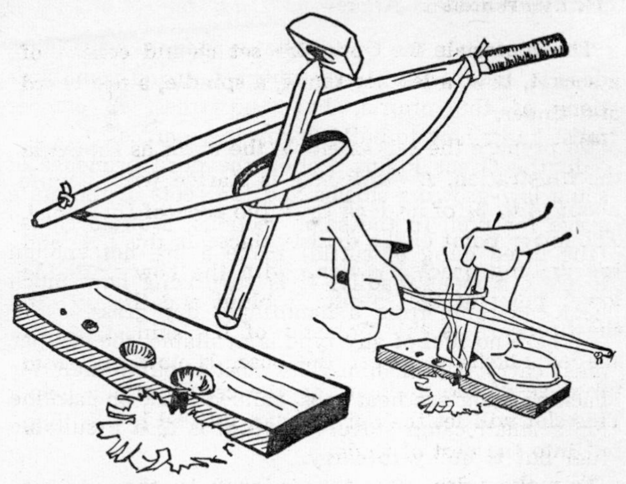

Fire by friction is another way to start a fire in an emergency. Make your own set.

The best trees for making fire sets are quaking aspen or poplar, large-toothed aspen, cottonwood, willow, white poplar, balsam, white cedar, red cedar, elm, linden, balsa, Arizona yucca and cypress. Some roots are superior to the limb or trunk wood of the tree. Elm, willow and cottonwood are listed among these.

Tinder may be made from red or white cedar bark, or the inner bark of chestnut, elm or cottonwood. The bark is pounded by a mallet or club until pulpy and then rolled between the hands until fluffy to get rid of the granular particles. Some fine grasses make good tinder. The down of cattail, milkweed, or the fluffy tops of dead asters or goldenrod, will serve as tinder. Some soft ropes when unravelled and fluffed, produce good tinder.

Fire in Woodless Areas

Such areas in the United States as the Great Plains, deserts, mountains above timber line and some sections of the prairie, have no trees. A camper must know how to build fire in these areas.

In the Great Plains section the dead branches of some low-growing shrubs and the roots of mesquite serve for fuel. In the same sections "Buffalo chips" (the dried dung of cattle) make a fire hot enough to cook a meal readily. It is surprising how much heat can come from a handful of dry grass.

Where no fuel of any type is available, the camper must carry it with him. The most popular fuels for back packing are heat tabs, canned heat, or gasoline for a small camp stove. Charcoal is also a suitable fuel but is bulky to carry.

Types of Fires

Fires are built for a purpose. They are used for cooking, for baking, heating, lighting, for drying clothing, or for companionship. The types vary with location as well as purpose. A good Scout and outdoorsman learns how to make several of the more common types, so that he may feel at home in any situation.

The Hunter's Fire

This is a cooking fire. Two small logs from three to six inches in diameter are laid side by side quartering into or at right angles to the wind. A space slightly smaller than the diameter of the cooking utensils separates these logs. The logs can be laid at an angle to one another, to accommodate several different sizes of frying pans or kettles at the same time. If the fire is for one or two meals, any logs will

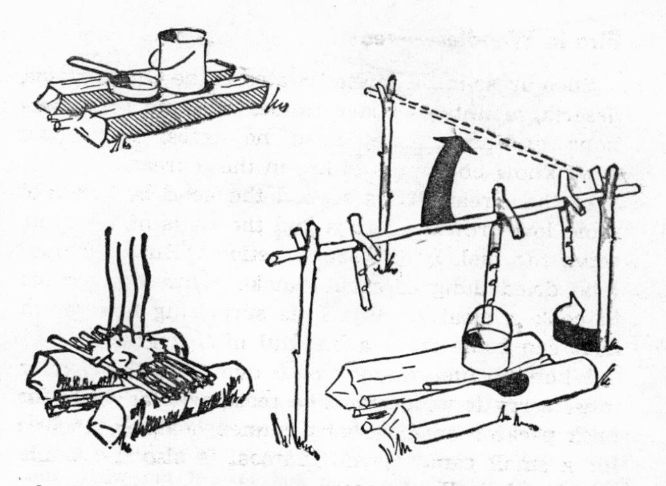

do—even those that are partially decayed. If the fire is to be used for several days, green logs will probably last the full time, without replacement. Logs should be flattened on the top side, so that the utensils will be less likely to upset. Kindling the fire the full length of the logs, makes it possible to cook several things at once. The fire may be controlled by use of a stick, or a rock for a chuck under the log on the windward side. If the log is raised, the air circulates underneath to fan the fire into an intense heat. The heat will die down if the log is lowered to the ground. A slow fire will result from scraping earth or sand against the outside of both logs to cut off all draft.

Garbage can be quickly disposed of by drying it on a grill made of a few sticks across the fire logs. When completely dried, it is dropped into the fire, where it will burn without odor.

The Hunter's Fire may be rapidly changed into a baking fire by driving stakes on the outside of one of the fire logs and rolling the other on top. When logs are not available, this type of fire may be made by arranging sod or rocks in a way similar to the two logs.

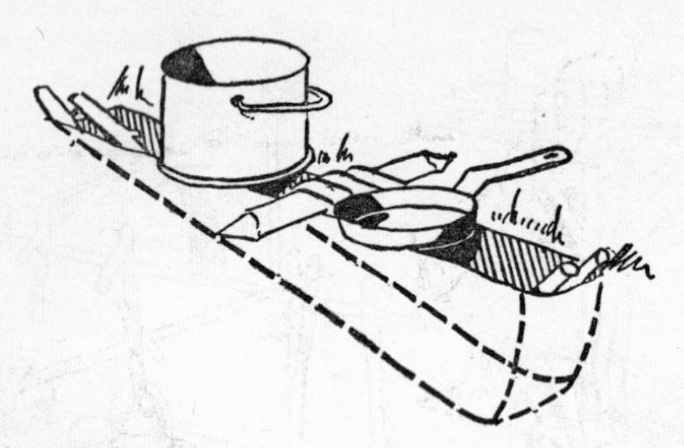

The Trench Fire

The Trench Fire is a cooking fire. It is made by digging a narrow trench that is eight to ten inches deep at one end and slopes up to ground level. The trench is dug so that it points into the wind, with the deep end toward the wind. The width of the trench is slightly narrower than the diameter of the cooking utensils. The fire is kindled in the deep end and is stoked from either end. The heat for cooking is controlled by location of the utensil on the trench. The heat is most intense directly over the fire. The fire can be controlled by placing a rock or pack as a windbreak on the windward side or by throwing dirt or sand on the bed of coals. Garbage is dried for burning by placing it on a few green twigs laid across the trench after the cooking is completed. Dishwater is poured into loose dirt at one end of the trench before filling it up at the end of the meal.

The trench fire is used when logs and rocks are not available, or in a situation where there is a strong, steady wind.

Fire in the Hole

This fire is good for windy or treeless country, and may be used for cooking and baking. It is made by digging a conical hole fourteen inches in diameter and from 14 to 18 inches deep. A good fire is made to heat the soil and produce a bed of coals in the bottom of the pit for cooking. The fire is fed by throwing short pieces of wood into the pit, or by placing

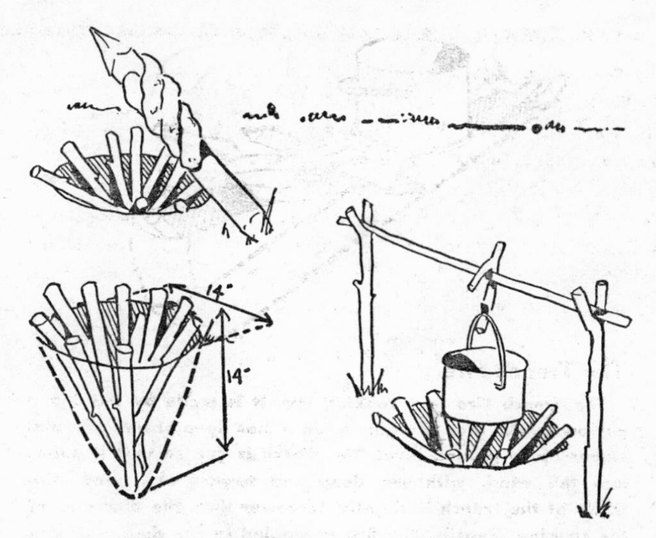

long sticks end first into the hole so that they will fall in as the ends burn off. The cooking is done over the edge of the hole, on two green sticks laid across the hole, or by using a crane.

A one-pot meal consisting of meat, potatoes, onions and carrots may be cooked by placing a pot with a dirt-tight lid on the bed of coals in the bottom of the hole. It is then completely covered with dirt. When the pot is dug out two hours later, the meal will be cooked. Only a slight amount of water need be used if the lid is tight fitting.

Fire for Reflector Baking

This is a baking and heating fire. It is made by building a "reflector" of logs, rocks or sod. The log reflector is built by driving two heavy stakes into the ground, both leaning slightly away from the reflector oven. Logs are then stacked horizontally one on top of the other, against the stakes. Green logs will last longer, but if these are not available, the logs may be covered with dirt, sod or mud.

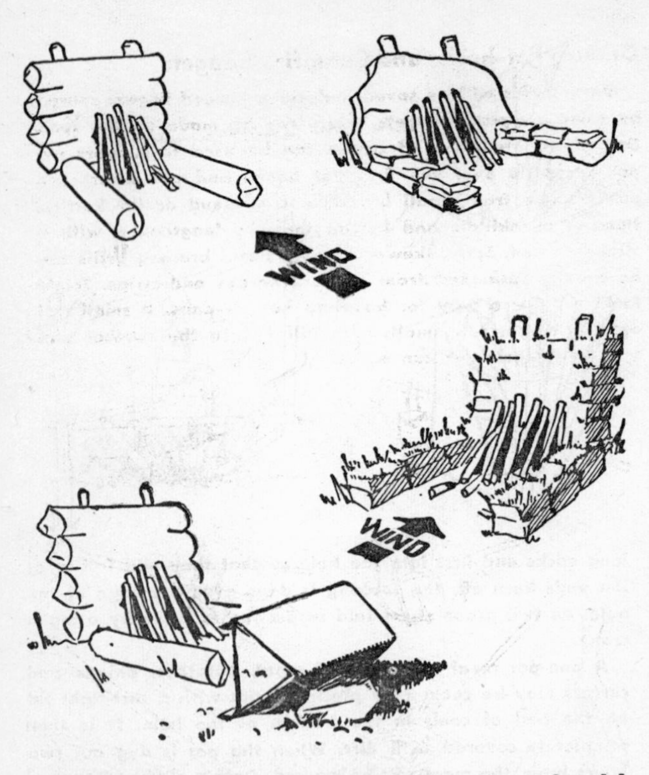

A reflector may be made quickly by propping a flat slab of rock on edge.

The fire for the reflector is built by standing the firewood on end against the back logs or stone.

To bake with the reflector, the oven is placed close enough to the fire to cause it to sizzle when a bit of water is flipped on it. This is just the right temperature to bake biscuits, toast bread or bake fish. Meat may be broiled by suspending it on a string or wire in front of the reflector. Twist on a pointed stick may be baked by placing it perpendicularly in front of the fire.

Cranes, Pot-hooks and Campfire Gadgets

Many meals will be saved and many burned fingers spared by using campfire gadgets, which can be made on the spot. One of several types of cranes can be used to support the pot or kettle over the fire. Pot hooks and pot lifters are easily made from small branches to suspend or lift kettles. Handles on skillets and kettles may be lengthened with a stick of wood. Spits, skewers, toasters and broiling grills can be readily fashioned from green branches and twigs. Triple forks provide a way for handling hot pie-pans. A small roll of wire and a few small nails will add to the number and type of gadgets you can make.

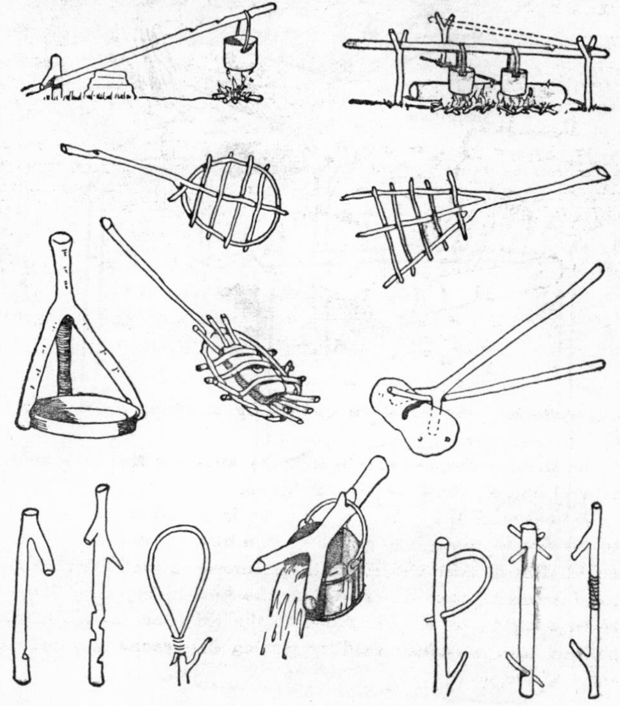

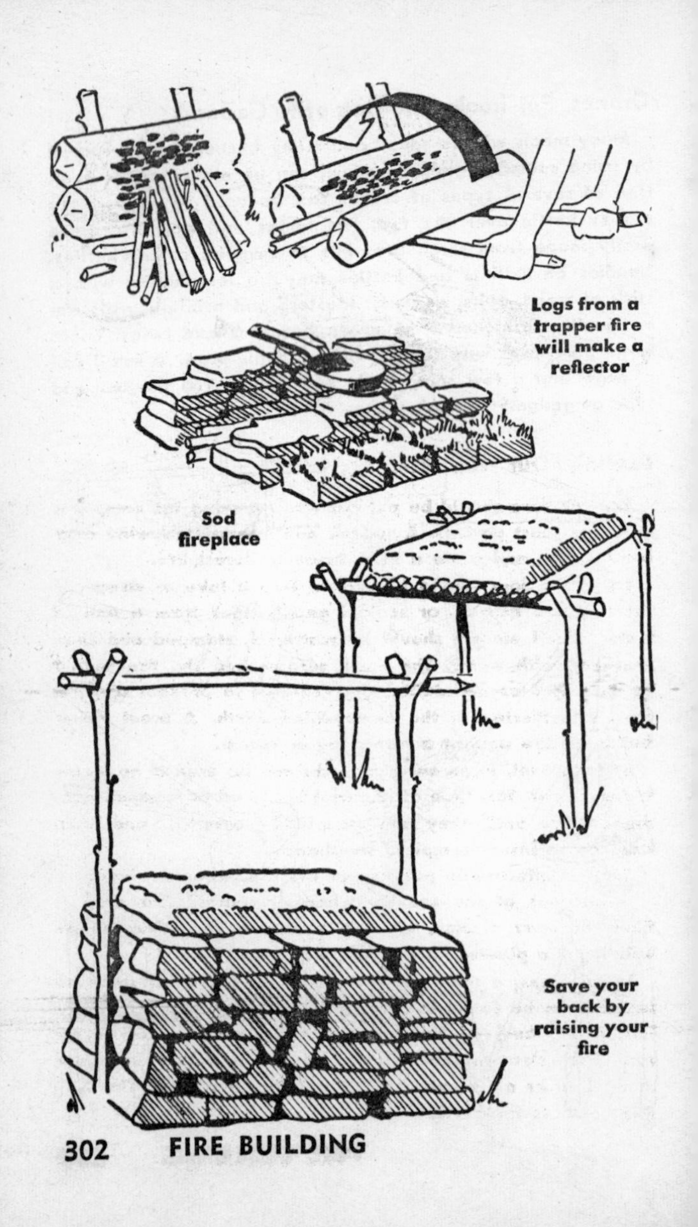

Logs from a trapper fire will make a reflector

Sod fireplace

Save your back by raising your fire

Putting Out the Fire

The campfire should be put out when leaving the campsite, even for short periods. A sudden and unexpected wind may blow sparks and cause a field, brush or forest fire.

Large fire logs should be thrown into a lake or stream if there is one nearby, or soaked on all sides from a pail of water. Small embers should be scattered, stamped and then drenched with water. The earth surrounding the fire should be saturated as an additional precaution to prevent a spark from smouldering in the humus-filled earth. A Scout never builds his fire against a rotten log or stump.

Sand, gravel, loose earth or rocks can be used if no water is convenient. This type of material is kicked or scooped over the embers until they are completely covered, and then stamped to insure complete smothering.

Snow is effective in putting out the fire, when available.

In sections of the country where a cleared fire area is likely to start erosion, cut and stack the sod cover before building fire places and carefully replace it later.

In all cases, a good Scout attempts to leave his campsite better than he found it. Burn all garbage and paper, burn, flatten and bury all tin cans, and erase all signs of human use. If the clean-up job is one of which you are proud, leave crossed sticks of unequal length over the dead fire. The long one points to the north.

Miscellaneous Suggestions

Always carry a good supply of matches—some in your pockets for immediate use, some in a waterproof matchbox, and a few waterproofed matches in each piece of duffle you carry.

Matches may be waterproofed by dipping them one at a time in hot paraffin or candle grease. They may also be waterproofed by dipping them in fingernail polish.

A waterproof matchbox is a good addition to your camp equipment. Match boxes are now made with a piece of metal attached to the side that throws a spark when scraped with the point of a knife. This spark is so hot that it will light cotton, milkweed down, or similar tinder.

Fire Wisdom

1. Start your fire with dead, soft wood—'dead but from a tree.' Standing wood is dry wood in most places.
2. Gather enough wood to cook your entire meal before you light the fire.
3. Split wood burns more readily than round—for quick burning all wood should be split.
4. Fires are controlled by draft. Lay the fire so you can control it—more air, more heat; less air, less heat.
5. Use soft woods for flames—for boiling, searing, quick frying and reflector oven baking. Soft woods are best for starting fires.
6. Hard woods make lasting coals for heating, broiling, stewing, slow frying and frying-pan baking.
7. Do not use shale and rocks from streambeds or along the seashore—they are likely to explode when heated.

CAMP COOKING

CHAPTER 17

First a bunch of tinder dry as it can be,
Then a little squaw wood—*dead but from a tree,*
Next some heavy firewood to make the kettle boil,
Now tasty food and pleasing warmth reward you for your toil.

—paraphrased from Ernest Thompson Seton's *Ballad of Fire.*

Every good outdoorsman becomes a good cook. He has to. It's a man-sized job. Most foresters, surveyors, mining engineers are good cooks as well as vigorous self-reliant woodsmen. Kit Carson, Davy Crockett, and Daniel Boone were famous cooks on the trail. A Patrol cooking its own meals is playing one of the most fascinating games in Scouting.

How to Go About Learning to Cook

Every time you eat a dish try to guess just what the ingredients are, and how it was flavored. Help cook a meal at home occasionally so that you learn the little secrets about preparing and cooking the various types of food. Watch your mother make pie and cake.

Making Your Cook Kit

A good cook kit is the first necessity for successful cooking on the trail. It must be large enough to take care of your needs but small and light enough to be convenient. It must contain all of those things that will be needed on a hiking or camping trip. This will include a skillet or frying pan, a pie pan, enough pots, kettles, buckets and pans to prepare a good meal all at one time; small airtight cans for flour, sugar, chocolate mix, tea or coffee, salt and pepper shakers which can be closed; a cup, plate, fork and spoon. All of these things should fit together as compactly as possible and slip into cloth bags with drawstrings.

A trip to the nearest five and ten cent store will usually give you a good start on your kit. The rest perhaps can be picked up around home. For lightness, all parts should be of aluminum except the skillet and cup. An eight-inch skillet of sheet iron with a folding handle fills the bill for a single person. There should be at least two pails with lids. The larger should hold approximately two quarts, and the other should fit inside it. The pans should be of the deep type with sloping sides. There should be at least two of these, in addition to the eight-inch pie pan which doubles as a cover for the skillet for cooking, and a plate for eating.

Square or rectangular airtight cans are preferable, since they pack more snugly. You may get these at

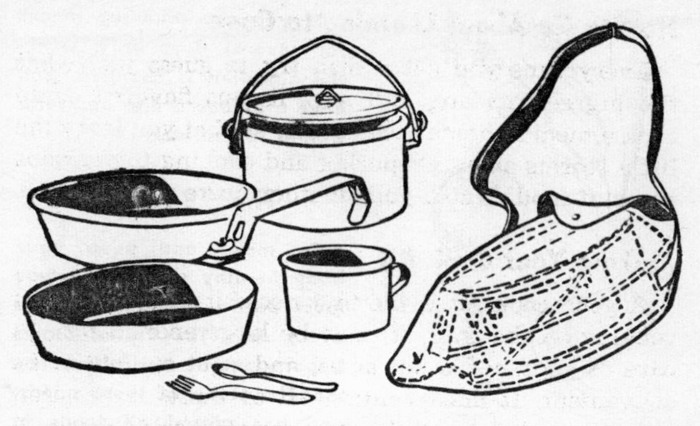

A personal cookkit has a fry pan, small pot, plate, cup and fork and spoon in it

home. Watch the cupboard shelves for the type wanted, and get them when they are empty. These cans should be metal and hold approximately a cup.

As salt rusts tin containers, make a good salt and pepper shaker from sections of a bamboo fishing pole. Some small tooth powder cans with chromium tops are also satisfactory.

Planning the Menu

If you are to cook just one or two meals out, planning the menu is easy. Just look over the pantry shelves to see what is available, and ask permission to take what you need. Take a pencil and a piece of cardboard and write down what you want for each meal. This will include a meat, two vegetables, bread, butter, a drink and dessert—which is usually fruit. As the foods are obtained in the right quantity, they are wrapped, placed in the pack and checked off the list. Salt, pepper, sugar, cocoa and the things that may be forgotten, should be already in your cook kit.

If you are planning menus for several days or a week, the situation is changed. You have a balanced diet and total weight to consider.

The "Basic 7"

To make and keep your body healthy and strong, you must eat a variety of foods every day. The United States Department of Agriculture has made a study of these needs, and has placed all foods in seven groups which they call the "Basic 7." These groups are given here. To plan your menus, check against the chart.

1—Vegetables — green, leafy and yellow—one big helping or more a day—some raw, some cooked

2—Oranges, Tomatoes, Grapefruit—one of these at least once a day

3—Potatoes, Apples, Bananas—or other vegetables or fruits every day

4—Milk—at least a pint a day —or cheese or evaporated or dried milk

5—Meat, Poultry, Fish—one or more servings daily. Eggs —at least 3 or 4 a week

6—Bread and Cereal—enriched bread, enriched flour, whole grain products, macaroni, spaghetti

7—Fats, Sweets—and seasonings as you like them

BALANCED HIKE MENUS for ONE PERSON for 3 DAYS

FIGURES INDICATE IN WHICH BASIC 7 GROUP THE FOOD BELONGS

BREAKFAST

1ST DAY		2ND DAY		3RD DAY	
Bacon		Oatmeal	(6)	Bacon	
Eggs	(5)	Scrambled Eggs	(5)	Pancakes	(6)
Orange	(2)	Orange	(2)	Stewed Apricots	(3)
Bread	(6)	Cocoa	(4)	Cocoa	(4)
Butter	(7)	Bread	(6)	Butter	(7)
Cocoa	(4)	Butter	(7)		

LUNCH

Chicken noodle soup		Pea soup	(5)	Potatoe soup	(3)
Sliced Ham	(5)	Sandwiches		Sandwiches	
Tomatoes	(2)	Cheese	(4)	Cheese	(4)
Bread	(6)	Peanut Butter	(5)	Peanut Butter	(5)
Butter	(7)	Bread	(6)	Bread	(6)
Milk	(4)	Butter	(7)	Butter	(7)
2 Cookies		Raisins	(3)	Candy Bar	

DINNER

Stewed beef	(5)	Corned beef	(5)	Ham	(5)
2 Potatoes	(3)	Cabbage	(1)	Fried potatoes	(3)
2 Carrots	(1)	2 Potatoes	(3)	Green beans	(1)
2 Onions small	(3)	2 Onions	(3)	Coleslaw	(2)
Cole slaw	(2)	Peanut Butter	(5)	Twist	(6)
Bread	(6)	Bread	(6)	Butter	(7)
Butter	(7)	Milk	(4)	Milk	(4)
Milk	(4)	Butterscotch pudding		Chocolate cream desert	
Dried Apricots	(3)				

Plan the menu for each camp meal well ahead of time. Then make a list of the different ingredients that you will need for the entire trip. Then determine which kind of foods are best for your needs—fresh, dried, dehydrated, canned. The chart on page 310 shows the comparative weights of the items included in the above menus.

BUYING LIST AND CHECK LIST SHOWING COMPARATIVE WEIGHTS BETWEEN FRESH, CANNED FOODS AND DEHYDRATED FOODS

(F)—FRESH (C)—CANNED
(D)—DRIED (DH)—DEHYDRATED

Article	No. of times it occurs	Total Amount	Heavy Weight	Light Weight
Bacon	II	½ lb.	8 oz.	8 oz.
Eggs	II	4	(F) 8 oz.	(DH) 2 oz.
Cocoa	III	¼ lb.	4 oz.	4 oz.
Bread	~~IIII~~ II	1 loaf (18 slices)	16 oz.	16 oz.
Butter	~~IIII~~ III	¼ lb.	4 oz.	4 oz.
Orange	II	2	(F) 12 oz.	(F) 12 oz.
Oatmeal	I	2 Tbsp.	1 oz.	1 oz.
Prunes	I	5	1 oz.	(D) 1 oz.
Pancake flour	I	½ cup	3 oz.	3 oz.
Apricots	II	10 apricots	2 oz.	(D) 2 oz.
Chicken noodle soup	I	1 pkg. or can	(C) 12 oz.	(DH) 1 oz.
Ham	II	½ lb.	8 oz.	8 oz.
Tomatoes	I	1 tomato	(F) 6 oz.	(F) 6 oz.
Cookies	I	2 cookies	2 oz.	2 oz.
Pea soup	I	1 pkg. or can	(C) 12 oz.	(DH) 1 oz.
Cheese	II		4 oz.	4 oz.
Raisins	I	2 oz.	2 oz.	(D) 2 oz.
Potato soup	I	1 pkg. or can	(C) 12 oz.	(DH) 1 oz.
Peanut Butter	III	¼ lb.	8 oz.	8 oz.
Candy bar	I	1	2 oz.	2 oz.
Beef	I	½ lb.	(F) 8 oz.	(F) 8 oz.
Potatoes	III	6	(F) 32 oz.	(DH) 4 oz.
Carrots	I	2	(F) 8 oz.	(DH) 1 oz.
Onions	II	7	(F) 14 oz.	(DH) 2 oz.
Cabbage	III	1 small head	(F) 24 oz.	(DH) 2 oz.
Milk	IIII	2 quarts	(C) 32 oz.	(DH) 8 oz.
Corned Beef	I	1 can	(C) 12 oz.	(C) 12 oz.
Green beans	I	1 small can	(F) 12 oz.	(DH) 1 oz.
Dessert	II	1 pkg.	2 oz.	2 oz.
Biscuit flour	I	1 cup	6 oz.	6 oz.
Mayonnaise for cole slaw	II	2 oz.	2 oz.	2 oz.
			Total 279 oz. or 17¼ lbs.	136 oz. or 8½ lbs.

Milk for the oatmeal, mayonnaise for the cole slaw, and an onion for the green beans are "hidden" needs that do not appear in the menu but are included in the check list above. Salt, pepper, flour and sugar are not included here as they are part of your regular cooking kit.

Check list for menus on page 309

Fresh and Raw Vegetables and Fruits

By "fresh," is meant just the way they came from the garden or orchard. If used reasonably soon, fresh fruits and vegetables are the best. "Raw" means uncooked.

Dried Vegetables and Fruits

Most of the moisture has been removed from dried products by drying in the sun or at moderate temperature. These foods are lighter in weight and more compact than fresh. They should be packed in an airtight container. Soak in water to restore moisture. These are raw foods, and after soaking they should be cooked the same as the fresh product. They are convenient and desirable for camping trips. Dried beans, peas, peaches, apricots and prunes are examples of this type.

Dehydrated Foods

All of the water has been extracted from dehydrated food by heat and vacuum. When completely dehydrated, the food usually weighs about one tenth of its original weight. When stored in moisture-proof containers, these foods will keep indefinitely. Their chief advantage is lightness in weight. They require no peeling or preparation, but must be cooked. Examples of dehydrated foods are potatoes, beets, cabbage, onions, soups, etc.

Canned Foods

These foods are cooked and vacuum packed. They are excellent in quality but heavy to carry, as they are packed in water and syrups. Their advantages are rapid, sure fire preparation and good flavor. They keep indefinitely if not opened or permitted to freeze. The disadvantages are bulk and weight. They are suitable for short trips. *Canned goods are not* to be used in meeting the Cooking requirements, as they are not raw foods.

Evaporated and Powdered Milk

Evaporated milk is canned milk, and if diluted when opened with an equal amount of water, is the equivalent of fresh milk, and may be drunk or used in cooking as fresh milk. Powdered milk may be mixed with water to make the equivalent of fresh milk. Use ¼ pound of dried milk powder to 1 quart of water for 1 quart of milk. Dried milk is convenient to carry and saves bulk, in weight, eight to one. It is mixed most easily by placing the powder on top of the right amount of cold water in a jar or can with a tight-fitting lid, and then shaking it.

Cooking by Yourself

It's fun to be able to cook a tasty meal over the open fire by yourself. Success depends upon three things; proper packing before leaving home, careful preparation before lighting the fire, continuous attention to the cooking while it is on the fire.

Do a Good Job of Packing

Packing is important. In addition to the necessary number of pots, pans, kettles, salt, pepper, sugar and flour, you should study your menus to be sure that some of those things that are not listed, such as grease for frying an egg, ingredients for salad dressing, syrup for pancakes, etc., are not forgotten. You will also need a piece of canvas or cloth to spread on

Get everything ready for cooking the complete meal before lighting the fire.

the ground while preparing food and eating, to help keep things clean. A trail tent or a light tarp to rig a cook shelter in case of rain, is desirable. Matches are necessary to light the fire. A pair of gloves is useful in handling hot pans. Make a check list so you won't forget any important items.

Food cooking over a camp fire requires constant watching. Meat must be turned, to brown it evenly and to keep it from burning. Skillets and pots must be moved if they get too hot. Food must be stirred regularly. Some foods must be cooked slowly—others rapidly. All must be seasoned.

Kitchen Police

While you are eating, heat water for washing and scalding the dishes. Dry and burn garbage at one end of the fire. If no baking is done, the total time for fire building, cooking, cleaning up and repacking should not exceed one hour for the average meal.

Cooking with a Buddy

When two or more people work together, organization is required. This is true when you cook with your buddy. One of you becomes the cook for the meal and the other becomes the assistant or "bull" cook as they say in the North Woods. The cook is responsible for putting out the ground cloth, unpacking the food, cooking and serving the meal.

The "bull" cook gathers the wood, builds the fire, gets the water, sets the table, cuts the bread, and does any other chores that the cook may need. He is the helper to the cook, so that the cook may give his undivided attention to preparing the meal. At the next meal the cook and "bull" cook exchange jobs.

Table of Measurements

Dash........a few grains—less than ⅛ teaspoon
Teaspoon....amount held in a teaspoon
Tablespoon...three teaspoonfuls
1 cup........16 tablespoonfuls
1 pint.......2 cups

All measurements are level. Draw a knife or stick across the top to be sure your salt, flour or sugar is level with the top of the spoon.

Cooking Terms and Definitions

BAKE ....To cook by dry heat, usually in an oven.

BATTER ....A half liquid mixture of flour, water, thin enough to pour.

BOIL ....To cook in water that is hot enough to bubble vigorously.

BROIL ....To cook in intense heat.

CREAM ....To thicken, by adding a liquid made of flour and water and boiling until smooth.

CUBE ....To cut into even-sided pieces.

DICE ....To cut into small cubes.

DOUGH ....A mixture of flour, water, seasoning, etc., so thick and heavy that it can be rolled.

FIRE

Hot ....The flames or hot bed of coals to cause rapid cooking.

Moderate ....The part of the fire that will cause moderate cooking.

Slow ....The part of fire that gives just enough heat to cook slowly.

FRY ....To cook in fat or grease.

GRILL ....A wire or green branch frame to hold meat while cooking.

PAN-BROIL ....To cook uncovered in hot skillet.

PAR-BOIL ....To cook in boiling water until half done.

ROAST ....To cook uncovered in oven without added moisture.

SOAK ....To cover and let stand in water.

SPIT ....A long, pointed green stick to hold meat for cooking.

STEEP ....Soak in hot water.

STIR ....

Constantly ....To mix without stopping.

Regularly ....To mix every minute or so.

Occasionally ......To mix every 3 or 4 minutes.

RECIPES

You may choose your "trail" meals from the following recipes which have been prepared to *help you* to meet your Second and First Class Cooking Requirements. You must use fresh or raw foods. This means that you may not use canned or partially cooked vegetables or "weiners," bologna, or any of the ready-to-eat meats.

Fruits

Fruits are an important part of our diet, as they supply vitamins, minerals, sugars, and roughage having a laxative action. Fruit may be used with breakfast or as a dessert with the luncheon or the evening meal. When fresh fruit is on hand, it is washed and eaten as it is. On longer trips where weight and space are important, dried fruits are more practical. The following suggestions will help you cook them in camp.

Prunes: Serving, 4 to 8 per person, depending on size. Preparation: Soak overnight, if possible, to reduce cooking time. Cover with water; add 2 teaspoonfuls of sugar per serving, simmer until swelled and cook until skins start to split, stirring occasionally. Continue cooking about fifteen minutes, until syrup over prunes thickens. A few drops of lemon juice and a bit of lemon rind add to the flavor. Serve hot or cold.

Dried Peaches: Serving, 2 to 4 halves per person. Preparation: Soak overnight if possible, to reduce cooking time. Cover with water, add 2 teaspoonfuls sugar per serving and simmer about fifteen minutes until tender. Stir occasionally. Peaches should be covered with a thick syrup when done. Serve hot or cold.

Dried Apricots: Serving, 4 to 8 per person. Preparation: Soak overnight if possible. Cook the same as dried peaches, but *double* the amount of sugar.

Dried Apples: Serving, ¼ cup dried apples will make one good serving when cooked.
Preparation: Soak overnight if possible. Cover with water and simmer. Apples swell as they cook so more water must be added. Cook until tender or mushy, thirty minutes. The flavor is improved by the addition of a dash of cinnamon and a lump of butter.

Cereals

Dry cereals are fine for permanent camps, but are too bulky for the trail. There is nothing that starts the day better, particularly if there is a long hike ahead or cold weather to face, than a big helping of hot oatmeal, cornmeal mush, or a wheat cereal.

Oatmeal: Serving, one person—3 tablespoonfuls.
Preparation: Use quick oats. Sift 3 heaping tablespoons of oatmeal slowly into one cup of boiling water, salted to taste (about ½ teaspoonful.) Stir constantly. Boil vigorously for 3 minutes. Remove and serve with milk and sugar.

Cornmeal Mush: Serving for one person—3 tablespoonfuls.
Preparation: Mix 3 tablespoons of cornmeal with ½ cup cold water. Stir this cornmeal mixture into one cup of boiling water salted to taste (about ½ teaspoonful). Boil and stir constantly for five minutes. Set on edge of fire and let simmer for 15 to 20 minutes more. Stir occasionally. Add a lump of butter the size of an English walnut to improve flavor. Serve hot with sugar and milk.

Meats

Meats supply the body with fat and protein, which furnish energy and build tissue. For the strenuous activities of camp life, you should have meat or its equivalent at least twice a day.

Bacon: Serving, 2 to 4 slices.
Preparation: Put in cold pan, fry slowly, pouring off grease into a container as it accumulates; turn slices regularly until brown or crisp as desired.

Broiling steak on a green forked stick

Avoid hot fire to prevent burning. Do not salt. (Grease may be used to fry eggs, pancakes, or to grease pans.)

Ham: Serving, one slice, ¼ to ½ lb.
Preparation: Ham may be purchased pre-cooked. The pre-cooked will spoil in a day or two in warm weather, so most campers carry the smoked type, which will keep longer without refrigeration. To cook, par-boil for about 5 minutes on each side; pour off water, and fry with a slight amount of grease over a moderate fire. Turn occasionally. The ham is ready to eat when slightly browned on both sides (about 8 minutes). Do not salt. Pre-cooked variety may be fried without par-boiling.

Hamburger: Serving, ⅓ lb.
Preparation: Wash hands. Mold chopped meat into cakes about 1 inch thick. Grease frying pan lightly, pre-heat and fry meat over a moderate fire, turning occasionally, about 5 to 7 minutes. Dry cracker crumbs or bread crumbs and a little water added to the meat will make it "go further." Chop an onion fine and add to flavor it, with ½ teaspoonful of salt, and pepper.

Steak: Serving, ½ to ¾ lb. per person.
Broiled: If your steak is tender, you may broil it. Place steak in grill or spit it on end of green stick. Sear in flame and broil slowly over hot coals. Cook about 15 to 20 minutes for a 1 inch thick steak. Remove, rub with butter, salt and pepper.

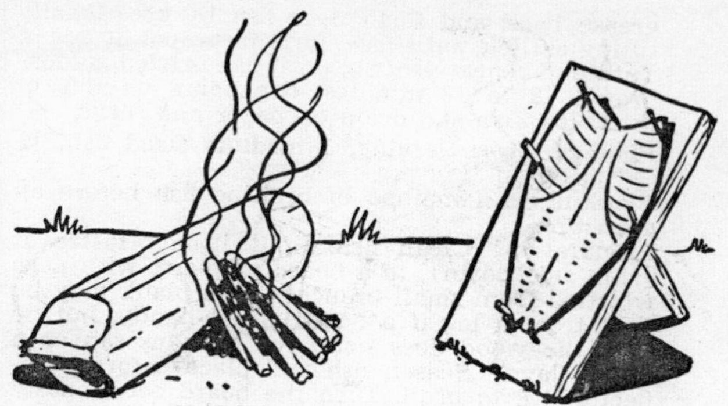

Planked fish, broiling before a fire

Pan-broiled: For tougher cuts, try pan-broiled or fried steak. Place skillet without grease on hot fire and heat until it smokes (extremely hot). Toss in steak and let it sear for a minute or more. Turn and sear other side. Cook over moderate fire. turning often (about 15 to 20 minutes). Remove, rub with butter, salt and pepper. No grease is used in the skillet during the entire operation.

Fried: Place skillet with tablespoon of grease (or piece of suet) over moderate fire and heat until grease smokes. Drop in steak. Turn occasionally, fry over moderate heat about 15 to 20 minutes till done; salt, pepper and butter and serve.

Pork Chops: Serving, ½ to ¾ lb. per individual. Preparation: Place chops in hot skillet; season; fry over moderate fire, turning occasionally. Cook until brown and well done, from 12 to 15 minutes, depending on thickness of chops. If chops are very fat, pour off extra grease as it accumulates. Pork should be thoroughly cooked.

Fish: Serving, ¼ to ½ lb. per individual.
Preparation:

Fried: Clean fish, wipe dry and salt and flour it this way: put in a paper bag with 2 or 3 tablespoonfuls of flour, pancake flour, bisquick or cornmeal, with teaspoonful of salt. Shake the fish gently in the mixture until well floured. Heat frying pan with 2 or 3 tablespoonfuls of grease until grease starts to smoke. Drop in fish. Work hot grease back and forth over fish by occasionally tilting skillet, until fish starts to brown at edges. Turn and repeat process, until fish is fried golden-brown (8 to 10 minutes, depending on size of fish). Remove and drain on paper and serve.

Planked Fish: Serving, 1 medium sized fish, ½ to ¾ lb

Planking is a method of broiling fish before an open fire.

Preparation: Clean fish. Split it and fasten it (skin side down), to a board or plank with pegs whittled from small branches. The plank may be split from a log if a board is not handy, but be sure the wood does not have resinous sap or a bitter flavor. Season fish and place before a reflector fire to broil. Turn the board occasionally to broil the fish evenly. Cook 15 to 30 minutes depending on the size of the fish and the heat of the fire.

Chicken:

Fried: Serving, ½ small frying or large broiling chicken.

Preparation: Cut into 2 or 3 pieces, roll in salted and peppered flour and fry in hot grease that covers the bottom of the skillet over moderate coals. Turn regularly until all pieces are a golden brown. Pour half a cup of water into the skillet, cover with a tight-fitting lid and simmer for 20 minutes, or until done. Thicken gravy with a little flour and water paste if desired. Serve hot.

Broiled: Serving, one small broiler.

Preparation: Season chicken inside and out by rubbing with a little salt mixed with bacon grease or butter. Spit chicken on long, green stick of sweet wood (not bitter wood). Arrange spit on forks before reflector fire or above good-sized bed of hot coals. Turn constantly until deep brown. The broiling should be slow enough to permit chicken to cook through prior to turning brown. A pan may be arranged below to catch the drippings. The time will be from 30 to 60 minutes, depending upon the size of the chicken.

Eggs: Serving, 1 to 2 eggs.

Preparation:

Fried: Heat skillet with one tablespoon of bacon grease, butter or fat. Break and drop in egg. Season. Fry over moderate fire until done, 2 to 3 minutes. Turn egg for those who do not wish "sunnyside up."

Scrambled: Melt in skillet one tablespoon fat (not as hot as for fried eggs). Break and drop in one or two eggs and stir with fork or spoon, add two tablespoons of milk for each egg. Cook over low fire—½ to 1 minute until eggs are firm.

Boiled: Place eggs in kettle in cold water over fire and bring rapidly to boil; about 3 minutes for soft boiled. Boil 10 minutes for hard-boiled eggs.

Vegetables

Vegetables furnish the bulk of the meal and supply starch, protein, roughage, vitamins and minerals, depending upon the vegetable. Only those in most common usage are mentioned here:

Potatoes:

Boiled in Jackets: Serving, 2 medium or one large potato.

Preparation: Wash, place in kettle, cover with hot or cold water and boil over hot fire 20 to 25 minutes. Test with fork. They must be tender to the center. Pour off water and dry by placing pot near fire for a few minutes. A bit of salt in the water helps season and prevents skins from boiling off. Peel, mash with fork, season with salt and pepper and flavor with butter or gravy.

Fried: Serving, 2 medium or one large potato.

Preparation: Peel, wash, slice thin or dice cold boiled potatoes. Fry in ham or bacon grease over moderate fire. Turn regularly. Season to taste while frying. Cook until brown, about 10 minutes. If raw potatoes are used, peel, slice ½ inch thick and fry about 15 minutes until brown. Turn them and cook on other side.

Baked: Serving, 2 medium sized potatoes.

Preparation: Potatoes must be covered to keep them from burning when baked in the coals of a fire. This may be done in many ways. Here are three common methods. Roll each potato in mud or clay; wrap it in paper that has been soaked in water at least 10 minutes; after the mud or paper has been balled around it, the potato should be more than double its original size. Bake in coals about 40 minutes. They may also be protected by placing them in a small tin can from which the lid has been partially removed, and filling this with dry sand. The lid is pressed down to keep the sand in the can. After preparation, the protected potatoes are buried in the coals. The fire is built on top and is kept going. Remove in 45 minutes, open, and find well-baked and *not burned* potatoes. Another method is to scrape aside embers and ashes from your fire to a depth of about 3 inches. Place potato in hole, cover with hot ashes, then hot coals. Cover with dirt. Dirt is necessary to keep potatoes from burning. Cook until done, about 45 minutes.

Beans

Green: Serving one cupful.
Preparation: Snap off ends and break beans into pieces approximately an inch long. Cover with water and bring to a slow boil over moderate fire. Cook until tender, from 12 to 15 minutes. For added flavor peel small-sized onion and slice into pot. Season to taste with salt, pepper and one tablespoonful of bacon grease. Cover pot.

Navy: Serving, ⅓ cup dry beans.
Preparation: Pick over beans to remove black or yellow ones. Soak overnight. In the morning pour off water, cover with plenty of fresh water, bring to slow boil. Add slice of bacon or piece of fat ham, and one small diced onion fifteen minutes after water starts to boil. Season with salt, pepper and one teaspoon of brown or white sugar. Continue cooking on moderate fire for an hour or an hour and a half, or until beans are soft. It will be necessary to add a little water and to stir occasionally. Beans should be nearly dry or in thick broth when done. Serve with catsup. If beans are soaked overnight, the cooking time will be reduced.

Carrots: Serving, 1 or 2 carrots.
Preparation: Carrots are at their best when cooked as a part of stew. To cook by themselves, cut in thin slices or dice. Cover with water, salt, and bring to a moderate boil. Stir occasionally. When tender, pour off most of the water and stir

in a piece of butter the size of an English walnut. Serve hot.

Onions: Serving, 2 medium, or one large onion.

Preparation: Onions are used chiefly for flavoring and seasoning. When fried with bacon or ham, they produce a flavor that may be used to season beans, spaghetti, chowder and many other dishes. They add a great deal to the flavor of liver, pot roast, stews and soups. They may be fried, stewed, buttered or creamed and served as a separate dish. When fried, they are usually cut in cross-wise slices about ¼-inch thick, and fried in fat for 10 minutes. For creaming, select small or medium-sized onions, peel, and cook whole in boiling salted water until tender, about 25 to 30 minutes. Save the water for gravy.

Corn: Serving, from 1 to 2 ears.

Preparation: This favorite vegetable may be prepared to eat in many ways. The favorites are:
Boiled: Shuck, remove silk, drop in kettle of boiling water for ten minutes. Remove, salt and butter and play like a mouth organ!

Roast: Soak corn in shucks in water for 10 minutes. Bury in hot coals for 15 minutes. Remove, shuck and eat.

Fried: Cut cold cooked corn from cob and fry in butter or bacon grease over moderate fire. Stir regularly. Salt, pepper and sprinkle with sugar. Fry until golden brown and serve hot.

Creamed: Cut corn from cob. Stew, season, sweeten, butter and add thickening when tender.

Trail Breads

The bannock of the North, and the sourdough of the West, and the hoe-cake of the South, are famous trail breads of the past. The new era has brought in prepared flours which are convenient to pack and carry, easy to prepare and nutritious to eat. These have taken much of the mystery and difficulty from camp baking, so that with little practice you can readily become expert at baking over the open fire.

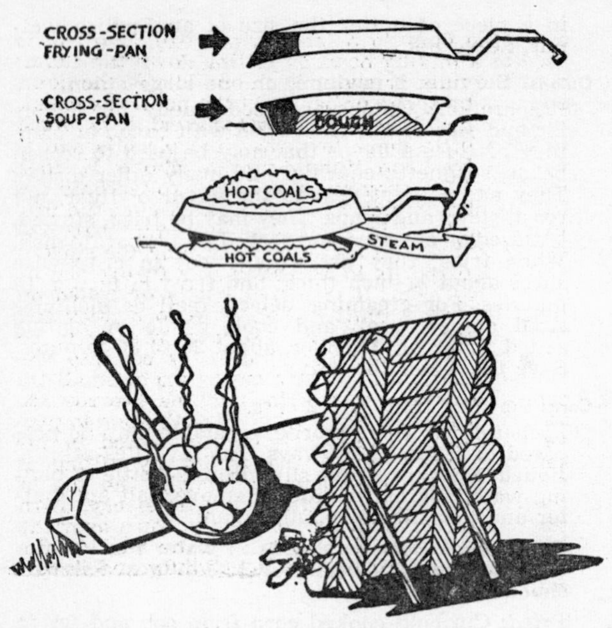

Two ways to bake trail bread

Pancakes or Griddle Cakes: Serving, ½ cup of prepared flour per person.

Preparation: Prepare the batter according to the instructions on the box. Melt grease until it covers bottom of frying pan and pour all excess back into grease can. Heat frying pan over medium fire until grease sizzles, then pour batter in center of pan until it covers two-thirds of bottom. Fry until bubbles appear and tip edges begin to brown. Turn with knife, or flip. Brown other side and serve with butter and syrup or jam. If pancakes are too thin, add more flour to batter; if too thick, thin with water.

Biscuits and Twist on a Stick: Serving, 1 cup of prepared flour per person.

Preparation: Use one of the prepared biscuit flours and prepare as instructed on the box. Some campers prefer to memorize the instructions and carry the flour in a large paper bag. The bag is used as a mixing bowl by rolling down the edges; pour the milk or water in the middle of the flour, and mix by spoon or hand, gently, not like cement.

If the dough is to be used for twist, it is mixed to be a little more firm than for biscuits and is worked by hand lightly into a ribbon ½ inch thick and 2 inches wide, and then rolled onto the baking stick which has been heated over the fire. Place the twist in front of or over the coals and carefully bake on all sides by turning the stick.

If the dough is to be baked in a frying pan or a reflector oven, it is patted gently or rolled on the dough cloth until it is about ½ inch thick and then scored into 1½ inch squares if it is to be baked as flat bread (one piece), or cut into biscuits by using the top of a cup, glass or small tin can. The skillet or pan to hold the biscuits for baking is greased and sprinkled with flour to prevent sticking. The dough is then baked in the reflector oven, or in the skillet by tilting it where the reflected heat will strike the top of the dough. Constant watching is necessary. Turn the pan to make all brown evenly. Turn over the biscuit or dough if it does not bake well on the bottom. Good biscuits are light, fluffy and flavorful.

Desserts

Desserts are the delight of the meal. They are rich in energy value and usually succeed in giving that pleasant full feeling even to a hungry Scout. Prepared pie and cake flours simplify baking on the trail, but this is still a little advanced for the beginner. The fruits previously mentioned make good camp desserts. The desserts mentioned below are easily carried and prepared.

Chocolate, Butterscotch and **Vanilla Pudding:** Serving, ½ of small package available at stores.

Preparation: Buy your favorite flavor at the corner store and follow the instructions on the box.

Jelly Horn: Serving, one per person.

Preparation: Prepare twist as mentioned above but wrap and bake on a rounded stick. Remove when done and fill with your favorite jelly or jam, or sugared banana—raw or baked. It's delicious.

Drinks and Beverages

Milk: Serving, one pint.

Milk is by far the most popular and healthful drink among boys of Scout age. It is difficult to carry on the trail as it is a liquid and bulky. Canned milk can be carried and thinned one-half with water before drinking, or the powdered milk may be used and mixed on the spot. Powdered whole milk may be purchased from any good outfitter and at stores.

Cocoa: Serving, 1 to 2 cups.

Preparation: Cocoa or chocolate mix containing cocoa, sugar and powdered milk is available at stores, restaurants, or soda fountains. Mix powder in a cup of hot water. A dash of salt improves the flavor.

Soup: Serving, one pint.

Cold-weather camping and hiking are made more enjoyable by including soups on the menu. For day hikes put up a vacuum bottle of homemade soup. If camping at a site where supplies are easily available use canned soups. For trail camping or hiking use dehydrated soup. Follow the directions on the package. Bouillon cubes are also easy to carry and prepare. Dissolve two cubes in a pint of hot water. For extra nourishment include one packet of a clear gelatine.

Fruit Ades and Flavorings: Serving, one pint.

Lemon, lime and orange ades from fresh fruit, sugar and water are tasty thirst-quenching drinks for hot-weather camping. Citric acid crystals are available for trail drinks. The crystals, as well as the popular imitation fruit-flavored ades, are dissolved in water and sweetened to taste. Follow directions on the package or container. Excellent warm-weather drinks may also be made from packages of fruit-flavored gelatine. Dissolve one package into three cups of water, stir and drink.

One-Pot Meals

Beef Stew:

Ingredients for one person ⅓ lb. stew beef, 2

medium-sized potatoes, 2 medium-sized onions, two medium-sized carrots.

Preparation: Cut beef into chunks about ½ inch square, place in pot with 1 tablespoon hot grease. Place over fire and brown beef. Turn occasionally. Peel potatoes and cut into ½ inch cubes. Wash carrots and cut into pieces ½ inch long. Peel two onions. Slice one onion into pot when beef is brown, and fry several minutes until the onion starts to turn brown. Add potatoes, carrots, the other onion which has been quartered, and 1 cup of water. Salt (about 1 teaspoonful) and pepper to taste. Cover pot and simmer over moderate fire for 45 minutes. Stir occasionally. Test meat and vegetables with a fork. When tender, the stew is done. It may be necessary to add water while cooking, but stew should be thick and not soupy when done.

Irish Stew:

Ingredients for one person, ½ lb. lamb, 2 medium-sized potatoes, 2 medium-sized onions and 2 medium-sized carrots.

Preparation: Same as Beef Stew.

Meat and Vegetables en casserole

This is a delicious meal which will cook itself while you are away from camp. It requires a pot or kettle with a tight-fitting lid. Prepare ingredients for beef or Irish stew using only ¼ cup of water. When boiling bury the pot in the ashes of a fire in a hole in the ground (be sure cover of pot fits tight). Place hot embers all around and on top of the pot, and cover it with earth. It is left in the hole for one hour or more. When dug up and opened the casserole is more delicious than stew, as all the natural juices have been retained.

Corned Beef and Cabbage:

Ingredients for one person, ⅓ lb. canned corned beef, 2 medium-sized potatoes, 2 medium-sized onions, ¼ small head cabbage.

Preparation: Cut potatoes in half, boil until half cooked, add corned beef cut into one inch cubes, onions peeled and quartered, cabbage cut in 2 or 3 pieces. The water should barely cover vegetables. Continue cooking until potatoes and cabbage are done. Salt cautiously, as the corned beef is salty. Pepper to taste. Serve piping hot. Drain off broth and serve as soup.

KABOB

Make a spit from a green stick (of sweet wood), as thick as a lead pencil. Sharpen the thin end. Cut one quarter pound of meat into one inch squares. Cut an onion in half and peel off the leaves. Skewer the meat and onion alternately on the stick. Pieces of bacon, slices of tomato or thin slices of potato may be used. Broil close to the fire, turning constantly.

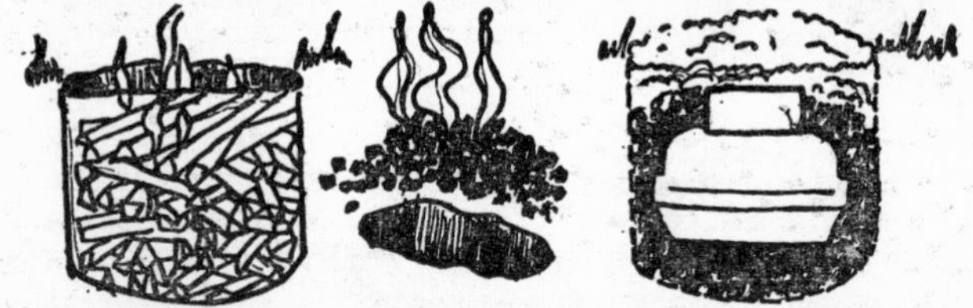

BEAN HOLE BEANS

Build a fire in a hole and get a hole full of hot coals. Place beans, bacon, molasses (see page 322) in a covered pot. Shovel out part of the coals, and place the pot in the remaining coals. Cover with coals. Cover the coals with dirt. If beans have been soaked over night, or partly cooked ahead of time, cooking takes about four to six hours.

IMU

Dig a hole and line with rocks. Build a fire in the hole and let it burn to hot coals, and until the rocks are thoroughly heated. Remove the coals, and place chicken and vegetables, wrapped in wet leaves in the bed of hot rocks. Cover with coals. Cover with a little dirt, then place an old tarp or burlap over the hole, and cover it with dirt. Cooking takes three to four hours.

Cooking Wild Plants

Most common edible wild plants may be prepared in one of three ways: boiled or steamed in water, like spinach or asparagus; roasted or baked like potatoes; steeped in boiling water, like tea. There are many wild plants which may be eaten raw. Wild fruits, such as strawberries, blueberries, raspberries, blackberries; many of the nuts and other seeds such as hickories, sweet acorns, pine seeds, walnuts; plants such as watercress, sorrel, peppergrass, shepherd's-purse, scurry-grass, purslane, and the plantains, all of which may be washed and eaten raw like lettuce.

Boiled Greens: Wild plants that may be boiled, steamed or stewed are numerous and common. Dock, purslane, chickweed, shepherd's-purse, mustard, canary-grass, roseroot, clover, mallow, waterleaf, goat's-beard, sweet coltsfoot, plantain, dandelion, and live-forever, are a few in this group.

Be careful to collect only the young and tender leaves. Pick over the leaves and throw away any that are old or tough. Then wash the leaves thoroughly.

In cooking, use as little water as possible, letting the greens simmer in their own juices. Add a little salt while the greens are cooking, and season later with salt and pepper to taste.

A small piece of bacon or salt-pork or a spoonful of bacon fat will add to the flavor of the greens.

If the first greens are too strong for your taste, next time try cooking them in a change of water. First cover the greens with water, and bring to a boil. Then pour off the water, add a little fresh water. Bring to a boil, and let simmer until tender.

Steamed Wild Plants: The following plants may be prepared like asparagus: bracken fern (new shoots) cattail (shoots) Solomon's seal (roots) common milk-weed (shoots), catbrier (new growth).

First wash the shoots in two or three changes of water. Then place in a little boiling water, and steam until tender. Add seasoning to taste, and serve with butter.

Baked or Roasted: Cattails, bur-reed, pond weeds, arrow heads, flowering rush, reeds, nutgrass, ground nuts, bugleweed, Jerusalem artichoke, wild salsify, prairie turnip, cow-lily and chufa grass are all plants that have roots or tubers which may be dug up.

The first step is to wash them thoroughly in two changes of water. All may be roasted or baked in coals, or in a reflector oven. If baked in the coals, first wrap the roots in several layers of large, sweet leaves that are first soaked in water. The wet leaves will first steam the roots, then as they dry out, the roots will be roasted or baked. Most of the roots will require no longer than an hour in hot coals. Practice will show you how long to cook these plants.

Camp Tea: Checkerberry leaves, mint leaves, elder flowers, sweet goldenrod leaves, basswood flowers, raspberry leaves, clover heads, black alder leaves, sweet gale leaves, sassafras root bark, slippery elm inner bark, sweet fern leaves, sweet birch leaves and strawberry leaves all may be used as camp teas.

First wash the leaves in cold water. Then place them in a cooking pot or large tin can, and cover with boiling water. Stir up for a few minutes with a spoon. Strain the tea through a clean handkerchief or cheese cloth and sweeten to taste.

The red clusters of fruit of staghorn sumac may be made into "lemonade"; soak in cold water for a few moments, then strain through a piece of cloth and sweeten to taste.

TENTS-OUTDOOR SHELTERS

CHAPTER 18

Out of every twenty-four hours in camp, you probably spend more time in your tent or other shelter than in any other one place. You sleep in it for at least eight or nine hours every night. You may flop down on your bunk for a short rest after lunch, or to rest your weary legs after a long hike. You may even sit on the foot of your bunk as you cook your meals over a fire which warms you while it cooks your dinner.

It is natural then, that you will want your tent and bed to be as comfortable as possible. You cannot expect all the comforts of home in a tent in the woods or prairies. But with a carefully chosen camp site, a well pitched tent and a comfortable bed, there is no reason why you should not enjoy the best fun there is in camping in the wilderness.

How to Choose a Campsite

The perfect campsite may never be found. But you should be able to find a spot that includes many of the good points of a desirable campsite. Here are the points to think about when selecting it. Try to find a place that has as many good points as possible.

Slope—The land where the camp is pitched should have enough slope so that rain water will drain off, but should be level enough for comfortable sleeping. If the land is flat, try to find a place where the soil will absorb any rain water. The ground should be soft enough so that tent pegs may be driven in, but not soggy or damp. The latrine should be located down hill from camp, the water supply and the eating area. It should be at least 100 feet from the camp kitchen.

Air and Wind—The camp should be pitched back to the prevailing winds and storm winds. It should be in a clearing where the sun can dry the ground and where free circulation of air will ventilate the tents. Low places may fill with fog or mosquitos at night. Pitch your camp high enough so that air will blow through it, but not on the highest point where lightning may strike.

Water and Wood—If possible, both the water and wood supply should be close enough to camp for easy transportation.

Layout—There should be enough space for tents so that each tent will have privacy. The camp kitchen and eating area should be conveniently located.

Safety—There should be no dead trees, nor live trees with dead branches, nor leaning trees, that may topple over in a wind storm and land in or around camp. If in mountainous country, check up-hill to see that there are no boulders that may topple down in a storm.

The camp should be far enough from any stream,

river or tide water so that it will not be washed away in a flash flood or long rain.

Pitch Your Tent

When you have thoroughly explored the area where you plan to camp and have chosen the best place for the Patrol campsite, or for your own individual campsite, lay it out. Before you drive a tent peg, decide on the exact place for each tent, for the camp kitchen and other camp features. Drive in small stakes to represent these features. Then look over the campsite and make any final changes that may be necessary.

The next job is to go to work on the exact spot where your tent will be pitched. Get right down on your hands and knees and go over every inch of the ground that will be inside the tent. Remove all stones, twigs and roots. They may be small during the day, but a tiny pebble in the middle of your back seems to grow all night, and by the crack of dawn has grown to boulder size.

Whatever kind of tent you use, there are a few general rules for pitching it. As you practice putting it up, you will be able to add a few rules of your own. For a starter, though, try this way:

First stake down the corners of the tent. Practice will show you how far apart to place the stakes. Then raise the pole or poles. Next look at the outside of the tent and decide how to place the other pegs, and rearrange the corner pegs so that the tent has a neat appearance.

You can usually tell whether the tent is pitched correctly just by looking at it. Well-made tents have a neat appearance, with no wrinkles. The material is tight, and there is a maximum of head room and floor

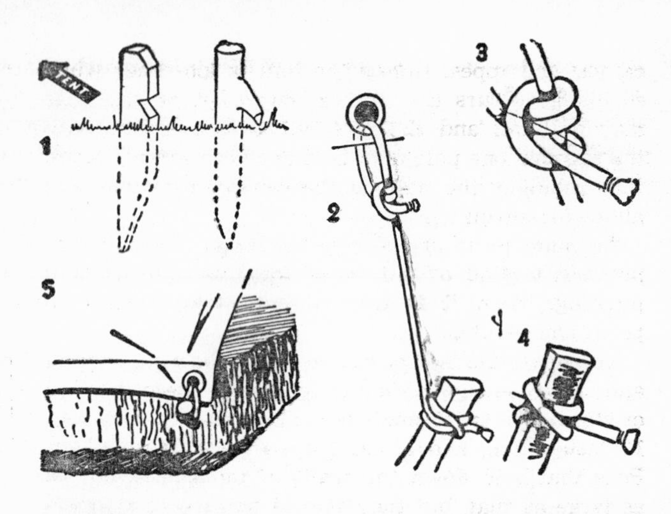

1—Two kinds of tent stakes. 2—Tie a tautline hitch (3) to the tent and a clove hitch (4) to the stake. (5) Tent wall should extend into the ditch.

space for the type of tent. If the tent is not pitched correctly, it may have an awkward appearance, seeming to be too wide for the height, or too narrow.

Another general rule for any tent is to use strong poles that are long enough. See illustrations on page 336 that show different ways of pitching different kinds of tents. You will notice in some cases, that outside poles are used. Most outdoorsmen prefer to use "scissors and springpoles" if possible. Inside poles cut down the amount of usable space in the tent and have a nasty habit of getting in the way during the night.

The other advantage of a scissors arrangement is that it is easily loosened in case rain shrinks the canvas and ropes. Unless the tent is loosened, when shrinkage occurs the canvas may tear, or the pegs may pull out and the tent will collapse. But with the scissors, one pole may be moved out a few inches, thus reducing the pull on the canvas and rope, and allow for shrinkage.

In many parts of the country, however, it is impossible to find or cut poles for this type of tent pitching. Then it is necessary to take your own poles and stakes.

The next rule is that stakes should be long enough and sturdy enough to hold the tent in place in wind or storm. For most small tents, pegs should be about 12 inches long and at least 1½ inches in diameter. Pegs that hold down the walls of tents need not be as large as that, but they should be large enough to hold the tent in place. Never underestimate the size of the stakes; it's better to have them too large than too small.

Good ropes are necessary. Check the rope on your tent and be sure that there are no worn places that may give way in a strong wind. Replace frayed ropes or old ones. Be sure to whip the ends of the ropes. Next practice tying the taut-line hitch so that you can tie it quickly and easily. It is probably the best knot to use on tent guy ropes. The knot will hold tight under strain, but will slip when the stress is released. It is easy to loosen guy ropes quickly, if this knot is used.

Ditching

In parts of the country where it may rain sometime while you are camping, it is best to ditch your tent. The ditch need only be about four inches deep and four inches wide to drain off rain water, and

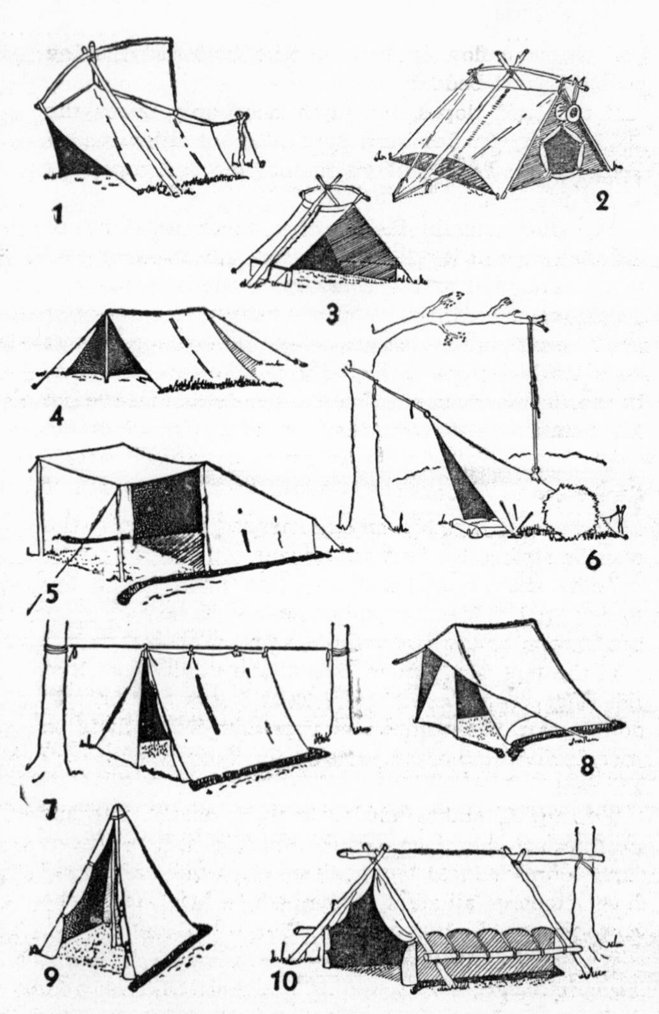

Tents—1—Forester. 2—Mountain. 3—Pup with a wall. 4—Pup. 5—Baker. 6—Trail. 7—Wedge. 8—Cruiser. 9—Miner. 10—Wall.

keep it from flowing through the tent and soaking you and your bedding.

If the land slopes, the ditch need only be on the uphill sides. In flat hard soils, dig the ditch on all sides. In some soils, ditching may not be necessary at all.

The ditch should be directly under the wall of the tent, so that it will collect rain water running off the tent as well as water on the ground.

Fill the ditch in front of the tent with pebbles or small stones, leaves, bundles of grass on sticks to keep the dirt from falling in and filling in the ditch. In country where soil erodes easily, do this all around the tent.

Clean-up

You can always tell an experienced camper by the way he strikes his tent and cleans up the camp site.

Tents should be absolutely dry before they are folded. All folds run along seams if possible, for tents wear on the folds, and seams are strong points.

If the tent has a floor, it should be folded so that the floor is on the outside. Tent floors are usually double thickness and water repellent. When it is on the outside of the folded tent, the floor will protect the tent.

Pull up all stakes and stack them neatly. Perhaps you can use them again some time. Fill in the ditches and mound the dirt two or three inches above ground level. Remove all signs of the bed. In brief, leave the campsite in a better condition than you found it.

Ground Beds

The kind of a ground bed to make depends upon the country and how long you are going to stay.

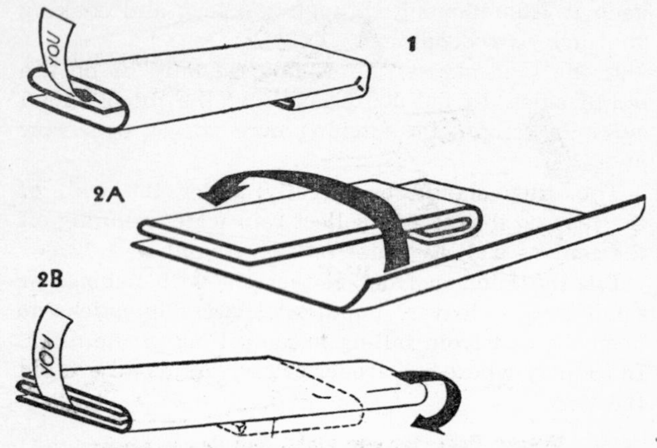

How to fold one blanket (1); and two blankets (2A & 2B)

If you are traveling light, and intend to stay one night, you may be satisfied with smoothing off the ground, digging shallow hip and shoulder holes, spreading out a water-proof ground cloth, and arranging your bedding on top.

For two or three nights in wooded country, you can collect a pile of dead leaves, wrap your ground cloth around them to form a mattress. For several days or a week, you can make a frame of notched or staked logs, and fill it with leaves. A ground cloth spread over the leaves, with your bedding on top, makes a comfortable bed.

In other parts of the country, boughs or grass may be used in place of leaves. Pile up the grass and cover it with the ground cloth, or take along a mattress cover, or large cloth envelope to hold the grass.

Air Your Blankets

Experienced campers air their bedding every day.

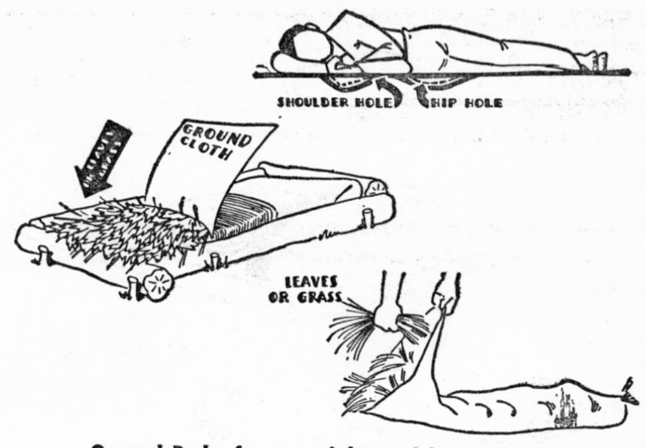

Ground Beds—for one night, and longer camps

They know that moisture given off by the body at night is absorbed by pajamas and bedding. So the first thing in the morning they throw their bedding over a rope or vine stretched between two trees, or over a low tree limb where the sun and air can dry it out. Bedding is much warmer when it is thoroughly dry.

Sleeping in Rain or Snow

If the ground is wet from rain, or covered with snow, your job of preparing a bed may be a little more difficult—unless you prefer to sleep in a puddle of water.

Usually though, an extra thick mattress of leaves or grass covered with a ground cloth will keep you dry.

In the case of snow, shovel away the snow down to the ground, if possible. Then make your bed as before. If the snow is too deep, lay some boughs on top of it, then cover them with your ground cloth.

HANDICRAFT

CHAPTER 19

At the trail's end, when it is time to set up camp, some fellows go about it without much fuss. Their packs are no larger than the average, perhaps even smaller. Yet these Scouts are soon at home in the wilderness, because they use their heads as well as their hands in improvising simple camp gadgets.

You, too, can have the fun of following in the steps of pioneer scouts who knew how to travel light and live off the land comfortably. You'll get satisfaction out of using equipment that you make instead of buy, and you can make it to fit your own needs.

There are many different types of tents, packs, cooking outfits and other equipment that you can make. The following ideas are suggested as a good beginning in handicraft—because they are rather easy to make, and very practical to use.

Trail Tent

The trail tent is easy to make. It is simply a cloth

about 9 feet square with tie tapes at the right points for pitching it in various ways.

Airplane cloth or balloon cloth are the best materials; but if you can't obtain these, get 10 yards of unbleached muslin or similar light-weight cloth with the closest weave possible. Ask at the store for material with a thread count of at least 68-72 per inch. You will also need a spool of No. 50 thread and 19 yards of 1-inch twill tape.

Let us assume you have unbleached muslin a yard wide. Since some cloth shrinks as much as 3½ inches in a yard, imagine what shape your tent would be in if you left the shrinking to the first rain. Shrinking and the first step of waterproofing the cloth can be done at the same time. Boil it for an hour in 2 gallons of water in which a pound of laundry soap is dissolved, and then rinse.

After drying without wringing, cut the cloth in three lengths to form a square when sewed together. In measuring allow for overlapping of the selvage

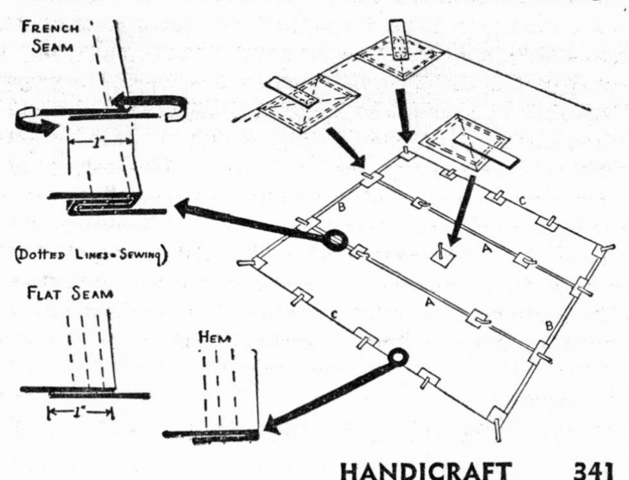

(uncut) edges at the seams (A), and for the folds to make the hems (B) along two sides of the tent. The other two sides (C) will be selvage edges and need no hemming. With a 1-inch overlap at both seams, the size of the tent will be reduced 2 inches if you use the flat seam, or 6 inches if you use the French seam.

Suppose you decide to use the French seam which is stronger and waterproof, and you find the muslin has shrunk 1 inch per yard. The tent will be three times 35 inches, minus 6 inches, or 99 inches square. So cut three pieces of muslin, each 101 inches long, which allows 1 inch at both ends to fold under for hems.

Next, sew the pieces together, side by side, with the French seam as shown on page 341. Then hem the two cut edges. A sewing machine, and perhaps mother's or sister's help, make this much easier.

At the spots where the tie tapes are to be fastened, sew reinforcements made of left-over muslin, stitched as indicated by the diagram. The corner and center reinforcements are 4 inches square, and the others along the edges of the tent are 2 inches by 4 inches. Finish the needle-work by sewing on the tie tapes. Each is a one-half yard length of twill tape, folded in the middle where it is sewed to the tent.

If you want to dye or decorate the tent with Patrol or Troop colors or emblems, this is the time to do it. Then finish the waterproofing by soaking the tent for four hours in a solution of ½ pound of alum and two gallons of hot water. Stir it and work the solution into the seams and hems. Or buy a commercial waterproofing and follow directions given on the container.

You and your tent are then ready for the trail. The diagrams show several ways to pitch it.

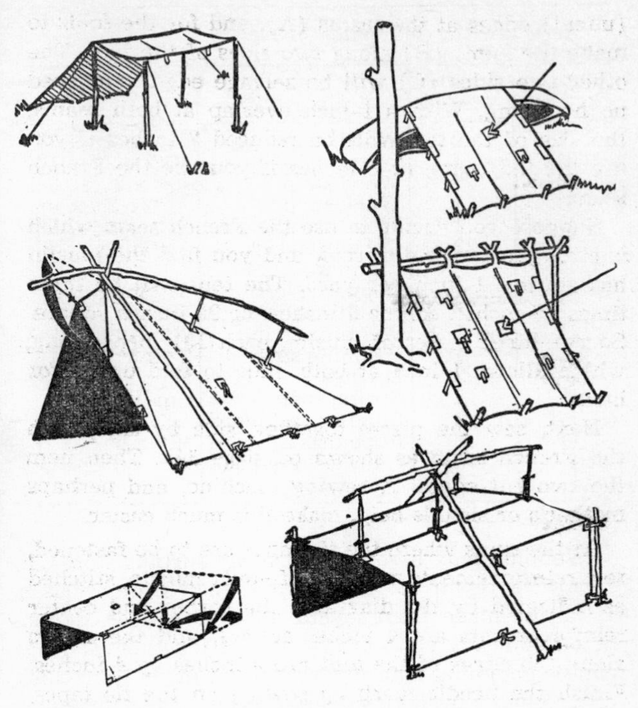

The trail tent may be pitched in many different ways

Dimond-O Pack Frame

A pack frame makes your load easier to carry by distributing the weight, preventing the pack from rubbing, and leaving your hands free for balancing as you swing along the trail. One of the best of several types for Scouts is the Dimond-O.

Use oak, ash or hickory ¼ inch thick, if possible. Otherwise, use straight grained pine ⅜ inch thick.

Here are the materials needed:

*Diagram Letter**	*Number Needed*	*Material*	*Size*
A	2	Wood strip	¼″ x 2″ x 24″
B	1	Wood strip	¼″ x 2″ x 16″
C	1	Wood strip	¼″ x 2″ x 10½″
D	1	Wood strip	¼″ x 2″ x 9½″
E	1	Wood strip	¼″ x 2″ x 8¾″
F	22	Copper rivets and washers	¾″ long
G	4	Copper rivets and washers	¼″ long
H	1	Webbing strip	2″ x 18″
I	1	Webbing strip	2″ x 3′
J	2	D-rings	2″
K	1	Spring snap	small
L	2	Rope or sash cord	⅛″ x 1′
M	1	Rope or sash cord for lashing pack to frame	⅛″ x 8′

* See diagram on page 345.

Webbing may be bought at army surplus stores, in furniture repair stores, or from mail order houses. It can be made from several folds of canvas, denim, or other heavy cloth cross-stitched together. D-rings can be bought at a hardware store or made from thick cold-rolled wire with solder on the joints of the rings.

The lengths of the uprights A and the bottom crosspiece B will depend on your size. Likewise the distances between crosspieces B and D will vary. The measurements given above are for an average-size Scout. When the frame is finished, B should be just below the belt, and D should be level with the shoulder blades. Have someone measure this distance on you. Add 6 inches and you have the length for uprights A. With a tape line measure from one hip bone around back to the other hip bone, and that's the length for crosspiece B.

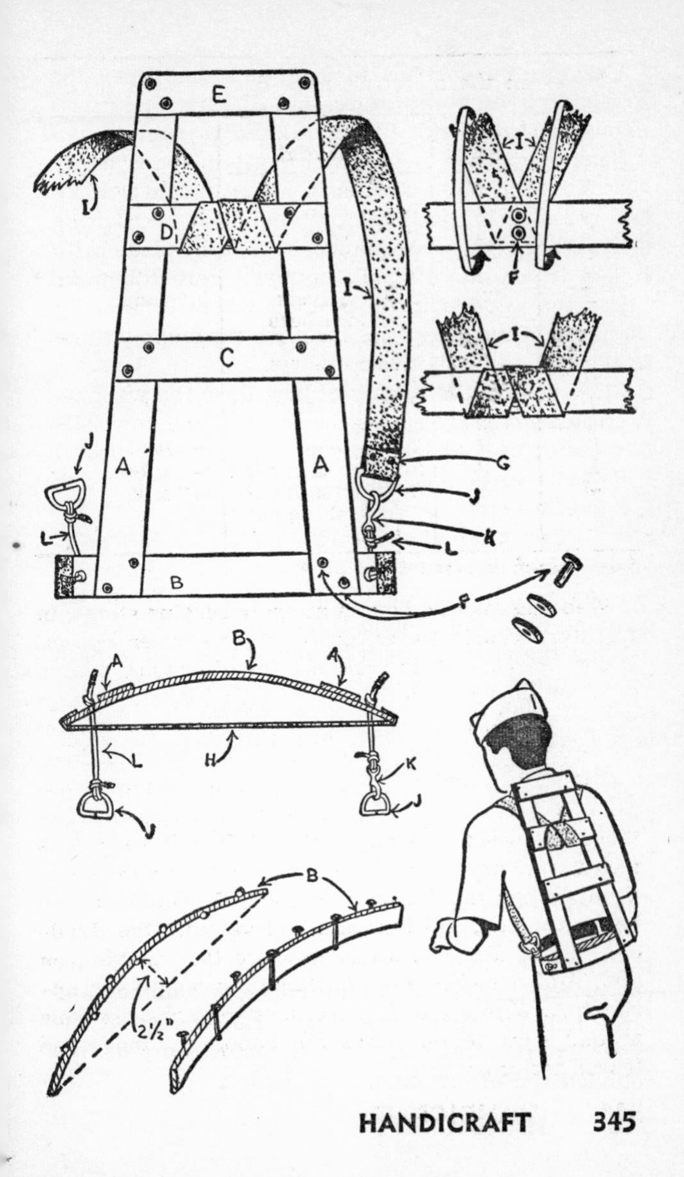
E
I
D
C
A
A
B
J
L
G
J
K
L
F
I
F
I
B
A
A
L
H
K
J
J
B
2½"

Cut the wood strips to size, and sandpaper the rough surfaces, sharp edges, and corners. Stain with oil stain or rub with linseed oil and turpentine.

Soak crosspiece B in water until it bends easily (2-4 hours in hot water or 24 hours in cold water). Put a 2½-inch bow in B by bending it and letting it dry thoroughly (24 hours) in a form made with spikes driven into a plank, as shown in the diagram.

Lay the wood strips in position and drill holes for the rivets. Rivet the strips together, putting a washer at the end to be flattened.

Rivet webbing H to ends of bow B, so the webbing is stretched tightly across the front of the bow. (Its purpose is to hold the pack away from your back.)

Rivet D-rings J to ends of webbing strip I, using the short rivets.

Fold strip I in half so it forms a V with a 45-degree angle. Rivet the webbing at the fold to the center and on the front side of crosspiece D. Wrap the webbing over and around D once.

Whip the ends of ropes L, and at one end of each tie a figure-8 or some other stopper knot. Thread the ropes through the holes in crosspiece B. Tie one rope to a D-ring, and the other to spring snap K, which snaps onto the other D-ring.

Double rope M and fasten to bow B with a girth hitch. Lay your pack on the frame, and lash with the rope as illustrated in Chapter 11.

Tin Can and Wire Crafts

The tools needed to work on tin cans and wire are tin snips for cutting, pliers for bending, a file for sharpening points or dulling edges, a hammer and large nail for punching holes, a can opener of the type that removes can ends without cutting off the rounded rim or leaving a ragged edge.

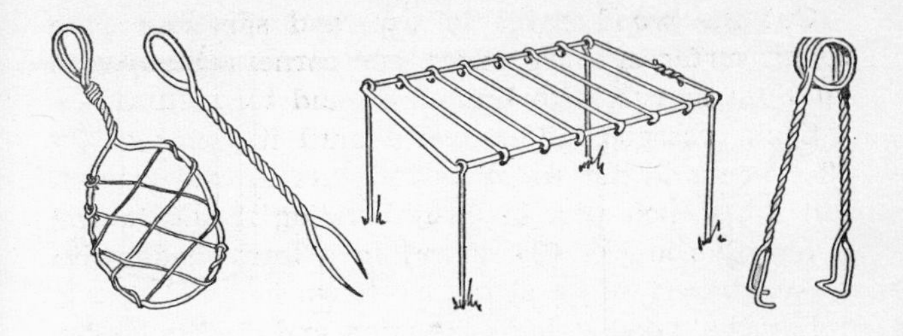

Bailing wire or old coat hangers with the paint rubbed off are used for the gadgets illustrated. Wire can be carried in a small roll in the pack, bent into gadgets in camp, and reworked from one gadget into another.

TIN CAN COOKER—Make from two No. 1/4 and two No. 2½ cans. Make smoke holes with triangular can opener. Stoke with pencil-size or smaller wood. Fry meat or egg, bake biscuit, boil cocoa, all at one time.

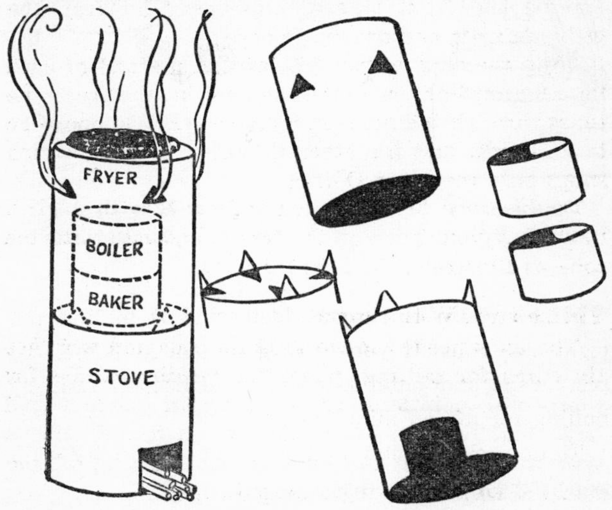

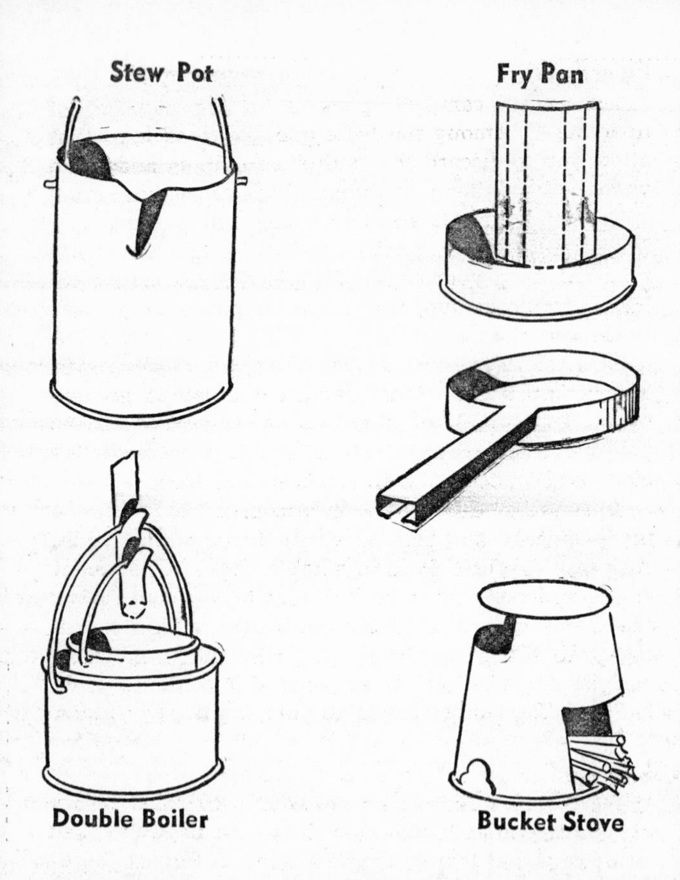

First step in tin can gadgeteering is finding the right size cans. If you can't get them at home, try restaurant and hotel kitchens. Sterilize all cans by boiling for fifteen minutes.

To do a careful job, first figure out and mark with pencil the lines you want to cut.

Food Bags

The expert camper's pack is "a big bag full of little bags." Among the little ones are food bags that allow you to discard the "store" containers and make your pack smaller and lighter. Make food bags from 1 and 2-pound salt and sugar bags; or cut material from larger bags to size and sew. Or get white material from your mother's "piece" collection. Two inches from the top, sew on a tie string of ¼-inch twill tape.

Bags for flour, sugar, and other dry rations must be dust-proof, and those for meat must be grease-proof. In both cases the treatment is the same—paraffin wax rubbed well into the weave of the cloth and smoothed with a warm flat-iron.

Waterproof, dust-proof, grease-proof bags can be made quickly and inexpensively from plastic cloth, such as Vinylite. It is available from department stores and mail order houses. Cut to size and fasten the seams with a good cement sealed with a warm flat-iron. Make the bags long enough so the tops can be folded over to prevent the contents from spilling. Use rubber bands to hold the flaps in place.

Lashings

Lashings are ropes bindings used with poles to construct tripods and tables, as shown on page 351, and bridges, signal towers, and lean-tos. A Square Lashing binds crossed poles together. If the crossed poles must be kept from springing apart where they cross, use a Diagonal Lashing. On parallel poles use a Shear Lashing.

Take your time, making every lashing firm and neat. The trick to this is to keep the rope tight as you go along.

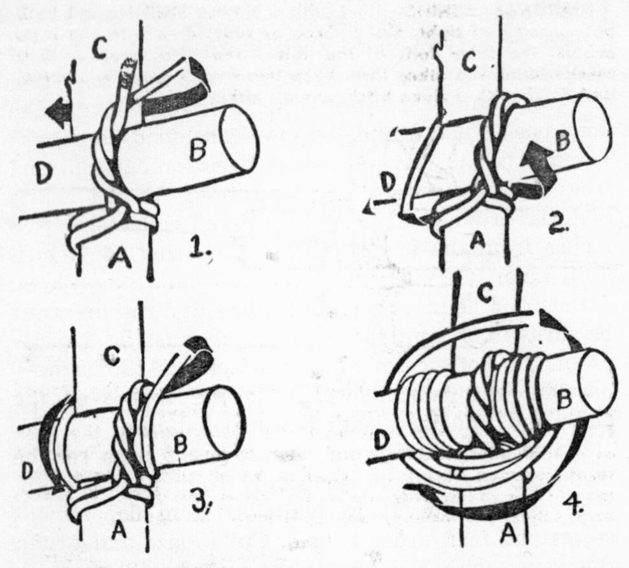

SQUARE LASHING—1. Start with a clove or timber hitch around the upright pole at A below the horizontal pole. Twist the short end of the rope around the long end for neatness. 2. Pass the rope over B, then around behind and under C, over D and under A. 3. Now you have laid a rope "trail" completely around the poles. Follow this same trail two or three times more, *always keeping the rope tight*. At A and C run the rope *inside* the previous trail but at B and D run it *outside* the previous trail. 4. Make three frapping turns, passing the rope between the spars and around the turns of rope already in place. Pull frappings tight and finish off with a clove hitch at B.

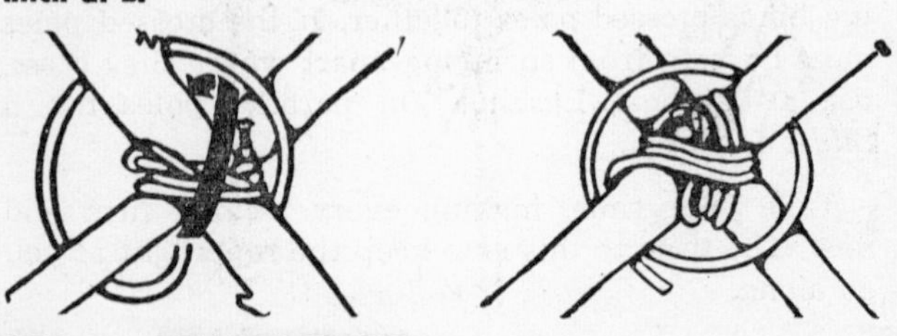

DIAGONAL LASHING—Start with a timber hitch around both poles, and pull tight. Make three or four turns with the rope around the same fork of the poles, and then three or four turns around the other fork. Take two frapping turns, tighten, and finish with a clove hitch around either pole.

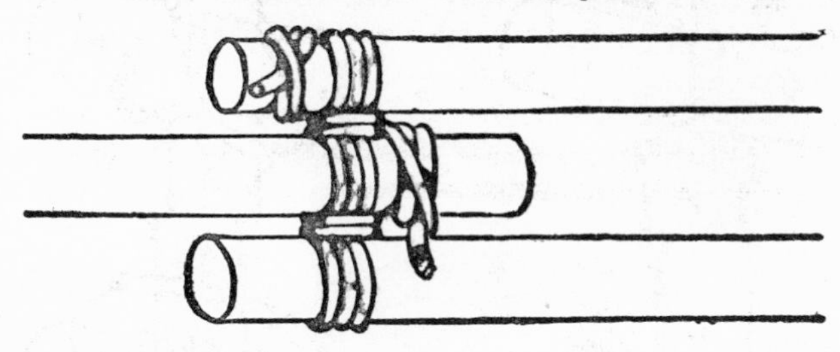

SHEAR LASHING—For a tripod, lay three poles on the ground as shown above. Begin with a clove hitch around an end pole. Take three loose turns around the poles, passing the rope over and under, and back and forth. Make two loose frapping turns between each pair of poles. Finish with a clove hitch around the center pole. Hoist the tripod into place. If necessary, adjust the lashing, making it looser or tighter.

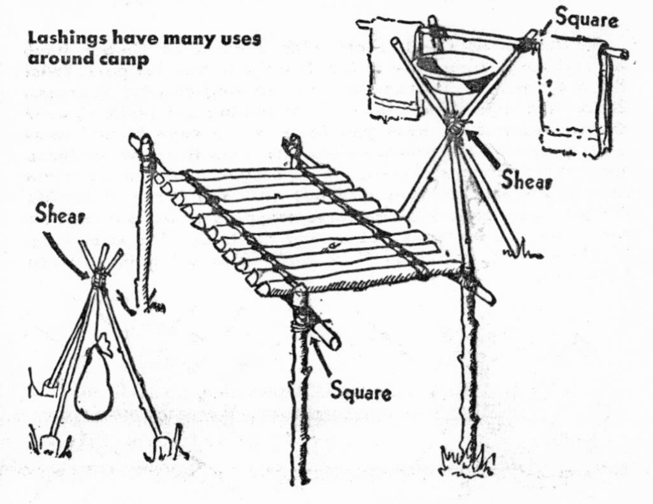

Lashings have many uses around camp

FIRST AID

CHAPTER 20

An old woodsman once said: "When you meet a bear in the woods there are two surprises: You have one and the bear has the other." There are also two surprises when you have an accident. The first is that the accident should have happened at all, and the second is that it should happen to you. But accidents do happen, and we have to know what to do before the doctor gets there.

First aid, then, is the **emergency care** given to anyone who is badly hurt or who is taken suddenly sick. It is also the immediate care that is necessary to prevent slight injuries from becoming much more serious.

There are four emergencies that must have instant attention to prevent death:

1. Where blood is spurting or gushing from a cut artery or vein. (pg. 358)
2. Where breathing has been stopped. (pg. 353)
3. Where poison has been taken. (pg. 370)
4. Where serious shock is present. (pg. 357)

Wait for nothing in such cases. JUMP TO THE JOB. The saved second may save a life.

Shock (pg. 356) can always be expected where injury is severe or very painful, but can often be prevented from becoming serious. Keep patient lying down, head lower than feet, face turned to side if he vomits. Cover him with enough blankets or coats to protect him from wind or cold. Talk cheerfully; try to put him at ease. Keep him quiet. That is a must.

SEND, OR CALL OR GO FOR A DOCTOR—Pages 65, 66. The doctor must be given correct information on how to get to the injured person. If there are one or more persons with you when the accident happens or is discovered, one should be sent to obtain the doctor's help. The best first-aider should stay with the injured person. In cities, hospital aid can be secured through police departments.

Asphyxiation or Stopped Breathing

We need three things to stay alive: Food, water, and oxygen (or fresh air). Now we can, if necessary, live for several weeks without food, or go for several days without water. It isn't comfortable, but we can come out of it alive. But we can only live a few minutes without oxygen. The stopping of breathing may be caused by being under water, by electric shock, deadly gases, mechanical strangulation, paralysis, or being smothered or buried. They all make us stop breathing, and unless somebody is present who immediately starts giving oxygen by means of artificial respiration, death comes in a very short time. We can't wait for a doctor or an ambulance in these cases. There isn't time.

When a person is pulled out of the water, his life depends on what is done **immediately**. He may be so near gone that the delay of a few seconds may make the difference between life and death.

If a person is overcome with exhaust gas (carbon monoxide) in a garage, you can't work on him until you get the gas out or get him out into the fresh air. Any attempt to work in the garage might also be fatal to you. Open the doors wide, smash a window if necessary so as to let the wind blow through. Call or send for help before you attempt to get the victim out into fresh air, so that you may be rescued in case you also get a dose of gas poisoning.

When a person has been knocked down by an electric shock there is always the danger that he is still in contact with a "live" wire. Call the police or the power company. Get experienced help. **Don't touch wires, even if they are insulated.**

Back-Pressure Arm-Lift Method of Artificial Respiration

1. Position of the Subject

Place the subject in a face down, prone position. Bend his elbows and place his hands one upon the other. Turn his face to one side, placing his cheek upon his hands.

2. Position of the Operator

Kneel at the head of the subject on either your right or left knee. Place your knee close to his arm and just at the side of his head. Place your opposite foot near his elbow. If it is more comfortable, kneel on both knees, one on either side of the subject's head. Place your hands upon the flat of his back in

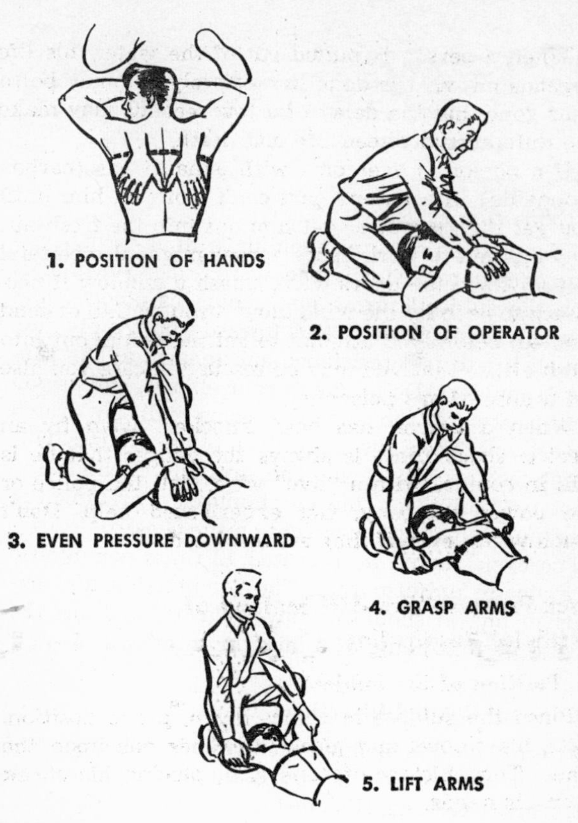

1. POSITION OF HANDS

2. POSITION OF OPERATOR

3. EVEN PRESSURE DOWNWARD

4. GRASP ARMS

5. LIFT ARMS

such a way that the heels of your hands lie just below a line running between his armpits. With the tips of the thumbs just touching, spread the fingers downward and outward.

3. Compression Phase

Rock forward until your arms are approximately vertical and allow the weight of the upper part of your body to exert slow, steady, even pressure downward upon your hands. This forces air out of the lungs. Your elbows should be kept straight and the pressure exerted almost directly downward on the back.

4. Expansion Phase

Release the pressure, avoiding a final thrust, and commence to rock slowly backward. Place your hands upon the subject's arms just above his elbows, and draw his arms upward and toward you. Apply just enough lift to feel resistance and tension at the subject's shoulders. Do not bend your elbows, and as you rock backward the subject's arms will be drawn toward you. Then lower the arms to the ground. This completes the full cycle. The arm lift expands the chest by pulling on the chest muscles, arching the back, and relieving the weight on the chest.

The cycle should be repeated 12 times per minute at a steady uniform rate. The compression and expansion phases should occupy about equal time, the release periods being of minimum duration.

Additional Related Directions

There should be a slight inclination of the patient's body in such way that the fluid drains from the respiratory passage. His head should be extended, not flexed forward, and the chin should not sag. A check should be made to be sure that the tongue or foreign objects are not obstructing the passages. A smooth rhythm in performing artificial respiration is desirable, but split second timing is not essential. Shock should receive adequate attention, and the subject should remain lying down until seen by a physician or until recovery seems assured.

Shock

Shock is that peculiar collapse which comes with every serious accident, and even with many little injuries. You suddenly feel faint, your face gets pale, your skin moist and clammy, your pulse weak and rapid. Your mind is dull and may go on to unconsciousness. There may be nausea and vomiting. It may come immediately after being hurt, or it may develop later.

The more serious the injury, the worse will be the shock; and it may even be so severe as to cause death, in cases of very severe pain or much loss of blood.

First Aid—Bleeding must be checked or shock will become worse. Place the person on his back, with his head low and feet raised. On sloping ground, place his head downhill. Persons in shock become chilled very rapidly and we must preserve their normal body temperature with blankets or other wraps both underneath and on top. Newspapers on the ground will help prevent chilling.

If an injured person is conscious and can swallow, give small drinks of hot tea or coffee with sugar. If he has already become chilled, you may need hot-water bottles to get him back to normal temperature, but be careful not to burn him.

Shock is so serious that you must get a doctor as soon as possible. In many cases the shock is more dangerous than the injury which caused it, so remember to keep every badly injured person lying down and warmed with blankets, so as to prevent shock if possible.

Fainting

This is so common that it is the one thing for which you are pretty sure to have to give first aid. Fainting

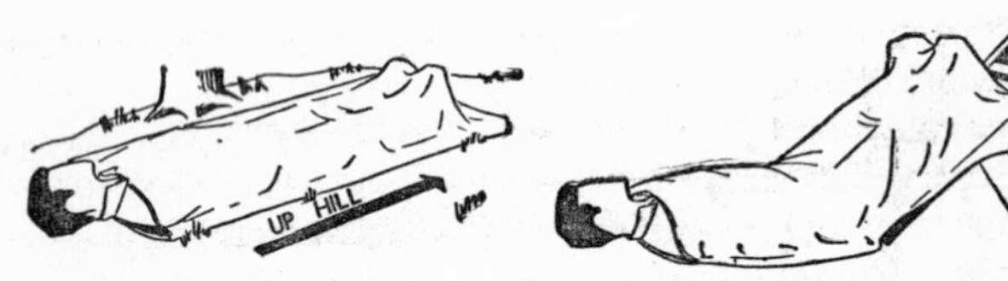

A person in shock must be kept warm and lying down

is due to a sudden loss of blood from the brain. Hunger, fatigue, bad air, standing still too long, fear, bad news, the sight of blood—any of these may make one person faint while others do not faint.

If you feel faint yourself, lie down or sit down, and bend over with the head between the knees, holding the arms tightly across the abdomen. If anyone faints, keep him lying down, head low, and feet raised. If he does not promptly become conscious, send for a doctor at once.

Wounds

A wound is an injury in which the skin is broken—either by a cut, a scrape, a puncture, or by being torn. Nearly all wounds bleed, some severely, some hardly any. Wounds with serious bleeding are not very common, but when they do occur our first job is to stop the bleeding.

Unless very severe, most bleeding can be stopped by holding up the injured arm or leg as high as possible. Pressure on the wound itself, with a sterile gauze compress held firmly against the wound, will stop all but the most severe bleeding. If you do not have a sterile compress, improvise one by scorching a piece of cloth with a match.

First Aid for Large Wounds: When a deep gash spurts jets of blood from a cut artery, or blood pours out from one of the larger veins, it is like a break in

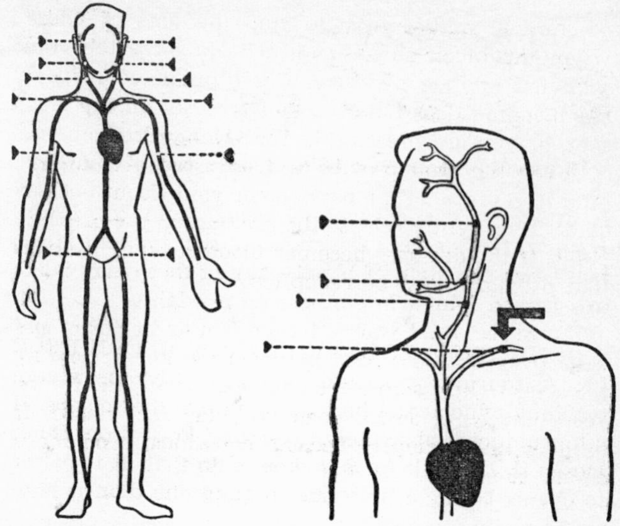

Pressure Points—triangles show where to press the artery to stop bleeding.

a water pipe. We may have to shut off the flow by pressure nearer the pump—the heart.

Know the pressure points shown in the diagram. These points are chosen because there is a bone over which the artery passes. When you press your hand against the bone you flatten out the artery just like

How to tie a triangle bandage on the knee

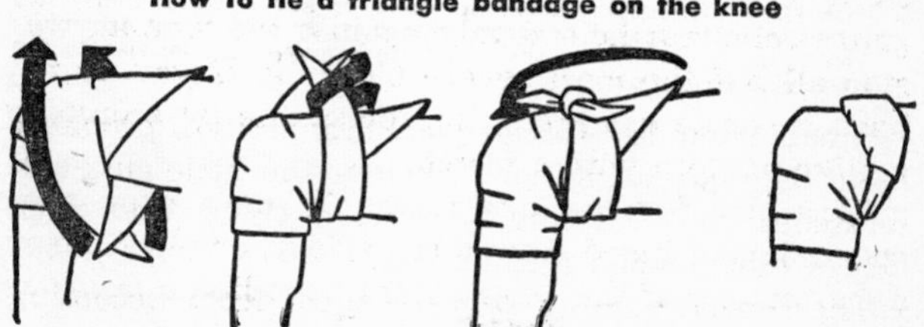

pinching a rubber tube to stop the flow of water. When the blood stops it means you have the right spot and enough pressure. Don't press too hard. If the bleeding does not stop, you are not on the right spot, or you are pressing in the wrong direction.

Cover the wound with a fresh sterile compress, bind it in place with a bandage or your Scout neckerchief. Then gently release the pressure at the pressure point. If the dressing becomes blood soaked, it means that pressure must be reapplied.

DON'T USE A TOURNIQUET IF YOU CAN HELP IT! A tourniquet should be used only for severe bleeding which can't be controlled by other means. If a tourniquet is absolutely necessary, keep it on. Don't loosen it. Leave it for a doctor to do that. It is better to chance losing a limb due to gangrene than it is to risk bleeding to death.

When a tourniquet must be used:

1. **Place the tourniquet close to the wound, but not at the wound edge. There should be unbroken skin between the tourniquet and the wound.**
2. **Make sure it is applied tightly enough to stop bleeding. Improperly applied, it may increase bleeding and hasten death.**
3. **Once the tourniquet is applied, it should not be released, no matter how long it has been in place, except by a physician. Physicians are prepared to control bleeding and replace blood volume adequately.**
4. **A notation should always be made and attached to the victim, giving the location and the hour of application.**
5. **Improvised tourniquets should be made of flat material about two inches wide (a cravat bandage, stockings, or a belt, for example). Don't use rope, wire, or sash cord; they may cause injuries to the underlying tissues and blood vessels.**

Small Wounds: Most of your first aid will probably be to take care of minor injuries—the little cuts and scratches, skinned knees, scraped shins, and such things that happen frequently.

These need care to prevent them from becoming

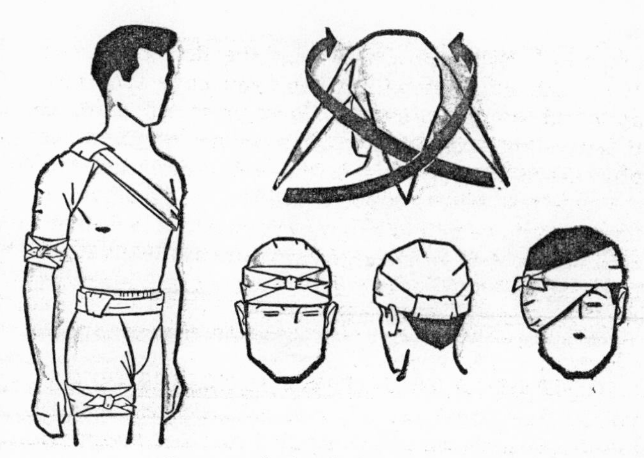

Cravat and triangle bandage uses

infected. You are not going to call a doctor out into the country just because you got scratched with a briar while on a hike. But the scratch should have prompt attention, and if it gets red and sore, you should see a doctor. This is especially true if you feel feverish and "sick all over."

Wash your hands first before you give first aid for

Some bleeding may be stopped by pressure on the wound

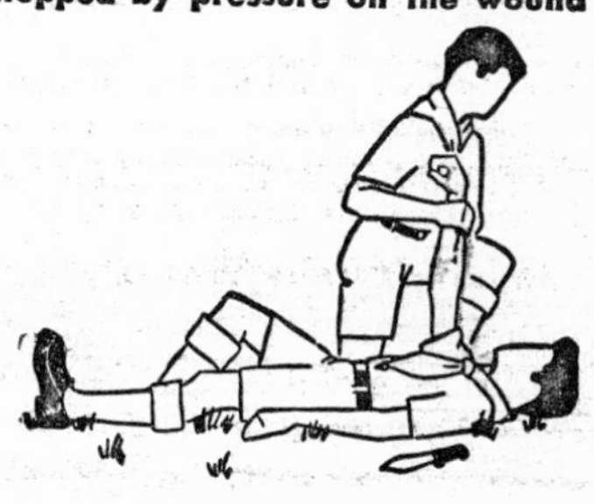

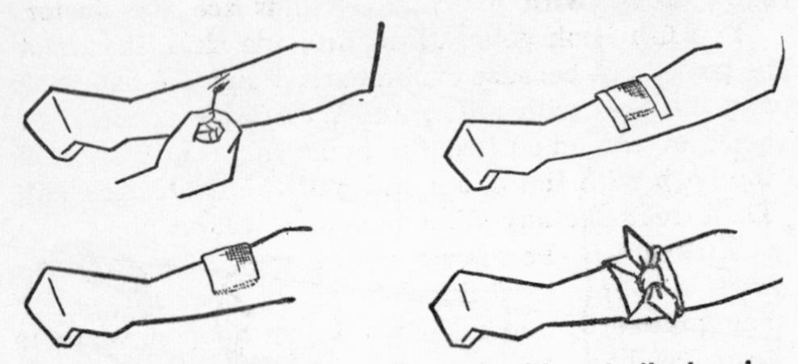

Apply a little antiseptic and cover with a sterile dressing. Then secure the dressing with adhesive or bandage.

wounds. If you cannot wash your hands, then you must be extra careful when you put on the dressing. In any case, whether you have washed or not, see that your fingers do not touch the side of the dressing which is to be placed against the wound.

If you have a small bottle of antiseptic solution in your first aid kit, a few drops may be put on small cuts, scratches, pricks or scrapes. (Don't use an antiseptic near the eye.) It may sting a little for a minute or two but it may help prevent infection. Let the antiseptic dry, and then carefully put on a sterile gauze dressing large enough to cover the wound. Then bind the dressing snugly in place with a bandage or with strips of adhesive tape. Never put adhesive directly on a wound without first putting on a sterile gauze.

Puncture Wounds: Wounds made by a pointed object which punctures a hole in the skin, such as a nail, wire, thorn, or even a bullet, are particularly dangerous. They do not bleed freely and cannot be cleaned easily. Tetanus or "lockjaw" is likely to develop from germs left in these closed-up holes. The first aid for these wounds is exactly the same as any small wound, but do not try to clean them out—you can't do it. **With puncture wounds see the doctor.**

If a fish hook gets jabbed into the skin, it cannot be pulled out because of the barb. Paint the fish hook and the skin with antiseptic. With a pliers push the hook on around so that the point comes out, snip off the barb with the pliers and pull the hook back out. Then treat like any other puncture wound.

Snake Bite—Poisonous snakes are rather rare except in a few localities. We rarely hear of anyone being bitten by one but when it does happen, we have to be ready to get busy and give proper first aid.

When a poisonous snake bites, there are usually two large puncture marks where the fangs went into the flesh. These spots rapidly become dark colored, and the pain is immediate, severe, and keeps getting worse for some time. There is swelling, and the person may become unconscious for awhile. He is usually very badly frightened, but he must be kept quiet. Above all, don't let him run, but go to work at once to try to remove the poison.

Snake bite—Put on a compression bandage. Apply antiseptic. Cut X marks on punctures, then apply suction

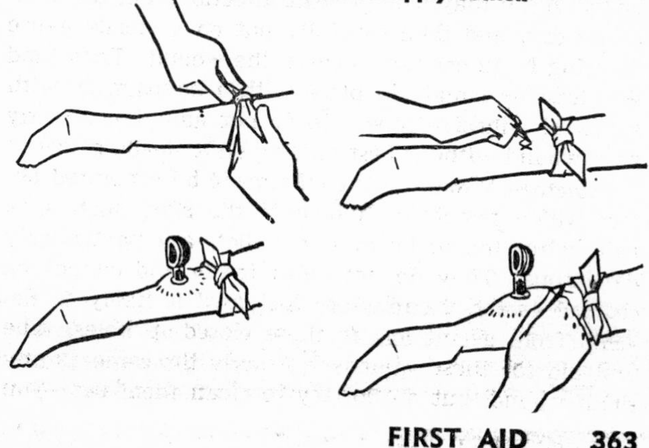

First put on a compression bandage a few inches above the fang marks, tied firmly enough to make the surface veins stand out, but not enough to shut off the deeper blood vessels. Do not twist this bandage, for it is not a tourniquet. The poison is just under the skin and we want to keep it from spreading into the body.

Second, take out your jacknife, open the sharpest blade and sterilize it with an antiseptic or over a flame. Paint a little antiseptic on the fang marks or wash with water. Cut across the fang marks in one direction. Then cut across each of them at right angles to the first cut. Carefully avoid cutting any veins. Usually the veins that you might cut lie just under the skin and are visible as blue lines.

Third, apply suction to draw the poison out of the cuts and the flesh around them. If you have a snake-bite kit with a suction cup, by all means use it, and if you know of any other nearby, send for it. If you have no suction cup, use your mouth and suck on the two cuts, spit out the blood and poison, and suck again, and continue to suck and spit for a half hour.

Call a doctor at once.

If the swelling moves up along the arm or leg, the compression bandage must be moved to keep ahead of the swelling. Make another ring of cuts around the first cuts and apply suction. Treat for shock, and give plenty of hot black coffee, tea, or hot water. Do not give alcoholic drinks. Do all you can to keep the person from being frightened, assure him that you are getting the poison out, and tell him that he will be all right if he keeps quiet.

As some of the poison is absorbed he may show signs of weakness, shortness of breath, faintness, and he may be sick and vomit. Keep up the suction until the doctor arrives, putting suction on each cut for about fifteen minutes every hour. Keep the other cuts moist with a solution of salt water on gauze.

Dog Bite—Dog bites and the bites of cats, foxes, skunks, or any mammal, would be just another wound were it not for the fact that any of these animals may become infected with the disease rabies or "hydrophobia," which is one of the most fatal of diseases known.

With proper medical treatment, rabies can be prevented. But if neglected and the disease develops, nothing can stop it.

If you should be bitten by an animal, do the necessary things at once. Immediately wash the wound and the skin around it very thoroughly with soap and water to get rid of the saliva. Apply antiseptic, let it dry, and put on a sterile dressing as in any other wound.

Then there are two more important things to be done. The dog or other animal should be taken care of at once. In most places the police or health department will take care of the animal. Where they cannot give this service the animal should be caught and shut up in a safe place where it cannot get out, so that it can be carefully watched to determine whether or not it has rabies. If the animal cannot be caught and has to be shot, it should not be shot in the head, for the head will be sent to the laboratory for examination of the brain to see if the animal had rabies. This should be done only by an experienced person, as there is danger of infection, no matter how small a scratch the animal may have made.

Nosebleed

Bleeding from the nose may result from a bump

or blow on the nose, but will sometimes start apparently without any cause. Most nosebleeds are not serious and will usually stop in a short time.

Sit down with the head slightly back, holding a gauze dressing or handkerchief against the nose to soak up the blood, and pinching the nostrils together. Breathe through the mouth and do not blow the nose, as this will disturb the blood clot and start it up again. Loosen the collar.

If this does not check bleeding, insert a small plug of gauze just inside the nostril from which the blood is coming, and press firmly on the side of the nostril. If bleeding continues, call a physician.

Blister on Heel

Because the feet are the hardest part of the body to keep clean, they are likely places for infections to develop. *Never neglect a skin break or blister on the foot.*

Blisters should not be opened except by a doctor. Do your best to prevent blisters. If you do get one, wash it with soap and water, or clear water. Cover with a sterile dressing held in place with adhesive tape.

If the blister has been broken, treat as any wound with antiseptic and a sterile dressing, and bring it to the attention of a doctor. Those small foot injuries are really dangerous and must not be neglected.

Ticks

Ticks are small, flat, brownish little "bugs" that get on an animal or person and then burrow in. They would do little harm if it were not that some of them become infected with "spotted fever" or "mountain fever." The percentage of infected ticks is very small, but we can't afford to take chances.

If you feel one crawling on your skin, brush him off and kill him with a stick or stone. Do not crush a tick with your fingers as that is not safe if he should be infected. If a tick has already started to suck when you find him, do not try to pull it off. It will let go and back out if you scorch its rear end with a lighted match or touch him with a drop of kerosene.

Chiggers

Chiggers or "red bugs" are tiny red spiders whose bites cause severe itching. Household ammonia or clear nail polish applied to the bites will relieve the itching. To keep chiggers and ticks off, dust your socks and around your waist with sulphur powder, or use a good insect repellent.

Burns

Burns are probably the most painful of all injuries, and therefore burns of a large area are always associated with severe shock. Frequently, the first aid most necessary is the prevention of shock.

Mild or first-degree burns, in which the skin is reddened, should not be too serious unless the shock is very great. For first aid, cover the burn with a sterile bandage. If one is not available, use a clean cloth. Don't put ointments, greases, or powder on burns. For scalds, remove clothing from scalded area. Wash chemical burns (except phosphorus) with large quantities of running water.

If your hands are burned, immediate relief from the pain usually results from putting them into lukewarm water and keeping them under water until someone can get the sterile bandages or clean cloth ready.

Severe burns, with blistered skin or the flesh actually burned and charred, are a more serious matter and may result in fatal shock. Get to a hospital or get the doctor at once. Cover the burned surface with sterile gauze and wrap in blankets and get going. Don't expose the person to cold air..

Most burned persons are thirsty and they may be given sips of water—not too cold or not too much.

Sunburn

For sunburn apply a burn ointment if the skin is reddened. A talcum or zinc oxide powder may be used for mild sunburn. If blisters are present, do not break them, but apply a sterile dressing because of danger of infection. Severe sunburn should always be treated by a doctor.

First Aid for Skin Poisoning

If you have been in contact with poisonivy, poison-oak or poisonsumac, try to wash it off. Yellow laundry soap, or any good soap powder, with warm water and lots of lather should get rid of most of the poison. Don't use a scrubbing brush, as that may scratch the skin, especially after the irritation begins.

Then make up a solution of baking soda or Epsom salts. Apply it to infected area with absorbent cotton, which must be thrown away after being used once. Calamine lotion may also be used to relieve itching in the early stages. In mild cases it is better to leave the inflamed areas exposed to air rather than to cover them with dry dressings. Ointments should not be used in early stages before seeing a physician because ointments with a fatty base tend to spread any poison remaining on the skin.

Cinder in the Eye

Cinders and small specks of dust may get into the

eye and lodge under the eyelid, causing pain and tears. The danger is that the object may cut, scratch, or become imbedded in the eyeball itself and start a serious infection. If the object still irritates, see the doctor at once.

If the object is loose, floating about in the space behind the eyelids, you may gently wipe it out with the corner of a folded piece of gauze or a clean handkerchief moistened with water. Never use dry cotton around the eye, as additional fine fibres may get in which are very hard to see.

If it is behind the upper lid, gently take the upper eyelashes in the thumb and finger, tell the person to look up, and while he does so, draw the upper lid out and downward over the lower lid, so that the foreign object may be wiped off by the edge of the lower lid. If a cinder still remains, see a doctor.

Do not rub the eyes. Do not use any instrument, such as a knife point, scissors, tweezers or toothpick, to try to remove cinders. Be gentle and clean. Wash your hands before doing anything about the eye.

Sprains

A sprain is an injury to a joint, in which the ligaments that make up the joint covering are torn or stretched. In some cases it is very hard to tell whether there may also be a broken bone. If in any doubt, treat for a fracture. Swelling is usually prompt and

Sprained ankle bandage

pretty severe, and there may be severe discoloration, but this will not appear for some time.

First Aid for Sprains: Elevate the arm or leg if possible and apply cold—either ice bags or ice or snow in a folded towel or let very cold water run on the joint.

Don't say to yourself, "Oh, it's just a sprain." See the doctor. He may find a small fracture or help to avoid a weak ankle that will give trouble.

Pain in the Abdomen

A stomach ache may come from eating too many green apples, but it may be something much more serious—perhaps appendicitis. Do not take any medicines unless given by a doctor, and do not take any laxative. If it should be appendicitis, taking a laxative could be very dangerous. Call a doctor. Until he arrives, remain quietly in bed; take no food, only small sips of water and no medicine.

Internal Poison

Send for a doctor—but go to work instantly. Wash the poison out of the stomach by giving luke warm soap suds, salt water, soda water, or even plain water. If the water is lukewarm, it is more likely to cause vomiting. Start with four or five glassfuls. If vomiting does not occur, tickle the inside of the throat with the finger. Then give two or three more glassfuls of the liquid. Repeat this process of washing out the stomach at least once more.

If burning or corrosive poison has been taken, such as bichloride of mercury, carbolic acid or lye, give milk or milk and raw eggs to drink after vomiting.

Treat for shock.

If breathing stops, give artificial respiration.

Sunstroke and Heat Exhaustion

Both these conditions come from too much heat, but are nearly opposite in character.

Sunstroke starts with headache, a red face and a strong pounding pulse. Then the skin gets red and dry and perspiration stops. The temperature goes up, and the person falls unconscious.

This is a very serious condition and a doctor should be called at once. Get the person into the shade, and do all you can to cool him off. Remove most of his clothing, pour cold water over him, or spray him with water from a hose. If you have ice available, rub his skin with ice wrapped in a neckerchief or towel. Wet cloths dipped in cold water and then swung around in the air will get colder by evaporation, and may help to cool him off, if nothing else is available.

Heat Exhaustion is really a form of shock from too much heat. The symptoms are pale face, weak, rapid pulse, moist clammy skin, low temperature. The first aid is practically the same as shock—a blanket to keep the normal temperature, feet raised and head low, hot tea or coffee with sugar as a stimulant.

Frostbite

It is easy to get frostbitten without knowing it. One warning is a feeling of intense cold and numbness. The frostbitten area is dead white. In a group, watch especially the cheeks, nose and ears of your friends for this tell-tale sign. Examine your own hands and feet if they become numb.

Cover the frozen part with woolen cloth or clothing. Keep the victim as warm as possible with extra clothing or blankets. Get him into a warm shelter as soon as possible and give him a warm drink. Handle the frozen part very carefully to avoid injury. Put it in lukewarm—**not hot**—water for a moment. But don't use hot water bottles or heat lamps, and don't get the frostbitten part near a hot stove or fire. Excessive heat may increase the danger. Above all, **do not rub with snow**; the frozen tissues may be bruised and gangrene will result.

Fractures

Fractures are divided into two kinds—simple and compound. A simple fracture is one in which the bone is broken but the skin around the break is not broken. These simple fractures are relatively safe because there is very little chance of infection. Compound fractures, on the other hand, are full of danger, for not only is the bone broken, but the skin is also.

If there is a wound, cover it with a sterile compress and bandage it lightly, just enough to hold it in place, taking care not to wiggle the bones while you are putting on the bandage.

Don't move fracture cases until the doctor gets there!

Unfortunately, there are times when this rule cannot be kept. If the injured person is in a place of danger, or great exposure, you may have to move him. So the rule is:

If he must be moved, put on splints first.

Even to turn him over on a blanket, or to help him to the sidewalk, it is necessary to put on some kind of splint. This may prevent a simple fracture from punching through the skin to become a compound fracture. Or it may prevent the sharp edges of bone from cutting blood vessels, nerves or muscles.

When an accident happens, you usually do not have any regular prepared splints at hand, so you have to use what is within immediate reach.

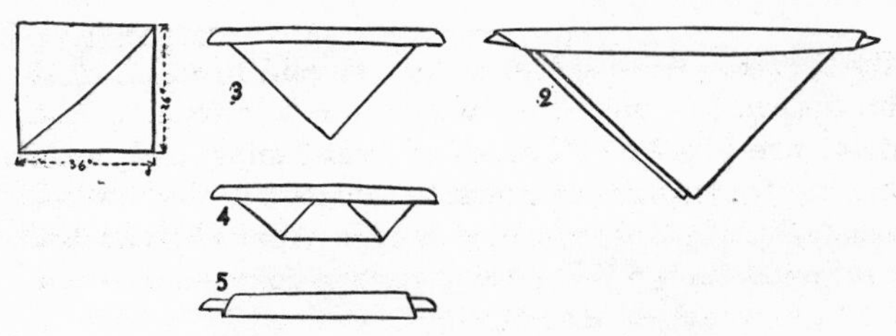

Use a neckerchief or square cloth to make a cravat bandage

For certain fractures, we can use the injured person's own body as a support to prevent the motion of fractures.

Collar Bone. When a collar bone is broken, the shoulder on that side may be a little lower, and there will be a very tender spot if we gently touch our finger tips along the bone. The best first aid is a sling to support the forearm and hand, with the hand raised a few inches higher than the elbow, and then a second triangle bandage or neckerchief folded in a wide cravat and tied around the person's body over the arm and sling, to try to keep the arm motionless.

Upper Arm. Here again we use the body to support the fracture. Make a narrow sling that will hold the hand and wrist, but do not include the elbow. We do not want to push up on the elbow when the upper bone of the arm is broken. Then take a couple of newspapers, or a large size magazine, bend it lengthwise to form a long channel which will fit around the outside of the arm as a splint, and bandage it in place with triangle or roller bandage, going clear around the body, the arm and the splint.

If you are on a hike and can't get papers or magazines, use a folded blanket, or several coats or shirts folded to make a similar long channel, and use some sticks or slats of wood on the outside to keep it rigid.

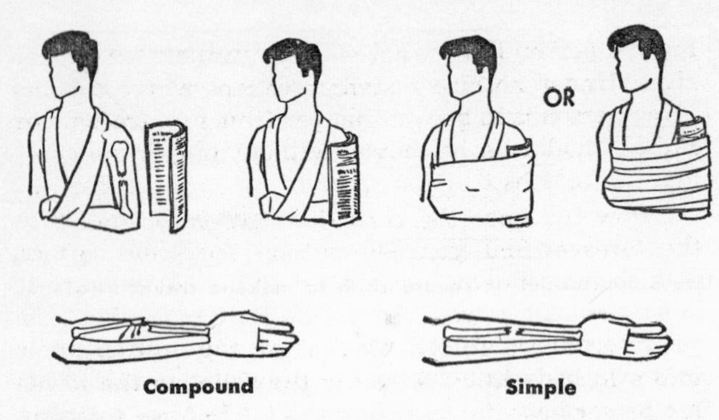

Use a magazine, folded newspaper or anything handy to make a splint. Apply a sling and use the person's body to support the injured arm.

Do not try to put the bandage around the arm and splint, as this will put pressure on the broken bone and may shut off circulation.

If the broken arm is straight, keep it that way. Make a long splint as already described and slip it around the arm. Have someone else support the upper arm and the splint while you are moving the arm to the side. Then bandage arm and splint to the body.

Forearm. This is one of the commonest fractures. Again we can use our newspaper or blanket splint. Bandage the splint around the forearm. The splint should be long enough to reach from the elbow to the finger tips, and the hand should be placed with the thumb up to prevent rotating the forearm and broken bones. Then use a sling to support the forearm, with the hand a few inches above the elbow.

The Leg. Fractures of the hip and thigh are so serious that they should be given first aid only by experienced persons with special training and equipment. As a Scout, your duty is to try to keep the injured person lying where he fell until expert aid arrives. Under no circumstances except where the injured person is in greater danger from fire, freezing or falling should he be moved without proper splints—and that means traction splints.

Below the knee the conditions are very similar to the forearm and you can put on the same sort of padded magazine or newspaper splint but be sure it is long enough to reach from the knee to the heel. Or you can take a folded blanket or a pillow, bend it into a long channel. To apply the splint to the lower leg be very careful in lifting the leg to have someone support both sides of the fracture while you pull a little on the ankle, and so move the leg over or slip the splint under and gently let the leg down into the channel. Then bandage the splint in place and bandage the two legs together for support. If the fracture is above the middle of the lower leg, then the splint must be long enough to go well above the knee.

Fractures of the wrist and ankle may be given the same first aid as those of the forearm or lower leg.

Fractures of the bones in the hand or foot are not likely to be serious, but without proper medical care, may result in a crippled hand or foot or a stiff or crooked finger or toe. A padded splint of stiff paper, magazine, cardboard or thin board is placed against the palm of the hand or the sole of the foot, extending beyond the finger or toe, and bandaged in place without pressure.

After putting on a splint it must be examined every half hour to be sure it is not too tight. Following a fracture a limb may swell rapidly and a splint that was put on properly may be too tight half an hour later. So if you have to wait for the doctor, watch that splint. If the injured person complains of much pain or if the extremity gets cold, try loosening the bandages just a little, but do not take them off or try to change splints. Some fractures are going to be painful no matter how skillfully the splints are applied.

All fracture victims will suffer some shock, so try to prevent it by keeping the person lying down, prevent him from getting chilled and after the splints have been applied, put him in shock position—head low, feet raised—except in cases with a head injury where the face is red.

Transporting Injured Persons

Proper transportation of the injured person is a very important part of First Aid. A good piece of First Aid may be completely undone by improper transportation. Head injuries, fractured skulls, broken backs and fractures of the lower limbs are often made much worse by improper handling.

A severely injured person should always be carried on a stretcher. Persons with head injuries and fractures of the skull, spine, pelvis, thigh or leg should be moved only in a lying position. And then only on a doctor's orders and with his direction, except in very unusual circumstances.

Do not be hurried into moving a patient. Very few cases require breakneck speed. Necessary First Aid should always be given and any tight clothing loosened before the patient is moved. Except when the patient's face is red, he should be covered with a blanket or other suitable covering to keep warm during transportation.

Improvised Stretchers—The ordinary stretcher known as the army stretcher is the most satisfactory for general use, if it is available. Usually, however, a stretcher has to be improvised.

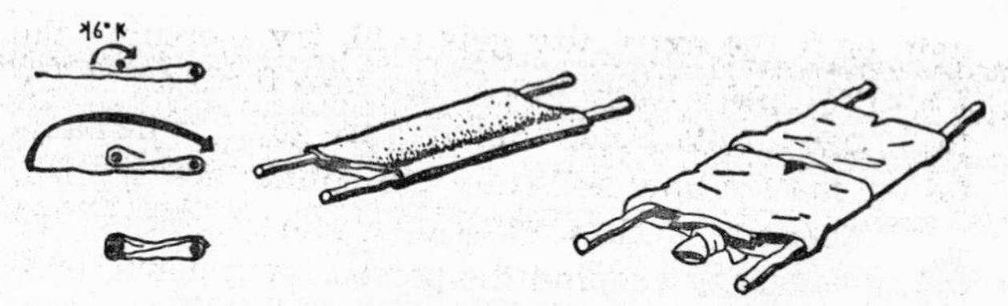

Use clothing, a blanket, shelter half or ground cloth to make a stretcher. Test the stretcher first.

The patient is carried feet first unless going up a steep grade. When the bearers of a stretcher with poles are not very strong, it may be advisable to use four bearers—one at each end of each pole.

Transportation Without a Stretcher—Frequently it is necessary to carry an injured person and no stretcher can be secured. Then one of the following methods may be used.

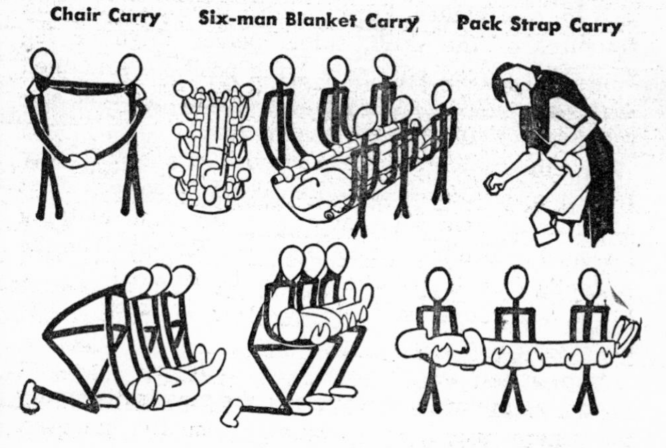

Three-man carry

SIGNALING

CHAPTER 21

Signaling is more than fun. Often it saves you a lot of time and work. In an emergency it may save life.

Take the example of a Troop starting on an over-nighter away from their base camp. The Silver Fox Patrol is part way up a mountain when they find that the meat that was to have been left in the cooler at camp till the last minute has been left there even longer. In fact it is still in the cooler instead of a Patrol pack.

Will the Scout with the short memory have to make the long trek to camp and back, while the rest of the Patrol wait? No, because the Lone Wolf Patrol has not left camp yet, and there are signalers in both Patrols.

One hiker ties his neckerchief to a staff, making a signal flag. Another removes the cover from his mess kit. They stand out on a point of rock in view of camp. Flashes of sunlight reflected from the shiny cover attract attention in camp. Then, by Morse with the flag, goes a request for the forgotten chow. The hikers get a "Roger" and "Wilco" from camp and go on their way, knowing that the Troop will have meat for supper.

A Scout's signaling skill was a lifesaver one evening when he was on a fishing trip with his father. In a wind storm a tree blew down, fell across their car, and knocked the father unconscious. After giving first aid, the Scout sized up the situation. The nearest help was at the village across the lake. An ex-Navy radioman ran the boat landing there. The car was facing in that direction, and the headlights still worked. The Scout began signaling "SOS. Doctor needed," by flashing the lights on and off. The radioman saw the flashes, read the message, and brought a doctor by boat in time to save the father's life.

Scouts use **Field Signals** and **International Morse Code** for communicating with each other.

Field Signals

Silent field signals have come down to us from the Indians. For instance, a large hunting party would maneuver by these signals to surround a herd of buffalo. When your Patrol or Troop uses field signals to get into various formations, you can say goodbye to noisy blasts of leaders' whistles. Onlookers will marvel at how quietly and quickly your group forms for a game or assembles for a parade. On hikes, many stalking games are possible with the signals. One test of your leadership ability is how you direct a Patrol or Troop with silent signals.

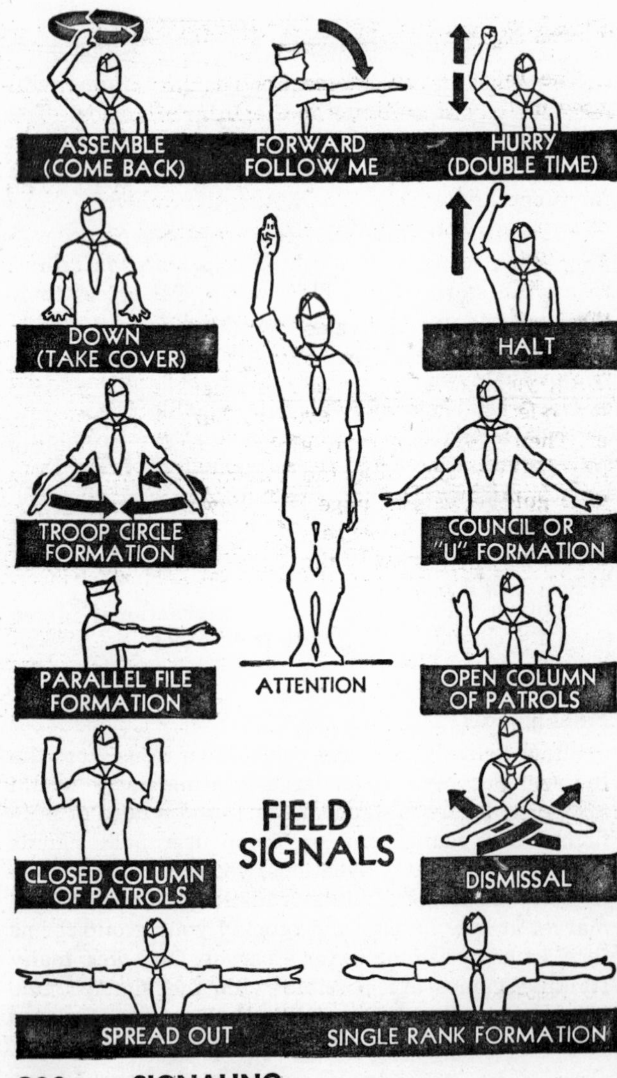
ASSEMBLE (COME BACK)
FORWARD FOLLOW ME
HURRY (DOUBLE TIME)
DOWN (TAKE COVER)
HALT
TROOP CIRCLE FORMATION
COUNCIL OR "U" FORMATION
PARALLEL FILE FORMATION
ATTENTION
OPEN COLUMN OF PATROLS
FIELD SIGNALS
CLOSED COLUMN OF PATROLS
DISMISSAL
SPREAD OUT
SINGLE RANK FORMATION

Morse Signaling

The International Morse Code is the most widely used method of getting a message through, and there are many ways of sending Morse: flag, red blinker light or heliograph by day; flashlight, lantern or torch by night; and at any time by buzzer, whistle, bugle, telegraph, drum or radio. You can invent others. For example, seated next to a friend, you can "talk" by a series of long and short pressures of the hand.

A radio instructor once said, "There is no easy way to learn Morse, but there is a less hard way." First, you and a buddy decide whether you are going to learn by ear or by eye—by buzzer, or by blinker. Then **throw away** any alphabet with dots (.) and dashes (—) alongside the letters. Instead, use the code guide given on page 386. Now you are on that "less hard" trail, because you are going to learn the Morse language without the useless step of translating it into dots and dashes.

"A" will be a short and a long period of sound, or a short and a long flash of light. Never think or say "dot dash."

Send the parts of a character close-spaced, leaving the pause between characters. Thus it is didah for "A" not dit-dah which would be "ET." A dah should be about three times as long as a dit.

LESSON GROUPS

Group I

E Dit
T Dah
A DiDah
O DahDahDah
I DiDit
N DahDit
S DiDiDit

WORDS USING LETTERS IN GROUP I

IS NO IT TO SET SIT TENT TONE NONE TOE SEA NEAT TEN ONE SENT SEAT STONE TIN SON INTO STAIN NONE TEA ANT TOAST SEASON EASE NET

A TENT IS SET. A SON IS IN A SEA. IT IS NOT TOAST. NONE IS SENT TO SINNIE.

Group II
H DiDiDiDit
R DiDahDit
D DahDiDit
L DiDahDiDit
U DiDiDah
C DahDiDahDit
5 DiDiDiDiDit

Group III
M DahDah
P DiDahDahDit
F DiDiDahDit
W DiDahDah
V DiDiDiDah
0 (number) DahDahDahDahDah

Group IV
Y DahDiDahDah
B DahDiDiDit
G DahDahDit
J DiDahDahDah
Q DahDahDiDah
4 DiDiDiDiDah

Group V
K DahDiDah
X DahDiDiDah
Z DahDahDiDit
1 DiDahDahDahDah
2 DiDiDahDahDah
Period DiDahDiDahDiDah
Comma DahDahDiDiDahDah

Group VI
3 DiDiDiDahDah
6 DahDiDiDiDit
7 DahDahDiDiDit
Question DiDiDahDahDiDit
End message DiDahDiDahDit
End communication DiDiDiDahDiDah

Group VII
8 DahDahDahDiDit
9 DahDahDahDahDit
Wait DiDahDiDiDit
Received O.K. DiDahDit

Learn one group at a time, then make up words and phrases from this group and send them. As soon as letters have been learned, practice by sending words and phrases only. After learning the Procedure Signs (pages 384-385), you are ready to handle messages in the field.

BLINKER		BUZZER OR RADIO		WIGWAG	
SENDER	RE-CEIVER	SENDER	RE-CEIVER	SENDER	RE-CEIVER
AA AA	K	CQ CQ	K	Waving overhead	K
BT	T	BT		BT	T
Campfire	T	Campfire		Campfire	T
starts	T	starts		starts	T
at	T	at		at	T
8	T	8		8	T
tonight	T	tonight		tonight	T
AR		AR		AR	

Wigwag Signaling

A wigwag flag is a two-foot square of red or white with a contrasting 8-inch square in the center and mounted on a six-foot staff. Use a red flag against a light background (sky, sand, snow) and a white flag against a dark background (dark trees or dark building).

Wigwag signals all start with the flag held straight up. Hold the bottom of the staff belt-high in the palm of one hand. With the other hand grasp the staff a foot above the bottom. A "dit" is made by swinging the flag in a 90-degree angle to the right and back. A "dah" is made by a similar swing to the left and back. An interval between words is made by dipping the flag forward and back.

Swing the flag smoothly, easily, without jerking. Keep it as flat as possible toward whoever is receiving the message. To avoid twisting the flag around the staff, swing it in a slight loop. Thus in sending "A" you make a slim figure 8 with the tip of the staff. When a wind is blowing, face slightly into or away from it to keep the flag flying fairly flat.

Meaning	*Explanation*
Attention	I have a message for you; make ready to receive.
Go Ahead	I am ready to receive.
Wait	Wait—I will be ready to receive you or to finish in a moment.
I cannot receive you	Radio: Your signals are too weak. Blinker: Your light not properly aimed. Flags: Move up Move down Move right Move left
Break	Beginning of text of message.
End of word	End of word.
End of sentence	Period.
Error	I have made a mistake and will repeat.
Word received	Made by receiver after each word to indicate received.
Repeat	Repeat.
Message received	Message is received completely.
End of message	Signing off — no more traffic.

SIGNS

Radio	*Blinker*	*Wigwag*
Call or CQ	Call or AA	Call or Waving Overhead
K	K	K
AS	AS	AS
QRJ	W	MU MD MR ML
BT	BT	BT
Space	Space	Front
AAA	AAA	AAA
EEEEEEEE	EEEEEEEE	EEEEEEEE
	T	T
IMI	IMI	IMI
R	R	R
AR	AR	AR

International Morse Code

Intervals denote sound	*Letters*	*Intervals denote light flashes*
di-dah	A	short-long
dah-di-di-dit	B	long-short-short-short
dah-di-dah-dit	C	long-short-long-short
dah-di-dit	D	long-short-short
dit	E	short
di-di-dah-dit	F	short-short-long-short
dah-dah-dit	G	long-long-short
di-di-di-dit	H	short-short-short-short
di-dit	I	short-short
di-dah-dah-dah	J	short-long-long-long
dah-di-dah	K	long-short-long
di-dah-di-dit	L	short-long-short-short
dah-dah	M	long-long
dah-dit	N	long-short
dah-dah-dah	O	long-long-long
di-dah-dah-dit	P	short-long-long-short
dah-dah-di-dah	Q	long-long-short-long
di-dah-dit	R	short-long-short
di-di-dit	S	short-short-short
dah	T	long
di-di-dah	U	short-short-long
di-di-di-dah	V	short-short-short-long
di-dah-dah	W	short-long-long
dah-di-di-dah	X	long-short-short-long
dah-di-dah-dah	Y	long-short-long-long
dah-dah-di-dit	Z	long-long-short-short

Numerals

di-dah-dah-dah-dah	1	short-long-long-long-long
di-di-dah-dah-dah	2	short-short-long-long-long
di-di-di-dah-dah	3	short-short-short-long-long
di-di-di-di-dah	4	short-short-short-short-long
di-di-di-di-dit	5	short-short-short-short-short
dah-di-di-di-dit	6	long-short-short-short-short
dah-dah-di-di-dit	7	long-long-short-short-short
dah-dah-dah-di-dit	8	long-long-long-short-short
dah-dah-dah-dah-dit	9	long-long-long-long-short
dah-dah-dah-dah-dah	0	long-long-long-long-long

Morse Signaling with a Buzzer

The first job to tackle is to memorize the code. Before wireless or code radio reached its present state of development, the beginner thought that the most important method of using it was by flag and soon found that he was badly handicapped with a great deal to "unlearn." Usually when you use the Morse Code, you will be using it as the code was originally intended, as a sonic or sound signaling system. The radio, field telegraph, buzzer or whistle will be the instrument. The fastest and most effective means of transmitting the code is by sound. Let's learn it that way!

The idea of learning by sound is that on hearing "dit," you know just by its sound that it is "E."

For equipment you will need something with which to make a sound—a buzzer, whistle or horn. You need paper and pencil. NO CHARTS.

How to Use the Key

To use the key properly, the secret of high-speed sending, have your hand, arm, and body in a comfortable, relaxed position. Your feet should be flat on the floor and the key placed so that the entire forearm rests on the desk, or on the same level with the key. Grasp the key lightly but firmly with your thumb and first two fingers. The thumb is not under the knob, rather on the side. Adjust the key so that there is an up and down motion of about one-sixteenth of an inch. Your elbow becomes a pivot and the entire forearm, flexing at the wrist, is used to send the characters. This allows the muscles of your arm to do most of the work and is less tiring than if the wrist alone were used. Allow the spring to bring the knob back into position; don't pull it back with your thumb or your sending will be "choppy." If you feel your arm and body tightening up, sit back and rest for a moment, because your sending will become an unintelligible mess, if you continue in a nervous tense state. A talk with a telegraph or radio operator may produce some valuable tips on sending.

Practice

You should start practice with another Scout who is in the same stage of code work. The two of you should have buzzers, and if you want to make the practice more interesting, a little time can be spent in hitching two earphones into your buzzer hookup so that you will have a rudimentary field telegraph system. It is not necessary, however, for the simple buzzer will serve admirably.

Send single letters at first. Send them slowly so that the listener may learn to recognize each character quickly and without hesitation. Always remember to divide the work evenly! It is easy to become lopsided, having a great deal more proficiency in sending than in receiving.

When the receipt of single letters seems to be coming easily, start the slow sending of complete words and then short and simple messages. Try to have the material sent at a slightly faster rate than you can copy easily. This will keep you alert and active.

Use one group of characters (pages 381-82) at a time; take it easy and learn by SOUND.

In copying, write each letter as you receive it. Do not write down dots and dashes! Print the letters. Script is too easily mixed up in rapid copying. If you miss a letter, leave the blank and go on, and don't worry about it or try to figure out what it might have been!

Don't practice too long at one session. Half an hour a day on a regular schedule is better than cramming exhausting labor into one evening. In a short time you will be sending and receiving well above the required rate of seven words a minute (approximately 35 letters).

After you have obtained reasonable proficiency, try tuning in on the radio. Many commercial sets have a short-wave receiving attachment by which you can tune into the lower bands which carry code work.

It won't be long before you find yourself recognizing word groups and copying them as a group. Write while listening to the next word. You will find that it is far more restful to listen and write at the same time. Good operators are usually copying several words "behind" the signals to which they are listening.

Signal Teams

A signal team, whether sending or receiving, should normally consist of four — team chief and observer, signalman, recorder and messenger. In sending, the recorder reads the message word-by-word or phrase-by-phrase, while the signaler uses the flags. In receiving, the signalman reads the letters as seen, to be written down by the recorder. The recorder should be a good signalman so that he can alternate to give his teammate a rest, or serve as signalman when the latter is absent.

SWIMMING

CHAPTER 22

A fish can swim but it can't travel on land. You can do both. You are like otters, beavers and other animals—an animal which can swim.

A fish can live only a few minutes out of water and a man can live only a few minutes under water unless he has special diving gear. Both men and fish must have oxygen but they get it in different ways. Fish take it from water passing over their gills, men from the air in their lungs.

Don't let anyone tell you that swimming is not a natural thing for a man to do. You may hear that a young baby can't swim, but a young baby can't walk either. He must learn, and that takes time. When the time comes for that same child to learn to swim, it's so easy that he can pick it up in a few hours. It's not unusual for a child of three years to be a good swimmer. If some folks wouldn't talk so much about

First get accustomed to the water

swimming being so hard to do a fellow would find it a whole lot easier to learn.

Swimming *is* natural, but it's different enough from land travel so that it takes a little while to get used to it. The same thing is true with playing baseball, shooting a gun or climbing a tree.

Let's Go!

Before you begin you should know two things about yourself and the water—floating and breathing. Almost all boys and about every girl can float with nose and mouth out of water, and without any movement of hands or feet, and that's all that is necessary. However, there are a few folks with large bones and heavy muscles who can't float without some slight movement of their hands or feet.

You would be surprised at the number of people who have had to be rescued because they became scared and forgot to float. A good many of those who drown would have been perfectly safe, if they had kept their hands under water and their chins high. If you practice floating and find you can't do it, don't worry. Some of the world's greatest swimmers can't float either.

Breathing

Before you try to float, learn about breathing. Practice it at home in a washbasin or pan. You need air with every complete swimming stroke, just as a gasoline engine must have air with every stroke of its pistons.

On land, you naturally breathe in and out through your nose. When swimming, you breathe in through the mouth and out through mouth *and* nose.

Breathe in through your mouth, then turn your head so your face is under water. Breathe out through your nose and mouth.

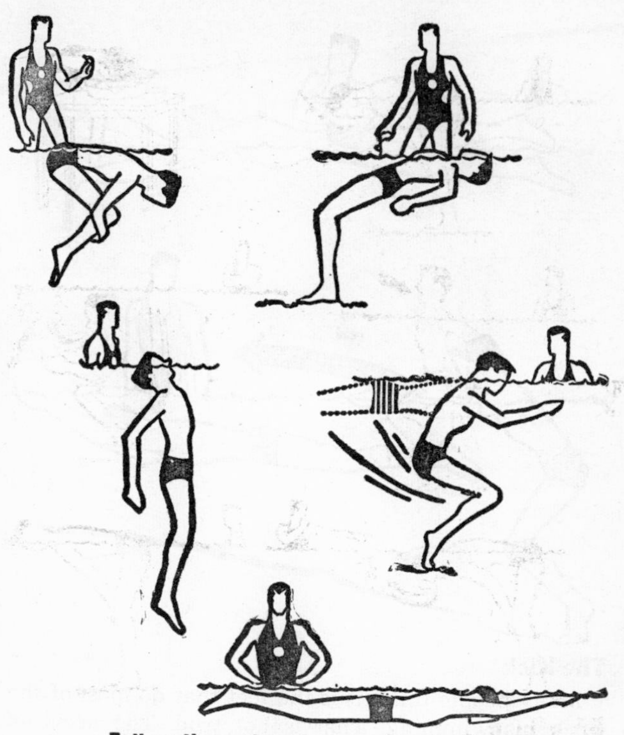

Follow these steps to learn how to float

Now Floating

With your Scoutmaster or a pal who can swim, (and be sure to have someone stand by to lend a helping hand if you need it) try to float in water about up to your lower ribs. The illustrations show the steps to follow. In learning to float be sure to keep your hands under water. When you raise your arms, you will sink. That is often the reason why people drown. If they keep their hands down under water they would be all right.

The Kick

Many people think it is the feet that do most of the work in swimming. That is not true. The arms do about two thirds of it. You should learn the leg stroke first however. And you can practice this at home before you go to the water at all. Look at the illustrations to learn how to do it.

Now Plunge

Stand in the water up to your lower ribs. Face your buddy who is about six feet away. Hook your toes in the bottom. Lean forward, take a breath, lower your head and plunge toward him. You will glide through the water like a fish.

When you have learned to kick, then practice using your arms and hands

Then Plunge and Kick

After plunging a few times with a little more distance each time, try the up and down leg kick. You'll just *zip* into your waiting buddy's hands.

Now Those Hands and Arms

In this crawl stroke you will see that the hands act like scoops or paddles. Reach one arm at a time out in front of you. Get an open hand hold on the water and pull it back toward your feet. When the Australian, Dick Cavill, first swam it, someone thought it looked the way a baby looks as he crawls across the floor. The stroke was named the "Crawl."

The stronger the pull with each arm, the faster you'll swim, *if* that pull is *right.* It takes practice. Try it at home in front of a mirror. Almost all great coaches use mirrors as aids in training their star swimmers. Watch the movement of each arm carefully.

Put them all together—legs, arms, hands and breathing

Put It All Together

Practice that arm stroke standing up in the water; then, leaning over, so your head is in the water. Try breathing with each stroke—breathe in on one side as the arm on that side leaves the water. Breathe out as that arm goes under water, and your face is under water. Now standing in the water up to your ribs, and facing shore, plunge toward shore. Start the kick, then start the arm stroke and the breathing. Practice and keep at it until you can do it without thinking.

Deep Water

You are almost ready for your deep water try. Be sure your buddy is standing by, as you will stand by some other beginner some day. Before you go out over your head, learn how to get yourself in a flat swimming position from a standing position in the water. It is almost like that plunge that you learned. Drop your head forward, extend both arms forward at the same time and start to kick. Then begin your arm stroke. With practice you will have no trouble when you get into deep water. Now is the time to

Practice jumping feet first into the water, leveling off for swimming and turning around in the water

take it easy. Think first, and don't do any thoughtless thing that may spoil your fun.

The best way to start deep water swimming is to swim beside a boat that is rowed along with you, or along the side of a pier or swimming pool, or across a narrow piece of deep water, with someone standing by with a pole to help you. Then after you have practiced this try your *jump off* in water about six feet deep, and learn to flatten out from a standing to swimming position.

That's the way to start. But there is more to learn before you will be a real swimmer and can take care of yourself. The good old-fashioned backstroke is a friend that has saved many a tired swimmer. You should know all about it. Then learn the side stroke and the trudgen for distance. Then some day you'll be able to swim a mile. You'll find those strokes described in the *Swimming* Merit Badge Pamphlet.

THE EIGHT-DEFENSE PLAN

1. **Medical Examination**—The first defense is a thorough physical examination.

2. **Trained Supervisor**—One who holds an up-to-date Lifesaving Certificate of a National Aquatic School, or of Red Cross or YMCA should direct the swim.

3. **Safe Swimming Area**—The bottom of the swimming area is examined to make sure that it's safe, with no deep holes, stumps or rocks. It's then marked off in three sections: Not more than three and a half feet deep for nonswimmers, up to just-over-head depth for beginners, deep water for swimmers.

4. **Life Guards**—Two older Scouts who are good swimmers are life guards. They're stationed ashore and equipped with a life line.

5. **Lookout**—A lookout stands at a point where he can watch all the swimmers.

6. **Ability Groups**—The Scouts are divided into three groups: nonswimmers who are learning; beginners who have swum 50 feet; and swimmers who have made 100 yards—25 of them on the back—and who can float. Each group stays in its area during swim.

7. **Buddy Plan**—Each Scout is paired with another boy of the same swimming ability. The two of you check in together, keep within ten feet of each other at all times, and check out together. Whenever a buddy signal is sounded, buddies grasp each other by the hand and hold their arms high, so that the lookout can check the number of buddy teams.

8. **Good Discipline**—The waterman sees to it that there's good discipline — with strict attention to the rules, but with a chance for a good time.

RESCUE IN THE WATER

"One of the very best rescue stories I ever heard," said Bill the old Life Guard, "was about a Brooklyn boy, Rocco Cassandra. Rocco and several other boys were riding bicycles on an old Newtown Creek pier.

"One boy's wheel skidded and he fell in. He couldn't swim. He tried to float, but he kept going down. Rocco was the only swimmer in the crowd. There were some men around, but they just stood there, looking.

"Rocco flung off his pants, sweater and sneakers and jumped in. The water was cold, but he swam out several feet and grabbed his friend. He got his right hand under the boy's body, and then managed to swim back to the poles which held up the pier, where he hung on for dear life.

"Meantime the boys on the pier had taken off their sweaters. They tied them together and dropped them to Rocco. He grabbed the tail of a sweater and the boys pulled. The sweaters slid apart. Then one of the men dropped a rope. Rocco wrapped his feet around Eddie's body, grabbed the rope and tied it round him. The men pulled them up.

"Smart piece of work, wasn't it?" asked Bill. "Rocco used his head. He didn't get excited but figured out one thing at a time, cool as could be.

"Most folks would have jumped overboard, clothes and all, and maybe both of them would have drowned. But not Rocco. He took 'em all off, even his shoes.

"And his knowing enough to jump gets me! I wonder where he learned that? That Creek is black and greasy and almost anything could have been sticking up under water to break his neck if he had gone in head first. Lots of people get killed that way."

Scout Rescues

Since Scouting started in America in 1910 more than 3600 Scouts have received awards from the National Court of Honor for saving lives at the risk of their own. Some of these rescues involved other kinds of accidents, but most of them were from drowning. Many other Scouts have saved lives, but no one except those Scouts and the persons they saved knew anything about it.

During 22 of these years—1911 through 1933—25 Scouts lost their lives in rescue attempts of which there is no formal record. Many Scout methods of rescue have been perfected and because they are trained, Scouts are able to save people with less risk to themselves and others because they are prepared.

How To Prepare

Work hard to improve your swimming. Go a little greater distance each time you swim. If you swim in a swimming pool, add a few more laps each day.

One hundred yards is a good beginning and a quarter mile even better. After you have done the quarter several different times, go after the half mile. Still later when you feel strong in the water, you will not find a mile too hard.

When you swim for distance, have someone, such as your Dad or Scoutmaster go along with you in a boat.

When Someone Needs Help

Whether you are a good swimmer or not, call *loudly* for help and keep calling to attract attention.

Usually water accidents happen close to shore. A stick, oar, pole, or rope will reach to the person in trouble. Often he can reach it. Sometimes planks, fence rails or the limb of a tree are nearby and can be pushed out.

If there is a boat handy, row or paddle it out and swing the stern of it around so it can be grasped. Stay with the boat. Excited persons sometimes row a boat out to make a rescue, then spoil their work by foolishly jumping out to give help. The best thing is to swing the boat into the struggling person's hands or reach out an oar or a hand to him.

When nothing is at hand, and a small child is in trouble in water that is not deep, you can wade out and pull the child in. But if you can't swim, it would be better to whip off your shirt and holding a sleeve or the tail, swing it out and into the child's hands and then pull him in.

If you swim well and a person is too far from shore to reach with a pole or rope, get out of your clothes quickly and run or jump into the water. *DO NOT DIVE.* Many boys and grownups have broken their necks that way.

Take your shirt with you and throw the end into the hands of the person in trouble and tow him ashore. While you are doing this talk to him. Say, "You will be all right; I'll have you ashore in a minute; don't fight me," or anything that will make him know help is at hand.

If there is nothing that you can carry out, then swim around behind him. Pull his head back, slide your hand across his chest and under the opposite arm. Then swim ashore.

If he has gone under water, call loudly for help. Dive under to bring him up. Tow him to shore and give him artificial respiration.

You must not get close enough to a struggling person to be kicked, clawed or grasped. That's the

reason you carry something with you if you can, or swim around behind him. If by mistake, you get in too close and he tries to grasp you, duck under the arm or push him away using a straight arm thrust against his chest. Then go around behind.

Things to Practice

Undressing You should never attempt a swimming rescue with your clothes on. Practice undressing as quickly as possible when you get ready for bed each night. Be able to get out of your street clothes down to underpants or swim trunks in less than 20 seconds. Before long you will do it in 15 and not a button lost.

Rope Throw Fix up a target for rope throwing practice, out in your yard. Use a stick 5 feet long to represent extended arms. In the middle, nail a tin can for the head. Use 40 feet of ¼ line. Throw 25, then 35 feet, at the rate of three throws in a minute. If the rope lands across the "head" 5 points; if between "head" and fingertips, 3 points.

Jump Jump into the water feet first without allowing your head to go under; then start to sprint to your buddy or an imaginary man 20 feet away.

Carry Disrobe quickly and carrying your shirt in your teeth, or a pole, oar or paddle in your hand,

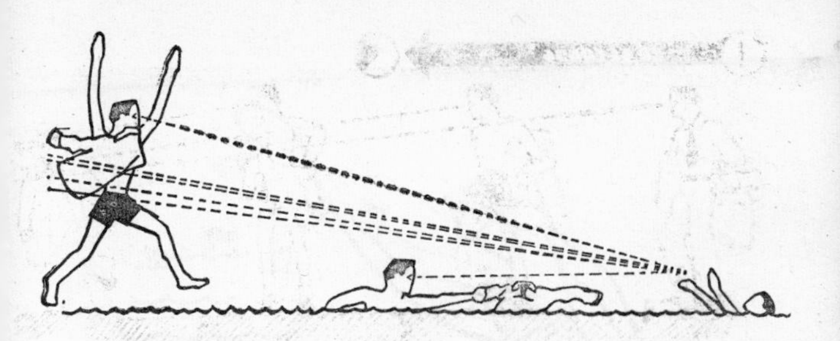

swim to your buddy 20 feet away. Let him grasp whatever you carry and tow him ashore.

Dive Dive from the surface in water 6, 7 and 8 feet deep to recover objects on the bottom. Keep your eyes open and protect your head with one hand if you can't see under water. If you have trouble going straight down practice turning somersaults at home. It will help you to double up and then go down headfirst in the water.

Cross-chest Carry Approach a person from the back when he is struggling, and get him in a cross-chest carry and take him ashore. Then give him artificial respiration.

Practice defending yourself against being grasped, kneed, kicked or clawed. Learn how to use a straight

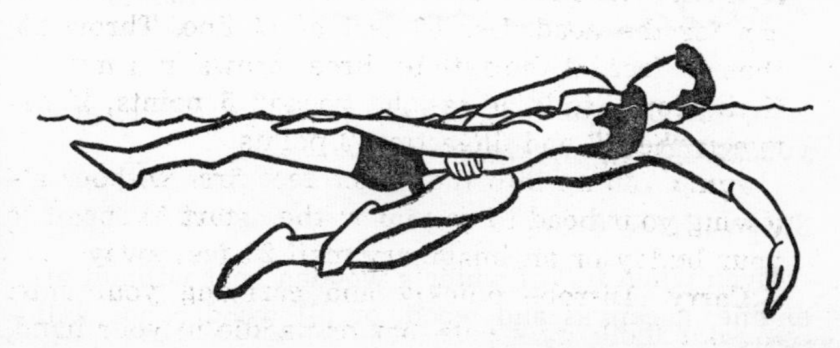

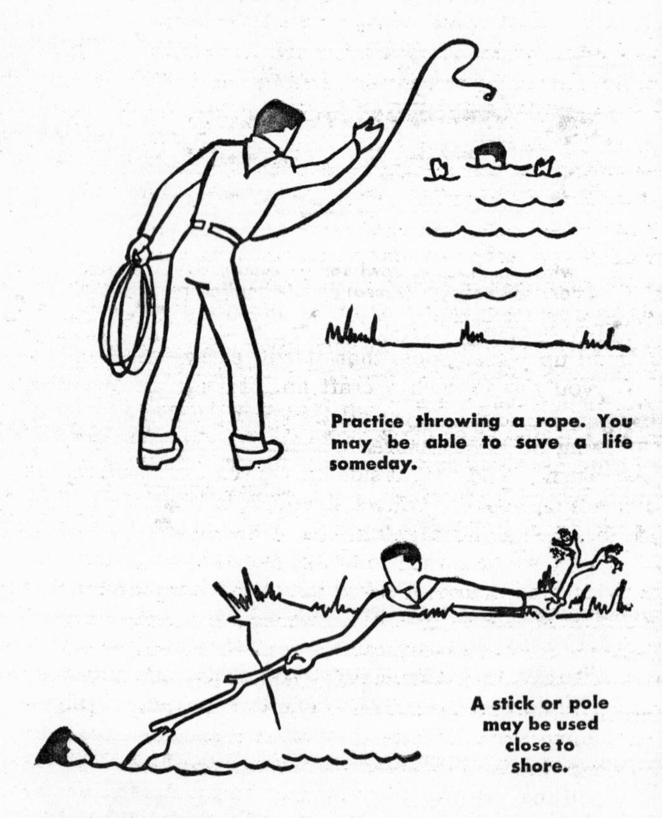

Practice throwing a rope. You may be able to save a life someday.

A stick or pole may be used close to shore.

arm, and how to duck in case someone tries to grab you round the neck.

Stay with the Boat

Even when full of water a wooden boat without an engine, a canvas and wood, or all wood canoe will

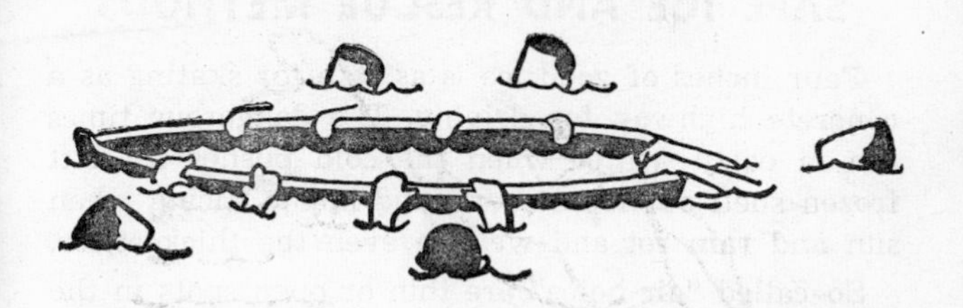

Stay with the boat—a rowboat or canoe, even if filled with water, will support several people holding on to the sides

hold up more people than it will carry when empty. If you are in such a craft and it leaks or is rolled over, be sure to keep all those who were in it from trying to swim ashore.

Turn the boat right side up. One or two weak swimmers can get in. Others should hold on to the sides. Everybody should keep as low in the water as possible. Two or three swimmers can hold on to the boat with one hand and take the boat ashore, swimming with one hand and both feet.

Metal boats and those made of plastics have either air tanks or some buoyant substance. After a time the tanks are likely to leak and the buoyant substance become lost. Because you can't always depend on these boats, it's better to test them first. Do this by filling the boat full of water and watching for air bubbles as you would if testing the inner tube of an auto tire.

If you want to become a good waterman, work hard on the requirements for Swimming, Life Saving and Rowing Merit Badges, quality as a "Scout Life Guard," be able to take care of yourself, and be fully prepared to help those who aren't so fortunate.

SAFE ICE AND RESCUE METHODS

Four inches of good ice is as safe for skating as a concrete highway for driving. The dangerous times are in early winter when the cold pushes its first frozen shell out from shore, and in the spring when sun and rain rot and weaken even the thickest ice.

So-called "air holes" are thin or open spots in the ice caused by strong currents or springs that bubble up from the bottom. The moving water is slow to freeze over and when it does it is weak. Such spots can be marked with red flags or bushes stuck in the holes or brush piled high enough to be seen. It is at these thin places that nearly all accidents occur. Young children go through them on sleds; over-daring skaters break through trying to go a little closer to the hole than the other fellow, and at night these air holes can't be seen unless well marked or lighted.

The drawings show ways of helping the fellow who has broken through the ice, and one way for you to help yourself should it happen to you.

If it's up to you to give aid, here are a few things that will help:

Call loudly for **help** if you are alone, and **keep on calling.**

Stay out of the water yourself if possible. If you can slide a pole, fence rail or board to the fellow in the water, he can rest the ends on solid ice on each side of the hole and climb out and roll to thicker ice or to shore.

Should you break through, you will get out with only a cold wetting, if you keep from becoming excited and frightened. Support yourself with one hand on the ice while you break off the thin edges with

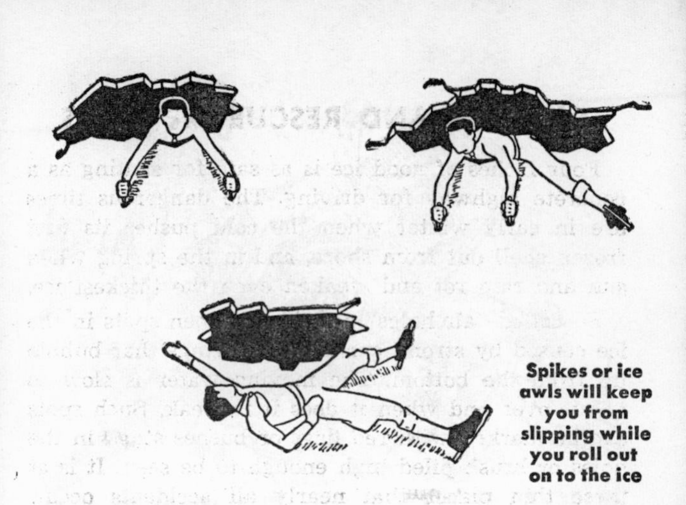

Spikes or ice awls will keep you from slipping while you roll out on to the ice

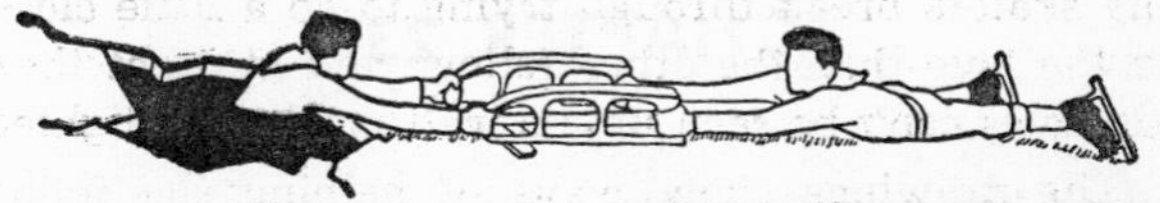

A sled, ladder or pole will help another fellow pull himself out of the water

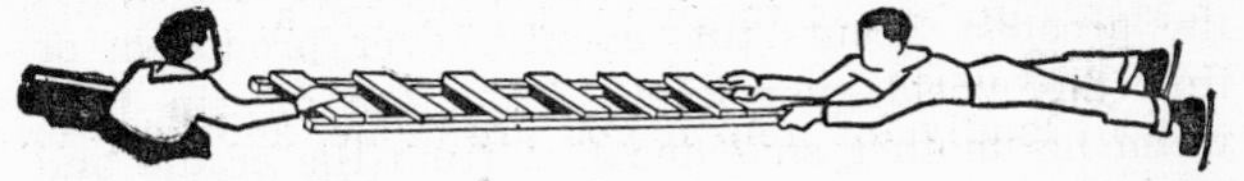

the other. When you have broken your way far enough so that the ice is strong, slide your arms up over the edges, kick your feet up and down close to the surface, to force yourself up and forward. As soon as your hips are out of water start to roll sideways away from the hole. This will spread your weight over a large surface and prevent another break through. An open knife dug into the ice or a pair of ice awls will help. It is a good idea to carry them whenever you go on ice.

PHYSICAL FITNESS

CHAPTER 23

God has given us a life to live, and we want it to be useful, happy, and full of action.

Frederick Burnham lived that way. He was one of the greatest Scouts this country ever produced, or that the world ever knew. From the day in 1862 when his mother snatched him from the cradle and hid him in a stack of corn to save him from Sioux Indian raiders, to the end of his life at eighty-six, his years were filled with daring deeds and remarkable experiences.

He was an Indian fighter; famed hunter; miner in Arizona, Africa and Alaska's Klondike; cattle rancher; scout and guide through two terrible Matabele wars in Africa, the second of which he himself brought to an end by hunting down the M'Limo, the dreadful high priest of the tribe. He was chief of scouts of the

British Army in the Boer War; holder of the D.S.O. (Distinguished Service Order); friend and teacher of Baden-Powell; and a clean-living, quiet-spoken gentleman.

For more than three-quarters of his lifetime, this mighty man of small stature—he was only five feet, seven inches tall—faced uncommon dangers. During those years and the less exciting ones that followed, he made it his business to keep perfectly fit by taking the best possible care of his health. He was able to get out of many a death trap when hunted by enemies, because of his daring, his keen mind, and a body that he always kept ready to do exactly what he wanted it to. He knew that to succeed and live through his scouting missions, he must always be in first-class physical condition. He did not smoke, drink, or weaken his body in any of the ways that caused the death of some of his friends.

When over eighty years of age, he was as alert as you would expect a great scout to be. And quick! There is nothing slow about a man able to snatch a fly out of the air with his fingers—and he could do that. Major Burnham was a great example of making the most of the body God gave him. He studied **keeping fit** as he did the skills of the scout.

Take Care of Yourself

There's a lot to this health business, but a fellow doesn't need to learn it all at one time. There are a few things that should be remembered every day. To start with, and before we get down to details, let's agree that just as fast as a fellow can do so, he ought to learn to **take care of himself.** Begin with little things such as taking care of small cuts, then gradually take on bigger things. It's wonderful practice for what is certain to follow. Everything we learn, we will use or know how to use, over and over again. Knowing we can take care of ourselves gives us self-confidence. We need a lot of that because it helps us to help other people when they need aid badly.

Scouting teaches that the sooner a boy learns to take care of himself, the easier it will be for him to face life as it is, and not let it get him down.

What has this to do with **physical fitness?** Well, it has a lot to do with **self-protection,** which is a big part of keeping fit. A good example is the Scout who was alone and, struck by a rattlesnake, took care of himself and saved his own life. Courage many times helps keep a fellow from getting laid up for a long time. One boy was so afraid of going to the doctor that he didn't tell his parents about the pain in his side until he fainted. Then he had to stay in the hospital for many weeks, instead of a few days, after his ruptured appendix was removed. Courage would have saved him all this.

Courage helps a fellow fight to get well when he is ill. Doctors say the will to get well is as necessary as any medicine.

Physical Fitness Means Ready

Good health means nothing wrong, but physical fitness means ready for anything. There's a big difference. Let's look at a lazy cat as an example. It sleeps all day long except when it wakes up to eat. There isn't a thing the matter with its health; it's just plain lazy. But it couldn't catch and kill a rat to save its life.

Maybe a boy or man could spend all of his hours indoors and never be sick, but he couldn't do that and be fit for hard play or emergency action.

It's not a boy's nature to worry too much over a thing like his health when he feels as frisky as a six-month-old pup, and he should not do so. But he should learn to avoid the things that will put him in bed when he has an important game to play, when the Troop's going camping, or the Patrol's going skating. And he certainly should not be scared by advertising into buying a special kind of health something-or-other which he doesn't need to stay healthy. If a fellow believed all that, he would swallow pills, gargle his throat, and take his temperature all day long.

It's natural to have a few aches and pains as you are growing up. A lot of times they are not very real and go away if a fellow gets busy and forgets. But if you have one that you know is real, tell mother or dad about it. If it gets too tough, ask them to take you to the doctor, particularly if it's down near what most folks call their stomach.

Examination by the Doctor

A good doctor is a great friend. Sure, he may put you to bed when all you think is wrong is a little sore throat, and "the old thermometer must be wrong." You can be sure he doesn't like to do it and is sorry if it happens when you had planned something important. Remember that only a few years back he was your age, and maybe had a doctor who pulled him through when the chances were pretty slim.

At least once each year go to your family doctor for a thorough check-up. An auto driver has a check-up on his car every few thousand miles, or a pilot on his plane after every few hundred hours in the air.

Suppose the doctor says to you someday, "Bud, those tonsils better come out before they get really bad." That's agreed on at home, and out they come, and the danger from those infected pests is over. If allowed to remain, they often become diseased; pus pockets form and make trouble in other parts of the body.

Now let's remember this: When we sit down with the doctor, we must **tell** him about the things that are troubling us. He can't see a pain or read our minds. A few such things which are quite natural often cause a lot of worry; and if your parents haven't explained them, your doctor can—if you ask. You don't need to hold back or hide things from him. Speak up, and you'll feel better for doing it, and he will help.

Suppose you wet the bed once in a while. Don't be afraid to ask him how to stop it. Suppose you are worrying because you have "wet dreams" or have practiced masturbation once in a while. If it has happened, don't let it scare you. If it's a habit, break it! Sure, it takes courage, and the best way is to keep busy with lots of work and play. But talk it over with your parents, religious leader or doctor; just open up to them and let them set you right.

Maybe he tells you that he thinks your eyes need attention. In that case, have them tested by an eye expert. You may get eye exercises or glasses to be worn only when you read. There are a lot of boys having trouble with their studies who would get along all right if they wore glasses. If you need them, don't mind the looks; some of the greatest athletes wear glasses.

There is a Scout Examination Form No. (1154) which you can use. Your Scoutmaster can get enough from the Scout Council headquarters for your whole Troop.

See Your Dentist

When your doctor gives you an examination, he will probably ask if you have had your teeth examined lately. They should be looked over every six months by a dentist. It's surprising how quickly pinpoint holes, unless filled, grow to big ones, and soon a tooth has to be pulled. That's not the worst of the bad-tooth business. Sometimes they become infected, and the poison they give off affects other parts of the body in painful and sometimes serious ways.

Sleep

How we all like sleep! It's nature's way of refueling us with energy when we are very tired. When we are sick, it helps us to get well. You need more sleep now than when you are older, because you are growing. Get from ten to eleven hours of sound sleep each night, with windows open enough to keep the air fresh. Pick up a little extra on Saturday morning if you can. It is possible to sleep too much just as it is possible to eat too much. You can't store up sleep, and too much at one time makes a fellow dopy.

Soap and Water

When you are nineteen or twenty years old, you will probably take a quick shower bath every day. Now two a week will do ordinarily. Keeping your skin clean is a part of keeping fit. A cut or scrape on a dirty skin is more likely to get sore and infected. Hands always need a washing with soap and warm water before every meal, and get out the dirt that shows black under finger nails. Wash your face with mild soap and water night and morning. Ears would be easier to clean if they were plain instead of fancy, but that's more reason why they need soap and water twice a day.

Feet

We should take care of those feet that carry our weight so much of the time. The chapter on Hiking tells how to do this. Another thing is to put powder between the toes every night. It helps dry up the moisture between them that probably causes what is often called "athlete's foot." If you have athlete's foot, your doctor can tell you how to stop it.

Food

Eating is something boys are famous for. While growing you should drink at least a pint of milk every day; and have fresh fruit, (or fruit juices), such as oranges, grapefruit, or tomatoes; and meat, fish or eggs and green vegetables, butter, bread and cereal.

Yes, it is hard to eat slowly, chewing food well, and drinking just as slowly; but swallowing your food whole is likely to cause an upset stomach—and what that stomach can do to a fellow when it's upset! It's easier to take a little more time. Go easy on candy and sweets of any kind—but not too easy on mother's best cake.

Bowel Movements

One bowel movement a day will do. Constipation, as difficulty with bowel movements is called, seldom bothers active people who drink five or six glasses of water each day, eat plenty of fruit, salads and green vegetables, and have a regular time for going to the toilet. Laxatives can do much more harm than good when taken without a doctor's advice. The habit of taking laxatives to cause bowel action is a very bad habit to get into, and no part of a physical fitness scheme.

Get Fit and Stay Fit

Suppose a great track star, perfectly trained and ready for tomorrow's meet, slips on the sidewalk. Not knowing how to relax and roll when falling, he injures his back and is out of an important race. Or suppose the greatest weight lifter, while alone, cuts an artery in his arm; and not knowing how to control it, loses so much blood before help comes that he cannot take part in a contest. Or suppose—but never mind more examples, you get the idea: That you must be able to **protect yourself** at all times to keep physically fit.

There are a few things you should learn that may even save your life some day.

A toothbrush, once you use it, is yours and yours alone, until its end. Use only **your own** and keep it for yourself only, and the same for towels and handkerchiefs. And never drink out of a cup or glass, or eat with spoon or fork that someone else has used. The germs of many kinds of illnesses, from common colds to tuberculosis, can be spread by careless use of such things.

Flies carry disease. Swatters made of old newspaper and D.D.T. spray kill flies. Keep 'em killed off to protect your family and yourself. If there are any choice fly meeting places around your home, clean them up.

Learn Skills

Personal first aid is what you do for yourself if you are hurt and there is no one to help you. It has saved many a man's life. It once saved the life of Burnham, the scout, when he was badly wounded, surrounded by Boer Commandos and with a mission—cutting a railroad—still to complete. He took care of his own wound, blew up the tracks, and escaped.

Swimming is a physical fitness, self-preservation skill. Don't be satisfied to just get by. Be satisfied only when you can swim for a mile. Thousands of men's lives were saved in the last war because they could swim, and other thousands lost theirs because they couldn't.

Learn to roll when you fall, forward, backward, sideways and over on your shoulder like a football player. It may save you from serious injury some day.

Learn balance. Practice walking a line on the ground, or a two-by-four plank set on edge, a rail fence, and maybe a tight rope. It's good for your leg muscles and may keep you from taking a serious fall some day.

Learn to jump forward, sideways, backward, and straight up in the air without "getting set"—just take off from where you stand. Sometimes they call that a rattle snake jump. Have you seen a man save his legs by a quick hop into the air when a steel cable snapped? It has happened.

Build up those back, shoulder, and arm muscles so that you can hang on or climb out of trouble if need be. For ten minutes a man hung by his fingers from the window sill of a burning building until rescued. Hundreds of men were saved or lost at sea in the war, depending on whether or not they could climb a rope or cargo net to safety.

Learn all of the good outdoor fun things you can. Things you can do when you grow up as well as now. To shoot a bow and a rifle, to catch fish on a pin or wooden hook or a dry fly. To sail, paddle, and row. Learn all you can about camping and nature lore and mountain climbing and winter sports and well you know—all the good physical fitness skill you can learn and have great fun doing it.

Yes, it's a lot of fun to be fit.

ON TO EAGLE

PART V

MERIT BADGE PROGRAM

CHAPTER 24

By the time you were old enough to be a Tenderfoot, you had found that you like to do certain things better than others. Perhaps you enjoy making a model plane, but not collecting stamps; or you may be a whiz at baseball, but basketball just isn't your game.

As you learned more Scouting you discovered that some of the things you never knew about before appealed to you a lot. Maybe it was first aid, or camp cooking. Formerly you were not interested because you knew nothing about it, but when you learned how to do it, you couldn't get enough.

Reason for Merit Badges

Two of the reasons for the Scout Merit Badge Plan are (1) to give you more skill in things you like to do; (2) to give you a chance to try out new activities, so that you can find new things which you really like.

The Merit Badge list in the Appendix includes more than a hundred activities which are popular with boys. Do you want to be an expert camper? The Camping and other outdoor Merit Badges will help you. If swimming is your hobby, the Swimming and the Lifesaving Merit Badges may start you on the way to being a champion. In a dozen different fields there are Merit Badges which will help lead you to the top.

If you live in the country, the projects in such Merit Badge subjects as Corn Farming, Dairying or First Aid to Animals include many things which will help you become a first-rate farmer.

Get a Hobby

Of course you want to get some new interests too. You start to make a cover for your Handbook and find you have opened the door to a brand new interest in Bookbinding. Collecting rocks and minerals on a Patrol hike for the Geology Merit Badge may start you on a hobby that will last you all your life. If you like to make things, the Merit Badges in Radio, Electricity and Farm Mechanics may be the start of a whole new field that you never thought of. Look over the list of Merit Badges.

Your Merit Badge Counselor

Older Scouts say one of the things they valued highly in their Merit Badge progress was the chance to meet the Merit Badge Counselor and talk their work over with him. He is a top-notch man in your community who gives his time and skill to help you, advising you with your projects.

The Merit Badge Pamphlets

Another good tool is the Merit Badge pamphlet prepared for each subject. These booklets make your work more fun and valuable to you. They may be obtained at your local Scout office or from the Boy Scouts of America, National Council, New Brunswick, N. J., at 25¢ each, or from your local library.

Maybe for All Your Life

Many men who were once Scouts feel that their entire lives were influenced by their Merit Badge work. Dr. Paul Siple, who when a Scout went with Admiral Byrd to the South Pole, first became interested in science through his Merit Badges. He has been with Admiral Byrd on three expeditions, and is now one of the nation's leading scientific explorers. There are hundreds of doctors, radio engineers, forest rangers and other men whose ambitions were first kindled while they were Scouts like you, earning a new Merit Badge.

Lots to Choose From

In choosing which Merit Badges you will work for, you will naturally select subjects at first that you are interested in, or that may seem easy for you. But *don't stop there.* Take some that you know will be hard; also a few subjects that you know nothing about, so as to have the fun of exploring.

First Class Scouts may earn any Merit Badge.

Merit Badges for Second Class Scouts

When you are a Second Class Scout, you want to become First Class just as soon as you can. But perhaps there are times during the week, between regular Patrol and Troop meetings, hikes and camping trips, when you can explore other fields of interest — especially your own hobbies. There are times, too, when weather, illness or other causes prevent you from completing your Scoutcraft requirements.

When the effort will not interfere with your progress toward First Class Rank, work for Merit Badges.

Second Class Scouts may earn any Merit Badges they wish, except that in the case of the following subjects the related First Class Scoutcraft requirements must be met first. The numbers in parentheses below refer to the First Class Scoutcraft requirements concerned on pages 110-114:

Astronomy (2a)
Camping (1a, 1b, 3, 7)
Canoeing (5)
Cooking (4)
First Aid (1c)
Lifesaving (5)
Pioneering (3)
Rowing (5)
Signaling (6)
Surveying (2)
Swimming (5)

Tenderfoot Scouts may not qualify for Merit Badges.

How You Qualify for Merit Badges

When you have made up your mind which Merit Badge you would like to tackle, ask your Scoutmaster for an application blank. If he feels you are ready to start working for the Badge, he signs the application and puts you in touch with your Merit Badge Counselor. Get a copy of the Merit Badge pamphlet in your subject and read it. Take it to your Counselor and talk over the requirements with him. He explains to you what you have to do and how you can get help. If you need advice in working out any of the projects you can consult your Counselor. When you have completed the requirements, make an appointment with him for examination. The Counselor gives you an examination and signs your application, if you are successful. You return the blank to the Scoutmaster. Later you will be awarded your Merit Badge, as explained in detail in Chapter 26.

Merit Badge Groups

1. **Animal Husbandry**
   - Animal Industry*
   - Beekeeping*
   - Beef Production*
   - Dairying*
   - Dog Care
   - First Aid to Animals*
   - Hog and Pork Production*
   - Pets
   - Pigeon Raising*
   - Poultry Keeping*
   - Rabbit Raising*
   - Sheep Farming*
2. **Aquatics**
   - Canoeing
   - Lifesaving
   - Rowing
   - Swimming
3. **Arts**
   - Architecture
   - Art
   - Dramatics
   - Indian Lore
   - Mechanical Drawing
   - Music
   - Photography
   - Pottery
   - Sculpture
   - Woodcarving
4. **Building**
   - Electricity
   - Farm Home and Its Planning*
   - Farm Layout and Building Arrangement*
   - Farm Mechanics*
   - Home Repairs
   - Machinery
   - Masonry
   - Metalwork
   - Painting
   - Plumbing
   - Woodwork
5. **Campcraft**
   - Camping
   - Cooking
   - Pioneering
   - Surveying
6. **Citizenship**
   - Citizenship in the Home
   - Citizenship in the Community
   - Citizenship in the Nation
   - World Brotherhood

7. Communication
Bugling
Journalism
Printing
Radio
Signaling

8. Conservation
Forestry*
Soil and Water Conservation*
Wildlife Management*

9. Crafts and Collections
Basketry
Bookbinding
Coin Collecting
Leatherwork
Stamp Collecting
Textiles

10. Nature
Astronomy
Bird Study
Botany
Chemistry
Geology
Insect Life
Nature
Reptile Study
Weather
Zoology

11. Outdoor Sports
Archery
Athletics
Cycling
Fishing
Hiking
Horsemanship*
Marksmanship
Skiing

12. Personal Development
Business
Farm Records and Bookkeeping*
Personal Fitness
Public Speaking
Reading
Salesmanship
Scholarship

13. Plant Cultivation
Agriculture*
Corn Farming*
Cotton Farming*
Fruit and Nut Growing*
Gardening*
Grasses, Legumes and Forage Crops*
Landscape Gardening*
Small Grains and Cereal Foods*

14. Public Service
Fingerprinting
Firemanship
First Aid
Public Health
Safety

15. Transportation
Automobiling
Aviation
Railroading
Seamanship

*These badges may be earned by a 4-H'er completing a club project in this subject. Or an FFA member may meet these or equivalent requirements through the FFA-supervised farming program.

MERIT BADGES REQUIRED FOR HIGHER RANKS

<table>
<tr><th>GROUPS</th><th>STAR</th><th>LIFE</th><th>EAGLE</th></tr>
<tr><td>Citizenship Group</td><td rowspan="2">Any 1</td><td>Any 2</td><td>Any 3</td></tr>
<tr><td>Public Service Gp.</td><td>First Aid</td><td>First Aid, Public Health, Safety, Firemanship</td></tr>
<tr><td>Campcraft Group</td><td rowspan="5">Any 1</td><td>Any 1</td><td>Camping
Cooking</td></tr>
<tr><td>Aquatics Group</td><td rowspan="2">Any 1</td><td>Swimming
Lifesaving</td></tr>
<tr><td>Outdoor Sports Gp.</td><td>Any 1</td></tr>
<tr><td>Nature Merit Badge</td><td rowspan="2">Any 1</td><td>Nature</td></tr>
<tr><td>Conservation Gp.</td><td>Any 1</td></tr>
<tr><td>Personal Development Gp.</td><td></td><td>Any 1</td><td>Personal Fitness</td></tr>
<tr><td>Animal Husbandry, Plant Cultivation, Communication, Transportation or Building Group</td><td></td><td>Any 1</td><td>Any 1</td></tr>
<tr><td>Additional Merit Badges which may be selected from any of the 15 Groups</td><td>Any 3</td><td>Any 2</td><td>Any 5</td></tr>
<tr><td>Total Required</td><td>5</td><td>10
Including the 5 earned for Star.</td><td>21
Including the 10 earned for Star and Life</td></tr>
</table>

STAR, LIFE AND EAGLE RANKS

CHAPTER 25

STAR REQUIREMENTS

To become a Star Scout you must be a First Class Scout and:

I. SCOUT SPIRIT

Satisfy your Scout leaders that you do your best in your everyday life, to live up to:

1. The Scout Oath or Promise
2. The Scout Law
3. The Scout Motto
4. The Scout Slogan

II. SCOUT PARTICIPATION

1. While a First Class Scout for a period of at least three months, show to the satisfaction of your leaders that you:

a. Are active in meetings, outdoor activities and service projects of your Unit and dependable in your Unit obligations.
b. Do your best to help in your home, school, church and community.
c. Take care of things that belong to you and respect the property of others.
d. Understand how to use wisely and conserve our natural resources (soil, water, forests, grasslands, wild life) and have taken part in a conservation project.

2. Have earned **one** Merit Badge from the CITIZENSHIP or PUBLIC SERVICE groups. See pages 424-425 for Merit Badge groups.

III. SCOUTCRAFT AND LIFE INTERESTS

1. Have earned one Merit Badge from any of the following groups: CAMPCRAFT, AQUATICS, OUTDOOR SPORTS, CONSERVATION or the Nature Merit Badge.
2. Have earned any ***three*** additional Merit Badges.*

LIFE SCOUT

To become a Life Scout you must be a Star Scout and:

I. SCOUT SPIRIT

Satisfy your Scout leaders that you do your best, in your everyday life, to live up to:

1. The Scout Oath or Promise
2. The Scout Law
3. The Scout Motto
4. The Scout Slogan

*This makes a total of five Merit Badges required for the rank (including *one* from the CITIZENSHIP or PUBLIC SERVICE groups).

II. SCOUT PARTICIPATION

1. While a Star Scout for a period of at least three months, show to the satisfaction of your leaders that you:
   a. Accept and carry out responsibilities in meetings, outdoor activities and service projects of your Unit.
   b. Do your best to help in your home, school, church and community.
   c. Take care of things that belong to you and respect the property of others.
   d. Have completed a conservation project approved in advance by your Unit leader.

2. Have earned the First Aid Merit Badge.

3. Have earned **two** Merit Badges from the CITIZENSHIP group.*

III. SCOUTCRAFT AND LIFE INTERESTS

1. Have earned the following Merit Badges:*
   One from CAMPCRAFT group;
   One from OUTDOOR SPORTS or AQUATICS group;
   Nature Merit Badge or one from CONSERVATION group;
   One from PERSONAL DEVELOPMENT group;
   One from any of the following groups: ANIMAL HUSBANDRY, PLANT CULTIVATION, COMMUNICATION, TRANSPORTATION, BUILDING.

2. Have earned any **two** other Merit Badges.**

---

*Merit Badges previously earned may be included.

**This makes a total of *ten* Merit Badges required for Life rank (including First Aid and *two* from the CITIZENSHIP group).

EAGLE SCOUT

To become an Eagle Scout you must be a Life Scout and:

I. SCOUT SPIRIT

Satisfy your Scout leaders that you do your best, in your everyday life, to live up to:

1. The Scout Oath or Promise
2. The Scout Law
3. The Scout Motto
4. The Scout Slogan

II. SCOUT PARTICIPATION

1. While a Life Scout for a period of at least six months show to the satisfaction of your leaders that you:
    a. Work actively as a leader in meetings, outdoor activities and service projects of your Unit.
    b. Do your best to help in your home, school, church and community.
    c. Take care of things that belong to you and respect the property of others.
2. Have earned **one** Merit Badge from the CONSERVATION group.*
3. Have earned three Merit Badges from the CITIZENSHIP group.

*Merit Badges previously earned may be included.

III. SCOUTCRAFT AND LIFE INTERESTS

1. Have earned the following Merit Badges:

Camping	Personal Fitness
Cooking	Public Health
Swimming	Safety
Lifesaving	Firemanship
Nature	First Aid

One from OUTDOOR SPORTS group:

One from any of the following groups: ANIMAL HUSBANDRY, PLANT CULTIVATION, COMMUNICATION, TRANSPORTATION, BUILDING.

Have earned any five other Merit Badges.*

Eagle Palm Awards

The Scout or Explorer of Eagle Rank who meets the requirements for five Merit Badges, in addition to the twenty-one required for Eagle Rank, may be awarded a Bronze Palm; for ten, a Gold Palm; for fifteen, a Silver Palm; for twenty or more such combinations of Bronze, Gold or Silver Palms as he may elect, to indicate the number for which awards have been made; provided, however, that no award of Palms may be made for more than five Merit Badges at any one time, and provided further that no award shall be made until after at least six months' satisfactory service as an Eagle, and that subsequent awards may be made for intervals of not less than six months' service following the previous award.

A Scout may elect to use any combination of the Bronze, Silver or Gold Palms to indicate the number for which awards have been made.

*This makes a total of 21 Merit Badges required for Eagle Rank (including *one* from the CONSERVATION group and *three* from the CITIZENSHIP group).

ALONG THE EAGLE TRAIL

CHAPTER 26

You are proud of your First Class Badge. It stands for your Scouting adventure, the skills you have acquired, the service you are prepared to give to others. To the people who see your badge it means that you are someone to be relied upon.

Climbing the Trail

You are older and probably wiser than when you were a Tenderfoot, and you realize what a lot there is still for you to learn, and that the more you learn the more you get out of Scouting and out of living. Maybe you once thought as you started up the Scout Trail that you could never hope to reach Eagle Rank. But the top of the mountain is in sight.

You Make Up Your Mind to Climb Higher

Your Scoutmaster is naturally proud of your achievements. He hopes that you will continue to advance not merely to get another badge, but to learn to be a better Scout and citizen. He would like to count on you to help train the younger Scouts, and he is proud that you reflect at home, at school, in church and in the community, the ideals of Scouting that he has tried to help you understand.

Your Requirements

The requirements for the higher ranks state that idea very directly. Star, Life and Eagle ranks are not recognition for Merit Badges alone. Merit Badges are only one-fourth of the requirements. These ranks are given in recognition of three other achievements — practice of Scout principles, active service, and leadership effort.

Evidence Required

The judgment of people who know you well is required as evidence that you are trying to live up to the Scout Oath and Law as you promised when you became a Tenderfoot. Your attitude in your home shows your parents what Scouting has meant to you. Your teacher judges from your actions in school. Your Sunday School teacher or pastor estimates the influence of Scouting upon you. Others, too, may be called upon. Your leaders will ask these people to write frankly whether or not you are a worthy Scout.

Active Service

As a Scout who is advancing, you continue to take an active part in the Troop, even if this sometimes means you must give up some other pleasure.

Leadership

Your leadership ability is another thing that counts largely towards your advancement. By the time you are First Class you should be a real asset in your Patrol and Troop. It is not easy to be a good leader, but you can try to learn. If you are modest, keep your sense of humor, and remember some of your own troubles when you were new in the Troop, it will help. Your Scoutmaster and other Troop Leaders will help you and give you a chance to try out in leadership jobs.

A fine way to practice leadership is to serve as Den Chief in a Pack of Cub Scouts. This counts on the service requirement for Citizenship in the Community.

A Scout Citizen

The three requirements — character, participation, and leadership — are the basis of good citizenship as well as good Scouting. You need not wait until you are twenty-one to practice citizenship. All around you are chances to be a good citizen now. Citizenship is more than voting or holding public office. It is doing your share wherever you are. It is your Scout spirit of helpfulness, plus the knowledge and skills that you carry with you every day.

Turn back to Chapter 9 and read again the section on citizenship. You are older now, and will understand better your heritage as an American Citizen.

How to Advance

Whatever Rank you are trying for, from Second Class to Eagle, you go through four steps. You may not have thought about it that way, but if you look back over what you have done, you will see that it breaks down like this.

(1) You learned how to do your stuff. This you had to do yourself, helped by your Patrol Leader, other Scouts, the Scoutmaster and special Troop instructors. (2) You met the requirements satisfactorily before the Scoutmaster or another leader. This was not like a school examination on book knowledge. Remember your Second Class Fire Building test? It was a final demonstration of what you had learned to do by practicing over and over again; really to know how to build a fire, you had to be able to build it on rainy days and on windy days, and under all conditions — not just happen to pass a test once by a lucky accident.

After learning and examining, you did two other things before you got your Badge. (3) You appeared before a Board of Review for review, and explained how you had met the requirements and what you had done, so the Board could be sure you had kept up the high standards of Scouting. Then (4), the award, when you received your badge before a Court of Honor.

Higher Ranks the Same

You go through these same steps for your Star, Life and Eagle Ranks. Your Scoutmaster gets the forms and blanks used to certify your advancement progress, and will tell you what you should do.

First you learn and practice your Merit Badge requirements with the help of your Counselor. Then he examines you. He approves your application.

Your Scoutmaster or other leader secures evidence

of your character, service and leadership ability as noted earlier in this Chapter.

When you have completed the required number of Merit Badges and have served the necessary length of time, your Scoutmaster makes out an application blank for you to appear before a Board of Review, as for Second and First Class Ranks. This may be in your Troop, your District or Council. Your Scoutmaster will tell you.

Merit Badge Helps

You will naturally find it easier to meet any and all Merit Badge requirements, as you climb the Eagle trail, if you have studied the related pamphlet, and thus obtained a well rounded view of the subject. Here our Scout Motto "Be Prepared" means everything. If you bring the pamphlet to your Merit Badge Counselor when you visit him, he will take this as evidence that you care enough to learn all you can about the subject.

These illustrated booklets are inexpensive. You can get them from your Scout Outfitter or through your local Scout Office. Many Troops have their own libraries, including many or all of these pamphlets. You can also get them in most public libraries.

The Board of Review

These men will not re-examine you, but they will question you on what you have accomplished. They will ask you about your service in the Troop and to the community. Their object is not to catch you up nor to embarrass you, but to make sure that you really do practice the principles of Scouting. They are your friends. Talk to them frankly.

The Board of Review then approves and sends your application to your Council office. A short time after, you may receive your certificate of advancement in rank. Your service record for your next rank begins on the date the Board of Review approves your application.

Court of Honor

Your badge of rank will probably be awarded in a public Court of Honor or ceremony. (Perhaps your certificate will also be presented then.) This is a proud moment for your Scoutmaster as well as your parents and friends. All of them had a share in helping you to earn your badge through their interest and their leadership, and you should feel that they share with you in one of the greatest occasions not merely of your career as a Scout, but of your whole life.

WHEN YOU'RE OLDER

CHAPTER 27

When you reach the age of Exploring (ninth grade or above and fourteen years of age, or fifteen years of age regardless of grade), you will face a decision as to whether to stay with the Scout Troop as a senior, or to join a separate Explorer Post. It is no longer possible to remain registered with the Scout Troop and also be an Explorer. You might discuss this with your parents, your Scoutmaster, and an Explorer Advisor. They can give you helpful ideas, but the decision is yours.

Opportunities in Your Troop

Your Scoutmaster would like to have you stay in the Troop to help him as he works with the younger boys. He recognizes you as one of his advanced Scouts —a young man who through association with the

Troop has gained many of the skills of Scouting — a young man who can pass this knowledge on to Scouts of lower ranks. He needs help in Scoutcraft skills, games, campfires, and in song leading.

If you remain in the Troop you can continue as a member of a Patrol, but probably you will assist the Scoutmaster more directly as a Senior Patrol Leader, Junior Assistant Scoutmaster, or Quartermaster or Scribe. These positions require mature, experienced Scouts to do a good job.

If you elect to remain in the Troop, you will be eligible to wear the "senior" strip on your uniform. This is the only uniform change. You will not wear the Explorer uniform unless you leave the Troop and join a Post.

The Explorer Advisor will tell you about the program of Exploring, and the fun and fellowship to be gained by working with a group of older boys. He will tell you about the advanced type of activity that Explorers do and their schedule of meetings.

When you joined Boy Scouting as a Tenderfoot, you set the Eagle Scout Rank as your goal. Whether you stay in the Troop, or continue on in Exploring, keep that Eagle Scout goal in front of you. It can be earned by both Scouts and Explorers. One of the commendable things about an Eagle Scout is that he has finished a job that he started. As a Tenderfoot you started for Eagle. Show that you have what it takes by finishing the job, whether as a Scout or an Explorer.

Exploring

When you become high-school age, you can choose to become an Explorer. You can do this by joining an Explorer Post, a Sea Explorer Ship, or an Air Explorer Squadron.

Exploring is a program especially designed to meet the interests, needs, and desires of high-school age boys. Its activities are selected and carried out by the boys themselves under the guidance of trained adult leaders with the help of qualified consultants.

Exploring offers the high school boys a balanced variety of experiences. It offers you the chance to serve other people by becoming a working citizen through service projects for your neighborhood, community, and nation.

Exploring calls you to adventure in the out-of-doors — to live ruggedly but comfortably in the wilderness, whether it's the forest, desert, plains, or mountains. You go to far away places, perhaps by paddle, saddle, awheel, or afoot.

Social events lead to more than good times and good manners in Exploring. They widen your circle of friends — among fellows, girls, and older folks. But more important, these social activities, stag or mixed, formal or informal, help you learn to get along with others. That's the sort of skill you'll use wherever you go, whatever you do, as long as you live. You grow socially in Exploring.

Exploring points ahead to your lifework. It urges you to think about earning a living. Through industrial tours, field trips, hobbies, part-time jobs, and vocational conferences you get a view of the world of work. You take a close look at your own interests and abilities and match them with the education and training needed for a career.

SPECIAL SCOUT OPPORTUNITIES

CHAPTER 28

The Religious Awards Program

Just as you keep yourself physically strong by training and healthful activities, so also you build yourself spiritually by practicing your religion.

Your Religious Award program will help you grow spiritually. It aids you to practice "duty to God," to be "reverent," and to be "faithful in your religious duties."

You learn your specific duties from your own minister, priest, or rabbi. You may begin either as a

Webelos Cub Scout, a Boy Scout, or Explorer; you advance to First Class and give at least one year of service to church or synagogue before receiving your award. You wear the medal in a place of honor over your heart, either centered or to the left of the Eagle Badge. You will find your Religious Award here.

Buddhist

The SANGHA AWARD is for Buddhists. Requirements are available from Dr. K. H. Taira, chairman, Buddhist Committee on Scouting, 661 F Street, Fresno, California, or your Council office.

Catholic

The words "Ad Altare Dei" from the opening prayer at Holy Mass, remind you that going to the "Altar of God" will bring joy to your youth. The AD ALTARE DEI AWARD is a bronze cross, suspended from a ribbon in papal and national colors.

Your record book *Ad Altare Dei Requirements* (Catalog No. 3093) can be obtained from your priest, Scout leader, or Council office. On pages 3, 4 and 5 you will learn how to earn this award. A *Catholic Manual for Scouts* (Catalog No. 3554) will help you prepare yourself. Your pastor certifies that you are fully prepared.

You send your application (Catalog No. 4423) properly signed to your Council. Your Scout chaplain will advise you when and where to come for the final examination and presentation ceremony in the church.

Eastern Orthodox Catholic

The ALPHA OMEGA AWARD is for Scouts and Explorers of the Eastern Orthodox Catholic Church. For information contact your Council office.

Jewish

Boy Scouts and Explorers of Jewish faith are eligible for the NER TAMID AWARD (Ner Tamid means Eternal Light). This is a bronze medal attached to a blue and white ribbon.

The Ner Tamid may be seen above the Holy Ark in every synagogue. It symbolizes Israel's eternal zeal in the service of God. The requirements for the award are found in the *Ner Tamid Award Record Book* (Catalog No. 3182), which you can obtain from your rabbi, Scout leader or Council office.

You will also find it helpful to get a copy of the *Ner Tamid Guide for Boy Scouts and Explorers* (Catalog No. 3178), since it contains basic information.

"Mormon"

Important to boys in the "Mormon" Church, the "DUTY TO GOD" AWARD program emphasizes spiritual development. On the badge, the buffalo skull represents the spirit of the pioneers in their great trek across the plains before the first transcontinental railroad was completed.

The medallion superimposed upon the buffalo skull shows the Salt Lake Temple, which is the symbol of the highest spiritual development of the Church.

Further information may be secured from the "Mormon" Relationships Service, Boy Scouts of America, Room 49, 112 South State Street, Salt Lake City, Utah.

Protestant

Requirements for Religious Awards have been set up by your church leaders.

To earn the GOD AND COUNTRY AWARD follow these steps: 1. Secure your *Service Record Book* (Catalog No. 4024) from your Council. 2. Enroll in program with your minister. 3. Fulfill requirements as directed by your minister. 4. Examination by your church board or minister. 5. Interview with Church Awards Committee in your area. 6. After approval of the Protestant Committee on Scouting, the Award will be presented to you at a worship service in your own church.

To earn the Lutheran PRO DEO ET PATRIA AWARD secure an application blank for enrollment as a candidate by writing to the Lutheran Committee on Scouting, 608 Second Avenue South, Minneapolis 2, Minnesota.

Den Chief

A Den Chief is a Boy Scout who leads the Cub Scouts in their games and handicraft, teaches them the program and helps the Den Mother run the Den. It is a high honor to be a Den Chief, and it is one of the finest Good Turns a Boy Scout can do, for his service means much happiness to a whole crowd of younger boys. If you are a Scout, talk to your Scoutmaster about being a Den Chief.

Associate Scout

Sometimes a fellow goes away from home to boarding school, or for some other good reason cannot attend Troop meetings regularly, but wants to keep his membership in his Troop. In this case, you can be an Associate Scout. You register with the Troop like other Scouts, promise to attend as many meetings as possible during the year and, of course, to observe the Scout Oath and Law and Daily Good Turn.

Awards by the National Court of Honor

The National Court of Honor makes awards for saving life at the risk of the Scout's own life and for other kinds of unusual Scoutlike service.

Gold Honor Medals and Certificates for Heroism

The highest special award in Scouting is the Gold Honor Medal for saving life. This is awarded by the National Court of Honor to Scouts who save life or attempt to save life at the risk of their own and show heroism, resourcefulness and skill. The Honor Medal is awarded with Crossed Palms in exceptional cases. A Certificate for Heroism may be awarded for saving life where there is less risk involved.

Medals of Merit and Certificates of Merit

A Medal of Merit is awarded by the National Court of Honor to Scouts who perform some outstanding act of service, putting into practice Scout skills, but not necessarily involving risk of life. Certificates of Merit may also be awarded for meritorious action.

Applications for these awards are made on behalf of Scouts by the Scoutmaster through the Council.

Hornaday Award for Distinguished Service to Conservation

One award which Scouts, Explorers and Scouters prize very highly is the William T. Hornaday Award for Distinguished Service to Conservation. It is given by the New York Zoological Society in honor of its first director, one of the staunchest pioneers for conservation of natural resources.

Whether you live in a city, in a small town, on a farm or in the wilderness, there is great work for you as a Scout to do. In fact there is conservation work for every Scout in America.

Wildlife protection alone is not sufficient to save

the country from a tragic loss of its life-supporting resources. Our life depends on soil conservation; on the protection of forests, grasslands and other plant life; on the conservation of water tables, lakes, streams and rivers. All are interdependent.

Scouts or Scouters interested in working for the Hornaday Award should write to the: National Council, Boy Scouts of America, New Brunswick, N. J. and ask for a Hornaday Award application.

On the application will be found many ideas for conservation projects. It is suggested that the applicant talk with a local conservation technician or agency and work for the Award under the guidance of an expert.

But remember that the Award is given for "Distinguished Service." This means that a high standard of accomplishment must result from your efforts. There are no requirements, as such, for the Award. Suggestions are made on the application form for the type of activity which will be considered outstanding. The number of hours spent on a project, while important, will not count as heavily as the importance of the results accomplished.

Order of the Arrow

The Order of the Arrow, national brotherhood of Scout honor campers, was founded in 1915 at Treasure Island Scout Camp. The purpose of the Order is: (1) to recognize those campers (Scouts, Explorers and Scouters) who best exemplify the Scout Promise and Law in their daily lives and by such recognition cause other campers to conduct themselves in such manner as to warrant recognition; (2) to develop and maintain camping traditions and spirit; (3) to promote Scout camping, which reaches its greatest effectiveness as a part of the unit's camping program, and to help strengthen the district and council camping program both year-round and in the summer camp, as directed by the Camping and Activities Committee of the Council; and (4) to crystallize the Scout habit of helpfulness into a life purpose of leadership in cheerful service to others.

The qualifications for membership are: registered Scout, Explorer or Scouter; a Scout Camper — 15 days and nights of camping, not more than seven of which may be a long-term camp; election by the membership of the home Unit; participation in the Ordeal and ceremonies; and First Class Scout.

There are now Order of the Arrow lodges in approximately 90 per cent of the Councils with an active membership of 120,000 Scouts, Explorers and Scouters.

Emergency Service Training

In times of disaster such as earthquakes, hurricanes, floods, or fires, Scouts have proved themselves resourceful and of practical help. Perhaps your Council has a plan for mobilization of Troops and Explorer Units for emergency service in case of disaster.

If you are part of your Troop's mobilization plan, you will want to do your share in making it work when you practice or take part in an actual emergency. Your skills developed in Second and First Class tests — and in Merit Badges — will be of great help to you.

Scout Lifeguard

If you are a First Class Scout you are eligible to be a Scout Lifeguard. If you meet the requirements.

Scout Lifeguard Requirements

1. Present medical examination certificate.
2. Hold the Merit Badge for Swimming.
3. Hold the Merit Badge for Rowing.

4. Hold the Red Cross Junior or Senior Lifesaving Certificate or hold the Lifesaving Merit Badge.

5. Instruct one First Class Scout for three hours in the Merit Badge requirements in Rowing, or Canoeing, or Lifesaving; or, instruct one non-swimmer for three hours in swimming.

6. Swim one-quarter mile in good form using any or all of the following strokes: side, back, breast or crawl.

7. a. Demonstrate twice his ability to remove (except underpants or bathing trunks) street clothes in 20 seconds or less.

   b. Watching "struggling" person constantly, remove street clothes on shore in 20 seconds, enter water feet first (by jumping or running), swim 30 feet, make correct approach, and tow victim 30 feet with cross-chest carry to shore.

8. Throw 15-inch ring buoy equipped with 60 feet of 3/16 inch line between two marks 5 feet apart, 30 feet from throwing mark three times in one minute, recoil, and leave ready for use.

9. Acting as coxswain of a lifeboat and using a pole, with a skilled oarsman rowing, approach a "struggling" person correctly, hold him at stern until rowed ashore and then assist him out of the water.

10. Answer ten questions selected by Counselor on waterfront safety and rescue methods.

11. Explain the plan for protecting a Troop swimming party, and, with two other Scouts, one acting as a drowning person, demonstrate the rope rescue method described in the plan.

12. Know and be able to explain plan of camp waterfront protection, including buddy and check plan.

SCOUT LIFEGUARD

Cloth; red, gold, white on blue background; worn on right side of swimming trunks

HISTORY OF SCOUTING

CHAPTER 29

You have already learned in the section on "Fun and Adventure in Scouting" how Scouting was started by Lord Baden-Powell, then a British General, to train his men in South Africa; how it was snatched up as a new game by boys back home in England, and was brought to the United States as the result of a Good Turn by an unknown English Scout.

The Boy Scouts of America was incorporated on February 8, 1910, the date which is now observed over the country as Boy Scout Anniversary Day.

That first year Scout Troops sprang up like mushrooms all over America because both boys and men were eager to have Scouting. Men from all national organizations interested in boys got together in June, 1910, and out of that meeting came the permanent organization plan of the Boy Scouts of America. Officers were elected; President Taft became Honorary President. (Ever since then, each President of the United States has been Honorary President of the Boy Scouts of America, and former Presidents have been Honorary Vice-Presidents.) Former President Theodore Roosevelt became Honorary Vice-President and Chief Scout Citizen, and Ernest Thompson Seton was Chief Scout. Dan Beard, author and artist, was a National Scout Commissioner, and James E. West became Chief Scout Executive.

In 1911 the first *Handbook For Boys* was published and the Scout Oath and Law were developed. The first Scout uniforms and badges were manufactured.

Scouts gave notable service in times of flood, fire, hurricane, and other disasters, as well as helping at parades and at civic gatherings during the years that followed. They justified their motto, "Be Prepared."

On June 15, 1916, because they had proved themselves such useful citizens, Congress granted a Federal Charter to the Boy Scouts of America, protecting the name and insignia, and authorizing the Scout uniform so that no one but Scouts might use the uniform of Scouting.

When the first World War came, Scouts rushed to help their country. They sold Liberty Bonds and Stamps totalling $406,859,262; located 20,758,660 feet of walnut for strategic purposes; collected 100 carloads of fruit pits needed for gas masks; conducted war gardens; distributed 30,000,000 pieces of Government literature, besides helping the Red Cross.

In 1920, 301 Scouts went to the First World Jamboree in England, camping with Scouts from 32 countries. The Second World Jamboree was held in Denmark in 1924; the Third in England in 1929; the Fourth in Hungary in 1933; the Fifth in Holland in

1937; the Sixth in France in 1947; the Seventh in Austria in 1951 and the Eighth in Canada in 1955.

In 1937 the First National Jamboree was held in Washington, D. C., at the invitation of the President. 27,232 Scouts and leaders took part in that big camp at the foot of the Washington Monument. During 1950, the Second National Jamboree was held at Valley Forge, Pennsylvania, and some 47,000 Scouts and leaders camped together on that historic site. Forty-five thousand took part in the Third National Jamboree on the Irvine Ranch in California in 1953. The Fourth was held at Valley Forge in 1957, with 52,000 attending.

The Boy Scouts of America continued to grow. In 1930 the Cub Scout Program for younger boys was added. To Sea Scouting, which had been popular almost from the beginning, were added Explorer Scouting and, in 1939, Air Scouting. This senior program became Exploring in 1949.

In World War II, Scouts lived up to their traditions. They helped Civil Defense as messengers, fire watchers, and aids to emergency medical units. They raised victory gardens. They salvaged wastepaper and collected scrap metal. They served as official dispatch bearers for important Government messages. They organized emergency service corps to aid the community.

In 1956 the Boy Scouts of America launched a Four-Year Program based on the theme "Onward for God and My Country." Scouting acknowledges its opportunity as a powerful force for freedom as well as a reinforcing influence in the life of each of its more than four million members.

MERIT BADGE REQUIREMENTS

Here are the requirements for all merit badges, including all revisions approved as this edition of the *Handbook for Boys* goes to press.

To obtain each of these merit badges, you must:

Agriculture*

1. Explain the nature of soil, its texture, its need of water, of air, and of plant and animal life; what the soil does for the plant and how the soil may be improved.

2. Make a seed tester and test the germination of three chosen varieties of seeds — 100 seeds of each variety.

3. Identify and describe ten common weeds of the community and tell how best to eliminate them.

4. Identify six common insect pests, tell what plants thev usually infest and how best to control them.

5. Have a practical knowledge, for your locality, of plowing, cultivating, harrowing, disking, draining, and harvesting and the purposes of each. Describe also the farm implements used in each case.

6. Tell how plants are propagated — by seeds, roots, cuttings, tubers, buds, and grafts. Explain where plants get their food and how they grow.

7. Read a weather map, know weather signals, and make local observations.

8. Name and distinguish ten common birds of your locality, and state their value to the farmer.

Animal Industry*

1. Name three breeds of draft horse and two breeds of light horse, and give the country or origin of each.

2. Name and give relative merits of four leading breeds of dairy cattle.

3. Name and explain the color markings and characteristics of five different breeds of beef animals.

4. Tell the requirements for the successful and profitable production of beef on a farm.

5. Describe how hogs are made profitable.

6. Name four leading breeds of sheep and describe them.

7. Demonstrate one first aid requirement in connection with farm animals.

---

*As a 4-H'er, complete a club project in this subject. Or as an FFA member, meet these or equivalent requirements through the FFA supervised farming program.

Archery

1. Name and explain the archery safety rules.
2. Do one of the following:

(a) Shoot with bow and arrows a Junior American round on a standard 48" target, and make a score of 250: 30 arrows at 50 yards; 30 arrows at 40 yards; 30 arrows at 30 yards.

(b) Shoot with bow and arrows a Chicago round on a standard 16" target, and make a score of 250:

30 arrows at 17 yards 2 feet	50 yards at 48" target
30 arrows at 13 yards 1 foot	40 yards at 48" target
30 arrows at 10 yards	30 yards at 48" target

(c) Shoot with bow and arrows an official field archery round and make a score of 50.

3. Rounds and shooting rules:

(a) Give the definition of the following: American round; Junior American round; the field rounds; clout shoot.

(b) Give the shooting rules used in target tournament. Explain how arrows are scored *or* give the shooting rules used in field archery tournaments. Explain how arrows are scored.

4. (a) Explain proper care and how to store: the bow; bowstring; arrows.

(b) Make a bowstring, whip the string, and adjust the bowstring with a bowman's knot.

(c) Explain the following terms: cast; weight of bow; fistmele; methods of aiming; spine; difference between target, field and hunting arrows.

(d) Discuss the history, romance, and development of Archery with your counselor.

Architecture

1. Present a satisfactory freehand drawing.
2. Draw without accurate measurements the five orders of architecture, the drawings being of the character of sketches, but preserving the proportions.
3. Write a historical outline of the important periods of architectural development, giving the names of the important recognized architects identified with the development of each style.
4. Submit an original design for a house of four or more rooms, giving an outline of specifications, the design to

consist of original working drawings at scale, drawn in ink on linen or paper suitable for making prints.

Art

1. Make a sketch of (a) some Scout equipment grouped together; (b) a camp scene from nature; (c) an event from memory or imagination. Draw one in pen and ink, one in pencil or charcoal, and paint one in color.

2. Design a decoration for some article of your own.

3. Tell how your art work would be reproduced— (a) by line cut; (b) by half-tone process; (c) by lithography.

Astronomy

1. Identify in the sky (a) ten conspicuous constellations, including at least four in the zodiac; (b) at least eight first-magnitude stars.

2. Chart the position of Venus, Mars, or Jupiter among the stars over a period of four or more weeks, *or* chart the Moon's path through four constellations in the zodiac.

3. Sketch the position of the Big Dipper and its relation to the North Star and the horizon early some evening and again six hours later the same night. Record the date and hour of the making of each sketch.

4. Indicate in the sky the limits of the group of stars which, as seen from your latitude, never set. By your own observations determine whether the Big Dipper or Cassiopeia ever set.

5. Draw a diagram showing the relation of the Sun, Moon, and Earth at new Moon, first quarter, full Moon, and last quarter. Draw a diagram showing the relation of the Sun, Moon, and Earth at an eclipse of the Sun, and another for an eclipse of the Moon.

6. Explain the principal cause of the tides. Draw a diagram showing the relation of the Sun, Moon, and Earth when we have the highest tides and the lowest tides.

7. Explain the principal difference between a reflecting and a refracting telescope. Illustrate by simple diagrams.

Athletics

1. Write an acceptable article of not less than five hundred words on how to train for an athletic event.

2. Give the rules for two track and two field events, and define an amateur.

3. Prepare plans for the holding of an athletic meet,

specifying duties of each required official.

4. Produce evidence of having satisfactorily served as an official in an athletic meet, or in a major athletic sport, such as football, baseball, or basketball.

5. Qualify in one event, according to your weight, in each of the following groups:

		Under 75 Lbs.	*Under 95 Lbs.*	*Under 110 Lbs.*	*Under 125 Lbs.*
1.	Running broad jump	10 ft. 2 in.	11 ft. 6 in.	12 ft.	13 ft.
	Running high jump	3 ft. 2 in.	3 ft. 6 in.	3 ft. 9 in.	4 ft.
	Standing broad jump	5 ft. 10 in.	6 ft. 3 in.	6 ft. 9 in.	7 ft. 2 in.
	Standing high jump	2 ft. 6 in.	3 ft.	3 ft. 2 in.	3 ft. 4 in.
2.	50-yard dash	8 sec.	7⅘ sec.	7⅗ sec.	7⅕ sec.
	100-yard dash				13 sec.
	6-potato race	36 sec.	28 sec.	27 sec.	26 sec.
3.	20-yard swim	19⅗ sec.	18⅖ sec.	17⅘ sec.	17⅕ sec.
	40-yard swim	47 sec.	40 sec.	39 sec.	38 sec.
4.	Pull up	3 times	5 times	6 times	8 times
	8-lb. shot-put	15 ft.	20 ft.	24 ft.	28 ft.
	Push-up from floor	7 times	9 times	10 times	12 times
	Rope climb 18 ft.	29 sec.	17 sec.	15 sec.	13 sec.
5.	1. Baseball throw for accuracy (3 strikes in 6 throws)	42 ft.	48 ft.	51 ft.	54 ft.
	2. Baseball throw for distance	120 ft.	150 ft.	175 ft.	195 ft.
	3. Basketball goal shooting (30 seconds)	5 in 8	5 in 8	6 in 9	7 in 10

		Under 140 Lbs.	*Under 160 Lbs.*	*Under 175 Lbs.*	*Under 200 Lbs.*	*Over 200 Lbs.*
1.	Run. broad jump	14 ft.	15 ft.	16 ft.	14 ft.	10 ft.
	Run. high jump	4 ft. 3 in.	4 ft. 2 in.	4 ft.	3 ft. 6 in.	3 ft.
	St. broad jump	7 ft. 4 in.	7 ft. 6 in.	7 ft. 4 in.	6 ft.	5 ft.
	St. high jump	3 ft. 6 in.	3 ft. 8 in.	3 ft. 5 in.	3 ft.	2 ft. 4 in.
2.	50-yard dash	7 sec.	6⅗ sec.	7 sec.	7⅗ sec.	8⅖ sec.
	100-yard dash	12⅗ sec.	12⅖ sec.	12⅘ sec.	14 sec.	15⅗ sec.
	6-potato race	25 sec.	24 sec.	28 sec.	32 sec.	36 sec.
3.	20-yard swim	16⅗ sec.	16 sec.	15 sec.	15⅘ sec.	18⅗ sec.
	40-yard swim	37 sec.	36 sec.	35 sec.	39 sec.	40 sec.
4.	Pull-up	10 times	12 times	10 times	6 times	4 times
	8-lb. shot-put	32 ft.	34 ft.	36 ft.	37 ft.	38 ft.
	Push-up from fl.	14 times	16 times	17 times	12 times	8 times
	Rope climb 18 ft.	11 sec.	14 sec.	17 sec.	20 sec.	25 sec.
5.	Baseball throw for accuracy (3 str., 6 throws)	57 ft.	65 ft.	70 ft.	60 ft.	50 ft.
	Baseball throw for distance	210 ft.	220 ft.	230 ft.	200 ft.	175 ft.
	Basketball goal shooting (30 seconds)	8 in 11	9 in 12	10 in 13	8 in 12	6 in 15

Automobiling

Be of legal age to drive a car and meet all other legal requirements of your state.

1. Carefully examine and check conditions of the folling safety features: (a) windshield wipers; (b) adjustment of rearview mirror; (c) headlights for all headlight switch positions; (d) elevation and focus of headlight beams; (e) tail and stop lights; (f) windshield and rear window visibility; (g) "play" in the steering wheel; (h) adjustment of brakes; (i) tires.

2. (a) List ten important things in your local or state motor vehicle regulations. (b) Give the necessary qualifications (including age) before a person can legally drive a car in your state.

3. Explain how the use of intoxicating liquor increases motor accidents, as, for example, in its effect on the driver's vision, judgment, and coordination.

4. A driver on a dry road, with brakes in good condition, sees danger ahead. Tell how many feet he requires to stop his car going 20 miles an hour; 40 miles; 60 miles.

5. Visit a traffic court (or traffic session of court) or interview a highway traffic officer and make a report on at least two accident cases. Tell from the evidence what driving and safety rules were violated and how accidents could have been prevented.

6. (a) List at least six sound driving practices which make for safety and courtesy on the road. (b) List at least four important characteristics of a good driver. (c) Demonstrate hand signals, using both single hand position and three position systems; explain their meaning.

7. Explain: (a) purpose of clutch, gearshift, accelerator, choke, and brakes; describe briefly how each works; (b) how to stop car on wet or icy road; (c) what to do when end skids to right; to left; (d) what to do when you first notice the shining stop light on rear of car ahead.

8. Change a tire.

9. (a) Start engine; put car in gear; shift gears. (b) Come smoothly to full stop from speed of 30 miles an hour. (c) Make right and left turns from proper traffic lanes, giving proper signals at proper time. (d) Park in a 20-foot space. (e) Start a car after stopping on an upgrade (away from curb); park on an upgrade and on a downgrade. Show how to drive down a steep hill *or* show how to get out of sand, mud, or snow. (f) Turn around in order to go in opposite direction between lines or markers 25 feet apart.

10. Show ability to stop a car going at a speed of 20

miles per hour so that nose of car fits into a chalk-marked, U-shaped box of 5-feet wide. Bumper should be over front line of the box and tires inside of side lines.

Aviation

1. (a) Describe briefly how aviation has "shrunk" the world. (b) List at least ten uses of aircraft in modern life.

2. (a) Identify real examples, models, or illustrations of each of the following general kinds of aircraft: landplane, seaplane, flying boat, amphibian, helicopter, blimp, dirigible, balloon. (b) Identify in the air, or from silhouettes seen for only five seconds each, at least six types of aircraft by name and model.

3. (a) With a model plane point out the forces which act on an airplane in flight. (b) Build a model airfoil wing section and demonstrate with it the principle of lift; *or* build demonstration airfoils which compare the drag effects of streamlined and nonstreamlined surfaces.

4. Show how the working control surfaces (ailerons, rudder, and elevators) of an airplane are operated for take-off, climbing, banking and turning, descending and landing.

5. Point out the following instruments on an instrument panel and explain the purpose of each: altimeter, air-speed indicator, compass, bank-and-turn indicator, tachometer, and oil pressure and temperature gauges.

6. Explain by use of models or illustrations the operation of piston, thermal-air jet, and rocket types of engines.

7. Point out six rules of safety to observe around airplanes and flying fields.

8. Build and fly a rise-off-ground model airplane (you may use a kit but must carve the propeller yourself). *or* Build two solid scale-model planes (kits may be used).

9. Do any two of these projects:

(a) Take an orientation flight in some type of aircraft.

(b) On a map mark a route for a proposed air tour of at least 3,000 miles, starting from the commercial airport nearest your home, and traveling over three or more different airlines. From airline timetables decide on scheduled times of departure and arrival for all stopover and connecting points. Prepare a list of important places of interest and geographical features to see en route.

(c) Visit a well-equipped airport and observe how facilities are used for sheltering, servicing, dispatching, and signaling aircraft.

(d) Make up a pilot's check list for a routine preflight inspection of a light airplane.

(e) Learn how to read an aeronautical chart.

(f) Measure a true course on the chart and correct it for magnetic variation, compass deviation, and wind drift in order to arrive at a compass heading.

(g) Build a gasoline-powered, rise-off-ground model plane that will fly at least 50 seconds. (A kit may be used.)

(h) Take part as a contestant or official in a recognized model air meet.

(i) Find out what lifework opportunities there are for a young man in the field of aviation. Look into the necessary qualifications and working conditions of one job in which you are especially interested, and into the possibilities it offers for reaching your goal in life.

Basketry

1. Plan and weave a large basket or tray, using reed, raffia, or splints.
2. Weave a seat for a stool or chair, using cane or rush.

Beekeeping*

1. Examine a colony of bees, remove the combs, find the queen, and determine the amount of the brood, number of queen cells, and the amount of honey in the hive.
2. Distinguish between the drones, workers, and eggs, larvae, and pupae, at various stages of development; honey, wax, pollen, and propolis. Tell how the bees make the honey and where the wax comes from; and explain the part played in the life of the colony by the queen, the drones, and the workers.
3. Have had experience in hiving a swarm or artificially dividing at least one colony. Explain the construction of the modern hive, especially in regard to the "bee spaces."
4. Put foundations in sections or frames and fill supers with frames or sections; and also remove filled supers from the hive and prepare the honey for market.
5. Write an acceptable article of not more than two hundred words on how and why the honeybee is used in pollinating farm crops. Name five crops in your area pollinated by honeybees.

---

* As a 4-H'er, complete a club project in this subject. Or as an FFA member, meet these or equivalent requirements through the FFA supervised farming program.

Beef Production

1. Name three beef breeds and show or explain markings and other characteristics for which each breed is noted.

2. Select a breed of beef cattle that would be your choice for your locality and give reasons for your choice. Give the history of the breed you choose.

3. Visit a farm or ranch and interview a farmer who produces beef cattle under any of these systems: (a) feeding market cattle for slaughter; (b) producing feeder cattle for sale to commercial cattle feeders; (c) producing purebred cattle for sale as seed stock to other breeders. Tell how the cattle were handled, what rations were fed, weight gains, time on feed, and other items emphasized by the farmer.

4. Explain fully what is meant by "baby beef production."

5. Submit to your counselor an actual (or typical) cost accounting record for a specific cattle feeding program. Include (a) date, price, weight, and grade of cattle when bought; (b) total feed consumed and value of feed; (c) miscellaneous expenses such as veterinarian's bills; (d) date, weight, price received, and grade of cattle when sold; (e) profit.

6. Sketch either a plan of a feed lot, hay and grain storage facilities, and loading chute for thirty or more fattening steers, or a corral plan with cutting and loading chutes for handling fifty or more beef cows and their calves at one time.

Bird Study

1. Produce a list of forty species of wild birds which have been personally observed and positively identified in the field and tell how to differentiate each from those other species with which it might be confused.

2. Produce a list showing the greatest number of species that you have seen in the field in one week.

3. Produce a list derived from personal reading of: (a) twenty species of birds particularly noted for their value to agriculture in the destruction of insects and weed seeds; (b) ten birds of prey particularly useful in the destruction of rats and mice; (c) ten species of fish-eating birds, and tell why they are not inimical to man's interests.

4. Describe at least two bird boxes or a birdbath and two feeding stations that have been constructed and erected by you.

5. (a) From personal observation name and describe the birds you have seen in three different habitats (open fields, woodlands, farmland, marsh, etc.) and tell why all birds do not choose the same habitat. Make at least three visits to each type of countryside. *or* (b) Make a census of the bird life of a 25-acre tract by systematically covering the ground on three separate days and listing the species and number of individuals of each observed.

6. State what you did to protect birds from slaughter and to promote the creation of bird preserves and sanctuaries.

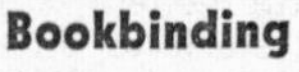

Bookbinding

1. Briefly describe the two principal sewing methods of binding or rebinding books by hand; tell when each should be used.

2. Make a scrapbook using binder's board and book cloth or a worthy substitute.

3. Rebind a book of four or more issues of a magazine, using binder's board and book cloth.

4. Visit a bindery and make an oral report to your counselor on the observed method of binding a book, pamphlet, or magazine. *or* Write an article of at least 200 words on bookbinding as a career.

Botany

1. Make five field trips of at least two hours each, to observe wild plant life. Keep record, based on field notes, of varieties of flowers found, with date, place, nature of locality (swamp, roadside, woods, meadow, etc.), and other observations such as seeds, seed pods, leaf arrangements, insect attraction. (If photographs or sketches are included, record will be more interesting.)

2. Identify from living specimens at least fifty plant specimens.

3. Identify in three or more specimens all parts of a perfect and complete flower. Explain (a) how plants are pollenized; (b) how ferns differ from flowering plants.

4. Identify specimens of at least ten families of flowering plants (other than trees), or submit properly labeled specimens of such families. (May be included as part of 8b.)

5. Know what plants are rare in your vicinity and what is being done or should be done to protect them.

6. Explain how plants use light, heat, water, oxygen, and carbon dioxide; how they manufacture their own food.

7. Submit or identify in field one specimen each of fungi, algae, lichens, and mosses. (Scouts living in regions where this requirement is not possible, may substitute five different species of ferns or desert plants.)

8. Carry out one of the following projects: (a) Submit a seed collection, properly labeled, of at least twenty different kinds of seeds gathered by yourself; germinate at least five species; find out all you can about different varieties of seeds and how they are scattered. (b) Submit specimens of at least thirty species of flowering plants. Include leaf, stem, flower and root (if not of rare plant). Mount neatly, label both with common and scientific name, date, place found, nature of locality. (c) Make a study of plant life in an area of not less than 15 square feet for at least two months. Keep record of species found, type of locality, insect attraction, seeds, etc. (d) Raise a wild flower or fern garden, including at least five different species of plants. Know: (1) both common and scientific names of each; (2) proper methods of transplanting and care.

Bugling

1. Sound properly on the bugle the following calls: First Call, Reveille, Mess, To the Colors, Officers, Drill, Assembly, Recall, Fatigue, Church, Fire, Swimming, Retreat, Call to Quarters, Taps.

Business

1. Write a satisfactory business and a personal letter.

2. Know simple bookkeeping or shorthand and typewriting.

3. Make a budget of your expenses including clothes and incidentals and keep a complete and actual account of personal receipts and expenditures for six months.

4. Be prepared to answer questions and problems in interest, percentage, and discount.

5. Present the certificate of your employers that for the period of six months preceding you have put into practice the Scout Oath and Law and shown efficiency in your application to business; that you have been prompt and regular in your attendance and have shown due regard for your general appearance by keeping your hair combed, your hands, nails, and teeth clean, your shoes shined, and your clothes clean and orderly; or serve satisfactorily for one year as troop scribe or Explorer unit secretary.

Camping †

1. (a) Prepare a check list of personal equipment necessary for a three-day camp. (b) Prepare a satisfactory menu and provision list for yourself and one or more companions for such a three-day camp. (c) Using your check list, assemble and pack this equipment and food properly for comfort and protection against bad weather.* (d) Carry this pack comfortably on your back. (e) Present yourself to your counselor for inspection, correctly clothed, wearing your pack, and with your check list, menu, and provision list. (f) Show proper care of the feet and discuss with your counselor the types of footwear for various weather conditions.

2. Improvise one emergency pack, using items readily available such as your clothes or rustic materials, keeping in mind that this pack should carry all gear and supplies needed for a three-day camp and meet requirements noted in 1c and 1d.

3. Show proper method for packing your full equipment on a pack frame or pack animal, using a diamond hitch or other suitable hitch.

4. (a) Lay out a camp site selected for yourself and one or more companions and give satisfactory reasons for your choice with consideration for weather, terrain, and water supply. Make a sketch of the camp site. (b) On this camp site construct a field latrine suitable for you and one or more companions for a three-day camp. (c) Working alone, pitch a tent properly with consideration for weather and terrain. Strike the tent and fold it neatly for packing. Tent may be a Forester, Explorer, or any other type of trail tent. (d) Show proper ditching and explain when to ditch and when not to ditch. (e) Make a comfortable ground bed and sleep on it for at least two nights. Native materials gathered nearby may be used if not contrary to local conservation practice. (f) Demonstrate how to dispose of garbage by burning and properly dispose of food cans.

5. Using natural material and/or items readily at hand, such as your pack frame: (a) Make a camp table or food storage container. (b) Make one of the following: (1) Tripod for suspending camp supplies and shear legs for rigging shelter, clothesline, or other camp convenience using proper lashing technique. (2) Make a six-foot rope or line, capable of supporting 50 pounds, from natural materials.

---

†A Second Class Scout must first qualify for First Class Scoutcraft Requirements 1a and b, 3 and 7 (see pages 110, 112, 114).

*NOTE: Where possible, the counselor should check the Scout's pack at the time he starts on an actual outdoor experience. When this is not possible, simulated provision items should be used to complete the packing of foodstuff in his pack.

6. Show the proper method for storing and protecting your full equipment against small animals, insects, and wet weather. Demonstrate how, on a rainy day, you would secure, prepare, and protect your firewood, as well as cook a meal.

7. (a) Demonstrate proper use of knife and axe in securing and preparing fuel, using natural material found on the spot. (b) Build two types of cooking fires and one fire for heating a tent or other type of open shelter.** (c) Show how to extinguish a fire properly.

8. Discuss with your counselor how you would protect yourself against cold weather and wet weather if caught out on the trail without equipment except what you are wearing and your knife and axe.

9. (a) Camp out a total of at least twenty days and twenty nights, sleeping each night under the sky, under a tent you have pitched, or improvised trail shelter you have made, and cook for yourself or your patrol at least twenty complete meals on these hikes or camps. (b) On all of these occasions leave a clean camp site with firewood neatly stacked and all rubbish disposed of properly.

10. Discuss with your counselor the application of the experiences you have had in earning the Camping merit badge in relation to: personal health and safety; survival; public health; good citizenship.

**NOTE: Where open fires cannot be built and established, camp stoves must be used. Demonstrate above fire lays, then build fire in the established camp stove.

Canoeing †

1. With a companion of about your weight and using a canoe not less than 14 feet in length: (a) Launch and get in the canoe properly from pier or shore (both if possible), giving directions to your companion. (b) Using a single-blade paddle while kneeling on one or both knees, in the bow position, paddle 100 yards, turn and paddle back, showing proper form in the following strokes: Bow Stroke, Diagonal Draw, Push Over, Reverse Sweep, and ¼ Sweep Stroke. (c) Change paddle to other side and repeat Requirement b. (d) While your canoe is afloat, properly change places with your companion who will now paddle in the bow. On one or both knees, paddle 100 yards and return, showing ability to keep canoe on straight course. (e) Make a proper landing.

2. While alone in canoe, using a single-blade paddle,

---

†A Second Class Scout must first qualify for First Class Scoutcraft Requirement 5 (see page 113).

paddle over a 100-yard course and return, demonstrating two kneeling positions for one man, and correctly do the following on one side going out, and on the other side coming back: (a) J Stroke, (b) Draw Stroke, (c) Push Over, (d)Stopping.

3. While fully dressed:* (a) Capsize a canoe in deep water and about 50 yards from landing place. (b) Right it and stow paddle and kneeling pad. Get in and paddle with hands or paddle for 25 yards. (c) Disrobe, secure clothing to thwarts, go overboard, and, holding on with one hand, swim and tow or swim and push swamped canoe to shore. (d) Properly land emptied canoe and put it away with assistance if necessary.

4. Using double-blade or single-blade paddle, assist a man who has capsized his canoe and is clinging to it. Empty it as explained in the merit badge pamphlet and steady it while man climbs aboard.

5. Discuss contents of a good emergency canoe repair kit and explain how to use it in repairing a one-inch hole in canvas.

---

*Wear clothing usually worn in canoeing in your territory according to the season of the year.

Chemistry

1. Do one of the following: (a) Collect ten compounds or elements found in the home and write the common name, chemical name, and formula or symbol for each. (b) In company with your counselor, follow a route selected by him and name fifteen compounds or elements found in nature or in objects seen along the way.

2. Perform experiments to illustrate four of the following chemical reactions: (a) neutralization, using an indicator; (b) precipitation of a solid from solution; (c) evolution of a gas; (d) combination of two elements to form a compound; (e) replacement of a metal in a salt by another metal.

3. Demonstrate and discuss the chemistry of a candle flame. Relate this knowledge to the burning of wood as in a campfire. Explain how water and sand act to extinguish campfires. Tell what methods are recommended for extinguishing fires involving: cooking fat, oil or gasoline, electrical equipment. Explain how each functions.

4. Explain the changes that occur in nature's (a) water cycle, (b) carbon-oxygen cycle, (c) nitrogen cycle. Describe the chemical reaction that takes place in carbon monoxide poisoning.

5. Explain what is meant by "hard water" and "soft water." Do one of the following: (a) Perform experiments to show how the hardness of water may be reduced. (b) Demonstrate the action of soap and synthetic detergents in hard water and explain any differences observed.

6. Tell how the chemical properties of iron, aluminum, copper, and silver influence their usefulness as cooking utensils, as tools, or for other purposes around the camp and home. Describe several means of preventing metal corrosion.

7. Do one of the following: (a) Visit an industrial plant that makes chemical products and describe the processes involved. (b) Visit a laboratory or a commercial establishment using chemical materials and find out how and why the materials are used. (c) Visit an experimental farm to learn how chemistry is meeting local problems of soil fertility and pest control. (d) Collect samples representing either the manufacture of chemicals from a common source, such as salt, sulfur, and petroleum, or the use of chemicals in the manufacture of a class of products such as textiles, drugs, or metals. Be prepared to discuss with your counselor the chemistry of the subject chosen.

8. Explain how principles expressed in the Scout Oath and the Scout Law are observed by scientists.

Citizenship in the Home

1. Discuss with your parents (or guardians) and your merit badge counselor: (a) the meaning of citizenship; (b) the importance of your home in your training for citizenship.

2. Submit a statement from your parents (or guardians) as evidence that you practice good citizenship at home by being courteous, fair, and helpful to other members of your family.

3. Prepare a list of your regular home duties or chores (at least five) and, for at least one month, keep a record of how often you do them.

4. Discuss with your family the rights and obligations you have in a democracy as compared with those under a dictatorship.

5. (a) Make a health and safety checkup of your home and help your family correct as many hazards as possible. (b) Work out with your family a plan of escape in case of fire in your home. (c) Tell how to get help in case of accident, illness, fire, and other emergencies in your home.

6. Do at least one major "Good Turn" for your home (not simply routine duties).

7. Make a budget and keep a record of your own income and expenses for two months.

8. Submit a report on a family group activity which you helped to plan, prepare for, and carry out.

NOTE: Merit badge counselors may adapt these requirements as necessary to meet special situations, such as not living in a family group.

Citizenship in the Community

1. Prepare a written outline of the history of your community, including such information as is known as to what Indian tribes once lived there, who the first non-Indian settlers were and when they came, important historical events, and people who figured prominently in the growth of the community.

2. Mark or point out on a map of your community: (a) chief government buildings; (b) fire station, police station, and hospital nearest your home; (c) nearby schools, churches, and synagogues; (d) main highways to neighboring cities and towns; (e) nearest railroad and bus stations and airport, if any; (f) chief industries or office of county agricultural agent; (g) historical and other worthwhile points of interest.

3. From newspapers, radio, television, forums, or other sources of public information and discussion, gather opinion on both sides of a public issue and then give your own ideas on it.

4. Draw a diagram of your state government, showing its executive, legislative, and judicial branches, and tell briefly what each does.

5. Do two of the following:

a. Draw a diagram of your village, town, city, or county government, showing top officials, courts, and administrative departments. Indicate which officials are elected and which are appointed.

b. Tell how to do seven of the following in your community: (1) report a fire; (2) report an automobile accident; (3) call an ambulance; (4) report damage to electric power, gas, or water supply system; (5) report damage to or need of repairs on streets, roads, bridges, or sewage system; (6) obtain a bicycle license; (7) obtain a dog license; (8) report a contagious disease; (9) report a mad dog scare; (10) obtain a building permit; (11) call a veterinarian; (12) obtain help from your county agricultural agent.

c. Visit one department of your local government and report on what services it provides for the community. *or* Attend a court session or a public meeting of a governmental body or political party and report on what takes place.

d. Know how much it costs to run your local government for one year, how this money is obtained, and for what it is chiefly spent. What kinds of taxes does your family pay in meeting this cost?

6. Discuss with your counselor the way in which Scouting helps to train you for citizenship and give examples of democracy at work in your troop or Explorer unit.

7. Vote regularly and take an active part in elections of officers and matters of business in your troop or Explorer unit, school, and other groups to which you belong.

8. List and briefly describe the work of five other volunteer organizations through which people of your community work together for the general welfare in such ways as: serving youth; safeguarding public health or safety; disaster relief; care of orphans; aid to the poor; provision of recreational facilities; promotion of good business or better farming; improvement of labor conditions; or general civic improvement.

9. Do one of the following: (a) Identify the principal political parties in your community or state and explain briefly their points of view on one public issue on which they disagree. (b) Describe at least one vocational opportunity offered in your community in some form of public service. Tell what personal qualifications you need for the job.

10. List and explain at least five privileges and forms of protection you enjoy as a citizen in your community, and describe your obligations to the community.

11. With the advice of your unit leader and counselor, plan your own program of community service and give at least ten hours of your time in carrying it out, or give ten hours of community service in a project carried out by your unit.

NOTE: In the District of Columbia, territories, and to some extent in rural communities, merit badge counselors may adapt these requirements as necessary to apply to the local situation.

Citizenship in the Nation

1. Read the Declaration of Independence and tell in your own words the meaning of the "self-evident truths" referred to.

2. Read the Constitution of the United States of America with its amendments, and: (a) explain its purpose as set forth in the Preamble; (b) draw a diagram to show the organization of our government into three branches as provided in Articles 1, 2 and 3; (c) describe and explain the purpose of the system of checks and balances in this organization; (d) tell how the Constitution may be amended as provided in Article 5.

3. Present newspaper or magazine clippings which show instances of how at least three of the privileges in our Bill of Rights have been protected in our country or how they have been denied in some other countries.

4. Take part in a group discussion (in your troop, Explorer unit, school, 4-H Club, family, or similar group) of an important national problem of the day.

5. Do one of the following: (a) Visit your national or state capitol, or a federal project which serves your community or region, or a place associated with a person or event which figured in the history of our nation. Prepare a report on your visit. (b) Correspond with someone, preferably a Scout or Explorer, who lives in another region of the United States or one of the U. S. territories. Exchange ideas, descriptive material, hobby items, etc.

6. Tell the names of the senators from your state and the representatives from your district in Congress and how you should address a letter to them at their Washington offices.

7. Tell what branch or department of the federal government is responsible for ten of the following: national parks; national forests; fish and wildlife protection; weather forecasting; flood control; investigation of violations of federal laws; judgment on such violations; minting of money; appropriations for government expenses; foreign policy; supreme command of our armed forces; soil conservation; child welfare; atomic energy.

8. Do the following: (a) Describe five ways in which the federal government serves you, your family, and your community directly. (b) Discuss with your parents (or guardians) and counselor the ways in which federal income, social security, excise, and other taxes, as well as import duties, affect the cost of living.

9. Have or obtain a birth certificate or other legal evidence of your citizenship. *or* If foreign born, learn what a person must do to gain United States citizenship.

Coin Collecting

1. Collect a type set of United States coins issued during the year of your birth (except commemorative, rare, and gold coins). Coins from any available mint will be acceptable.

2. In your birth year collection: (a) point out the mint mark (if any) on each coin and identify the mint; (b) point out the initials (if any) of the designer on each coin and identify the designer.

3. Collect a type set of United States coins minted during the twentieth century (except commemorative and gold coins).

4. Do any one of the following: (a) Collect a type set of United States coins minted from 1853 through 1900 (except commemorative and gold coins). (b) Make rough sketches of both sides of five different denominations of United States coins minted from 1792 through 1852 and of both sides of five different colonial or state coins issued prior to 1792. Show all designs, dates, and lettering clearly. (c) Collect, classify and mount fifty different coins minted by at least ten different countries outside the United States. ("Classify" means by country, denomination, date, and any special reason for issue.)

Cooking †

1. (a) Build a fireplace out of stone, brick, clay, logs, or other locally gathered material. (b) Build a fire in the fireplace. (c) Give evidence satisfactory to the counselor that you have cooked over this fire a satisfactory meal for at least four persons, including hot soup, meat or fish, two fresh vegetables, a dessert which requires cooking, and a hot beverage, timing your cooking so that the courses will be ready to serve at the proper time. (d) Order and pack properly for transportation the necessary materials to make this meal. (e) Dispose of garbage in a proper manner, clean utensils, put out fire and clean up the site thoroughly.

2. Mix dough and bake biscuits or other bread for four or more persons outdoors in a reflector oven, clay or Dutch oven, or other improvised outdoor oven.

3. Give evidence that you have carved properly and served correctly to a patrol or family group at table.

---

†A Second Class Scout must first qualify for First Class Scoutcraft Requirement 4 (see page 113).

Corn Farming*

1. Grow a patch of corn of not less than 300 square feet, if planted to some standard variety, or a smaller plot if devoted to a new, experimental variety. (Speak to your merit badge counselor before planting.)

2. Keep an accurate and complete record of costs, hours of work, seed, other materials, and yield.

3. Have your corn patch inspected at least once by your merit badge counselor.

4. Submit your record, with samples of yield, to your counselor and describe the modern methods of corn farming.

Cotton Farming*

1. On a map of the United States block in the sections where cotton is successfully grown.

2. Grow a patch of cotton successfully on the basis of instructions given by the county agent representing the United States Department of Agriculture and your state college of agriculture.

3. Demonstrate how to test cotton seed for vitality.

4. Give the domestic and commercial uses of cotton and cotton seed; name some of the more important by-products.

5. Name the more important insect pests that damage cotton and give recommendations as to their prevention and control.

6. Name the important cotton plant diseases and explain fully control measures for each.

7. By arrangement with the owner of a cotton plantation, take part in four operations in connection with a cotton crop and explain fully how you did the work.

8. Make a written report from personal observation on a cotton gin in action and on the conditions and operations of the nearest local cotton market.

9. Demonstrate how you would detect cotton goods made from long staple cotton.

10. Draw a plan for a moderate-sized cotton plantation, showing field layouts and plan for three or four years rotation of crops with the cotton.

---

*As a 4-H'er, complete a club project in this subject. Or as an FFA member, meet these or equivalent requirements through the FFA supervised farming program.

Cycling

1. Ride twenty-five consecutive miles on each of two days each month for a period of three months; in other words, six rides of twenty-five miles each during the three months. You must submit to the merit badge counselor a report of the rides taken, including dates, routes traveled, and interesting things observed.

2. After the three-month conditioning period in Requirement No. 1, ride a bicycle fifty miles in ten hours.

3. Repair a puncture.

4. Take apart and clean a bicycle and put it together again properly.

5. Know and demonstrate safety precautions on the road.

6. Go on a scouting expedition over a route selected by the merit badge counselor and make a report.

7. Read and follow a course laid out on a map.

8. Demonstrate proper method of receiving, safeguarding, and delivering messages by bicycle.

NOTE: Bicycle must be equipped with all necessary safety features as required by your state and local traffic laws.

Dairying*

1. Understand the management of dairy cattle.

2. Be able to milk.

3. Understand pasteurization of milk and care of dairy utensils and appliances.

4. Test the milk of at least five cows, for ten days each, with the Babcock test, and make proper reports.

*As a 4-H'er, complete a club project in this subject. Or as an FFA member, meet these or equivalent requirements through the FFA supervised farming program.

Dog Care

1. Present a statement signed by a parent or guardian describing the care you have given your dog (or a dog under your supervision) during a period of at least two months. Include these items: feeding schedule, kinds of food used, housing, exercising, grooming, and bathing. State what has been done to keep the dog alert and healthy.

2. Present a written report showing the approximate cost of feeding and caring for your dog for a period of at least two months.

3. Point out on a dog (or on a sketch) at least ten parts, giving the correct name of each.

4. Describe from personal observation, or point out from pictures, some of the distinguishing characteristics of ten breeds of dogs. *or* Give a brief history of some one breed of dog, including the origin if possible.

5. Explain precautions to take in handling an injured dog; demonstrate how to apply an emergency safety muzzle. Explain how to treat wounds, including use of the tourniquet. Show how to apply simple dressing and bandage to the foot, body, or head. Explain what action to take when a dog is struck by an automobile.

6. Do at least two of the following: (a) Describe what should be done to remove fleas, ticks, and lice from your dog. (b) Describe the symptoms of the following and explain what you would do if your dog showed these symptoms: distemper, rabies, mange, ringworm. (c) Describe the proper treatment for: sore ear, sore eye, fits, removing an object swallowed by a dog, removing an object stuck in its throat. (d) Explain first aid treatment for a dogbite and list the items needed in every dog owner's first aid kit.

7. State the dangers of home treatment of a serious ailment when the services of a veterinarian are available and report on a visit to a veterinary hospital. *or* Report on a visit to a shelter of your local humane society or SPCA, if available.

8. Explain in general the proper method used in obedience training. Demonstrate, if possible, with your dog, at least three of these commands: "Come," "Sit," "Down" (lie down), "Heel" (walk closely at owner's left side), "Stay" (remain in position); "Take it," "Drop it," "Get it" as used in retrieving work.

9. Know the laws and ordinances involving dogs, including ownership, registration, control, and humane treatment, in force in your own community.

Dramatics

Do any five of the following:

1. Show that you are familiar with the outstanding periods in the history of the drama, beginning with the Greek drama.

2. Submit evidence that you have taken part in a play given by your troop, school, Sunday school, or other group, before an audience of at least fifty persons, such part to be of sufficient importance to give you opportunity to display dramatic ability.

3. Submit a satisfactory play written by yourself of at least two acts and of at least twenty minutes' duration preferably on a subject connected with Scouting; submit a diagram of a stage, set for one of the acts in such play,

indicating left, right, off stage, backdrop, proscenium, etc.

4. Through an oral quiz, using your own play (Requirement No. 3) to illustrate, exhibit a knowledge of the fundamental elements of a play, namely, plot, character, dialogue; point out some of the elements that enter into the development of the plot, such as conflict, surprise, rising action, climax, etc.; show how characters reveal themselves by words and actions and why the dialogue should be natural and brief and accompanied by action.

5. Direct a play of at least twenty minutes' duration given by your troop or other group, selecting the cast and planning or actually supervising the scenery, properties, costumes, lighting, and all other details with reference to the actors and materials available. (This may be your own play in Requirement No. 3.) Arrange to have the counselor, or someone designated by the counselor, present at the performance.

6. "Make up" as an old man, an Indian, and "straight."

7. Present to the counselor a list of five entertainment features which you can arrange to give at a moment's notice, either alone or with others, suitable for campfire, troop meeting, or general gathering and present any two selected by the counselor from such list.

Electricity

1. Do an experiment showing the law of electrical attraction and repulsion; make and operate a simple electromagnet.

2. Explain the difference between a direct and an alternating current and the common uses of each. Give one method of identifying the currents.

3. Make pencil sketches showing the construction and operation of a battery cell and an electric bell.

4. Explain why a fuse blows out and how to detect a blown fuse in your own home. Demonstrate how to safely replace it.

5. Explain the meaning of overloading a household electrical circuit. Tell what you have done to make sure that this unsafe condition does not exist in your home.

6. Properly splice and tape two pieces of insulated wire. *or* Repair a frayed electrical cord where it enters an appliance or wall plug.

7. Demonstrate how to rescue a person in contact with a live wire in the home and show proper first aid treatment if the patient is unconscious from electrical shock.

8. Sketch the floor plan of a room in your home, showing light sockets, switches, and convenience outlets. Find out which fuses protect these.

9. Read correctly a watt-hour meter and compute a residence bill.

10. Explain ten electrical terms in common use, such as volt, ampere, watt, ohm, resistance, induction, circuit breaker, fuse transformer, main switch, insulation, cycle, rectifier, magnetic field, etc.

11. Do any two of the items listed: (a) Mount and connect a buzzer, bell, or light with a battery; have a key or switch in the line. (b) Make and operate a simple electric motor, not from a kit. (c) Construct a simple rheostat; show that it works. (d) Construct a single-pole double-throw switch; show that it works. (e) Make a proper connection of electric train equipment to a standard house circuit and show how it operates.

Farm Home and Its Planning*

1. Make a sketch of a farmhouse, showing location and relation of house to farm buildings, pens, yards, garden, fields with proper landscape effect.

2. Present a landscape plan for a farmhome showing both front- and back-yard effect and show drainage plans.

3. Present a drawing plan of sewage disposal for a country home.

4. Describe the value of windbreaks for a rural home and the kind of trees of most value for such purpose in your section.

5. Tell where and when you would plant nut and fruit trees for a country home.

6. Name seven suitable shrubs, plants, and vines for the farm dooryard.

Farm Layout and Building Arrangement*

1. From measurements made by yourself, draw a map of your own farm or a nearby one.

2. Make a scale drawing of a satisfactory rearrangement of the buildings, fields, windbreaks, etc., on the farm in Requirement 1. Explain the advantages and approximate costs of the changes you plan.

3. Draw a detailed set of plans for a new major building (such as an all-purpose barn, dairy barn, poultry plant, hog house, etc.) for the farm in Requirement 2. Show how you have made ample provision for light, ventilation, sanitation, feed storage, etc.

*As a 4-H'er, complete a club project in this subject. Or as an FFA member, meet these or equivalent requirements through the FFA supervised farming program.

Farm Mechanics*

1. Make a list of mechanic's tools usually found in a well-equipped farm shop. Explain the uses of at least four.

2. Select any farm machine and explain how power is transferred to do a job.

3. Do ONE of the following: (a) Put a new handle in any tool found on the farm, such as an axe, hammer, hoe, fork, or shovel. (b) Sharpen any cutting tool found on the farm, such as a hoe, cultivator tooth, pruning shears, or a section on a mower sickle bar. (c) Construct for the home shop a tool rack and suitable place to store nails, bolts, washers, etc.

4. Do ONE of the following: (a) Make an adjustment on a piece of farm equipment or machinery (for example, adjust cultivators on a tractor or garden power cultivator, adjust tractor fan belt, adjust and check a seeder or planter for proper seeding rate, register a mower or combine cutter bar). (b) Select a piece of farm machinery or equipment. Check all nuts, bolts, and screws, tightening any that are loose and replacing those that are missing, worn, or damaged. Prepare a list of items you tighten or replace. (c) Repair a piece of farm machinery or equipment (for example, replace broken or worn mower cutter bar sections, replace worn ledger plates on mower guards).

5. Do ONE of the following: (a) Perform the following types of services on a tractor in the presence of your merit badge counselor, farm manager, or parent: lubricate tractor, change oil and oil filter, remove and clean air cleaner, drain and flush cooling system, clean radiator fins. (b) With any farm machine, perform a daily service check for field use (check fuel, water, battery, lubrication, tires or tracks, worn or loose parts, and perform other operations necessary for best field performance). (c) Prepare any farm machine (does not have to be power-driven) for winter storage.

6. Visit an implement dealer. Prepare a list of the safety features found on a tractor and one other farm machine displayed there. Explain the purposes of these safety features.

Farm Records and Bookkeeping*

1. Explain fully what kind of records and books should be kept for a general purpose and

*As a 4-H'er, complete a club project in this subject. Or as an FFA member, meet these or equivalent requirements through the FFA supervised farming program.

stock farm. Tell which of these are kept on your farm.

2. Make and submit a poultry and egg production record for one month.

3. Make out a bill of sale for the following to Jones Produce Company, Chicago, Illinois.

160 lbs. of spring fryers	$ .30 per lb.
32 doz. eggs	.42 per doz.
1 cockerel for breeding purposes	5.75
24 pullets	2.50 each

4. Make a seven-day milk record for a herd of cows (your own or a neighbor's).

5. Make out a sample of one year's birth record for three colts, twenty-seven calves, and fifteen pigs.

6. Explain what records are needed in making out an income tax report for your state or federal income tax.

Fingerprinting

1. Take a clear and legible set of fingerprints, including the rolled and plain impressions, on a standard 8 x 8 fingerprint card.

2. (a) Name the surfaces of the human body on which friction or papillary ridges are found. (b) Explain why plain impressions must necessarily be taken on a fingerprint card.

3. Show that you can identify the eight pattern types in which fingerprints are grouped; collect a specimen of at least six of these types.

4. Give a brief history of identification by fingerprinting and distinguish between civil identification and criminal identification, pointing out the useful purposes served by each.

5. Obtain the fingerprints of five persons and present evidence that these fingerprints, together with complete descriptive data, have been accepted for the civil identification file.

Firemanship

1. Explain how heat, fuel, and air are necessary to cause fire. Describe how the elimination of any one of these will extinguish fire.

2. Explain five causes of fire in the home and tell how to guard against each.

3. Explain how fire might start from: (a) a pile of oily or paint-covered rags, (b) wet hay in a haymow, (c) elec-

trical wiring and equipment, (d) gas connections and appliances, (e) oil-burning stoves and portable kerosene heaters.

4. With the help of your parents make a thorough fire-safety inspection of your home. Then prepare the following in writing: (a) List all those things you have found in your home that could start a fire. A standard home firesafety check list may be used. Have one of your parents sign this list. (b) Tell what you have done to correct these defects. (c) List all equipment of any sort in your home that can be used to extinguish fires.

5. (a) With your parents, list the amount and location of any gasoline, kerosene, cleaning fluid, paint, thinner, turpentine, etc., in your home, including outbuildings. (b) Tell which of these materials were stored unsafely and what you did to correct those conditions.

6. (a) Visit the fire station nearest your home. Identify the most important pieces of equipment there and describe the purpose of each. (b) Describe the ways of turning in an alarm in your community. (c) Explain the fire problems in your local area and what is being done to solve them.

7. Make a rough sketch of the sleeping area in your home and show which persons are in what rooms. Then explain: (a) what to do if you smell smoke when you wake up at night, (b) what you should do to save yourself and your family, (c) a home fire escape plan that you have discussed with your entire family.

8. Show what you would do to save a person whose clothes are on fire.

9. (a) Tell how to set up a camp and make it safe from fire. (b) Describe the fire equipment you should have available before lighting a fire. (c) Bring a note from your unit leader stating that you have properly put out a campfire. Describe where and how you did this.

10. (a) Tell whom you should notify in case of a serious fire on camping trips. (b) Explain how to fight a grass or brush fire with improvised equipment. (c) Tell how forest fires may start. Explain what is done to prevent them and what you may do to help.

First Aid †

1. State what first aid is and why it is important.

†A Second Class Scout must first qualify for First Class Scoutcraft Requirement 1c (see page 110).

2. (a) Describe the causes and signs of shock. (b) Demonstrate on another person the first aid for shock.

3. (a) Explain what should be done for severe bleeding. (b) Tell under what extreme circumstances the use of a tourniquet may be justified. (c) Demonstrate how to stop bleeding from a severe cut of the lower leg and wrist.

4. (a) State under what circumstances artificial respiration may be needed and explain how you can tell that a person has stopped breathing. (b) Demonstrate the back-pressure arm-lift method of giving artificial respiration* for three minutes and additional first aid. (c) State what you can safely do to rescue a person from one of the following: contact with a live electric wire in a home, from a room containing carbon monoxide and other fumes or smoke, and from drowning.

5. (a) State how poisoning by mouth can be prevented. (b) Describe the first aid for poisoning by mouth and why quick action is necessary.

6. (a) Describe the signs of a broken bone and give general rules for first aid for fractures. (b) On a person lying down, and using improvised materials, demonstrate the first aid for any two of the following fractures: forearm, upper arm, wrist, collarbone, upper leg, lower leg, crushed foot.

7. (a) State the purpose of bandages and sterile dressings. (b) Demonstrate, using dressings when needed, the following bandages: (triangular) arm sling, foot, head; (cravat) eye, knee, hand.

8. (a) Tell the dangers in moving a seriously injured person. (b) If a sick or injured person must be moved, tell how you would decide what method to use. (c) Demonstrate alone and with assistance one carry for a mild injury and one for a serious injury.

9. (a) State the first aid for the following: sunburn, burn with blisters on the back of the hand, deep burn of the forearm, frostbitten ear or foot. (b) Demonstrate the proper way to extinguish flames on a person whose clothes are on fire and what you would do after the flames are out.

10. (a) State some causes and proper first aid for unconsciousness. (b) Explain how to prevent simple fainting and describe first aid for simple fainting and epileptic convulsions.

11. (a) Describe proper first aid for one of the following: puncture wound, animal bite, poisonous snake bite, eye injury. (b) Explain what to do for one of the following: pain in the belly, blisters caused by rubbing, boils

---

*Note: The old prone pressure method has been replaced by the newest back-pressure arm-lift method.

and pimples, colds, arm and leg cramps, bruises, earache, hiccup, choking on food, insect bites, tick bites, poison ivy.

12. (a) Make a list of materials to be included in a home first aid kit, first aid equipment for an automobile, or a patrol first aid kit. (b) Assist in teaching first aid (such as First Class first aid requirements to one or more persons).

First Aid to Animals*

1. Prepare and explain a schedule for the proper management of at least one farm animal, covering a period of one month, to show what must be done to prevent illness, blemishes, defects, and disease arising from improper or unsanitary surroundings.

2. Be able to recognize the symptoms and explain the proper treatment for the following: Horses — (a) lameness; (b) exhaustion from overheating; (c) distemper. Cows — (d) milk fever. Sheep — (e) foot and mouth disease; (f) anthrax. Hogs — (g) cholera. Dogs — (h) distemper; (i) rabies.

3. Explain fully what you would do for the animal in the following emergencies: (a) wire cuts; (b) choking; (c) colic; (d) bloat; (e) when a horse falls in stall or on the highway; (f) cruelty or neglect of domestic animals.

4. Demonstrate on an animal how to treat: (a) a broken bone; (b) a sprain; (c) serious bleeding; (d) an open sore.

5. Present evidence that you have: (a) assisted in the care of an injured or sick animal for a period of at least four days; *or* (b) cooperated with humane society or local officials in behalf of animals; *or* (c) cooperated with local officials in prevention of hog cholera or other infectious diseases to which farm animals are subject.

*As a 4-H'er, complete a club project in this subject. Or as an FFA member, meet these or equivalent requirements through the FFA supervised farming program.

Fishing

1. Catch three different kinds of fish by any legal, sportsmanlike method and identify them. (One of the fish must be taken on an artificial lure using any type of rod.) Clean properly for cooking.

2. Identify the different parts of a fly rod, or a casting rod, or a salt-water rod, or a spinning rod; and the main parts of a fly, or casting, or salt-water, or spinning reel. *or* Show how to take care of your fishing tackle so that

it will remain in good condition for the longest period of time. *or* Tell where the chief kinds of fish are likely to be found in your area, at different times of year, different times of day, in different kinds of weather.

3. Catch and identify three kinds of live bait.

4. Give the open seasons on game fish in your area, explain how and why they are protected by law, and tell briefly what fish conservationists are doing to improve fishing for you.

Forestry*

1. Point out fifteen different species of forest trees or wild shrubs in the field and tell their names and chief uses. (If less than fifteen kinds grow locally, identify and tell the uses of those that may be found.)

2. Do one:

(a) Collect leaves or winter twigs of fifteen forest trees or shrubs; mount them in a notebook, writing the name of each, where it grows in the U. S. and the chief uses.

(b) Obtain wood samples of ten different trees and tell some of the uses of each kind of wood.

3. (a) Describe the value of forests in protecting soil and building fertility, regulating the flow of water, wildlife management, and as recreational areas. Tell from what watershed or other source your community obtains its water. (b) Describe briefly the part that forest products play in our everyday life.

4. (a) Make a diameter tape or Biltmore stick. Show how to determine the height and diameter of trees. Estimate the board foot volume of three trees selected by the counselor. *or* (b) Examine ten stumps or logs and discuss the reasons for variations in the rate of growth from the rings.

5. Describe what is meant by sustained yield forestry.

6. Do one:

(a) Mark a ¼-acre plot for an improvement cutting (using chalk or paint to mark trees for removal) and tell why you would remove the marked trees.

(b) Help your counselor or a forester make an improvement or harvest cutting.

(c) Grow and tend for one year seedlings of forest trees or shrubs.

(d) Plant 100 seedlings for future lumber production, pulpwood, or for soil and water conservation.

*As a 4-H'er, complete a club project in this subject. Or as an FFA member, meet these or equivalent requirements through the FFA supervised farming program.

(e) Collect twenty mature cones from a coniferous tree, extract seed, and run a germination test on the seed.

(f) Assist in planting a shelter belt or windbreak and tell why the work is important.

(g) Help in some range improvement project approved by your counselor.

7. (a) Describe the damage to forests and watersheds resulting from fire, insects, tree diseases, overgrazing, unwise cutting practices. Tell what is being done to reduce this damage. (b) Tell what to do if a fire is discovered in woodlands. (c) Take part in a forest fire prevention campaign or build a fire lane of at least 100 yards at a location designated by a local fire warden or forester, or counselor.

8. Do one:

(a) Visit a logging operation, pulp or paper mill, wood preserving plant, furniture factory, veneer plant, mill working plant, sawmill, turpentine still, or some other wood-using industry and write a report of about 500 words telling what the raw material is, where it comes from, and how the finished product is made, how products are used, and how waste materials are disposed of.

(b) Visit a managed public or private forest area or watershed area with its manager or supervisor. Write a story of about 500 words on how they manage the forest to grow repeated crops of timber, to protect the watershed, or to provide other services and benefits.

(c) Help a forester, wildlife expert, or your counselor in some forest project that will benefit wild animals.

(d) Help a forester mark a hiking or ski trail, improve a campground, or make some other improvement for recreational use.

(e) Help your counselor or a forester with some other type of improvement, or furnish evidence acceptable to the counselor of some other activity or accomplishment of benefit to the forest or related resources.

(f) Help a grazing officer make a survey.

Fruit and Nut Growing*

1. (a) Point out on a map of the United States the chief regions where ten different kinds or varieties of fruits and (or) nuts are grown. (b) List the kinds and varieties of fruits and nuts that can be grown economically in your locality.

2. Select a suitable site for a fruit or nut orchard, vineyard, or berry patch and submit a plan for planting it.

3. Take full care of fruit or nut trees, grapevines, or berry plants throughout a crop season or for one year. Keep accurate records of costs, observations and yield. *or* Help take care of a fruit or nut orchard or vineyard of at least one acre through a full crop season.

4. Prune a tree, vine, or bush properly. Explain why pruning was necessary.

5. Describe three of the most harmful insect pests and two diseases most harmful to fruit or nut crops in your locality. Explain how you would control each without hurting birds or other wildlife or destroying useful insects.

6. Do one of the following: (a) Plant at least five fruit or nut trees to improve your home grounds, Scout camp, or other appropriate site in years to come. (b) Bud or graft a fruit or nut tree successfully with some better variety. (c) Pick or gather your fruit or nut crop (Requirement 3). Show how to grade and prepare it for market. Figure out its current market value in your locality. (d) Exhibit your crop at a fair, or visit your state or county fair and compare samples of your crop with those exhibited. (e) Help preserve some of your crop for sale or future home use.

Gardening*

1. Grow at least six vegetables in the family garden, or other suitable plot, from preparation of soil through harvesting.

2. State the food value of nine common vegetables, including three root or tuber crops, three vegetables which bear (fruits) above ground, and three leafy greens.

3. Tell what you did to control insects or diseases which attacked your garden. Tell where and how to use a contact insecticide, a stomach poison, and a fungicide.

4. Do three of the following: (a) Test 100 garden seeds for germination. (b) Make a hotbed or cold frame, or grow plants in same. (c) Clean, grade, bunch, or pack any three vegetables for market. (d) Exhibit one or more of the vegetables you have grown at a harvest festival, fair, or other suitable occasion. (e) Make a storage bin or pit for home use. (f) Preserve or store a portion of the crop grown and describe the process. (g) Carry out equivalent project approved by the counselor.

---

*As a 4-H'er, complete a club project in this subject. Or as an FFA member, meet these or equivalent requirements through the FFA supervised farming program.

Geology

1. Do one: (a) Make a collection of different ores, rock-forming minerals, and fossils and label with name and use (or age) of each specimen. (Minimum total twenty specimens.) (b) Make a collection of different sedimentary, igneous, and metamorphic rocks and name the important minerals found in each. Tell what use can be made of these rocks? Minimum total, ten (specimens).

2. Do one: (a) Visit a mine; quarry; oil or gas field; a gravel, clay, sand, or shell pit; or other similar operation. Explain the nature of the deposit and how the product is removed, transported, sold, and used. What safety precautions are used in this operation? (b) Visit your local water supply system and describe the source, quality, and amount of water required for your community and its relation to the geology of your area.

3. Find out if there is a topographic map of your home area and how it is obtained. Study the map, explaining the important geological features shown on it. (If a local map is not available, study one of another area that is familiar to you. Air photos may be used instead of a topographic map.)

4. Do one: (a) Prepare a report including maps or sketches on the geological features on or below the surface of the region where you live, your Scout camp, or an area that you know. (b) Describe how the soil of your area was formed and the kinds of rock from which it came. (c) Describe the earth materials used in your home (or a public building) and tell how they were obtained; or list those which you use every day and give their source.

ALTERNATIVE: In place of 4a, 4b, or 4c, the Merit Badge Counselor may choose a project of like merit, that will make use of some of the interesting geological features of the area in which you live.

Grasses, Legumes and Forage Crops*

Meet three out of five requirements as indicated in each of the four divisions, or a total of twelve requirements out of the twenty.

Grasses — any three

1. Show samples of five kinds of perennial grasses and

*As a 4-H'er, complete a club project in this subject. Or as an FFA member, meet these or equivalent requirements through the FFA supervised farming program.

explain their uses for feed purposes, soil conservation, and control of erosion.

2. Show how to prepare a seedbed for a lawn, pasture, or meadow.

3. Show: (a) samples of three annual grasses used both for hay and pastures; (b) samples of three large seed grasses, explaining the practical use of each.

4. Make a blotter, plate, or rag doll seed tester and show how to use in testing seeds for vitality.

5. (a) Make an exhibit of the six most important grasses common to your locality. Identify and explain the use of each; (b) explain the difference between "bunch grasses" and "sod-forming" grasses and their uses.

Legumes — any three including Requirement 1 or 3

1. Show samples and name the five most important legume crops grown in your section.

2. Name three small seed legumes and three large seed legumes. Explain use of this for feed, soil conservation, cash crop, and for maintaining soil moisture.

3. Show how to fertilize, lime, prepare seedbed, seed, and manage a crop of legumes grown in your locality.

4. Explain: (a) how legumes, such as soybeans, cow peas, alfalfa, and clover may be used to build soil fertility and control erosion; (b) under what conditions legumes deplete the soil.

5. Explain: (a) what is meant by inoculation of legumes; (b) how this is done, and why it is important.

Pastures — any three including Requirement 3 or 5

1. Explain the best method for improvement of old pastures and how to manage and maintain pasture fertility in your section.

2. Explain under what conditions grasses, legumes, and hayfields may be used for pastures.

3. Make an exhibit or collection of five poisonous or undesirable grasses and weeds which are injurious to pastures or poisonous to livestock.

4. Explain from personal observation how cows, horses, and sheep differ in their grazing methods or habits.

5. Prepare an exhibit of at least five pasture grasses, showing whole plant with stem, leaf, flower, and seed.

Hay Crops — any three

1. Explain how grasses such as legumes and grain crops may be used for hay or feed for livestock and wild game.

2. Give directions on how to store hay crops safely in barns, stacks, sheds, and in bales. Explain how to prevent hay barn fires and combustion.

3. Make a mounted exhibit of five kinds of properly cured hay crops; explain the qualities of "succulent" or "well-cured" hay.

4. Show samples of not less than two kinds of hay crops best suited to different livestock, such as dairy cows, horses, sheep, deer and beef cattle.

5. Show how to operate one haymaking machine and one hand tool; name five tools and machines used for haymaking in your locality; explain the purpose of each.

Hiking

1. Take five hikes of ten continuous miles each, on five separate days.

2. After sufficient training, take one hike of twenty continuous miles in one day.

3. Within a month of the final hike submit a short report of each of the six hikes, containing dates, routes traveled, weather conditions, and interesting things observed.

4. Demonstrate proper walking techniques with and without a pack. Explain the main points of good hiking practice, including care of feet and toenails, type of clothing, footwear and stockings, prevention and care of blisters, safety on the road and in the use of water for drinking.

5. Submit a written plan for a ten-mile hike, based upon a map (preferably a topographical map), including description of route, list of necessary clothing and equipment, and list of ingredients of a suitable luncheon meal.

Hog and Pork Production*

1. Explain to your counselor the importance of hog and pork production nationally and in your own state. Describe the type of hog in greatest demand by the consumer. Submit a rough sketch showing the principal cuts of pork.

2. Give satisfactory evidence that you have raised or helped raise hogs. Give four rules for success in hog production based on your own experience. Outline what you consider general good management in breeding methods and care in ensuring healthy litters, with minimum loss before weaning, including labor-saving methods.

3. Write an essay of at least 200 words on sanitation, food, water, shade, and pasture and explain why grains alone are not an adequate food. Outline in writing the proper feeding from the breeding period through weaning of a litter of pigs. Discuss fattening and growth.

---

*As a 4-H'er, complete a club project in this subject. Or as an FFA member, meet these or equivalent requirements through the FFA supervised farming program.

4. Describe two breeds of hog with which you are personally familiar. Name at least two other breeds. Visit a farm where hog raising is a major project, or visit a packing plant or stockyards; describe your visit.

5. Describe symptoms of two hog diseases and two parasites. Tell what you should do on discovering these symptoms. Explain how roundworm infestation can be prevented.

6. Tell how to prepare and show a hog for exhibit in fair or stock show.

Home Repairs

Do fourteen of the following:

1. Paint a door or a piece of furniture.
2. Whitewash or calcimine a wall or ceiling.
3. Repair an electric plug or lamp socket.
4. Repair a sash cord.
5. Replace a faucet washer.
6. Solder.
7. Hang pictures.
8. Repair a window shade.
9. Clean a Venetian blind.
10. Hang curtains and repair rods.
11. Lay linoleum.
12. Mend clothing or socks.
13. Repair upholstery.
14. Repair furniture.
15. Mend china.
16. Sharpen knives.
17. Repair gate or sagging door.
18. Repair screen on window or door.
19. Install a radio aerial.
20. Wax or polish a floor.
21. Replace a broken pane of glass.
22. Clean out a sink trap.

Horsemanship

1. Demonstrate ability to lead a horse from a stall, corral or field, and saddle and bridle properly.

2. On level ground continuously execute the following movements correctly, at ease and in sympathy with the horse:

(a) Mount. (b) Walk horse in a straight line for at least 60 feet. (c) Make half circle of not over 16 feet in radius at walk. (d) Trot in a straight line for at least 60 feet. (e) Make a half circle at trot of not over 20 feet. (f) Canter in a large circle 20 feet or over in radius on proper lead. (g) Change direction either by reversing at canter and changing leads or coming down to a walk reversing and taking up canter on proper lead. (h) Halt straight. (i) Back up straight four paces. (j) Halt and dismount.

3. Demonstrate ability to properly groom, pick out feet, and generally care for horse after riding.

4. Describe the symptoms of colic and four other common horse diseases.

5. Name three principal defects of feet or legs and explain how to detect.

6. Describe the correct method of feeding the horse that you use for this test. Explain why the amount and type of feed will vary according to the work the horse does and the type of horse he is.

7. Demonstrate the proper care of saddle and bridle and name the principal parts of the saddle and bridle.

8. Name at least fifteen principal points of a horse.

9. Name four leading breeds of horses and explain fully for what each breed is noted.

10. Show how to safely approach and remove a horse from a stall in case of fire.

Indian Lore

1. Give history of the Indian tribe that once lived nearest your home, telling something of their customs and habits, where the survivors remain, and their present condition. Visit them if possible.

2. Make an Indian costume complete and correct as to detail for one of the tribal groups, to consist of headdress, shirt, leggings or kilt, and moccasins. *or* Make and decorate authentically three of the following articles, using Indian methods in so far as possible: drum (tom-tom), rattle, bow and arrows, quiver, coupstick or lance, pipe, pipe bag, belt, war bonnet, crow belt or "bustle" war club, totem pole, council seat or canoe paddle.

3. Make a model of a tepee, or of any other type of Indian dwelling.

4. Take part in an Indian pageant, entertainment, or campfire ceremonial in which at least three dances based on authentic Indian themes are used.

5. Sing three Indian songs including the "Omaha Tribal Prayer" and tell something of their meaning.

6. Demonstrate three Indian games that can be played in camp or at meetings.

7. Know at least fifty signs in the Indian sign language and with them carry on a conversation for three minutes, or tell a story in sign talk that will take at least that much time.

Insect Life

1. Watch the insects at a pondside or brook, ant's nest, clump of flowers, wasp's nest, rotted log, or other center of activity for three hours. Make notes on what you see.

2. In the field — or if this is impossible, from mounted specimens — tell to which order insects of six different orders belong. Explain how you recognize each order.

3. (a) Make a spreading board and three specimen boxes; (b) collect, mount, and label twenty-five different kinds of insects including three beneficial and three harmful to man. Exhibit this collection at a troop meeting.

4. Know something about the life histories and habits of the twenty-five insects collected in Requirement No. 3; that is, where each is likely to be found, what it eats, the different stages of its life, how it sees, hears, smells, feels (if it does these things), and with what plants, animals, birds, and other insects it is associated.

Journalism

Do any nine of the following:

1. Write stories covering satisfactorily the following assignments, demonstrating that you know the principles of good news writing, including the elements of a good lead paragraph: (a) a news incident; (b) a routine club or society meeting; (c) a lecture, sermon, or political address.

2. Write: (a) an editorial; (b) a feature or human interest story; (c) a review of a play, motion picture, radio or television show, concert, book, or art or photography exhibit.

3. (a) Explain how the articles in Requirements 1 and 2 differ. (b) Secure the publication of at least one of these articles.

4. (a) Prepare a simple set of headline styles which will serve all needs of a small newspaper, indicating type size and approximate count for each. (b) Using this schedule, write good headlines for the three stories in Requirement 1.

5. Present photographic or cartoon copy, or the suggestions for such copy, as an illustration for a news story and write the caption for it.

6. Read and correct proof, using the conventional proofreader's signs.

7. Show that you know what is meant by the following

terms: point, font, pica, face, case, linotype, hand-set, galley proof; halftone, electrotype, screen, stereotype mat.

8. (a) Explain the steps necessary to copyright a book, magazine, or newspaper; tell what rights are granted by a copyright and for what period. (b) Explain what is meant by freedom of the press and why we have libel laws. Tell what plagiarism is.

9. Prepare a dummy for the printer of an eight-page newspaper or magazine, including the placing of different-size advertisements to cover the equivalent of two pages.

10. Explain the process of preparing a modern newspaper for publication, demonstrating a satisfactory knowledge of the various departments and executives and their functions. Explain the importance of the deadline.

11. Have contributed as a reporter, or as editor, or a member of the editorial or business staff (either voluntary or paid) on a newspaper or a local council troop, school, trade, farm, or club publication for at least six issues.

12. Present a scrapbook, including unpublished copy as well as clippings of published material, filed under date and place of publication.

Landscape Gardening*

1. Describe two examples of landscape gardening in your locality and tell what improvement, if any, you would suggest.

2. Explain how at least five trees have been used for landscaping in your community. Give several of their advantages and disadvantages.

3. Give the main characteristics of at least fifteen shrubs used either in formal or informal landscape work.

4. (a) Make a working drawing or model of a portion of the grounds around your own home using planting of your own selection — to blot out some untidy place such as laundry yard, garbage can, compost heap, back porch, or other ugly view. Carry out this project *or* (b) make a working drawing of a flower garden, arranging plants so there will be continuous showing of flowers for a season. Plant and take care of it.

5. Keep a record of the project (4a) or garden (4b), showing time it took, cost of shrubs, seeds, plants, trellis, wood, etc.

*As a 4-H'er, complete a club project in this subject. Or as an FFA member, meet these or equivalent requirements through the FFA supervised farming program.

Leatherwork

1. Collect samples of at least five different kinds of leather: calfskin, cowhide, pigskin, etc. Point out the chief characteristics and best uses of each.

2. Make one or more articles of leather which involve the technique of: (a) preparation and transfer of a pattern; (b) cutting the leather; (c) punching holes; (d) lacing; and (e) decoration by one or more means, such as tooling, embossing, stamping, carving or burning.

3. Submit evidence that you take proper care of your shoes and other leather wearing apparel.

4. Do two of these projects: (a) Learn (from observation if possible) the process of tanning, curing, and finishing leather. (b) Tan or cure the skin of a small animal. (c) Demonstrate proper care of leather goods and make minor repairs on a damaged suitcase, piece of harness, or other article. (d) Sole and heel a pair of shoes or boots. Keep a record of costs and time spent. (e) Plait or braid an article of leather or leather substitute — such as a whistle lanyard, belt, or dog leash. Make a terminal Turk's-head. (f) Find out what lifework opportunities there are in the leather industries. Choose one specific job in which you are interested and report on the qualifications you must have for the job and what the working conditions are.

Lifesaving †

(These tests must be performed before a counselor who holds the senior life saving certificate of one of the following organizations: American Red Cross, National Collegiate Athletic Association, Y.M.C.A., or who holds an Aquatic School certificate of the Boy Scouts of America for lifesaving.)

To obtain this merit badge, you must first have met the merit badge requirements for Swimming, must have spent at least six hours in preparation and practice, and must demonstrate the following:

1. Demonstrate twice your ability to remove street clothes (except underpants or bathing trunks) in 20 seconds or less.

2. Demonstrate correct approach to drowning persons who are in the following positions: (a) back to you — back approach; (b) face to you with head above water — underwater approach.

3. With the aid of a buddy and a subject, demonstrate

†A Second Class Scout must first qualify for First Class Scoutcraft Requirement 5 (see page 113).

the following rope rescue both as line tender and as rescuer:

As rescuer — Carrying the looped end of 50 feet of ⅛-inch rope across shoulder and chest, enter water with run or jump, swim 50 feet to struggling person whom you grasp with one hand, grasp rope with other hand, and be towed ashore.

As line tender — Chain knot rescue line. Tie and place loop around rescuer's shoulder, pay out rope, and pull rescuer and subject ashore.

4. Watching struggling person constantly, enter water feet first (by jumping or running) and — (a) swim 30 feet, make correct approach, and tow victim 30 feet to shore with hair carry; (b) swim 30 feet, make correct approach, and tow victim 30 feet to shore with cross chest carry.

5. Swim 30 feet, make correct approach to a tired person and, using tired swimmer's carry, push 30 feet to shore.

6. In water at least 6 feet deep, demonstrate how to block effectively and avoid by ducking the following grips of a struggling person: around neck with right arm, with left arm, with both arms. In each case, turn struggling person around and place him in a position for towing ashore.

7. Demonstrate resuscitation, 1½ minutes, back-pressure arm-lift method.

8. Surface dive in 6 to 8 feet, recovering various objects three times and a 10-pound weight once.

9. In deep water, remove street clothes (except underpants or bathing trunks) and swim 100 yards.

Machinery

1. Explain the proper way to use the following hand tools: screw driver, ball-peen hammer, pliers, cold chisel, center punch, file, calipers, hacksaw, rule, combination square. Also these types of wrenches: open end, adjustable, monkey, pipe, box, and socket. Demonstrate to your counselor the use of any eight of the above tools.

2. Assemble or construct wooden or metal models of these: lever inclined plane, screw, wedge, wheel and axle, block and tackle, and gears.

3. Make and present a rough sketch showing the operation of: diesel engine, steam turbine, four-cycle gasoline engine. Explain how — in a factory or machine shop — the power is commonly transmitted to the machines.

4. Make and present a satisfactory sketch showing the

construction of a drill press and a metalworking lathe. Explain three operations that can be performed on each.

5. Make a metal object from a plan or blueprint using a machine lathe and a drill press.

6. Visit a machine shop, trade school or factory; note the benchwork, power equipment, machine tools, and safety devices to protect workers; take notes and describe your visit. *or* If no such shop is available, submit a chart or outline showing at least five mechanical occcupations and listing the work and training required for each.

Marksmanship

1. (a) Pledge your word that you will live up to the Scout Marksman's Code. (b) Explain your understanding of the meaning of each of the rules of safety in the Scout Marksman's Code. (c) Explain what different kinds of weapons are meant by the word "gun" as it is used in the Scout Marksman's Code.

2. Demonstrate with a rifle or shotgun: (a) the very first thing you must do whenever you take up a gun or whenever a gun is handed to you by another person; (b) the proper way to carry a gun afield if you are walking with two companions [show how each of the three persons should carry his gun (1) when walking single file and (2) when walking abreast]; (c) how to properly hand a gun to another person; (d) how to properly take a gun from an automobile; (e) how to properly handle a gun when it is necessary to cross a fence; (f) the proper care a gun requires after use — (1) when in daily use and (2) when storing it for a long period of time.

3. Describe what "rifling" is and explain its function.

4. In what direction should the rear sight of a gun be moved to move the striking point of the bullet: (a) from right to left? (b) from too low to "on target"?

5. (a) Make not less than 30 points in the offhand (standing) position out of a possible 50 points (5 shots) on each of four targets. (b) Make a score of not less than 40 points in the prone position out of a possible 50 points (5 shots) on each of six targets.

NOTE: You may qualify for Requirements 5a and 5b on any one of the following courses of fire: (1) 50-foot course may be fired with .22 caliber rim-fire rifles using .22 short, long, or long rifle ammunition, using official 50-foot targets on a 50-foot range. (2) 25-foot course may be fired with .22 caliber rim-fire rifles using .22 caliber CB or BB caps, or pneumatic or gas type air rifles not greater than .22 caliber, using 50- or 25-foot targets on a 25-foot range. (3) 15-foot course may be fired with any spring-type air rifle (BB gun) using official 15-foot air rifle targets on a 15-foot range.

Specifications: Range distance of 50, 25, or 15 feet is measured from firing line to face of target. Sights can be any not containing glass. Targets must be official NRA, official BSA, or those issued by the director of Civilian

Marksmanship. Rifle sling may be used in connection with arm and hand supporting the fore end. No other use of the sling is permitted.

The Scout Marksman's Code

1. A Scout *always* treats every gun, whether it is a rifle, a shotgun, an air gun, or a handgun, as a *loaded gun*— even though he has personally unloaded it.
2. A Scout points the muzzle of a gun in a safe direction when picking it up and laying it down.
3. A Scout opens the action of a gun immediately and makes sure that it is unloaded.
4. A Scout opens the action of a gun before he passes it to another person.
5. A Scout never points a gun, loaded or unloaded, toy or real, at any human being under any circumstances.
6. A Scout always follows the principles and practices of wildlife conservation and lives up to the spirit and letter of all game laws.
7. A Scout takes every precaution for the safety of others before shooting in the open.
8. A Scout cares for a firearm properly before he lays it aside.
9. A Scout is sportsmanlike when engaged in contests of skill with firearms and whenever handling firearms.
10. A Scout pledges never to shoot at anything he cannot positively identify.
11. A Scout knows and complies with the laws governing the use of firearms in his community and state.

Masonry

1. (a) Prepare or read correctly plans for a permanent, useful masonry structure such as a wall, small dam, outdoor fireplace, or trash burner. (b) Mark out the site on the ground, dig a foundation trench, and pour a foundation of solid concrete mixed by yourself. (c) Prepare mortar correctly. (d) Using a mason's tools correctly, complete the structure.
2. Point out examples of coursed ashlar, random ashlar, and rubble construction.
3. Do any three of the following projects: (a) Lay a stepping stone or flagstone walk. (b) Build a useful concrete structure, such as a wall, small dam, pond, floor, sidewalk, or post. (c) Design and mold in a form an ornamental concrete object, such as a birdbath, window box, garden seat, or sundial. (d) Make major repairs in a masonry structure. (e) Build a useful, dry masonry structure, such as an outdoor fireplace, incinerator, or grease trap. (f) Plaster or stucco a wall or ceiling. (g) Visit a

rock quarry or a factory where cement, brick, tile, concrete block, or other masonry material is made. Observe and report on operations from beginning to end. (h) Find out what lifework opportunities there are in masonry and allied trades. Choose one specific job in which you are interested and report on the qualifications you must have for the job and what the working conditions are.

Mechanical Drawing

1. Make a preliminary rough sketch drawn to approximate scale and from it submit a finished accurate scale floor plan of your troop meeting room, or a room in your church building, school, or home, such drawings to be properly titled and to indicate by accepted conventional symbols, all openings, equipment, safety devices, etc. List drawing instruments used.

2. Submit an accurate scale drawing of some piece of craftwork for use in home, school, troop meeting place, or camp, which is sufficiently clear and detailed to be used by someone else as a working basis for making the article; drawing to include a bill of material with an estimate of cost for such craft article.

3. Submit drawings made by yourself of each of the following: (a) orthographic projections and an isometric projection, of an object other than those specified in Requirements No. 1 and No. 2; (b) reduce or enlarge a simple scale drawing approved by your counselor, indicating the scale of enlargement or reduction you have used.

4. Make ink tracing of craft article in Requirement No. 2 and submit cost of reproducing drawing by blueprinting, or photostating, or other method of reproduction.

5. Describe the subject of your drawing in Requirement No. 2 in ink printing of not less than twenty-five words, using single stroke vertical or slant Gothic letters.

Metalwork

1. (a) Collect and label samples of ten metals or alloys and describe the source, chief qualities, and most important uses of each. (b) Learn how ores are mined and how the metals are extracted, reduced, and refined. (c) Explain how metals are shaped for shipment to industry.

2. Make three useful articles from tin cans.

3. (a) Make one or more simple articles of metal in which you use at least six of the following operations: annealing, bending, casting, coloring, cutting, drilling, fil-

ing, grinding, hammering, pickling, piercing, planishing, polishing, riveting, sawing, soldering, stamping, welding. (b) Take proper care of the tools used. (c) Keep a record of time and costs involved.

4. Do any two of the following projects:

(a) Forge a chain hook ring, and at least three links of round iron or soft steel; join the parts by welding.

(b) Make a cold chisel of at least ⅝-inch hexagonal tool steel; harden and temper.

(c) From a working drawing, make a pattern of a small machine part. Make a satisfactory benchwork mold from this pattern using any convenient flask. Make proper allowances for draft and machining. Pour the metal; remove and clean the casting. Submit drawing, pattern, and casting to counselor.

(d) Make or repair three metal toys (or metal parts of toys) and, after submitting them to your counselor, contribute them to needy children.

(e) Visit a metalcraft, forge, foundry, machine, or similar shop, or a mill. Observe and report on its operations from beginning to end. Note what safety precautions are taken to protect the workers.

(f) Operate one piece of metal machining equipment (such as lathe, planer, or drill press), carefully practicing all safety precautions.

(g) Find out what lifework opportunities there are in the metal trades. Choose one specific job in which you are interested and report on the qualifications you must have for the job and what the working conditions are.

Music

1. Sing or play a simple folk song, art song, or hymn selected by your counselor. (You should be able to read all the signs and terms of the score and to sing or play it on a standard musical instrument in an acceptable musical manner with respect to technique, phrasing, tone, dynamics and rhythm.)

2. Name the four general groups of musical instruments and briefly describe how tones are obtained from one example of each group.

3. Do two of the following:

(a) Attend a concert, recital, oratorio, opera, or other classical or semiclassical music performance, or listen to at least three hours of such musical programs on radio, television, or phonograph. Report on what compositions were heard, who their composers were, and who performed and conducted them. Know the story of any program music or opera included. Discuss your own impressions of the music with your counselor.

(b) Outline in your own words the development of music in the United States. Show that you are familiar with the lives and works of at least five of this country's better known composers and musical artists.

(c) Serve satisfactorily for at least six months as a member of a school, church, Scout unit, or other community musical organization, such as a band, orchestra, chamber group, drum and bugle corps, glee club, or choir. *or* Participate as a soloist in at least six public functions.

4. Do one of the following:

(a) Teach three songs to a group of Scouts or other persons and, using proper hand motions, lead them in singing the songs.

(b) Compose and write the score for a piece of music of at least twelve measures.

(c) Make a primitive musical instrument and learn to play satisfactorily on it.

(d) Catalogue properly your own or your family collection of at least twelve phonograph records. Show how to handle and store records correctly.

Nature

1. After personal investigation, select for study one typical wildlife community, approved by your counselor (forest, field, marsh, pond, desert, mountain top, ocean shore, etc.) near your home, *or* your favorite camp site. Take at least two hikes within that area and do the following:

(a) Submit a list of the most commonly found plants (trees, shrubs, flowers, grasses, etc.) and animals (mammals, birds, reptiles, amphibians, fish, insects, mollusks). (b) Report on kinds of soils and most commonly found rocks. (c) Describe springs, streams, lakes and other waters found.

2. From reading or talks with your counselor tell how temperature, wind, rainfall, altitude, geology, tide, *wild* or *domestic animals* or *man* help make the selected area what it is. Tell what is meant by the term "plant succession." From reading or talks with your counselor, tell briefly what successions have occurred in the selected area in the last hundred years and what would probably happen in the next hundred years if the area is undisturbed by man.

3. Do all of the requirements in two of the following fields:

Birds

(a) Identify in the field twenty species of birds. (b) Recognize ten species of birds by calls or songs, or determine their presence by nests or other signs. (c) Make and set out three birdhouses or two feeding stations and tell what birds used them; or photograph nests of four species of birds.

Mammals

(a) Identify in the field six species of wild mammals. (b) Recognize in the field the signs of six species of wild mammals. (c) Make plaster casts of the tracks of three wild mammals; or photograph two species of wild mammals.

Reptiles or Amphibians

(a) Recognize the poisonous snakes in *your* area and identify in the field six species of reptiles or amphibians (snakes, turtles, lizards, frogs, toads, salamanders). (b) Recognize three species of toads or frogs by their voices; or identify three reptiles or amphibians by their eggs, dens, burrows, or other signs. (c) Raise tadpoles from the eggs of some amphibian, or raise adults from tadpoles; or keep an adult reptile or amphibian under conditions that keep it healthy for one month.

Insects or Spiders

(a) Catch and identify thirty species. (b) Collect and mount thirty species. (c) Raise an insect from the pupa or cocoon or raise adults from nymphs or keep larvae until they form pupae or cocoons; or keep a colony of ants or bees through one season.

Fish

(a) Catch and identify four species of fish. (b) Collect four kinds of natural animal food eaten by fish; or make an artificial lure and catch a fish with it. (c) Develop a simple aquarium containing fish and plant life and keep it successfully balanced for one month.

Mollusks and Crustaceans

(a) Identify five species of mollusks and crustaceans (clams, mussels, snails — shrimp, crabs, crayfish). (b) Mount at least six shells. (c) Make an aquarium and keep in it two species of mollusks or crustaceans under such conditions that they stay healthy for a month.

Plants

(a) Identify in the field fifteen species of wild plants (trees, shrubs, ferns, grasses, mosses, etc.). (b) Collect and label correctly seeds of six plants; or collect, mount, and label leaves of twelve plants. (c) Build a terrarium of at least three species of plants and keep it successfully for one month.

Soils and Rocks

(a) Collect and identify soils found in three soil profiles; or ten rocks representative of the area. (b) Find at least six species of animals that live in soil. (c) Grow seeds for one month in two kinds of soil and describe difference in rate of growth.

4. Select one species of plant, mammal, bird, fish, reptile or amphibian and, from personal observation and reading, write a simple life history (how and where and when it originated; how it grows; what it eats; what eats it; migratory habits if any; how and where it spends the winter; its natural home, etc.).

Painting

1. (a) Explain at least three ways in which a coat of paint can improve a surface. (b) Explain the chief uses of oil, water, and rubber base paints, also enamel, shellac, varnish, and lacquer. Tell what qualities of each make it suited to these uses.

2. Prepare and paint any two of the following items or similar ones approved by your counselor, using satisfactory fillers, priming coats, covering coats, and finishing coats as necessary:

An exterior surface	A boat or canoe
An interior surface	A floor
An article of furniture	A porch rail or fence
A concrete or cement wall	A lawn mower

3. Prepare an old painted surface, containing holes and uneven surfaces, to receive and retain a new coat of paint.

4. Add colors to a white paint base so as to produce paints of two predetermined colors that harmonize. With these paint properly one of the following items in two colors: model plane, birdhouse, furniture, serving tray, dollhouse, picture frame, or similar useful item approved by your counselor.

5. Demonstrate the proper methods of using, cleaning, and storing a paintbrush, paint roller, or spray gun.

Personal Fitness

*1. Before you attempt to meet any other requirements, have your doctor give you a thorough health examination, including a vision test, using the standard Scout medical examination form. Describe th examination to your counselor and tell him what questions you asked about your health, what advice and recommendations your doctor made, and what you have done about them.

*2. Have an examination made by your dentist and submit a statement certifying that your teeth have been examined and properly cared for.

3. Demonstrate that you have a good understanding of physical and mental health by answering questions asked by your counselor on the following: (a) Reasons for being fit. (b) Normal differences in rate of growth and development. (c) What it means to be mentally healthy. Discuss three healthy personality traits. (d) The need for pasteurization of milk, the sanitary control of water, and the sanitary disposal of human waste. (e) Basic foods essential to the daily diet of a person of your age. (f) Cleanliness of the hands, food, and dishes in the control of illness. (g) Effects of tobacco and alcohol. (h) Illnesses against which you may be immunized.

4. Present a list of your personal health habits including: (a) number of hours of sleep; (b) care of your skin, hands, fingernails, toenails; (c) care of your eyes; (d) care of your teeth; (e) prevention of accidents in your home.

5. Demonstrate six exercises suitable for all-round physical development, including those that strengthen the muscles of your arms, shoulders, chest, abdomen, back, and one to increase your endurance.

6. Demonstrate proficiency in two individual sports such as the following: badminton, bowling, canoeing (one man), diving, golf, handball, horseback riding, rowing (one man), skating, skiing, squash, tennis, table tennis, track or field sports, tumbling, wrestling.

7. Swim 100 yards.

8. Demonstrate proficiency in one of the following team events played according to the published rules of the game: baseball (hardball or softball), basketball, football (eleven-man or six-man), hockey, lacrosse, soccer, volleyball.

9. Demonstrate that you can meet the following physi-

---

*In keeping with established policy, it is understood that where compliance with the health and/or dental requirements, Nos. 1 and 2, is in violation of the religious convictions of the individual, such requirement or requirements will be set aside on the presentation of a certification by the boy's parents and proper church official that: (a) a definite violation of religious conviction is involved, and (b) the parents accept full responsibility for any consequence of such exemption and release the Boy Scouts of America from any responsibility.

cal fitness tests after you have trained for each of them regularly on at least four days a week for four weeks.

	AGE			
	11-12	13-14	15-16	17 and over
Push-ups	12	15	18	21
Pull-ups	4	5	7	8
Sit-ups	35	40	45	50
Vertical wall jump	11″	14″	16″	18″

Running

Present evidence that you have trained for this run for four consecutive weeks in the following way: (a) For two weeks (minimum — four days each week) run or jog at least the prescribed distance without checking time. (b) For the next two weeks (minimum — four days each week) run the distance for time, gradually increasing speed. Submit a record of all these time trials.

Standard to be met at the end of training period:

	AGE			
	11-12	13-14	15-16	17 and over
Distance	½ mile	¾ mile	1 mile	1 mile
Time	4 min.	6 min.	7½ min.	7 min.

Pets*

1. Present evidence that you have cared properly for one or more pets for a period of at least four months, after approval of the project by your counselor.

2. Present an article of at least two hundred words, explaining your responsibility in the care, feeding, housing, etc., of your pets over a two-month period; tell some *interesting* facts about them and why you have this particular kind of pet. Include a statement on local laws and ordinances, if any, relating to the pets you keep.

3. Show that you have completed reading a book or pamphlet, approved by your counselor, covering your kind of pet.

4. Do any one of the following: (a) Exhibit your pets in some pet show, amateur or professional. (b) Start a friend raising pets similar to yours; advise him, and help him get a good start. (c) Breed your pets as a project and show their offspring to the counselor. (d) Train a pet in three or more tricks or *special abilities*.

*If you have earned merit badges for Dog Care, Nature, Rabbit Raising, Reptile Study, Zoology, Hog and Pork Production, Pigeon Raising, or Poultry Keeping, work done on any of these will not qualify you for the above requirements.

Photography

1. Submit at least sixteen black-and-white photographs, *or* thirty color transparencies, *or* a 100-foot reel of 16 mm. movie film, *or* a 50-foot reel of 8 mm. Picture taking must be done by yourself, and results must be acceptable to your counselor from the standpoint of selection of subject and background, composition, focus, exposure, light and shade, and tone quality or color harmony. Tell what types of camera, film, and filter were used for your pictures, and why.

2. Do one of the following:

(a) Develop your negatives and make your own prints of sixteen black-and-white still photographs taken by yourself. Tell what kind of film negative developer, paper, and paper developer you used and why you selected those materials.

(b) Submit a plan for a series of at least thirty color transparencies on some phase of Scouting, family, school, church, or community activity. Plan should call for a presentation of about four minutes and should include: (1) a "shooting" script (a written description of what the series will cover and how they will be photographed); (2) an outline of the commentary to accompany the slides, or a list of titles necessary for an effective presentation; (3) a list of equipment and properties required.

(c) Submit a plan for a complete how-to-do-it movie on some phase of Scouting, family, school, church or community activity. Plan should call for a running time of approximately four minutes (100 feet of 16 mm. film, 50 feet of 8 mm.) and should include: (1) a "shooting" script (a written description or plan of what the movie will cover and how it will be photographed); (2) an outline of the commentary to accompany the movie, or a list of titles necessary for an effective presentation; (3) a list of equipment and properties required.

3. Do one of the following:

(a) Enlarge to 8" x 10" and properly mount on 16" x 20" mounts at least two black-and-white pictures taken by yourself and exhibit them in a regular photography exhibit or at a Scout or Explorer meeting.

(b) Submit a series of at least ten black-and-white pictures that tell a how-to-do-it story.

(c) Prepare glossy prints of two of your photographs in suitable form, with captions to be submitted to a publication.

(d) Take the series of thirty color transparencies planned under 2b and present it to an audience.

(e) Take the movie planned under 2c, edit and title it, and present it to an audience.

(f) Demonstrate your ability to set up and put on an effective film presentation before a group, including operation of a standard 16 mm. sound projector. Show proper advance preparations covering local license or permit (if required), safety precautions, seating arrangements, choice of screen size and surface, electrical requirements, house lights, ventilation, care of film, and trouble shooting.

(g) Demonstrate your ability to set up and put on a presentation similar to 3f, but calling for operation of a slide or filmstrip projector with sound or narrator.

4. Investigate and report on the opportunities open to you for finding a career in some aspect of photography.

Pigeon Raising*

1. (a) House and care for at least two pairs of pigeons for three months. (b) Keep an accounting on cost of birds, feed, equipment, etc., and of income received from sale of squabs or birds for this same period. (c) Keep complete production records of eggs laid, squabs hatched, sickness, deaths, etc., for this same period.

2. Submit a photograph or drawing of your loft and flypen.

3. List the four fundamental requirements for successful pigeon raising.

4. If you live in city or town, give its ordinances regulating the keeping of pigeons.

5. Describe two breeds of utility pigeons used for squabbing; two fancy breeds used for exhibiting; and two breeds used for flying (racing or high flying).

6. Do one: (a) Pick, dress, and cook at least one squab raised by you. Visit a squab farm and write a 300-word report on it. (b) Enter at least one pigeon owned by you in a pigeon show. Visit a pigeon show and write a 300-word report on it. (c) Enter at least one pigeon owned by you in a pigeon race. Visit a racing loft, or racing club meeting, and write a 300-word report on it.

*As a 4-H'er, complete a club project in this subject. Or as an FFA member, meet these or equivalent requirements through the FFA supervised farming program.

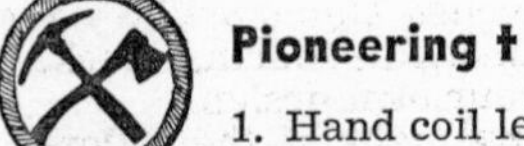

Pioneering †

1. Hand coil length of rope. Describe (a) kinds of rope; (b) care of rope; (c) weakening effect of knots.

†A Second Class Scout must first qualify for First Class Scoutcraft Requirement 3 (see page 112).

2. Tie quickly twelve knots and hitches and explain their specific use in pioneering.
3. Make a long, a short, and an eye splice.
4. Lash spars together properly using square, diagonal, and sheer lashings.
5. (a) Build, without the use of nails, spikes, or wire, a bridge or derrick (capable of supporting two hundred pounds in weight) or other practical pioneering project such as signal tower, monkey bridge, gateway. *or* (b) Build a shack of one kind or another suitable for three occupants. *or* (c) Using lashings only, make a model bridge at least 18 inches long and explain the principles involved in its construction.

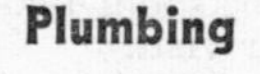

Plumbing

1. (a) Submit a sketch and explain the operation of the hot and cold water supply system in your home or that of a neighbor. Tell how you would make the system safe from freezing. (b) Submit a sketch and explain the drainage system of the plumbing in a house, including the use of drains and vents.
2. Show how to use five important plumber's tools.
3. Identify and describe the use of each of the following: washer, cap nut, float, force cup, half-and-half solder, flux, elbow, tee, nipple, coupling, plug, union, trap, drainpipe, water meter.
4. Tell what kinds of pipe are most used in a plumbing system and why. Cut thread and connect two pieces of pipe or connect two pieces of copper tubing.
5. (a) Replace a washer in a faucet. (b) Clean out a sink or lavatory trap.
6. Submit to your counselor a list of five important local health regulations related to plumbing.

Pottery

1. Explain the properties and ingredients of a good clay body for craft pottery.
2. Make and submit two drawings of pottery forms, to be on paper at least 8½ by 11 inches. One must be a recognized pottery type, such as American Indian, Greek, or Chinese. The other must be of your own design.
3. Explain the meaning of any eight of the following terms, as applied to pottery: bat, wedging, throwing, leather dry, bone dry, green ware, bisque or biscuit ware, terra cotta, grog, slip, earthenware, stoneware, porcelain, pyrometric cone, glaze.

4. Do any three of these, the pieces to be painted, glazed, or otherwise decorated by you and approved by your counselor: (a) Make a flat tray or dish. (b) Make a box or similar item, using the slab method. (c) Make a vase or jar, using the coil method. (d) Make four different tiles of original design. (e) Make a human or animal figurine or decorative book ends. (f) Throw a simple vase on a potter's wheel. (g) Make an acceptable pottery form and help to fire it.

5. Submit a rough sketch of a potter's wheel and tell how it works.

6. Explain the scope of the ceramic industry in the United States and tell some of the items produced, exclusive of craft pottery. *or* Visit a pottery, brickyard, ceramic plant, trade school, or workshop; take notes on pottery processes; and describe your visit.

Poultry Keeping*

Complete the requirements in one of the following groups:

Rearing Pullets

1. Raise and take care of twenty or more chicks (straight run or pullet) for five months.

2. Keep records on all management practices (feed consumption, mortality, medications, vaccinations) and present them to your merit badge counselor.

3. Tell how to identify three poultry diseases common in your area and how you prevent your pullets from contracting these diseases.

4. Make one piece of equipment (waterer, feeder, brooder, for example) and put it to good use.

5. Describe the brooding house in which you raised your pullets. Explain how you provided for proper sanitation and ventilation.

Flock Management

1. Manage a flock (your own or a neighbor's) of ten or more pullets or hens for six months. Birds should be at least five months old at the start.

2. Keep daily egg production records and records on feed consumption and mortality. Turn these records in to your merit badge counselor.

3. Tell how to identify three poultry diseases common in your area and how you prevent your birds from contracting these diseases. Explain culling.

---

*As a 4-H'er, complete a club project in this subject. Or as an FFA member, meet these or equivalent requirements through the FFA supervised farming program.

4. Make one piece of equipment (feeder, waterer, catching hook, roosts, for example) and put it to good use.

5. Candle, grade, and pack two dozen eggs for market.

Poultry Meat Production

1. Raise twenty or more broilers, fryers, roasters, caponettes, capons, turkeys, or ducks to market age.

2. Keep accurate records of feed consumption, mortality, weight gains, etc., and turn them in to your merit badge counselor.

3. Write a concise report on the management of your birds. Include information on brooding, housing, sanitation, feeding, and disease control.

4. Make one piece of equipment (feeder, waterer, catching hook, disposal pit, for example) and put it to good use.

5. Kill and dress two birds for market.

Printing

1. Set a paragraph of type by hand from manuscript copy.

2. Read and mark proof correctly.

3. Set type from original copy for a display card or advertising handbill for practical use.

4. Run 100 copies of the job in Requirement 3 on a 10 x 15 or smaller job press. Demonstrate the correct method of inking, setting gauge pins, use of make-ready, accuracy of feeding, and washing up press. *or* Using a stencil screen and base made by yourself, print at least 50 copies of a poster, greeting card, or other material by the silk-screen process.

Public Health

1. Tell how people contract five of the following diseases and what you and the health department can do to prevent their spread: typhoid fever, diphtheria, malaria, hookworm, Rocky Mountain spotted fever, tetanus (lockjaw), rabies, whooping cough, scarlet fever, tuberculosis, smallpox.

2. (a) Name two diseases common to animal and man that can be caught by a person through the drinking of unpasteurized milk. (b) Name two diseases that can be

caught by drinking polluted water. (c) Name two diseases that can be spread by rats.

3. Explain how flies may be controlled and their breeding places destroyed.

4. Name three diseases against which an infant should be immunized and two diseases against which boys of Scout and Explorer age should be immunized.

5. Do two of the following: (a) Visit your state, county, or local health department and prepare an outline of its principal functions. (b) Visit your water treatment plant and prepare an outline of the major steps in the water treatment used to protect your community from diseases that may be spread by water. (c) Prepare a simple sketch of a home sewage disposal system and tell how it should be located and constructed to protect against the pollution of nearby wells or springs. (d) Visit a dairy farm and prepare an outline of the measures taken to produce clean milk for pasteurization. (e) Visit a milk pasteurization plant and prepare a brief statement on the pasteurization of milk. (f) Visit your community sewage treatment plant and prepare a brief statement about sewage disposal.

6. Do the following: (a) Filter one full canteen of muddy water, using clean cloth or other materials, and then make the water safe for drinking either by treatment with suitable chemical or by boiling water. (b) Dig and make ready for use either a straddle trench latrine or a "cathole" latrine; then fill in properly. (c) Properly dispose of garbage and rubbish from a camp site. (d) Describe how milk could be pasteurized in your home and make a quart of raw milk safe to drink.

7. Explain two purposes of the "recheck" examination given to Scouts by a medical doctor when they arrive at a council camp.

Public Speaking

1. Give an original talk of not less than five minutes, from notes or complete text, to an audience of at least twenty-five persons, on some phase of Scouting.

2. Read a selection of 500 words or more, to show your ability to read at sight material you have never seen before.

3. Describe clearly and simply a technical process, game, science experiment, or instructions for making an article of handicraft.

4. Talk extemporaneously for at least two minutes on a subject of interest to you, chosen for you by the counselor.

Rabbit Raising*

1. Properly house a litter of rabbits, from mating of doe until marketing time for the litter.
2. Explain the use of your breed and know about one breed used for meat, one for fur, and one for wool.
3. Keep a breeding record, a feeding schedule, and a financial record.

*This badge may also be earned by completing a 4-H Club project in this subject.

Radio

1. Draw a basic wiring diagram of a one-tube receiving set. Use correct symbols and show all essential parts. Describe purpose of each part.
2. Make a working one-tube receiving set and demonstrate its operation by receiving from at least five different stations.
3. Explain how to install an antenna for use in receiving equipment and how to ground it properly and protect it against lightning and power wires.
4. Receive and send correctly a straight text of not less than five words (or twenty-five letters). Text will be assigned by merit badge counselor.
5. Name five of the most frequently used "Q" signals and explain the meaning of each.
6. Tell five basic requirements for a federal license to operate a transmitting station.

NOTE: The holding of an amateur operator's license will exempt the Scout from examination on all requirements above, except 1 and 2. Such license must be in force at the time the Radio badge is awarded.

Railroading

1. Outline the major steps in the growth and development of railroads in the United States and discuss the importance of the railroads to our daily life.
2. Name the railroads which directly serve your community (or the station nearest your home) and on a map indicate connecting routes to at least one city in each of the following sections of the United States: East, South, Middle West, and Far West.
3. Explain briefly how each of the three kinds of locomotives (steam, electric, and diesel) develops power.
4. Identify examples, models, or pictures of six different locomotive types and ten different kinds of rolling stock

(passenger or freight or both), explaining the use of each.

5. List the principal duties of the men who make up the engine crew and train crew of a freight or passenger train.

6. (a) Demonstrate five arm or lantern signals commonly used by trainmen.

(b) Tell what the several aspects of one type of semaphore or light signal system mean.

(c) Identify the meanings of five train whistle signals.

(d) Describe two emergency methods of signaling a train to stop in order to prevent a disaster.

7. Explain at least six rules of safety to observe aboard and around trains and with respect to hazards around railroad tracks, platforms, yards, crossings, trestles, etc.

8. Do any three of the following (the last five are especially suited to the interest of model railroaders):

(a) Outline the general organization of a railroad company and briefly describe the functions of its major departments.

(b) Identify freight cars of at least ten different railroads by their report heralds or symbols.

(c) With one or more adults, plan and take a railroad trip of twenty-five or more miles; purchase your own ticket and read the timetables and accompanying notes correctly.

(d) Explore the lifework opportunities open to a young man in the field of railroading. Describe the necessary qualifications and working conditions of one job in which you are especially interested.

(e) (1) Know name, scale to foot, proportion, and track gauge for four standard model railroad gauges. (2) Demonstrate proper method of cleaning and lubricating a model locomotive and other model equipment.

(f) Draw to scale the layout of your own model railroad, or a layout which could be built in a suitable place in your home. Your layout must include at least a point-to-point or continuous loop road with a variety of routings, a turnaround, a terminal, a classification yard, and one or more sidings.

(g) Alone or with others, construct a model railroad layout. Lay track with realistic ties, ballast, and scenery. Make proper wire connections from power supply to track and accessories.

(h) Make an acceptable scale model of a locomotive with or without motive power or two pieces of rolling stock. (Kits may be used.)

(i) Draw scale plans and construct two model accessories, such as a station, bridge, trestle, tunnel, roundhouse, or turntable.

Reading

1. Have read at least twelve books within the past year (not more than three of these from school outside reading requirements). The twelve books to include at least one each from three of the following classifications — fiction, adventure, Scouting, biography, technical or scientific reading, travel, poetry, the arts or books on hobbies. Present list of books read and authors.

2. Indicate the places in your community or county from which you may borrow, rent, or purchase books, and present library card or other evidence of how you secured the books read in Requirement No. 1.

3. Explain how you became interested in your favorite hobby and how you acquired the information or material to make your hobby worth while. Make a list of books, pamphlets, and magazines which you could suggest to a friend just starting this hobby.

4. List the books you own as a start toward a personal library.

5. Report on newspapers or news magazines you read to keep posted on current events.

6. Be a subscriber or a regular reader of a magazine for at least the preceding six months. Report any other magazines read.

7. Locate and deliver reading matter to some shut-in or sick person; *or* help someone find books on his hobby; *or* render service to your school or public library; *or* perform some similar service.

Note: Books and magazines must be approved by counselor.

Reptile Study

1. Make sketches from your own observation, showing markings and color patterns of seven reptiles and three amphibians found in your state and record the habitat and habits of each species.

2. Know approximately the number of species and general distribution of reptiles and amphibians in the United States.

3. Describe how reptiles and amphibians reproduce themselves.

4. Give ten superstitions about snakes and a correct explanation in each case.

5. Describe in detail six poisonous snakes and lizards found in the United States and their habits. Name those found in your own state. Demonstrate first aid treatment for snake bite.

6. List ten reptiles or amphibians useful to man either as food or in controlling insects or rodent pests and state how food is taken. List food habits of each species. If there are laws in force in your state for their protection, tell the reasons each is protected.

7. From actual observation describe how reptiles move forward. Describe the functions of the muscles, ribs, and belly plates.

8. Describe the outstanding differences between (1) alligators and crocodiles; (2) toads and frogs; (3) newts and the other species of salamanders; (4) salamanders and lizards.

9. Maintain in a terrarium, aquarium or properly constructed cage, one or more reptiles or amphibians for at least a month, recording the food accepted, the method employed in eating, changes in color or skin shedding, and general habits during this period. *or* Keep the eggs of one amphibian or reptile from the time of laying until hatching and record the length of time required for hatching and method of hatching.

10. Go out at night and identify three kinds of toads or frogs by their voices. Stalk each with a flashlight and discover how each sings, and from where (water, in tree, etc.). Imitate for counselor the song of each. *or* Take a recognizable photograph of a turtle, a snake, and an amphibian. Photographs must be from living specimens. *or* Give a brief, informal talk to a small group on reptiles or amphibians, using at least three living specimens for illustration purposes.

NOTE: The Scout should use nonpoisonous reptiles only in fulfilling 9 and 10.

Rowing †

1. Row properly without assistance, with your counselor in stern: (a) In a straight line for a quarter of a mile,* stop, make a pivot turn, and return to starting place. (b) Back water in a straight line 220 yards. Make a turn under way, still backing water, and return to the starting point.

(Feather after each stroke. Pin rowlocks must not be used.)

2. Demonstrate how to launch and land as follows:

(a) Launch and land a rowboat properly from and to

---

*If a quarter-mile straight course is not available, shorter courses may be used. The Scout will then row back and forth in a straight line until a quarter mile has been covered.

†A Second Class Scout must first qualify for First Class Scoutcraft Requirement 5 (see page 113).

shore. (b) Bring rowboat alongside pier, properly assist a passenger into it, row 50 feet, stop, pivot, come back to pier, and assist passenger safely from the boat. (c) Moor a rowboat using (1) clove hitch, (2) two half hitches, (3) bowline.

3. Alone or with one other person, turn a swamped rowboat right side up, get in, and paddle it for 10 yards with your hands or an oar. Tell why you should hang on or get in a swamped boat.

4. Alone in a rowboat, shove off from shore or pier; approach a swimmer and maneuver boat so that the swimmer may hold on to the stern while he is being towed ashore.

5. Identify and describe:

(a) Two or more of the following types of boats: fisherman's dory, St. Lawrence skiff, Mississippi River John boat, ship's longboat, punt, and dinghy; (b) carvel and clinker type of planking; (c) two of the following types of rowlocks; tholepin bow rowlock, ring rowlock, open top rowlock. Give one or more reasons why pin-type rowlocks are not recommended.

6. Explain the advantages gained by feathering oars while rowing and answer any two of the following questions: (a) How would you handle a rowboat if caught in a sudden storm or high wind? (b) How would you calculate the number of persons who may safely be carried in any given lifeboat under oars, using a U.S. Steamship Inspection formula? (c) What lights are required on a rowboat at night, both with and without outboard motor? (d) How would you haul out and stow away a rowboat which is not to be used during the winter, and how would you prepare it for use in the spring?

Safety

1. Write a report of not less than 150 words on one of the following topics or come prepared with notes to discuss them with your merit badge counselor: (a) Accident figures in the U.S. for one year. Include number of deaths and injuries in the four principal accident classes (work, motor vehicle, home, public) and costs of accidents. Explain how a serious accident to you or your parents can change your life. (b) Unsafe actions

---

*NOTE: This requirement must be waived when it involves conflict with local or state law relating to ownership and use of firearms. In all other cases evidence must be produced that all practice and the test have been conducted under a range officer whose appointment has been approved by the local or National Council. (This requirement does not necessitate Scout's supplying gun.)

and accidents. Explain how at least five unsafe actions can cause death or injury. (c) Safety and daily living. Explain how safety information acquired in Scouting can help you in daily living. Also tell how safety helps you enjoy adventures.

2. Watch drivers and pedestrians at or near an intersection for a total of three hours (can be done half hour, one hour, etc., at a time). List the unsafe practices you see and explain what would have been the safe practice in each case.

3. Demonstrate or list five important safety practices for each of the following: Walking, bicycle riding, automobile driving in town, automobile driving in the country.

4. Do one: (a) Assist in an organized safety campaign. (b) Visit and report on a local traffic court. (c) Add reflective material to farm equipment used on the highway.

5. Using a safety check list, complete a safety inspection of your home and premises. Explain what hazards have been corrected and how.

6. Describe safety practices in the home that help prevent falls, burns and scalds, and poisonings.

7. Explain to your counselor safety precautions related to the following: Dogs or other pets, firearms, hiking and camping, hand tools, electric wires, blasting caps, outdoor fires, swimming, excavations, winter sports or summer sports (except swimming).

8. List safety precautions that should be followed in two work areas where boys of Scout age might be employed, either in after-school or vacation jobs.

9. Do one: (a) Report on a safety project in which you participated at school, at church, or in the community. (b) Get permission and accompany a building or fire inspector on a safety inspection tour of a public building. Make a report of the tour. (c) Get permission and accompany a safety director, safety engineer, or safety inspector of an industrial plant on a safety inspection tour of his plant. Make a report of the tour.

10. Discuss with your counselor how you can contribute to the safety of yourself, your family, and your community.

Salesmanship

1. Analyze an article of merchandise from each of five retail stores and make a report of what happens to each article of merchandise investigated from the time it leaves the manufacturer until it reaches the consumer.

2. Explain the value of a salesman between manufacturer and jobber, between jobber and retailer, or between manufacturer and retailer.

3. Sell a definite quantity of merchandise, the total sales value of which is in excess of $10.00, and give your actual selling experience, telling the methods you used to influence people to buy your merchandise and how you overcame "selling resistance."

4. Indicate the place or importance of selling in business.

5. Explain how ideas are formed and how a salesman can lead a customer to decide to buy.

6. Sell at a profit something you have made or grown. Keep the necessary records to enable you to fix the right selling price and tell how much profit you have made.

7. Obtain, and hold for three months, a selling job for the hours after school, Saturday afternoons, or vacation. Describe what is necessary to sell the things you handle.

8. In uniform, visit a business concern and learn how their product is sold. Describe the selling process. Take with you an outline of at least ten questions prepared in advance.

9. Name five fundamental requirements of successful salesmanship.

10. Go to some successful practical salesman in your community and find out what he thinks of selling as a lifework. Write out in 500 words or more your conclusion of what the salesman tells you of salesmanship as a lifework.

11. (a) Explain what you understand to be the meaning of the statement that "Every man is a salesman. He must sell himself, his time, his ideas, his service." (b) Explain why truthfulness about an article is one of the outstanding requirements of all good selling. (c) Explain what it is that every salesman sells to his employer. (d) Explain how courtesy to prospective customers aids selling. Be prepared to give examples.

Scholarship

1. Present evidence from the principal* of your school that during the past year (a) your attitude toward school, based on behavior, leadership, and service, has been better than average and (b) that you have been on your class honor roll or have maintained an average grade of 82 or above for at least one term or semester.

*Alternates: dean, vice principal, student adviser or counselor, guidance director or home-room teacher.

2. Show that you have taken an active part in at least two extracurricular activities, such as athletics, music, school publication work, dramatics, student council. Explain your part in these activities.

3. Write and submit to your counselor for approval an essay (at least four hundred words) on "How School Training Will Be of Value to Me in My Future."

4. Submit a list of the educational resources other than your own school in your community (public library, museums, historical shrines, churches, extension service office, etc.). Visit two of these places and report to your counselor on how you used their facilities for self-education.

Sculpture

1. Model in clay or plasticine, or carve in wood, soft stone, soap, or other soft material: (a) a full-size human head of a type or nationality; (b) a small scale model of a group of animals or people in action.

2. (a) Make a plaster cast mold of an apple, pear, or any other fruit or vegetable. (b) In this mold cast a replica of the fruit or vegetable.

Seamanship

1. Using at least one-inch (circumference) rope, demonstrate correct (a) whipping of rope, (b) coiling, and (c) flinging. Describe the characteristics of three different types of rope commonly used by seamen.

2. Using at least one-inch (circumference) rope, make: (a) at least three kinds of knots used by seamen; (b) two bends; (c) two kinds of hitches; (d) a short splice; (e) and an eye splice. (Explain practical uses in seamanship of each type of knot, bend, hitch, and splice demonstrated.)

3. Demonstrate on sailcloth use of palm and needle in making: (a) a herringbone stitch and (b) both flat and round seams.

4. Demonstrate: (a) making a line fast to a cleat, ringbolt, and pile correctly; (b) a simple whip; (c) a single block tackle; (d) a double block tackle. Describe and explain uses of: (1) a snatch block; (2) a becket.

5. Describe: (a) at least two kinds of anchors and (b) the uses and outstanding features of a lead line.

6. Box the compass to 32 points. Explain: (a) The quarter point and degree systems; (b) compass deviation;

(c) compass variation. Know the importance of the North Star to seamen.

7. Have a working knowledge of: (a) weather and tides; (b) coast and geodetic survey charts. Understand buoyage system as used on coastwise harbors, rivers, and bays.

8. Know what lights and other equipment are required by law for: (a) a power-driven pleasure boat of Class 2; (b) a power-driven motorboat under 26 feet; (c) sailing vessels.

9. Understand proper flying of the ensign, jack, and two other flags commonly used on commercial or pleasure craft.

10. Name the working sails of a schooner from bow to stern. Know the name of the line used for: (a) hoisting a sail or a flag; (b) for trimming a sail to make it set properly. Explain the following terms: starboard tack; port tack; running free; reaching; abaft; abeam.

11. Know: (a) what the danger section is when two vessels are approaching; (b) what signals are used when a vessel is passing (1) to left, (2) to right, (3) a sailing vessel lying at anchor in fog, (4) a power-driven vessel; (c) two types of distress signals commonly used at sea other than radio.

12. (a) Fully dressed (in shoes, trousers, and jumper or coat), jump overboard in deep water, undress and, accompanied by a boat, swim 100 yards under supervision of counselor. (b) Demonstrate proper use of life belt and life buoy.

13. Handle correctly some type of boat or canoe under sail on all points of sailing, getting under way, reefing, docking, and anchoring.

14. Handle a rowboat (a) with a pair of oars; (b) with a single oar (sculling).

15. (a) Launch and land a rowboat or canoe properly from and to shore; (b) bring rowboat or canoe alongside pier, properly assist a passenger into boat, row 50 feet, pivot, come back to pier and assist passenger safely and properly from boat; (c) make rowboat or canoe fast to pier properly, using clove hitch, two half hitches, and bowline.

Sheep Farming*

1. Explain the use of sheep for domestic purposes, for commerce, and industry.

*As a 4-H'er, complete a club project in this subject. Or as an FFA member, meet these or equivalent requirements through the FFA supervised farming program.

2. From stock actually observed, name and explain characteristics of four leading breeds of sheep shown. Explain which is your favorite and why.

3. Give origin and history of one breed of sheep.

4. Visit two meat markets and obtain information for making a drawing of a sheep, then mark off the meat grade sections of the animal.

5. Exhibit and explain four of the different grades of wool from sheep.

6. Explain what wool is used for in home, commerce, and industry.

7. Make an exhibit of pictures of at least five sheep breeds and show samples of wool produced by each.

Signaling †

1. Make an electric buzzer outfit, wireless, blinker, or other signaling device.

2. Send and receive in the International Morse code, by buzzer or other sound device, a complete message of not less than thirty-five words, at a rate of not less than thirty-five letters per minute.

3. Demonstrate an ability to send and receive a message in the International Morse code by wigwag and by blinker or other light signaling device at the rate of not less than twenty letters per minute.

4. Send and receive by Semaphore code at the rate of not less than thirty letters per minute.

5. Know the proper application of the International Morse and Semaphore codes; when, where, and how they can be used to best advantage.

6. Discuss briefly various other codes and methods of signaling which are in common use.

†A Second Class Scout must first qualify for First Class Scoutcraft Requirement 6 (see page 114).

Skiing

1. Present yourself properly equipped and clothed for skiing.

2. Know the Skier's Safety Code.

3. Demonstrate ability to ski correctly on the level, with both the one step and the two step, and demonstrate the proper use of poles.

4. Demonstrate ability to climb correctly, using: (a) side step; (b) diagonal with both left and right kick turns, and (c) herringbone.

5. (a) Demonstrate correctly the "snow plow"; (b) do four continuous snow plow turns.

6. Do a right and left Christiania turn to a standstill from a direct descent.

7. (a) Jump turn to the right and left. *or* (b) Telemark turn to the right and left.

8. Choose any two of the following: (a) Run a slalom course with no falls through four pairs of flags, zigzagged not more than 40 feet apart, each set of flags requiring a 90 degree turn. (b) Make a direct downhill or diagonal run of at least 100 yards under complete control. (c) Make a 400-foot vertical ascent and descent under complete control with a pack of at least fifteen pounds. (d) Demonstrate ability to jump by completing three successive no-fall jumps of not less than 12 meters.

9. Choose any one of the following: (a) Show how to make an emergency toboggan out of several pairs of skis with only such materials as one would have on a ski trip. Explain treatment of frostbite. (b) Explain the correct method of waxing skis for different snow conditions. Demonstrate ability to wax a pair of skis. Describe care of skis during the off season. (c) Diagram a slalom course which will fairly test a skier's ability. Explain rules and describe how a slalom race is run; or explain rules for and describe the conduct of a down-mountain race. (d) Build a pair of skis, bindings, or poles.

Small Grains and Cereal Foods*

Qualify in all of the following:

1. On a map of the United States show where the following crops are grown in volume: rye, oats, barley, wheat, rice, flax, corn, soybeans, sorghum.

2. Run a germination test of 100 seeds each for two of the above crops raised in your area. Tell how you would treat these seeds to control disease.

3. Submit a sketch of a field on which grain is to be grown, showing how you would control soil erosion. Describe crop rotation, strip farming and contour farming.

4. Demonstrate in an outdoor seedbed or large box filled with soil the preparation of a seedbed and plant wheat and oats or any two small grains native to your section.

5. Explain steps farmers take to protect crops from diseases and insects and stored crops from rodents.

*As a 4-H'er, complete a club project in this subject. Or as an FFA member, meet these or equivalent requirements through the FFA supervised farming program.

6. Make an exhibit of three or more grain crops and display at a school, fair, or Scouting event. Must include root systems, stems, leaves, and seeds.

And qualify in any three of the following:

7. Collect, bottle, and label samples of three grain seeds grown in your area. Mark on label the variety, where grown, and the number of days from planting to harvest.

8. Do a soil conservation project; describe how it was done and give the results.

9. For two grains grown in your area, explain how you would prepare the field. Give dates and methods of planting and the amount of seed per acre; define "certified" seed.

10. Assist in harvesting a crop of grain; describe a combine and how it works.

11. Visit a grain elevator, a seed sales plant, or a grain marketing center. Take notes and write an acceptable article on what you learned.

12. Visit your grocery store and list the grain products sold; describe how one of these products is manufactured.

13. Prepare and serve a hot cereal food at home or camp; describe protein and other food ingredients in cereal and grain products and tell how they contribute to health.

Soil and Water Conservation*

1. Determine the depth of topsoil in at least two contrasting areas, such as grazed and ungrazed woods; cultivated fields and fields left in grass, grazed pastures and ungrazed haylots; well-kept lawn and heavily cropped garden; etc.

2. Plant two bean seeds in a flowerpot of topsoil, and two bean seeds in a flowerpot of subsoil. Tend them for a month and report on difference in rate of growth in two pots, appearance of plants, and other differences.

3. (a) Describe the different types, causes, and results of soil erosion. (b) Show snapshots or rough sketches of two examples of erosion in your community. (c) Explain what is meant by soil depletion.

4. Explain the meaning of the following terms: (a) contour farming; (b) strip cropping; (c) rotation of crops; (d) terracing; (e) cover crops.

5. On a road map or similar map, point out the watershed area for your community.

6. Make a diagram-sketch showing how rain water

*As a 4-H'er, complete a club project in this subject. Or as an FFA member, meet these or equivalent requirements through the FFA supervised farming program.

falling to the ground eventually gets to your kitchen faucet.

7. Explain how man's use of land in the watershed affects your community's water supply.

8. Do one:

(a) Help build a stock pond or farm pond.

(b) Make a study of plant, animal, and fish species in a pond and, if necessary, carry out such practices as will increase the fish population.

(c) Carry out a bank erosion control or other improvement project on a stream, pond, or lake.

(d) Control a gully by building necessary diversion ditches and brush dams or other structures and planting to grass and shrubs.

(e) Take an active part in removing the cause of pollution of a stream, pond, or lake.

(f) Help to plan, survey, and lay out a drainage or irrigation system for a field or other area that needs drainage or irrigation.

(g) Help build drainage or irrigation ditches on a field.

(h) Find out what is done with domestic and industrial waste in your community and write at least 500 words on the methods used to prevent pollution and to purify your water supply.

(i) Help to plan, survey, or lay out contour furrows or water-spreading dikes on pasture or range land.

(j) Carry out any other water management project approved by your counselor or representative of the local soil conservation district, national forest, or Taylor grazing district.

9. Do one:

(a) Help carry out a soil conservation project on a farm or Scout camp cooperating with the local soil conservation district.

(b) Plant 100 tree or shrub seedlings on school grounds, park, camp, or other eroding area that is unsuited for cultivation, or as a windbreak for buildings or a blowing field.

(c) Test the soil, fertilize, and, as needed, lime and plant grass or perennial legumes on ¼ acre of lawn, school grounds, camp, or other eroding area that is unsuited for cultivation.

(d) Take an active part in the program for a Farmer's Field Day, Face Lifting, or other soil conservation demonstration project.

(e) Trace a conservation survey map of a local farm or Scout camp and describe the different land classes found on it and tell what each different area should be used for and what conservative measures are needed on it.

(f) Help survey and lay out a plot of land for terracing, or strip cropping, or contour ploughing.

(g) Help construct terraces on a field.

(h) Help plan, lay out, or construct a grass waterway for a field or other eroding area where a waterway is needed.

(i) Carry out any other soil conservation project approved by your counselor or representative of the local soil conservation district, national forest, or Taylor grazing district.

(j) Reseed one acre of pasture or range land on which the present grass cover is insufficient to guard the soil against erosion.

Stamp Collecting

1. Mount and exhibit in a commercial album or an album of your own making: (a) a collection of 750 or more different stamps from at least thirty countries; *or* (b) a collection of 150 or more different stamps from a single country or a group of closely related countries; *or* (c) a collection of 75 or more different stamps on some special subject such as birds, trees, great men, music, aviation, etc. (stamps may be from any number of countries); *or* (d) a collection of 200 or more special items such as precanceled stamps, postage meters, revenue stamps, covers, postal stationery, etc.

2. Demonstrate the use of the *Standard Postage Stamp Catalogue*, or a catalogue particularly related to your collection in Requirement 1, to find at least five items selected by the counselor.

3. Show stamps to support brief definitions of the following terms: perforation, imperforate, roulette, cancellation, cover, mint stamp, coil stamp, overprint, surcharge, engraving, and printing process other than engraving.

4. Exhibit one stamp in each of the following classifications and explain the purpose of each: regular postage, commemorative, semipostal, air mail, postage due, envelope, special delivery, precancel, and revenue.

5. Explain the meaning of good condition of a stamp and show one stamp that is well centered, fully perforated, clearly cancelled, clean, and undamaged by tears or thin spots.

6. Demonstrate a knowledge of the following stamp collector's tools: (a) Use a perforation gauge to determine, on a stamp supplied by the counselor, the perforation measurement in accordance with the accepted standard. (b) Use a magnifying glass for careful exami-

nation of design and condition. (c) Use the watermark detector to show how a watermark may aid in identifying a stamp. (d) Use stamp tongs and stamp hinges correctly in mounting a stamp in an album.

Surveying †

1. Map correctly from the country itself the main features of half a mile of road, with 440 yards each side, to a scale of 1 inch to 200 feet, and afterwards draw same map from memory.

2. Measure the width of a river.

3. Measure the height of a tree, telegraph pole, or a church steeple, describing the method adopted.

4. Be able to measure a gradient.

5. Understand the use of the plane table.

†A Second Class Scout must first qualify for First Class Scoutcraft Requirement 2 (see page 111).

Swimming †

1. Swim 150 yards in good form using the following strokes for at least the distance specified: (a) side stroke — 50 yards; (b) elementary backstroke (only) — 50 yards; (c) breast stroke — 50 yards.

2. Surface dive in 6 feet of water and recover object on bottom.

3. In water 6 feet or more deep, while dressed in cotton shirt and cotton trousers, remove trousers, tie overhand knot in the bottom of each leg, inflate trousers and float motionless for one minute using them for support. *or* While dressed as above, tread water, inflate shirt, and float motionless for one minute.

4. Rest motionless in the water, or as nearly so as possible, at any angle, for one minute.

5. Enter water without sound, swim silently for 50 feet (with breast stroke or dog paddle), leave water without sound.

6. While swimming, submerge quickly (use both surface dive and feet first method), swim three strokes forward under water, return to the surface, and at signal repeat three times.

7. Demonstrate a rescue in one of the following ways: (a) Disrobe on shore, enter the water feet first (jump or run) carrying outside shirt in teeth or hand, swim 30

†A Second Class Scout must first qualify for First Class Scoutcraft Requirement 5 (see page 113).

feet, swing one end of the shirt to the hands of presumably drowning person and tow him ashore. *or* (b) Make rescue under same conditions as above, using instead of shirt, a pole, branch of tree, paddle, or oar to shove to presumably drowning person.

Textiles

1. (a) Submit samples of the following yarn, thread, or fiber: cotton, wool, synthetic silk and linen. Discuss their sources, including the chief countries that produce them. (b) Tell how at least three of these fibers differ in character. Show one good method of testing fibers so as to recognize them.

2. Submit samples of woven fabrics containing cotton, wool, silk, linen, acetate, rayon, and nylon. Discuss the various qualities and common uses of each, including the garments you are wearing.

3. Submit two or more samples of knitted goods and discuss briefly the qualities of those as compared to woven fabrics.

4. Explain the principal operations used to manufacture any fiber into a fabric. Name the machines used and tell briefly what each machine does.

5. Discuss the types of dyes in general use and explain why some fabrics require different dyes than others. Discuss spun, stock yarn and piece dyeing. Discuss the qualities of a vat dye.

6. Do one of the following: (1) Visit a textile mill, clothing factory, or dye plant and report fully to your counselor on this experience. (2) Waterproof a piece of fabric. (3) Weave an article on a simple loom that you have made yourself.

(b) Investigate and report on the career opportunities that are open to you in the textile or clothing manufacturing industries.

7. Explain ten of these textile terms: fiber, filament, yarn, short staple, ply yarn, burning test, fiber blends, warp, filling, pick, cloth count, pick glass, selvage, nap, gray goods, mercerized, color printing.

8. Show that you know something about the purchase and care of your own wearing apparel as follows: (a) Tell the meaning on labels of "reprocessed," "Sanforized," "preshrunk," and "water repellent." (b) Remove a grease spot from a piece of fabric by dry cleaning, using precautions against fire. (c) Give rules for proper cleaning and storing of your own garments. (d) Wash underwear and socks properly under camping conditions.

Weather

1. Have a general knowledge of the composition of air, referring to both constant and variable elements of the air and what function each performs.

2. Develop quite broadly the subjects moisture, fog, hail, rain, and snow.

3. Explain points connected with electrical and optical phenomena in the air, i.e., have a knowledge of the following: rainbow, mirages, looming, halos, northern lights, St. Elmo's fire, lightning and thunder. Describe as many of the above as you have seen.

4. Have a knowledge of the use and construction of and demonstrate your ability to read a barometer, thermometer, anemometer, psychrometer, and rain gauge. Have constructed a weather vane. Know the weather signals or storm signals.

5. Outline in writing a simple statement of the climate of the United States and of your own state.

6. Explain the value of weather prediction. Write a brief account of the United States Weather Bureau, stating what daily, weekly, and monthly publications are sent out by this bureau. Be able to interpret the charts and graphs contained in their publications.

7. Keep a daily record for a month of the following: dew or frost in the morning; at a specific hour each day (this hour must be the same every day), the direction of the wind, the temperature, kind of clouds (if any) in the sky. (State if it rains or snows at this hour.)

8. Name some places where, during severe thunder storms, the danger from lightning is great, some places where the danger is small.

Wildlife Management*

1. Do one:

(a) On a rough sketch of a five-acre area — (1) Show and identify the chief types of plant cover; (2) Show the location (and identify) nests, dens, runways, droppings, feeding, and other animal signs.

(b) On a five-acre area — (1) Identify three of the chief tree, three of shrub, or three ground cover species used by animals for food, shelter, or cover. (2) Identify by signs, or sight, ten of the animal species found in the area.

*As a 4-H'er, complete a club project in this subject. Or as an FFA member, meet these or equivalent requirements through the FFA supervised farming program.

2. Describe the value of three wild animals, each as sources of food, clothing, and recreation; and the role of three animals each in insect, weed, and rodent control.

3. (a) Describe the damage to wildlife resulting from wildfire, overgrazing, unwise forest practices, soil erosion, unwise drainage, "slick and clean" farming, and water pollution. (b) Explain the relationship between wildlife and the natural habitat and how man controls the natural environment.

4. Explain who makes laws setting definite seasons and bag limits on hunting, fishing, and trapping in your state and the reason for the laws.

5. Do one:

(a) Make a wildlife count on each of two contrasting approximate five-acre plots. Grazed versus ungrazed wood lots; or strip cropped versus solid planting; or burned-over versus not burned-over area; or other contrasting areas.

(b) Visit a state or federal or private game refuge or game management area with a wildlife technician and write at least 500 words on what is being done to make the area better for wildlife.

(c) Visit a game farm or fish hatchery with a wildlife technician and write a report of at least 500 words on the pros and cons of game stocking against habitat improvements as means of increasing wildlife populations.

(d) Attend a recognized camp for at least a week where conservation is a major part of the program and describe how you will use the information you learned.

(e) Go out for at least two days with a commercial fisherman and describe his catch and methods used.

(f) Select one wildlife species common to your neighborhood and find out what management practices are used, or the practices that may be necessary to maintain the species.

6. Do one:

(a) Help build, stock, or fertilize a farm pond.

(b) Plant stream or ditch banks to control erosion.

(c) Build a fence or plant a "living fence" to exclude stock from a wood lot, stream, or pond banks, or other easily damaged wildlife habitat.

(d) Set out 200 food plants for birds and mammals.

(e) Build three check dams, deflectors, or cover devices in a stream or lake to provide shelter for fish and to help reduce erosion.

(f) Study the fish species in a pond or lake and, if necessary, carry out such practices as may be necessary to benefit the fish.

(g) Build and set out in suitable places ten nesting boxes or "den pipes."

(h) Plant a windbreak or hedge or other suitable winter cover for wildlife.

(i) Help plant a gully, road cut, fill or eroding area, to reduce erosion, build up soil fertility, and at the same time provide shelter for wildlife.

Woodcarving

1. Make, with only a knife for a tool, three handy camp articles, such as pothooks, fork, spoon, tent pegs, coat hooks, or candleholder, all articles to be made from natural material.

2. Plan and carve an appropriate design in low relief on some simple object such as book ends, a tray, a pair of bellows, a chest, a screen, a clock case, a letter opener, or a box. *or* Plan and carve in the round, smooth and finish a simple object such as a totem animal figure, or model.

3. State the qualities of hardwood and softwood and the best woods to use in woodcarving; name, describe, and explain how to sharpen the different kinds of woodcarving tools, including knife and axe, and explain methods of handling the grain of the wood in designing and carving.

Woodwork

1. (a) Describe briefly how timber is grown, harvested, and milled and how lumber is cured, seasoned, graded, and sized. (b) Collect and label sample blocks of six kinds of wood useful in woodworking; describe the chief qualities and best uses of each.

2. (a) Demonstrate proper care and use of all woodworking tools and equipment which you own or are permitted to use at home or school. (b) Sharpen correctly the cutting edges of two tools.

3. Make a useful article of wood which calls for use of saw, plane, hammer, and brace and bit. Cut parts from lumber which you have measured and squared correctly according to working drawings.

4. (a) Submit, for approval of your counselor, a working sketch of a carpentry project, along with a list of material needed. (b) Complete the project and submit a report of time spent and cost of materials.

5. Do any two of the following projects:

(a) Make working drawings of some article requiring

(1) beveled or rounded edges, or curved or incised cutting; and (2) miter, dowel, or mortise and tenon joints. Construct the article.

(b) Make an article for which you have to turn duplicate parts on a lathe.

(c) Make a cabinet, storage box, or some other article with a door or lid attached with inset hinges.

(d) With other members of your patrol or troop, take part in a project of making and repairing wooden toys for needy children; or help carry out a carpentry service project in your community.

(e) Build a miniature, accurate scale model of a house, barn, or other frame structure.

(f) Talk with a skilled cabinetmaker or carpenter and find out what are the employment opportunities and conditions (required training, apprenticeship, work hours, pay rates, union organization, etc.) for woodworking craftsmen in your locality.

World Brotherhood

1. (a) Tell how the Scout movement began and point out on a map at least thirty countries which have Scouting. (b) Describe or demonstrate at least three ways in which Scouts or Explorers of most countries can recognize one another.

2. (a) Tell briefly how modern transportation and communication have "shrunk" the world during the past hundred years and have made nations more dependent upon one another. (b) Tell how natural resources, commerce, and trade affect a nation's economy and relationship among nations. (c) Find and list at least eight different everyday articles that were imported or made from different materials imported from other parts of the world. Identify the countries from which these come.

3. (a) Describe the form and structure of government of one nation on each continent. (b) Review the story of at least three national heroes of other lands.

4. Tell the purpose and functions of at least two international organizations of which the United States is a member (such as the Postal Union, Pan American Union, International Red Cross, United Nations, the International Court of Justice).

5. Do one of the following: (a) Carry on a simple, understandable conversation with another person in a modern foreign language for at least five minutes and translate at least 200 words of simple text in that language.* (b) Correspond with someone in another country,

exchanging at least three letters each way.

6. Prove by deed that you belong to a world brotherhood by doing two of the following: (a) Hike or camp with boys from other countries. (b) Make friends with new arrivals from abroad. (c) Help with collecting relief supplies to be sent abroad. (d) Help an organization which promotes world brotherhood, such as foreign missions and the International Junior Red Cross.

*A Boy Scout or Explorer who has earned the World Brotherhood merit badge and who has qualified for optional Requirement 5a is entitled to wear the Interpreter's badge for the foreign language used.

Zoology

1. Make five field trips of at least two hours each (preferably at different seasons) to observe wild animal life. Keep records of such trips, listing all animals seen, with date, place, nature of locality, and observations of animals and their habits. (Photographs, sketches, track casts, etc., will add to the interest of this record.)

2. Using the "keys" of the modern system of classifying animal life, show ability to classify at least five animals of different phyla which you yourself select.

3. Find out the life processes that are common to all animal life (birth, self protection, feeding, breathing, etc.). Keep record from personal observation of the life cycle and habits of at least two animals of different phyla.

4. On a map of your locality (showing such things as forests, plains, streams, marshes, arid areas, etc.) indicate animals found in each habitat. Know what is being done in your state to protect wild animal life.

5. Carry out one of the following projects: (a) Keep a young animal (completely weaned from mother) such as a squirrel, white rat, rabbit, or guinea pig for at least three months. Keep a weekly diary of its habits, food requirements, gain in weight, general health, etc. *or* (b) Maintain an aquarium or "toad pen" for at least three months. Stock from local ponds, streams, or marshes. Watch development from egg on, of frogs, toads, turtles, fish, or whatever animal you have chosen for special observation. Keep record of life cycle and habits. *or* (c) Submit at least ten photographs or sketches based on your own observation of microscopic animal life in the field for a period of at least three months. Present at least three properly prepared slides of microscopic life.

NOTE: Animals, in the zoological sense, include all living organisms other than plant life, from amoeba up through man. However, since birds, snakes, and insects are covered in other merit badge subjects, choose other examples of animal life for these requirements.

Pepsi-Cola
Pepsi-Cola

Here's how you can enjoy a lifetime of shooting FUN!

HOW TO USE YOUR TARGET RIFLE. Get to know the correct shooting positions. Try the prone position first. Then sitting. The kneeling and off-hand positions are also fun, but tougher. Be relaxed, comfortable. Line up your sights. Inhale a breath. Exhale most of it and slowly "sque-e-ze" the trigger, and PRACTICE.

HOW TO SELECT AMMUNITION.
Pick the right ammunition for your gun. For target shooting and plinking, use Remington standard velocity 22's. For pests, or shooting at long ranges, you need the maximum power of Remington "Hi-Speed" 22's.

Remember your safety rules at all times.

REMINGTON'S MODEL 521T—a sharp-shooting combination hunting and target rifle. Smooth action and smart, racy lines. A swell 22!

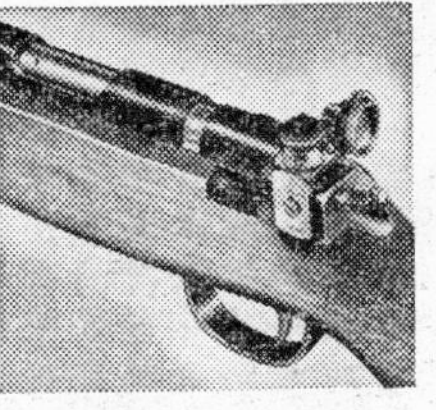

Micrometer rear sight with quarter-minute click adjustments for windage and elevation. Patridge-type blade front sight. A grand aid to your accuracy.

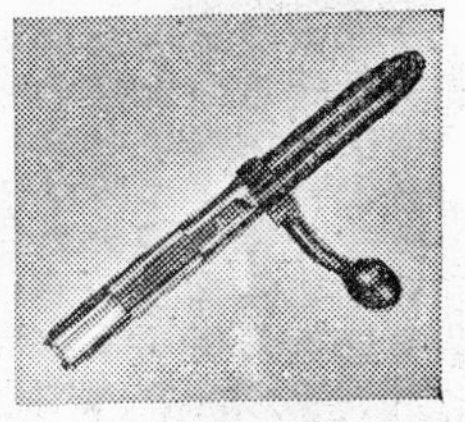

Self-cocking bolt with double-locking lugs provides correct head-spacing that means years of accurate shooting. Red firing indicator shows you when the rifle is cocked.

"Hi-Speed" is a trademark of
Remington Arms Company, Inc., Bridgeport 2, Conn.

"If It's Remington—It's Right!"

Remington

BOOKS TO READ

Backwoods Engineering

Ashley Book of Knots, The. Clifford W. Ashley. Doubleday & Co., Garden City, N. Y.

Axe Manual. Peter McLaren. Fayette R. Plumb, Inc., Philadelphia, Pa.

Knots and How to Tie Them. Donald A. Smith. Boy Scouts of America. See local Scout distributors. No. 3166.

Ropework. James M. Drew. Webb Publishing Co., St. Paul, Minn.

Woodcraft. Bernard S. Mason. A. S. Barnes and Co., New York. Out of print; see your library.

Woodsmanship. Bernard S. Mason. A. S. Barnes and Co., New York.

Birds

Birds. Herbert S. Zim and Ira N. Gabrielson. Simon and Schuster, New York.

Field Guide to the Birds, A. Roger Tory Peterson. Houghton Mifflin Co., Boston.

Guide to Bird Songs, A. Aretas A. Saunders. Doubleday & Co., Garden City, N. Y.

Guide to Bird Watching, A. Joseph J. Hickey. Oxford University Press, New York.

Our Amazing Birds. Robert S. Lemmon. Doubleday & Co., New York.

Camping and Hiking

Boy's Complete Book of Camping. Stanley Pashko. Greenberg Publisher, New York. Out of print; see your library.

Camping and Woodcraft. Horace Kephart. Macmillan Co., New York.

Handicraft. Lester Griswold. Prentice-Hall, Englewood Cliffs, N. J.

Hiker's Handbook. Douglas Leechman. W. W. Norton & Co., New York.

How to Survive on Land and Sea. United States Naval Institute, Annapolis, Md.

Junior Book of Camping and Woodcraft. Bernard S. Mason. A. S. Barnes and Co., New York.

Let's Go Camping. Harry Zarchy. Alfred A. Knopf, New York.

Manual of Walking, A. Elon Jessup. E. P. Dutton & Co., New York. Out of print; see your library.
Wildwood Wisdom. Ellsworth Jaeger. Macmillan Co., New York.

Citizenship

American Citizen's Handbook, The. Joy E. Morgan. National Education Association, Washington, D. C. Out of print; see your library.
Democracy and You. Charles E. Merrill Co., Columbus, Ohio. Out of print; see your library.
Flag of the United States, The. Harrison S. Kerrick. American Legion, Indianapolis, Ind.
Stars and Stripes. M. Garrison. Caxton Printers, Caldwell, Idaho.

Cooking

Camp Cookery. Horace Kephart. Macmillan Co., New York.
Complete Book of Outdoor Cookery. H. Brown and J. Beard. Doubleday & Co., Garden City, N. Y.
Cook It Outdoors. James Beard. M. Barrows & Co., New York.
Jack-Knife Cookery. James A. Wilder. E. P. Dutton & Co., New York.
Outdoor Chef, The. Paul W. Handel. Harper & Brothers, New York.
Outdoorsman's Cookbook, The. Arthur H. Carhart. Macmillan Co., New York.
Young America's Cookbook. Charles Scribner's Sons, New York.

Emergencies and First Aid

Complete Book of First Aid, The. John Henderson, M. D. Little, Brown and Co., Boston.
Disaster on Your Doorstep. Paul W. Kearney. Harper & Brothers, New York.
First Aid Textbook for Juniors. American Red Cross. Doubleday & Co., Garden City, N. Y.
Hurricane Damage Prevention (pamphlet). Federation of Mutual Fire Insurance Companies, Chicago.
Manual of Lifesaving and Water Safety. Charles E. Silvia. Association Press, New York.

Fishing

Boy's Complete Book of Fresh and Salt Water Fishing. O. H. P. Rodman and E. C. Janes. Little, Brown and Co., Boston.

PAUSE
FOR
COKE
REG. U.S. PAT. OFF.
SIGN OF GOOD TASTE
Coca-Cola
REG. U.S. PAT. OFF.

Field Book of Fresh Water Angling. John A. Knight. G. P. Putnam's Sons, New York.
Fresh Water Fishing. M. E. Shoemaker. Doubleday & Co., Garden City, N. Y.

Insects

Field Book of Insects. Frank Lutz. G. P. Putnam's Sons, New York.
How to Know the Insects. H. E. Jaques. William C. Brown Co., Dubuque, Iowa.
Insect Friends. Edwin Way Teale. Dodd, Mead & Co., New York.
Junior Book of Insects. Edwin Way Teale. E. P. Dutton & Co., New York.

Nature

Book of Nature Hobbies. Ted S. Pettit. Didier, Publishers, New York. Out of print; see your library.
Field Book of Nature Activities. William Hillcourt. G. P. Putnam's Sons, New York.
Field Book of North American Mammals. H. E. A. Anthony. G. P. Putnam's Sons, New York.
Meeting the Mammals. Victor Cahalane. Macmillan Co., New York.
Wildlife in Color. Roger Tory Peterson. Houghton Mifflin Co., Boston.

Physical Fitness

Boy's Book of Body Building. Stanley Pashko. Grosset & Dunlap, New York.
Here's Power for You. David Manners. Sentinel Book Publishers, New York.
How to Be Fit. Robert Kiphuth. Yale University Press, New Haven, Conn.

Reptiles

Boy's Book of Snakes. Percy A. Morris. Ronald Press Co., New York.
Field Book of Snakes. K. P. Schmidt and D. D. Davis. G. P. Putnam's Sons, New York.
Handbook of Frogs and Toads. A. A. and A. H. Wright. Cornell University Press, Ithaca, N. Y.
Handbook of Salamanders. Sherman Bishop. Cornell University Press, Ithaca, N. Y.

Rocks and Minerals

Field Book of Common Rocks and Minerals. F. B. Loomis. G. P. Putnam's Sons, New York.

Badges: (reading left to right) Athletics, Rowing, Cycling; Life Saving, Horsemanship, Skiing; Swimming, Canoeing.

Why wear a supporter? There are a couple of good reasons:

1. It protects you where you need it most.

2. It helps you fight fatigue.

Ask any top athlete—he'll tell you he wouldn't play a minute without wearing a supporter.

Which supporter? BIKE! *More star athletes have worn Bike than any other brand.* Make sure you wear one, too, when you go after these merit badges.

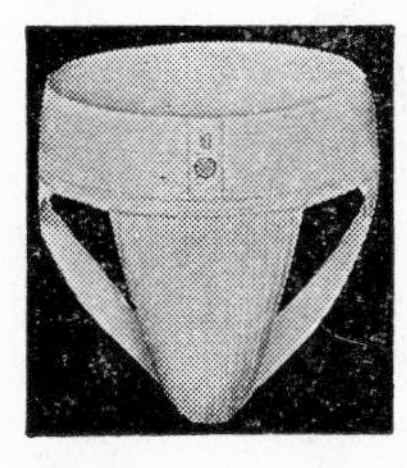

BIKE®

THE KENDALL COMPANY

BIKE WEB SALES DIVISION

Rock Book, The. C. L. and M. A. Fenton. Doubleday & Co., New York.

Singing

Boy Scout Songbook. Boy Scouts of America. See local Scout distributors. No. 3226.
Camp Songs 'n Things. Boy Scouts of America. See local Scout distributors. No. 3249.

Signaling

Learning the Radio Telegraph Code. American Radio Relay League, West Hartford, Conn.
Bluejackets' Manual, The. United States Naval Institute, Annapolis, Md.

Stars

Beginner's Star-Book, A. K. McKready. G. P. Putnam's Sons, New York.
Discover the Stars. Gaylord Johnson. Sentinel Book Publishers, New York.
Primer for Star Gazers, A. Henry M. Neely. Harper & Brothers, New York.
Stars. Herbert S. Zim and Robert H. Baker. Simon and Schuster, New York.

Tracking and Stalking

Animal Tracks. George F. Mason. William Morrow and Co., New York.
Scout Field Book. Boy Scouts of America. See local Scout distributors. No. 3649.
Tracks and Trailcraft. Ellsworth Jaeger. Macmillan Co., New York.

Trees and Flowers

Beginner's Guide to Wild Flowers. E. H. Hausman. G. P. Putnam's Sons, New York.
Best Loved Trees of America, The. Robert S. Lemmon. Doubleday & Co., Garden City, N. Y.
Edible Wild Plants. O. P. Medsger. Macmillan Co., New York.
Field Book of American Trees and Shrubs, F. S. Mathews. G. P. Putnam's Sons, New York.
Field Book of American Wild Flowers. F. S. Mathews. G. P. Putnam's Sons, New York.
Flowers. Herbert S. Zim and Alexander C. Martin. Simon and Schuster, New York.
Learn the Trees from Leaf Prints. David S. Marx. Botanic Publishing Co., Cincinnati, Ohio.

Earn Your Marksmanship Badge

with your

DAISY AIR RIFLE

SCOUTS: Any Daisy Air Rifle may be used to earn your Marksmanship Merit Badge! Ask your local Merit Badge counselor now!

LEADERS: Send 10¢ coin for new 16-page "Club Brochure" on BB gun shooting!

with 2 Daisy BB Packs!

THE FAMOUS DAISY PUMP GUN

King of all air rifles! Take-down model. Daisy's pump-action, forced-feed repeater is full 37″ long—very accurate. Combination peep-and-open sight adjustable for windage, elevation. "Ramp-type" front sight. Gold-filled "engraving" on jacket. Full oval stock.

Remember... Daisy spring-type air rifles give you the *most* fun for the *least* money!

Prices Subject To Change Without Notice

Duty added in Canada

No. 25

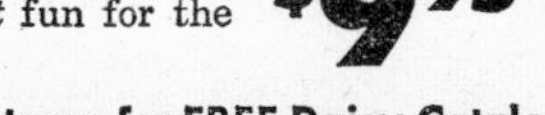

$9.95

Send 3¢ stamp for FREE Daisy Catalog

DAISY

Manufacturing Company

DEPT. BS-8, ROGERS, ARKANSAS—U. S. A.

This Green World. Rutherford Platt. Dodd, Mead & Co., New York.
Trees of the Eastern United States and Canada. W. M. Harlow. McGraw-Hill Book Co., New York.

Water Fun

Basic Swimming. Robert Kiphuth and H. M. Burke. Yale University Press, New Haven, Conn.
Canoeing. Carle W. Handel. A. S. Barnes and Co., New York.
Swimming and Diving. American Red Cross. McGraw-Hill Book Co., New York.

Weather

Eric Sloane's Weather Book. Eric Sloane. Little, Brown and Co., Boston.
How About the Weather? Robert M. Fisher. Harper & Brothers, New York.
Weathercraft. Athelstan F. Spilhause. Viking Press, New York.

Fishermen favor the fast-moving new Sea-Horse 10 . . . water skiers scoot with the new Sea-Horse 35

New! Only Sea-Horse has Dynautical Design

Goes better with your boat . . . makes your boat go better!

You'll see the difference! All new Sea-Horses are white and clean as a hound's tooth. You'll *feel* the difference the first time you run one—smooth, quiet power—more fun than ever before. That's Dynautical Design—inside and out! See the '59 Sea-Horses at your Johnson dealer's now. Sizes from 3 to 50 hp.

For FREE catalog, write to Johnson Motors, 500 Pershing. Rd., Waukegan, Illinois

Johnson . . . first in dependability

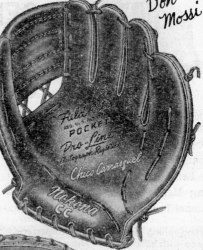

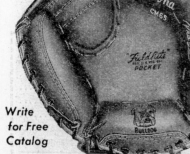

Sleeping bag shown below available at your local Boy Scout distributor.

*"Dacron" is Du Pont's registered trademark for their polyester fiber.

Best buy for camping!

Sleeping bags filled 100% with DACRON Fiberfill

REG. U. S. PAT. OFF

They're lighter to carry . . . easier to roll . . . more comfortable to sleep in . . . that's why these man-sized sleeping bags filled 100% with "Dacron"* polyester fiberfill are tops with campers everywhere. "Dacron" Fiberfill gives off lasting warmth . . . is non-allergenic, moth and mildew resistant, too!

BETTER THINGS FOR BETTER LIVING
. . . *THROUGH CHEMISTRY*

DU PONT

REG. U. S. PAT. OFF.

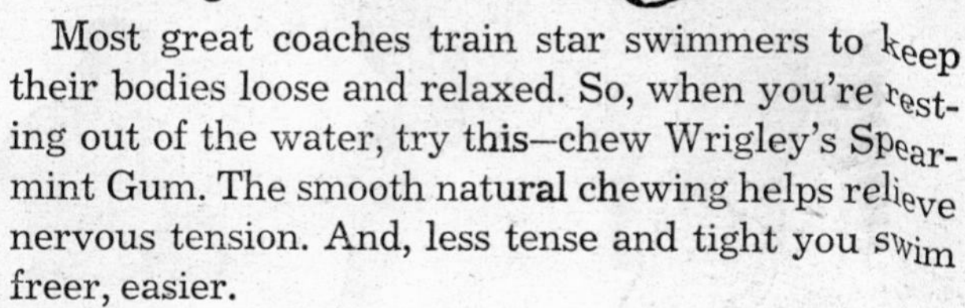

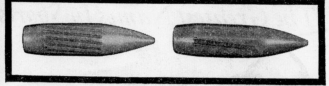

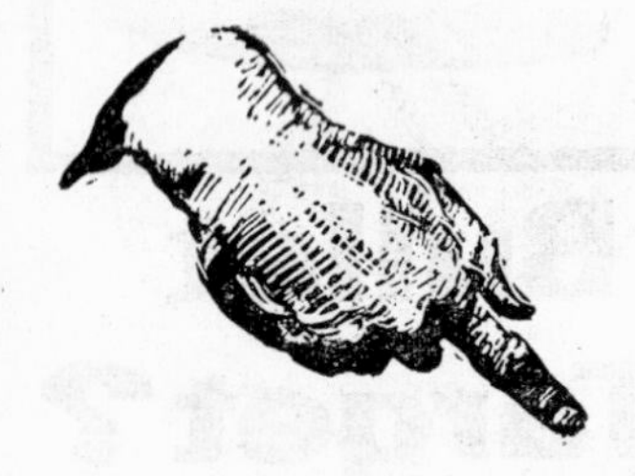

INDEX

A

B

C

D

E

F

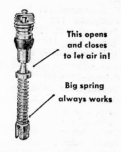

L

M

N

O

P

R

S

w illustrated
talog of Mossberg
les, shotguns and
escope sights.
you like guns,
u should have
Send today.

NEW
Model **320K**
*$17.95**

Hammerless bolt action 22 caliber single shot. Accurate, fast-loading —a real beauty, a rifle to be proud of. 4-power scope shown mounted (Model 4M4) only $10.95 additional.

* $18.95 west of Rockies

O. F. MOSSBERG & SONS, Inc.
928 ST. JOHN STREET
NEW HAVEN 5, CONNECTICUT
Please send catalog to:

NAME

ADDRESS

CITY

STATE

GOOD SCOUTS CARRY
MARBLE CAMPING EQUIPMENT

FAMOUS SAFETY AXES

Only axes with safety guard that folds into handle. Head can't fly off. Extra tough, extra sharp blade.

Hickory handle . . $6.75
Metal handle . . . $11.25

BELT AXE
14" long. Hickory handle. **$5.50**

NEW "*Sportsman*" KNIFE

Beautiful stag handle. Tough, sharp 4-inch blade. Embossed leather sheath included. **$5.50**

Seven other models $4.25 to $12

WATERPROOF MATCH BOX
Keeps your matches dry. Non-breakable brass, nickel-plated. Only **95¢**

COMPASSES
Pin-on, pocket, wrist models. Guaranteed accurate. **$2.25** to **$3.50**

At your sporting goods store

MARBLE
ARMS CORPORATION
286 Delta Ave., Gladstone, Mich.

T

U

W